volume

Created by
OSAMU TEZUKA

Adaptation by
SATOSHI SHIKI

どろろと百鬼丸伝

どろろと
ひゃっきまる
でん

THE LEGEND OF
DORORO AND
HYAKKIMARU
VOLUME 5

CONTENTS

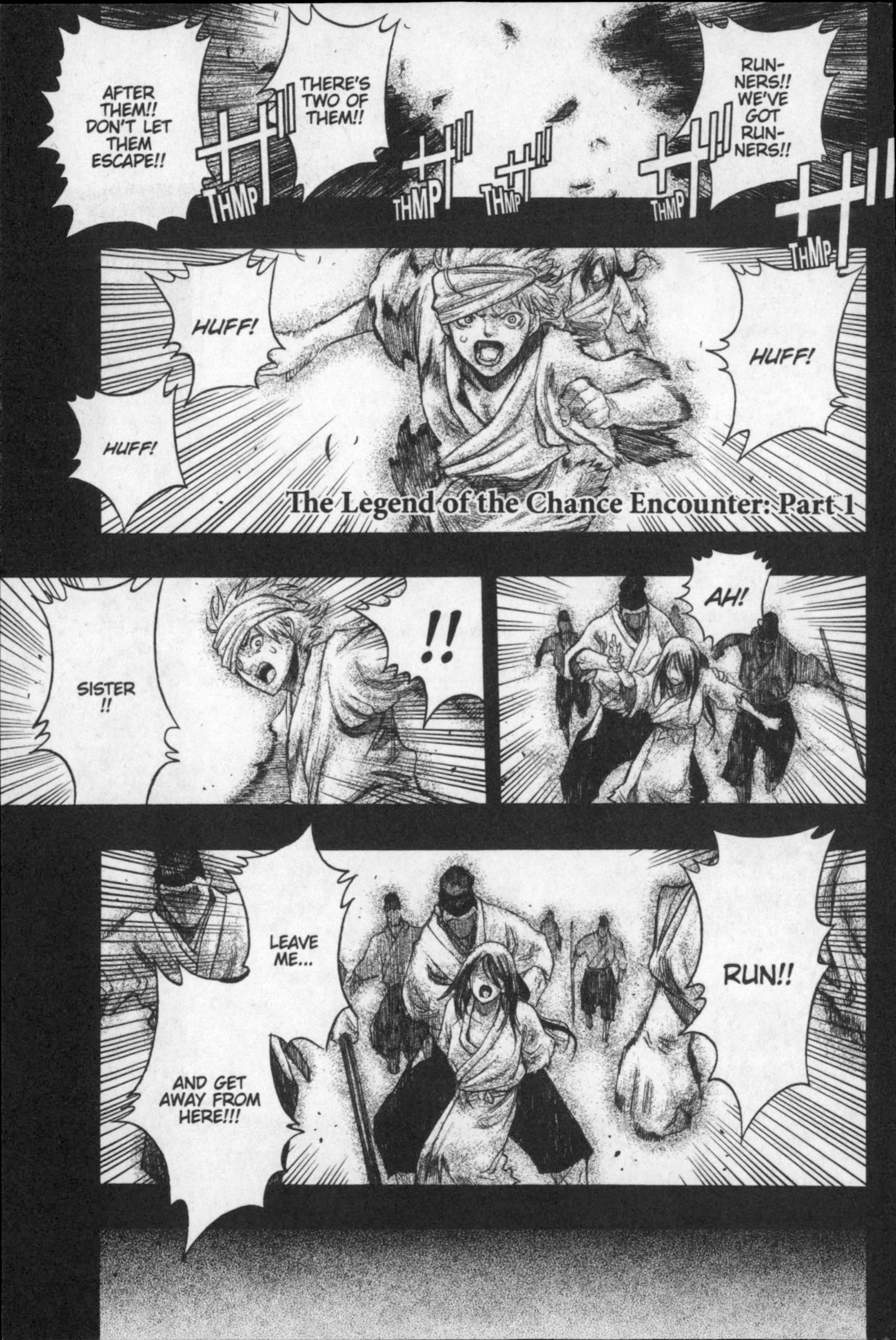
RUN-NERS!! WE'VE GOT RUN-NERS!!
THMP
THMP
THMP
THMP
THERE'S TWO OF THEM!!
THMP
AFTER THEM!! DON'T LET THEM ESCAPE!!
HUFF!
HUFF!
HUFF!
The Legend of the Chance Encounter: Part 1
AH!
!!
SISTER!!
RUN!!
LEAVE ME...
AND GET AWAY FROM HERE!!!

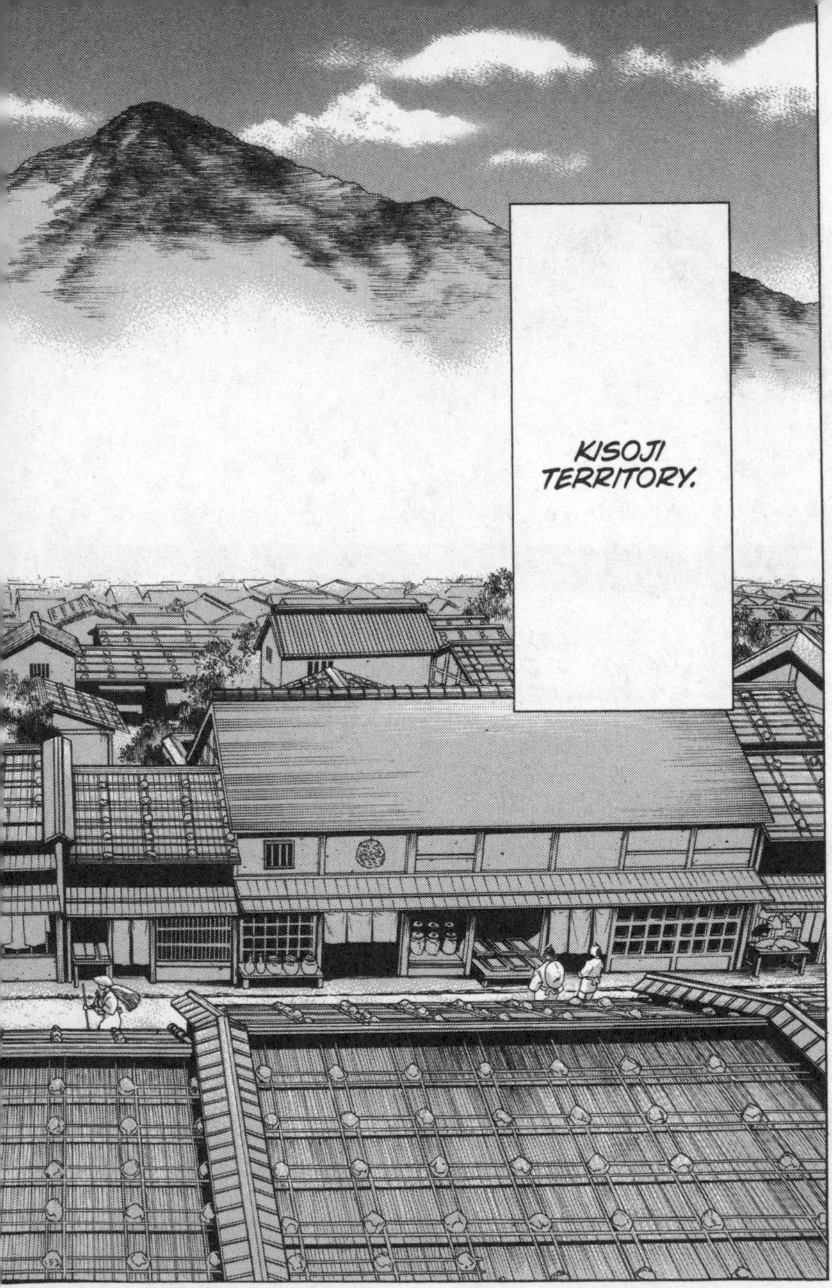
KISOJI TERRITORY.

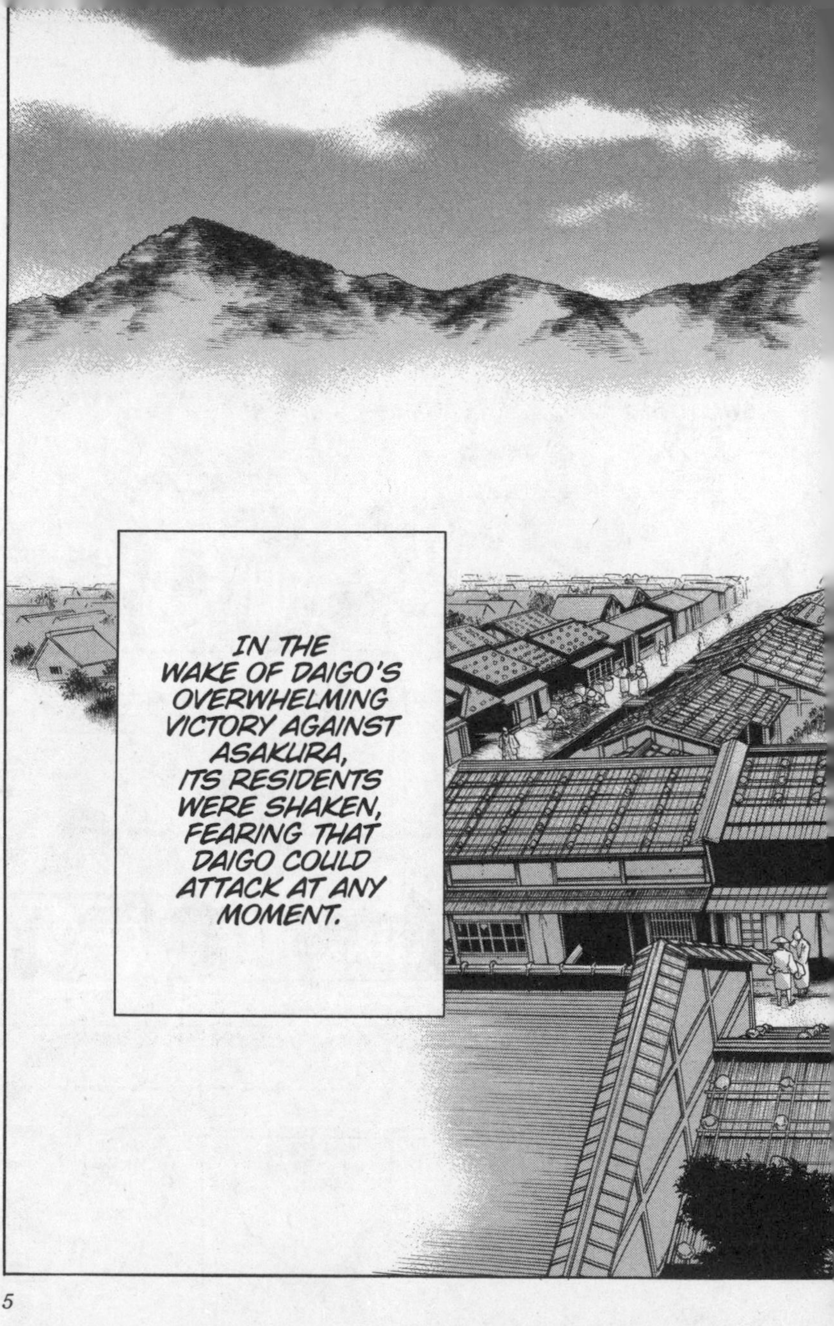
IN THE WAKE OF DAIGO'S OVERWHELMING VICTORY AGAINST ASAKURA, ITS RESIDENTS WERE SHAKEN, FEARING THAT DAIGO COULD ATTACK AT ANY MOMENT.

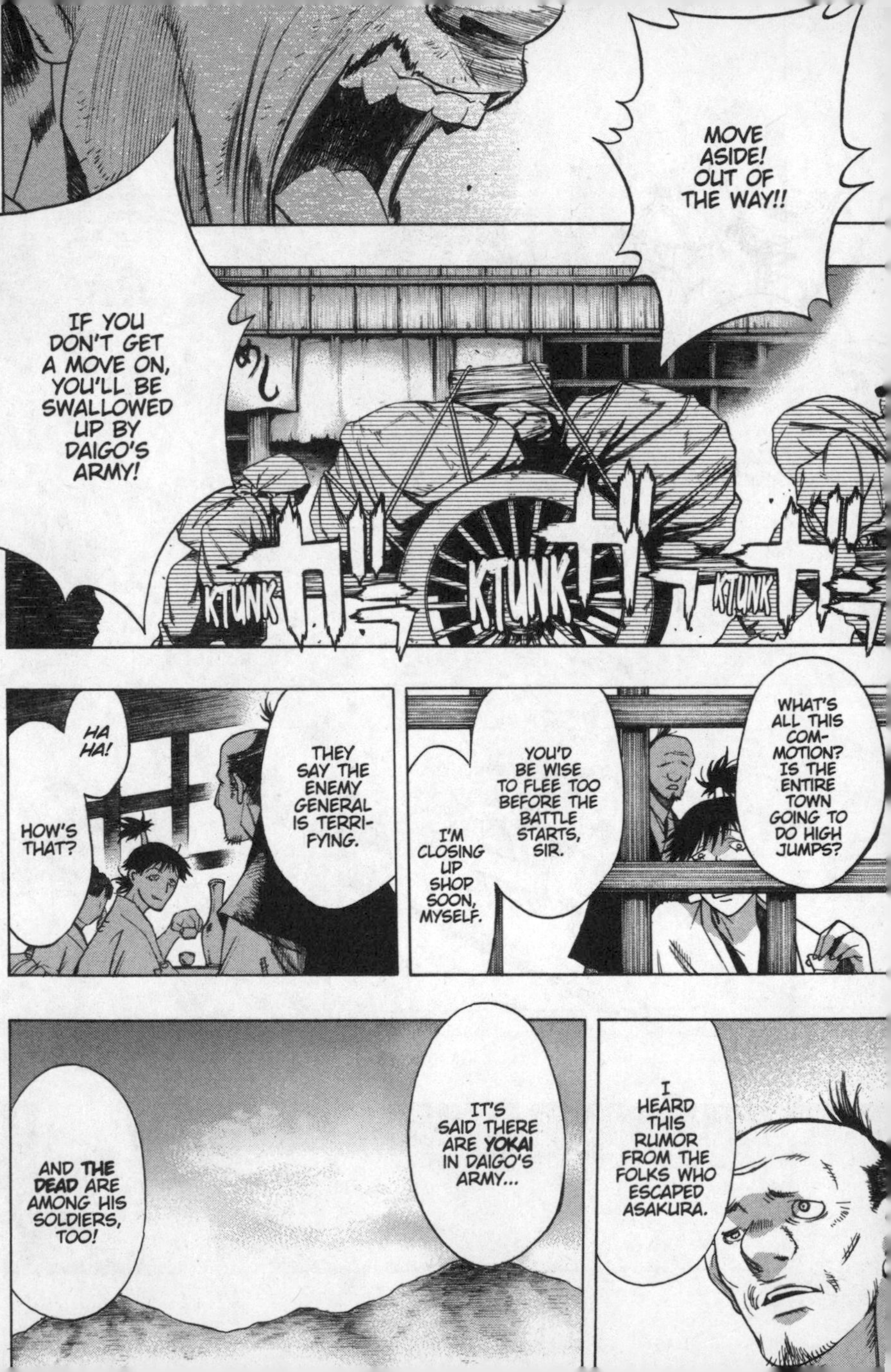
MOVE ASIDE! OUT OF THE WAY!!
IF YOU DON'T GET A MOVE ON, YOU'LL BE SWALLOWED UP BY DAIGO'S ARMY!
めし
KTUNK
KTUNK
KTUNK
WHAT'S ALL THIS COM-MOTION? IS THE ENTIRE TOWN GOING TO DO HIGH JUMPS?
YOU'D BE WISE TO FLEE TOO BEFORE THE BATTLE STARTS, SIR.
I'M CLOSING UP SHOP SOON, MYSELF.
THEY SAY THE ENEMY GENERAL IS TERRI-FYING.
HA HA!
HOW'S THAT?
I HEARD THIS RUMOR FROM THE FOLKS WHO ESCAPED ASAKURA.
IT'S SAID THERE ARE **YOKAI** IN DAIGO'S ARMY...
AND **THE DEAD** ARE AMONG HIS SOLDIERS, TOO!

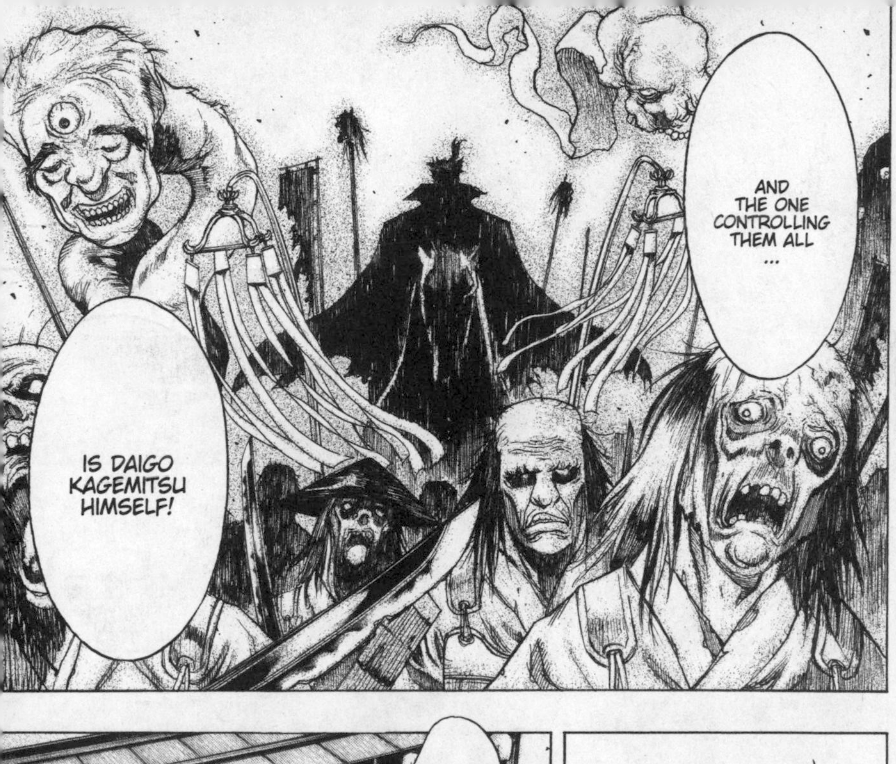
AND THE ONE CONTROLLING THEM ALL ...
IS DAIGO KAGEMITSU HIMSELF!

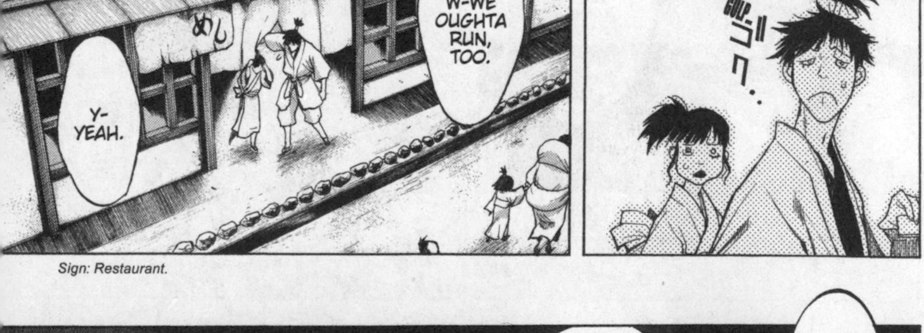
GULP
W-WE OUGHTA RUN, TOO.
めし
Y-YEAH.

Sign: Restaurant.

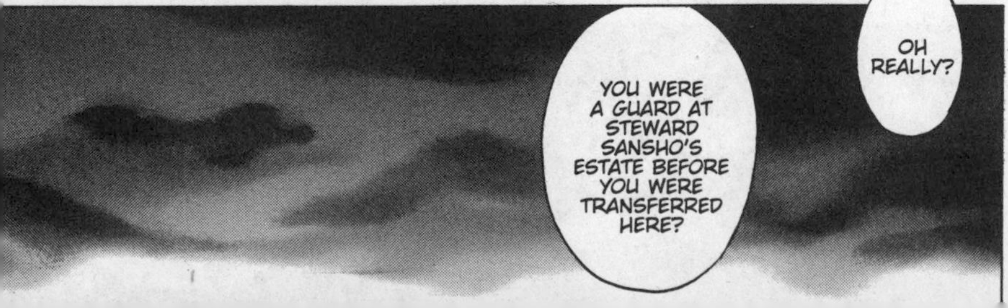
OH REALLY?
YOU WERE A GUARD AT STEWARD SANSHO'S ESTATE BEFORE YOU WERE TRANSFERRED HERE?

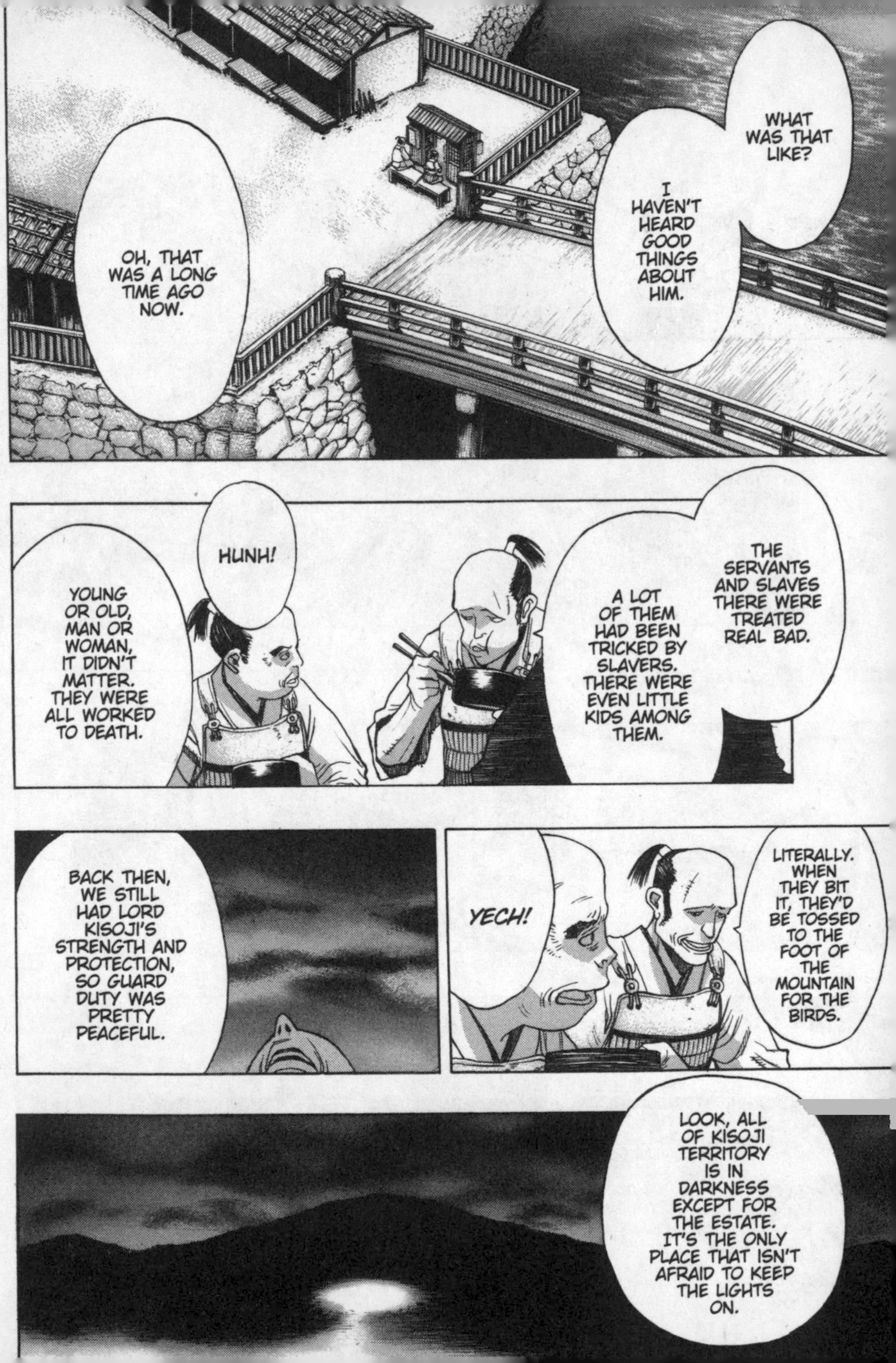
WHAT WAS THAT LIKE?
I HAVEN'T HEARD GOOD THINGS ABOUT HIM.
OH, THAT WAS A LONG TIME AGO NOW.
THE SERVANTS AND SLAVES THERE WERE TREATED REAL BAD.
A LOT OF THEM HAD BEEN TRICKED BY SLAVERS. THERE WERE EVEN LITTLE KIDS AMONG THEM.
HUNH!
YOUNG OR OLD, MAN OR WOMAN, IT DIDN'T MATTER. THEY WERE ALL WORKED TO DEATH.
LITERALLY. WHEN THEY BIT IT, THEY'D BE TOSSED TO THE FOOT OF THE MOUNTAIN FOR THE BIRDS.
YECH!
BACK THEN, WE STILL HAD LORD KISOJI'S STRENGTH AND PROTECTION, SO GUARD DUTY WAS PRETTY PEACEFUL.
LOOK, ALL OF KISOJI TERRITORY IS IN DARKNESS EXCEPT FOR THE ESTATE. IT'S THE ONLY PLACE THAT ISN'T AFRAID TO KEEP THE LIGHTS ON.

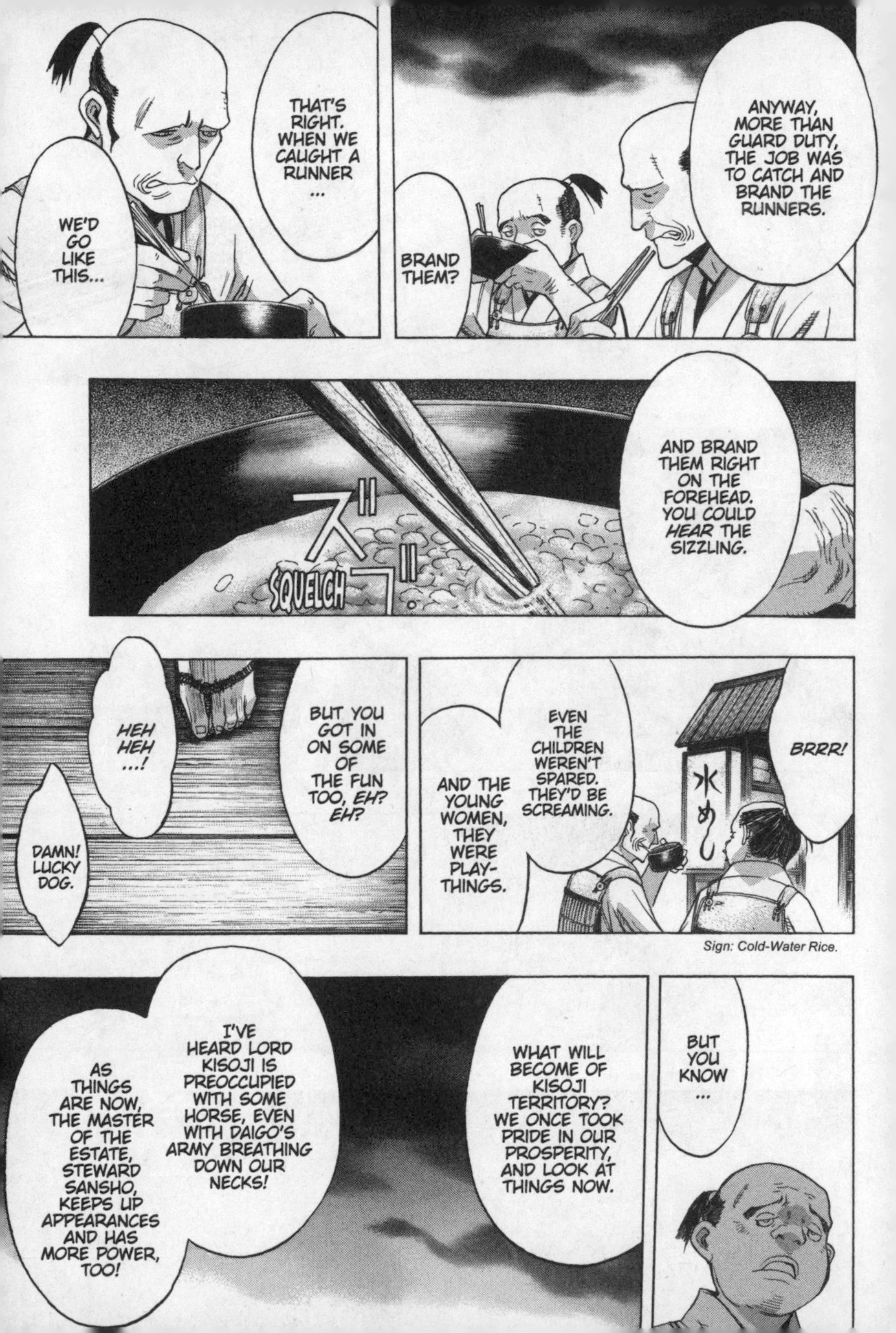
ANYWAY, MORE THAN GUARD DUTY, THE JOB WAS TO CATCH AND BRAND THE RUNNERS.
BRAND THEM?
THAT'S RIGHT. WHEN WE CAUGHT A RUNNER ...
WE'D GO LIKE THIS...
AND BRAND THEM RIGHT ON THE FOREHEAD. YOU COULD *HEAR* THE SIZZLING.
SQUELCH
BRRR!
EVEN THE CHILDREN WEREN'T SPARED. THEY'D BE SCREAMING.
AND THE YOUNG WOMEN, THEY WERE PLAY-THINGS.
水めし
BUT YOU GOT IN ON SOME OF THE FUN TOO, *EH? EH?*
HEH HEH ...!
DAMN! LUCKY DOG.
BUT YOU KNOW ...
WHAT WILL BECOME OF KISOJI TERRITORY? WE ONCE TOOK PRIDE IN OUR PROSPERITY, AND LOOK AT THINGS NOW.
I'VE HEARD LORD KISOJI IS PREOCCUPIED WITH SOME HORSE, EVEN WITH DAIGO'S ARMY BREATHING DOWN OUR NECKS!
AS THINGS ARE NOW, THE MASTER OF THE ESTATE, STEWARD SANSHO, KEEPS UP APPEARANCES AND HAS MORE POWER, TOO!

Sign: Cold-Water Rice.

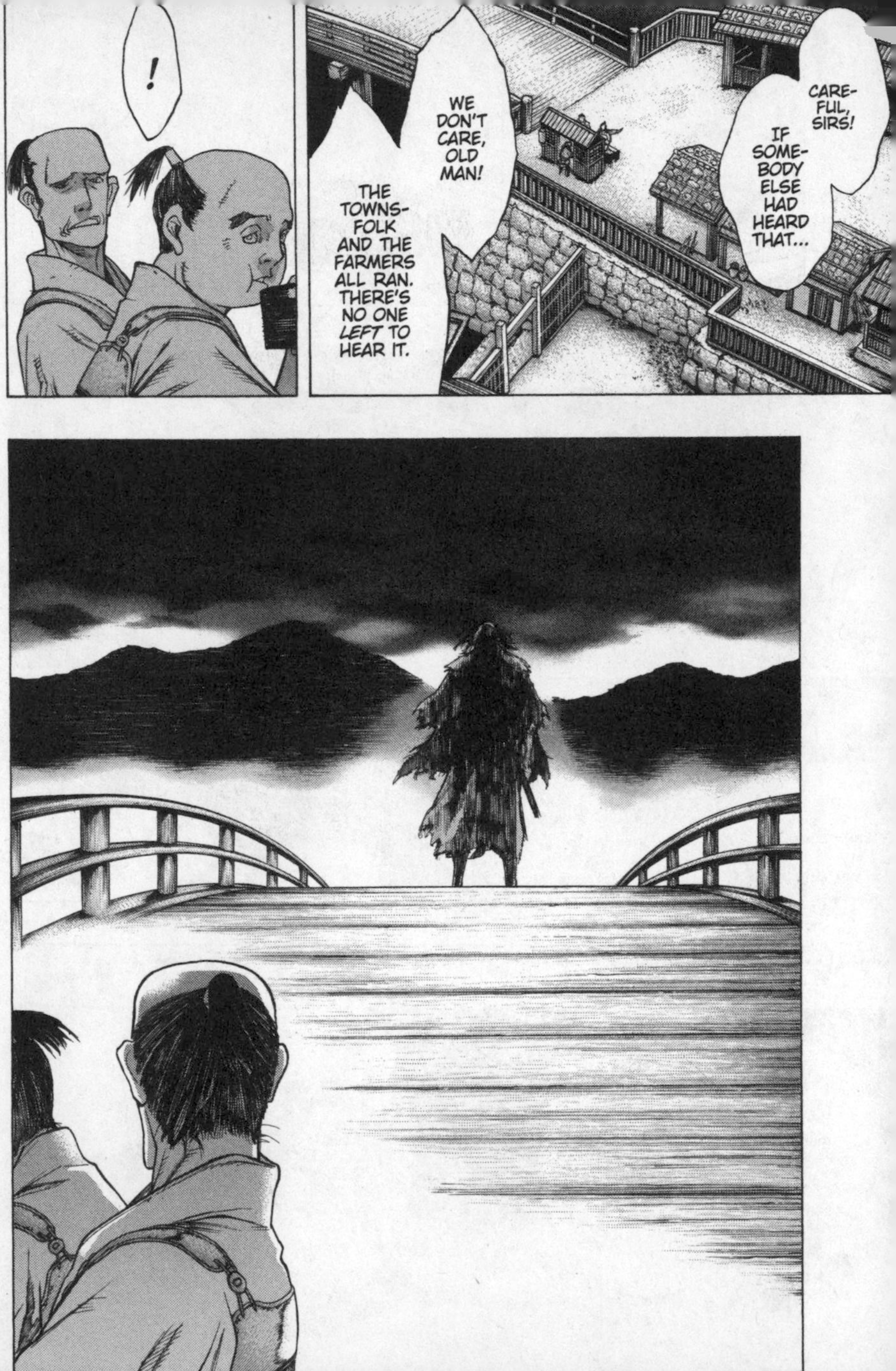
CARE-FUL, SIRS!
IF SOME-BODY ELSE HAD HEARD THAT...
WE DON'T CARE, OLD MAN!
THE TOWNS-FOLK AND THE FARMERS ALL RAN. THERE'S NO ONE *LEFT* TO HEAR IT.
!

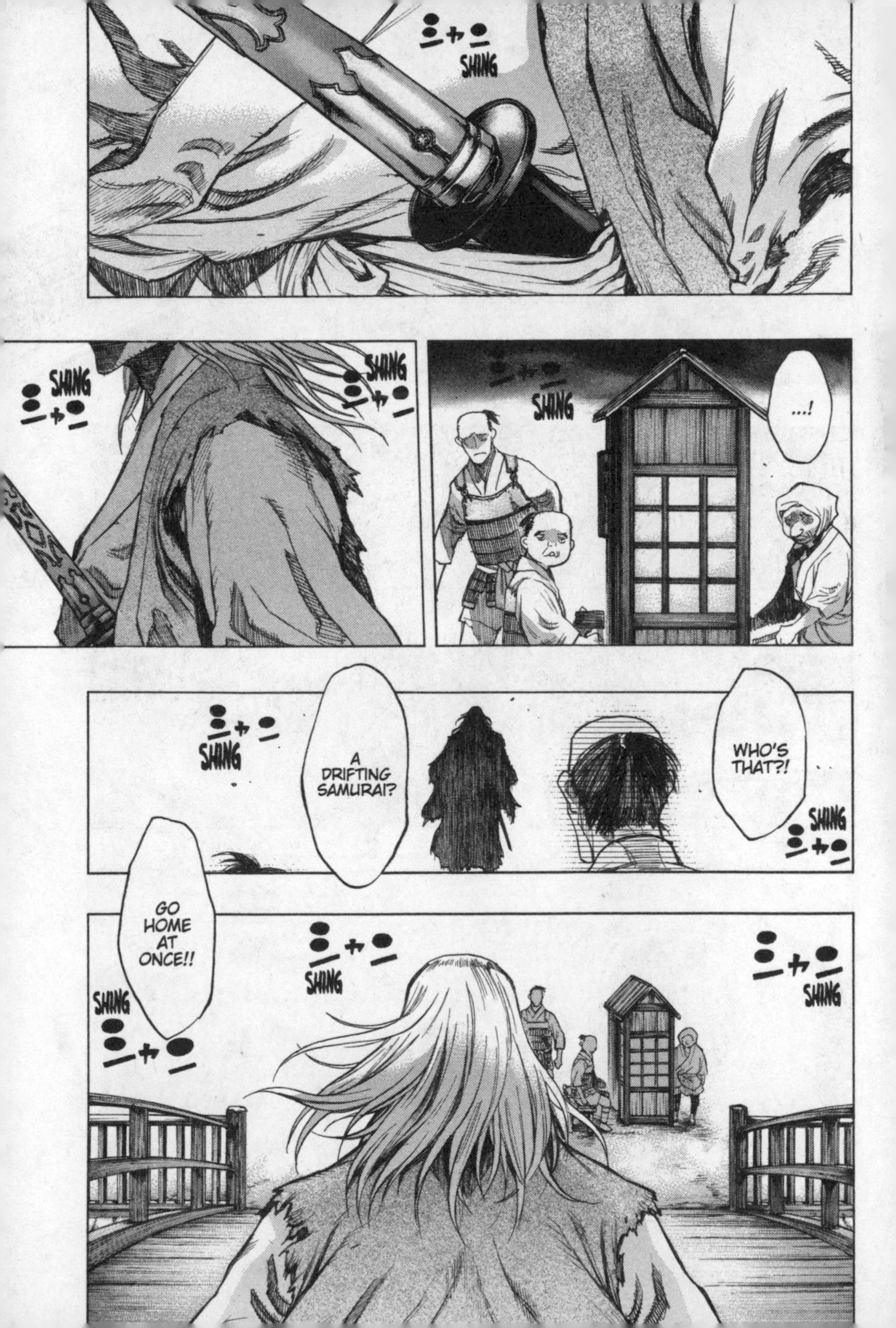
SHING
SHING
...!
SHING
SHING
WHO'S THAT?!
SHING
A DRIFTING SAMURAI?
SHING
SHING
GO HOME AT ONCE!!
SHING
SHING

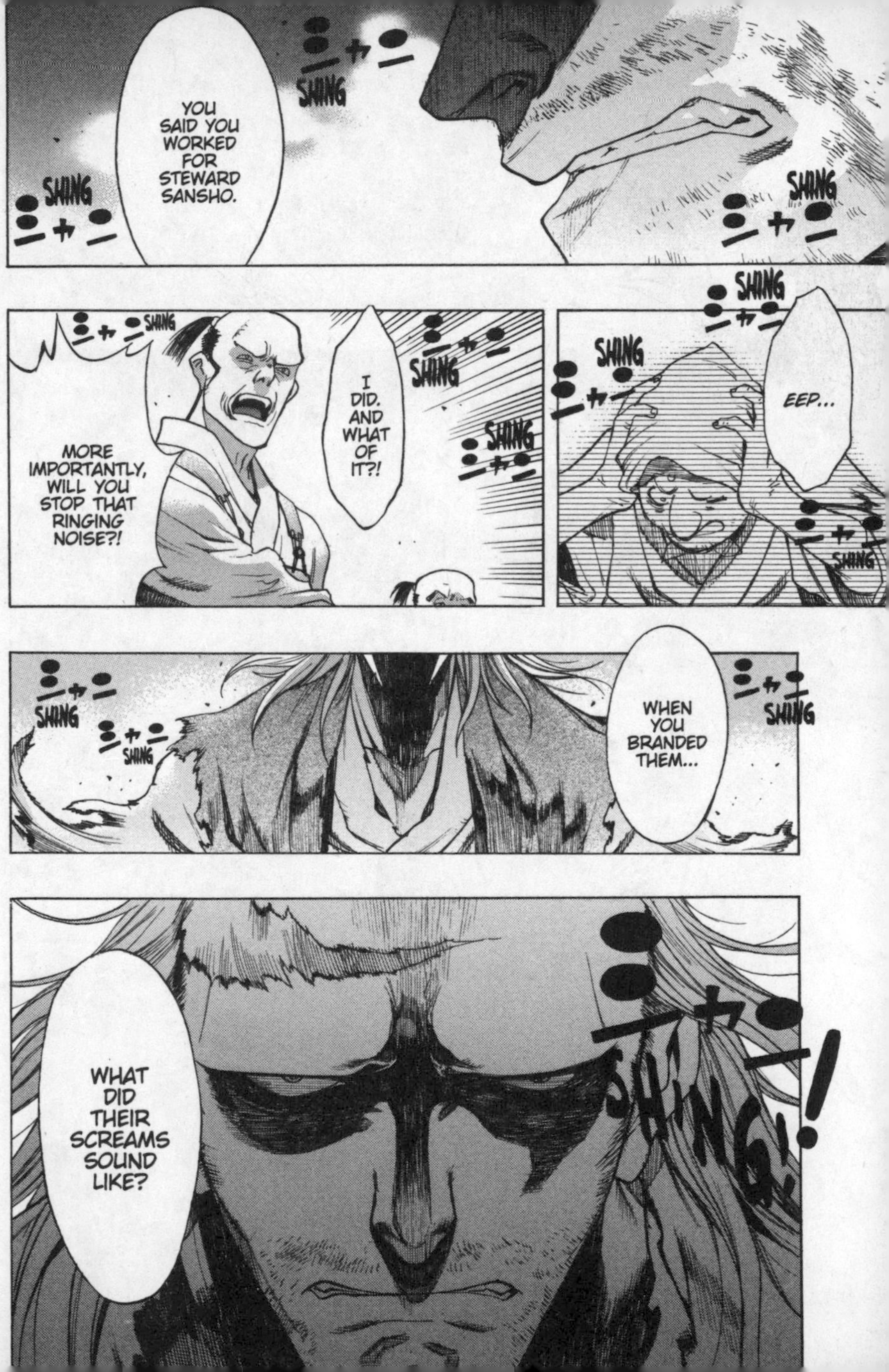
SHING
SHING
YOU SAID YOU WORKED FOR STEWARD SANSHO.
SHING
SHING
SHING
EEP...
SHING
SHING
SHING
I DID. AND WHAT OF IT?!
SHING
MORE IMPORTANTLY, WILL YOU STOP THAT RINGING NOISE?!
SHING
WHEN YOU BRANDED THEM...
SHING
SHING
SHING!!
WHAT DID THEIR SCREAMS SOUND LIKE?

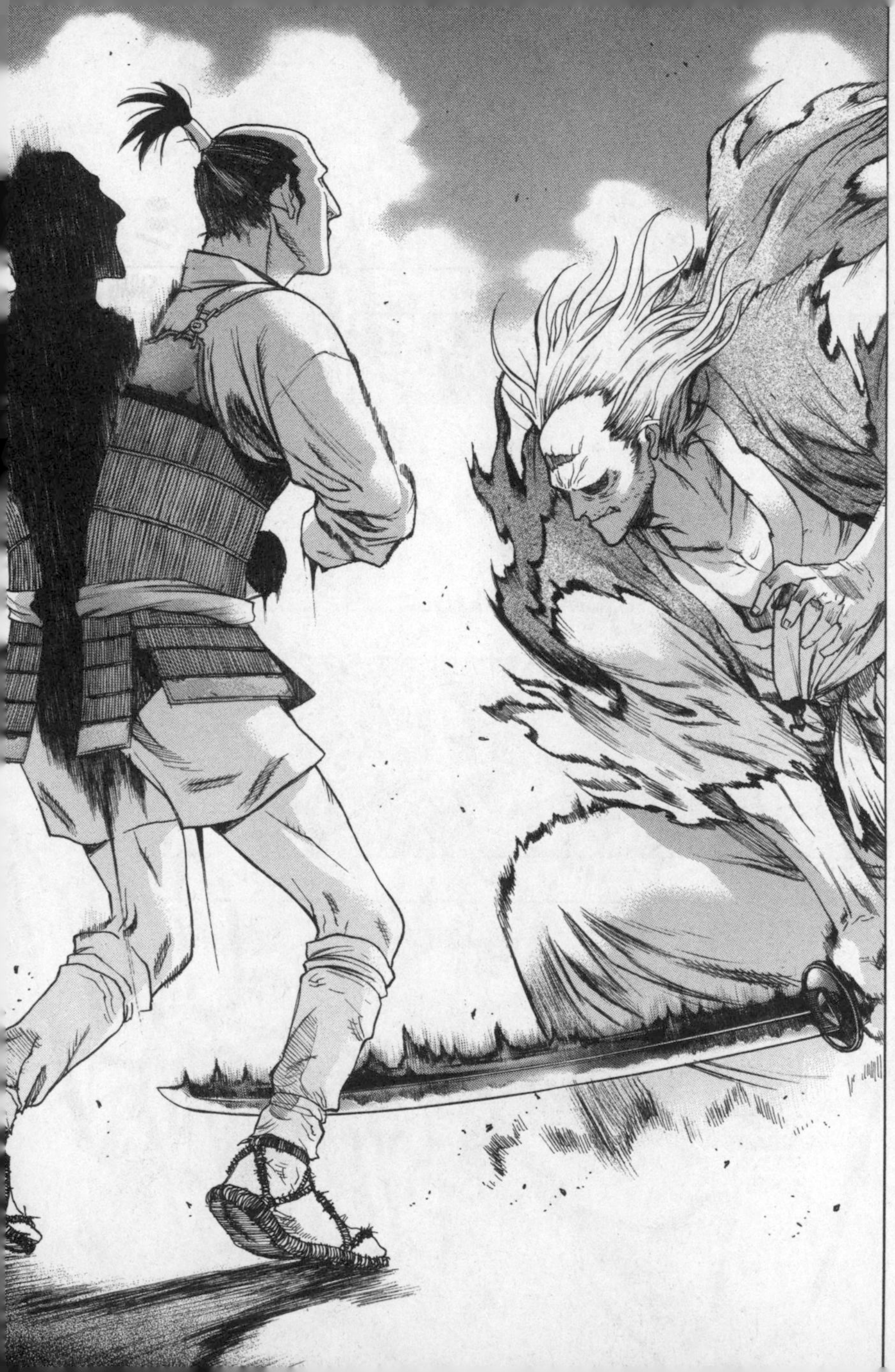

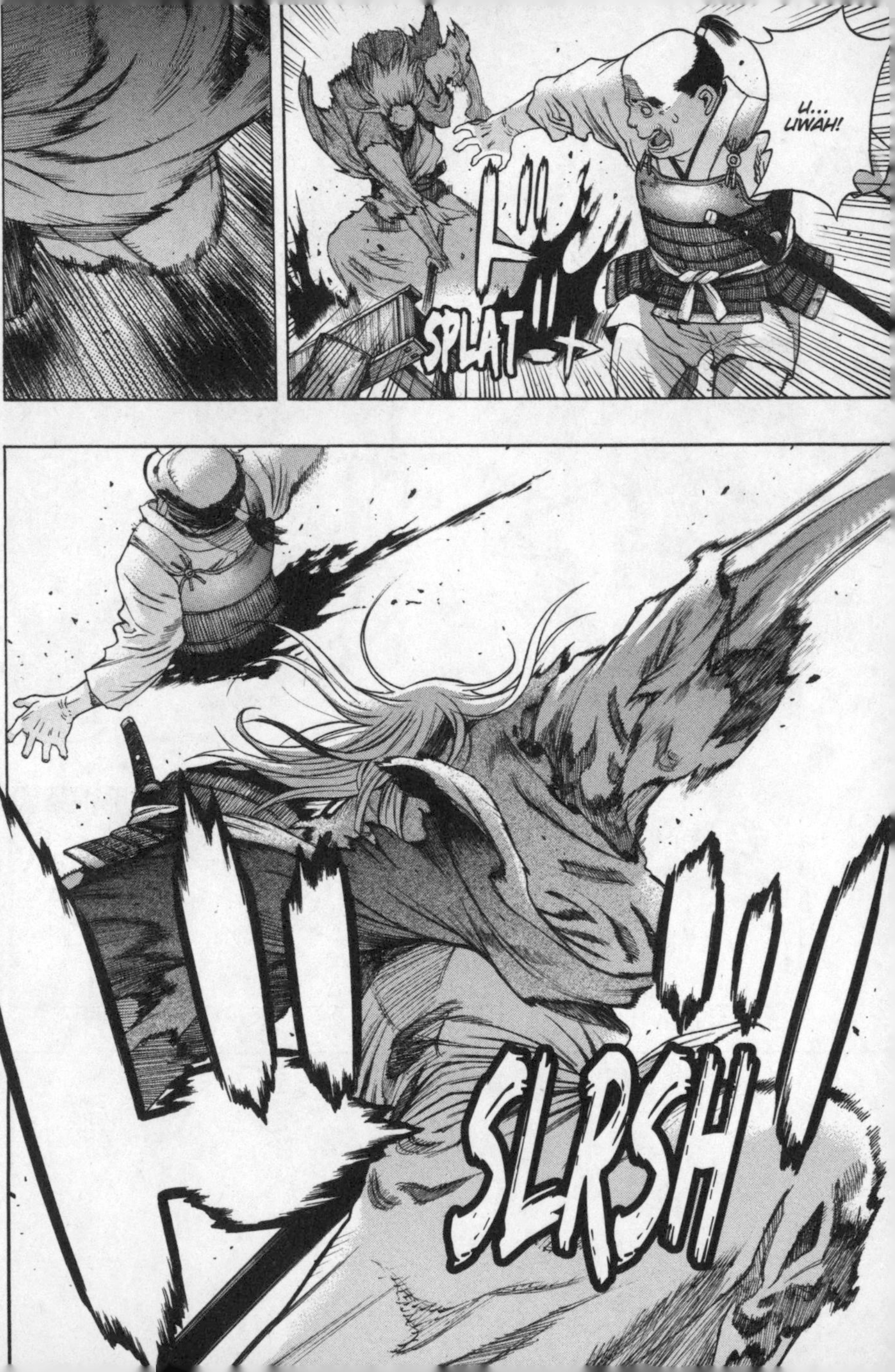
U... UWAH!
SPLAT
SLRSH

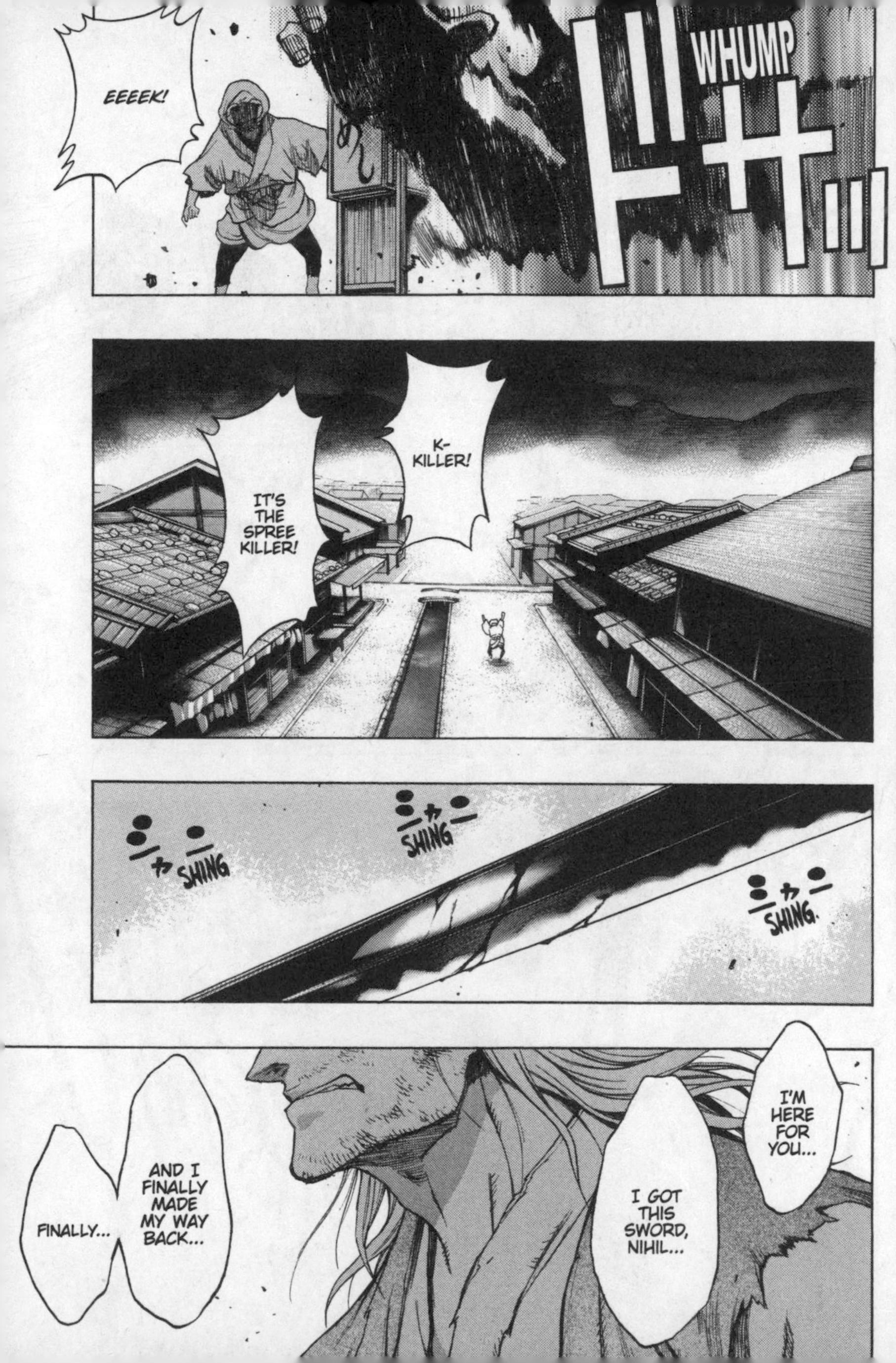
WHUMP
EEEEK!
K-KILLER!
IT'S THE SPREE KILLER!
SHING
SHING
SHING
I'M HERE FOR YOU...
I GOT THIS SWORD, NIHIL...
AND I FINALLY MADE MY WAY BACK...
FINALLY...

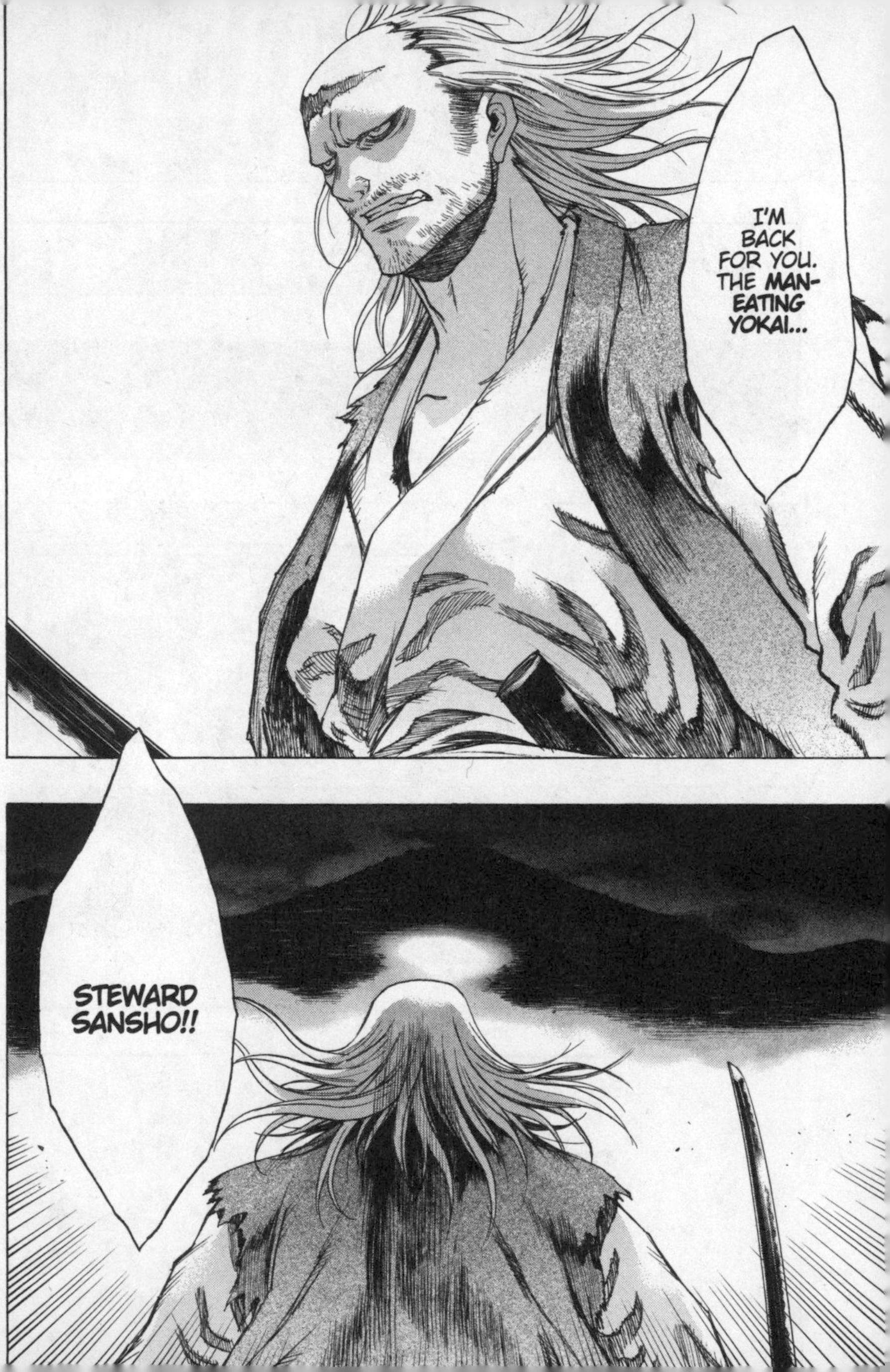
I'M BACK FOR YOU. THE MAN-EATING YOKAI...
STEWARD SANSHO!!

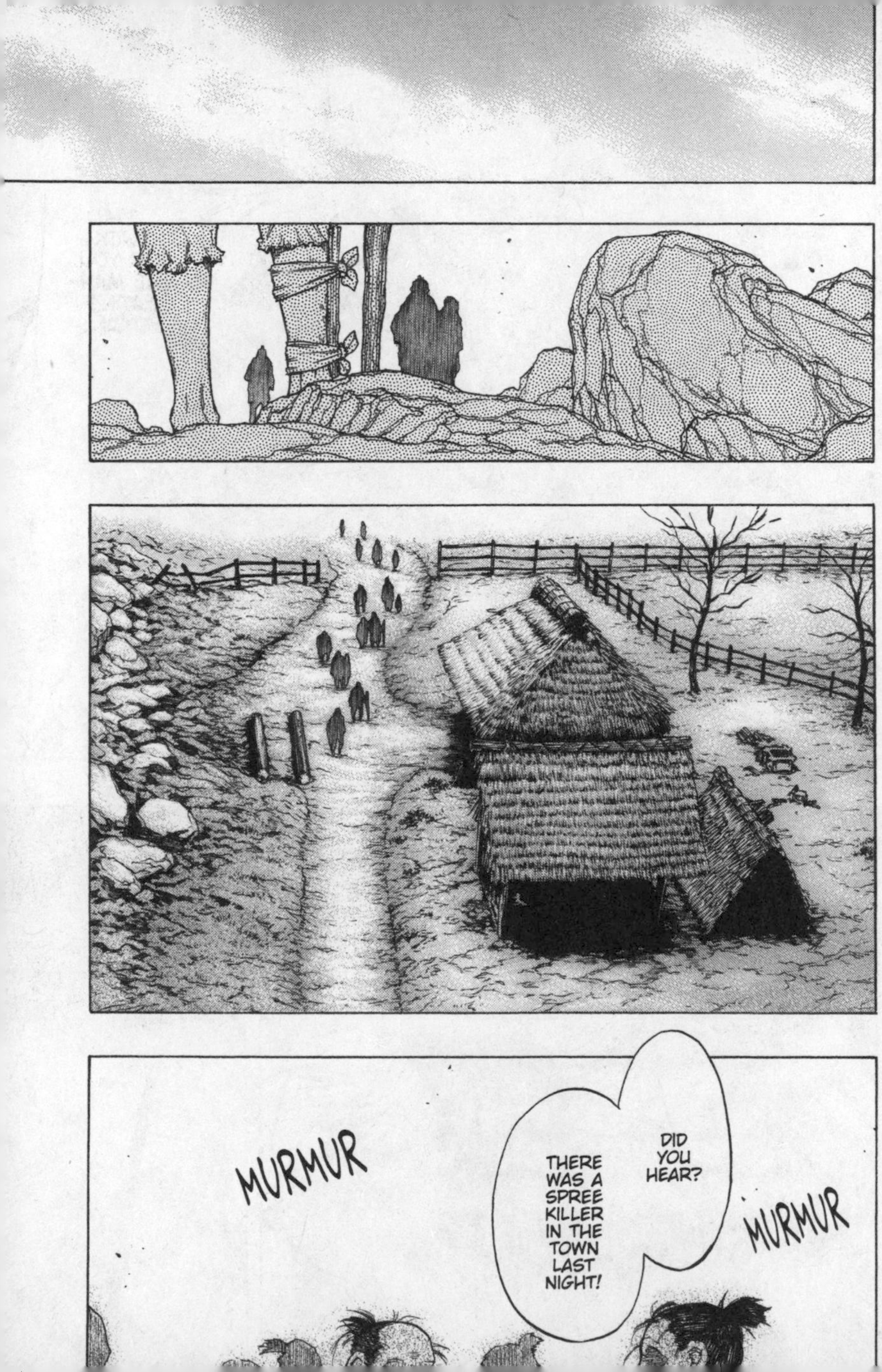
DID YOU HEAR?
THERE WAS A SPREE KILLER IN THE TOWN LAST NIGHT!
MURMUR
MURMUR

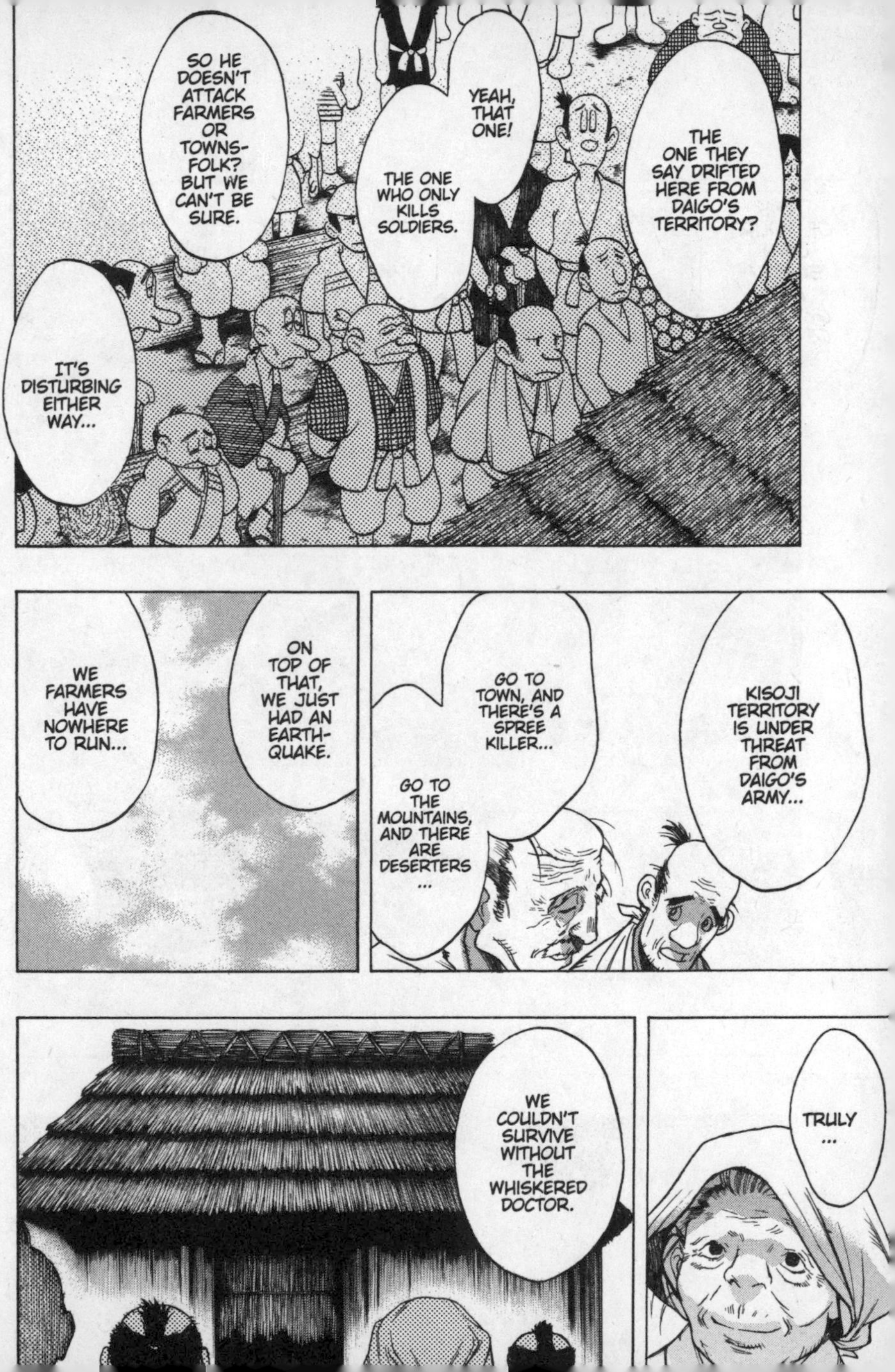
THE ONE THEY SAY DRIFTED HERE FROM DAIGO'S TERRITORY?
YEAH, THAT ONE!
THE ONE WHO ONLY KILLS SOLDIERS.
SO HE DOESN'T ATTACK FARMERS OR TOWNS-FOLK? BUT WE CAN'T BE SURE.
IT'S DISTURBING EITHER WAY...
KISOJI TERRITORY IS UNDER THREAT FROM DAIGO'S ARMY...
GO TO TOWN, AND THERE'S A SPREE KILLER...
GO TO THE MOUNTAINS, AND THERE ARE DESERTERS ...
ON TOP OF THAT, WE JUST HAD AN EARTH-QUAKE.
WE FARMERS HAVE NOWHERE TO RUN...
TRULY ...
WE COULDN'T SURVIVE WITHOUT THE WHISKERED DOCTOR.

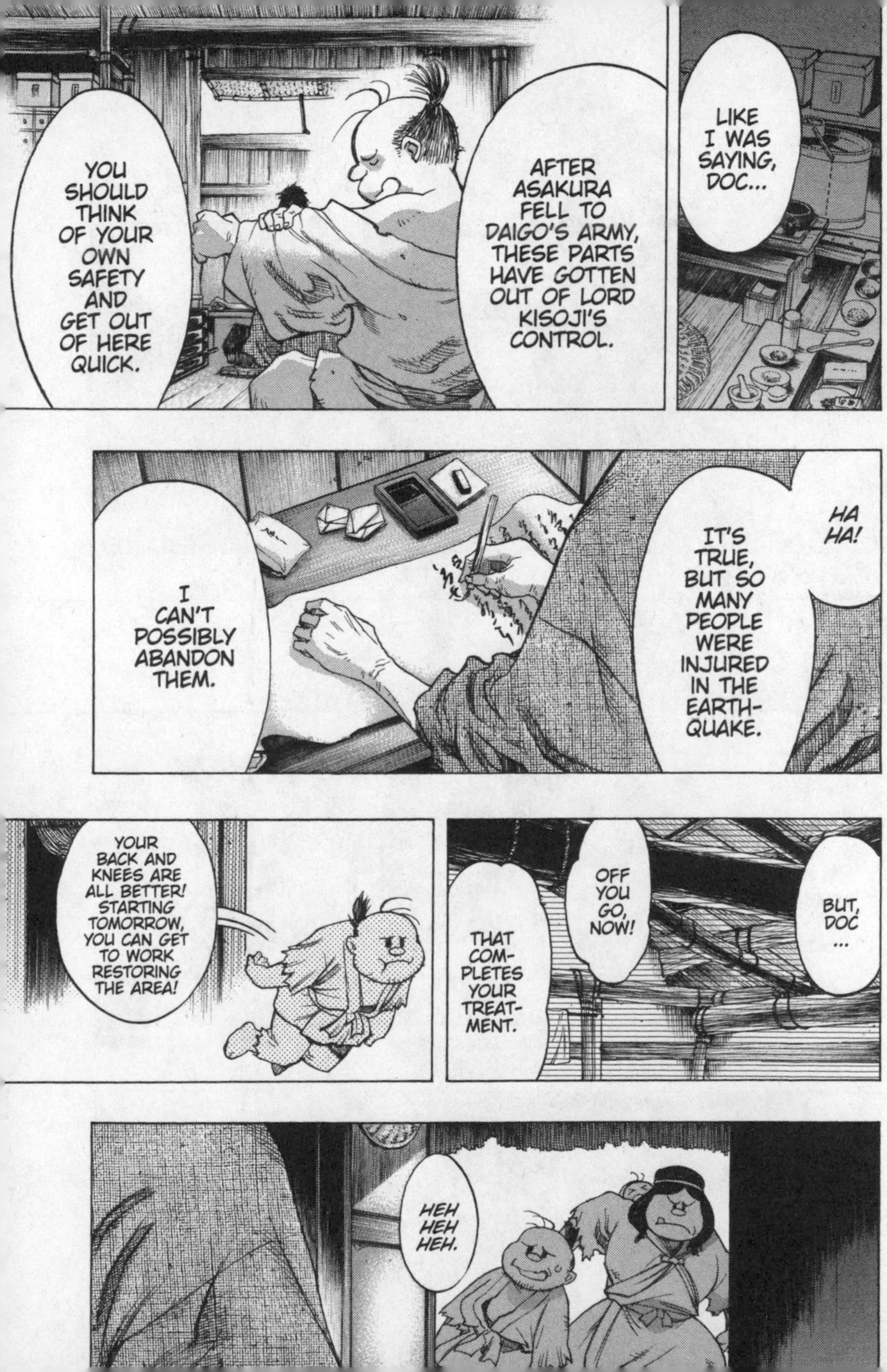
LIKE I WAS SAYING, DOC...
AFTER ASAKURA FELL TO DAIGO'S ARMY, THESE PARTS HAVE GOTTEN OUT OF LORD KISOJI'S CONTROL.
YOU SHOULD THINK OF YOUR OWN SAFETY AND GET OUT OF HERE QUICK.
HA HA!
IT'S TRUE, BUT SO MANY PEOPLE WERE INJURED IN THE EARTH-QUAKE.
I CAN'T POSSIBLY ABANDON THEM.
BUT, DOC ...
OFF YOU GO, NOW!
THAT COM-PLETES YOUR TREAT-MENT.
YOUR BACK AND KNEES ARE ALL BETTER! STARTING TOMORROW, YOU CAN GET TO WORK RESTORING THE AREA!
HEH HEH HEH.

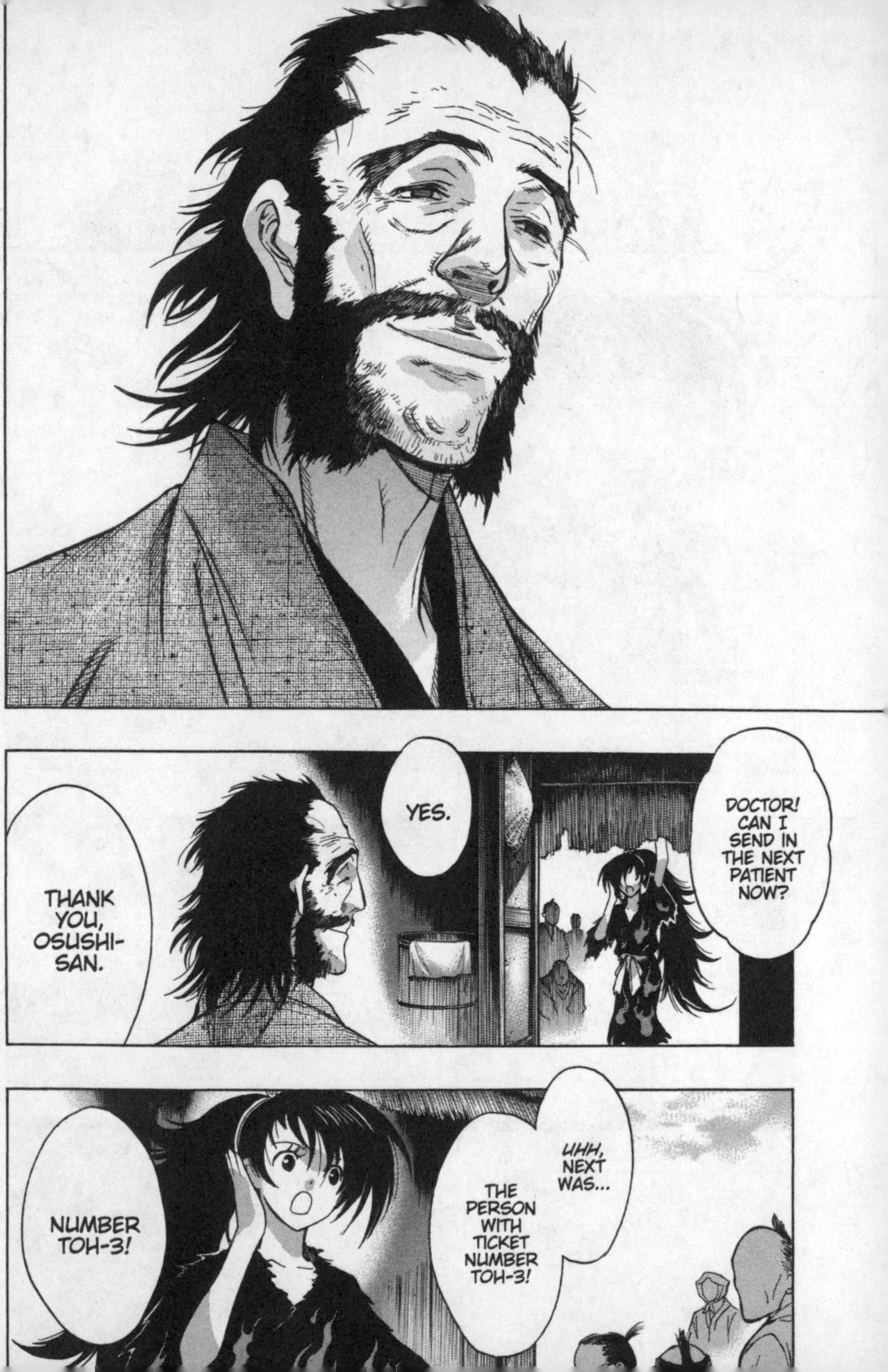
DOCTOR! CAN I SEND IN THE NEXT PATIENT NOW?
YES.
THANK YOU, OSUSHI-SAN.
UHH, NEXT WAS...
THE PERSON WITH TICKET NUMBER TOH-3!
NUMBER TOH-3!

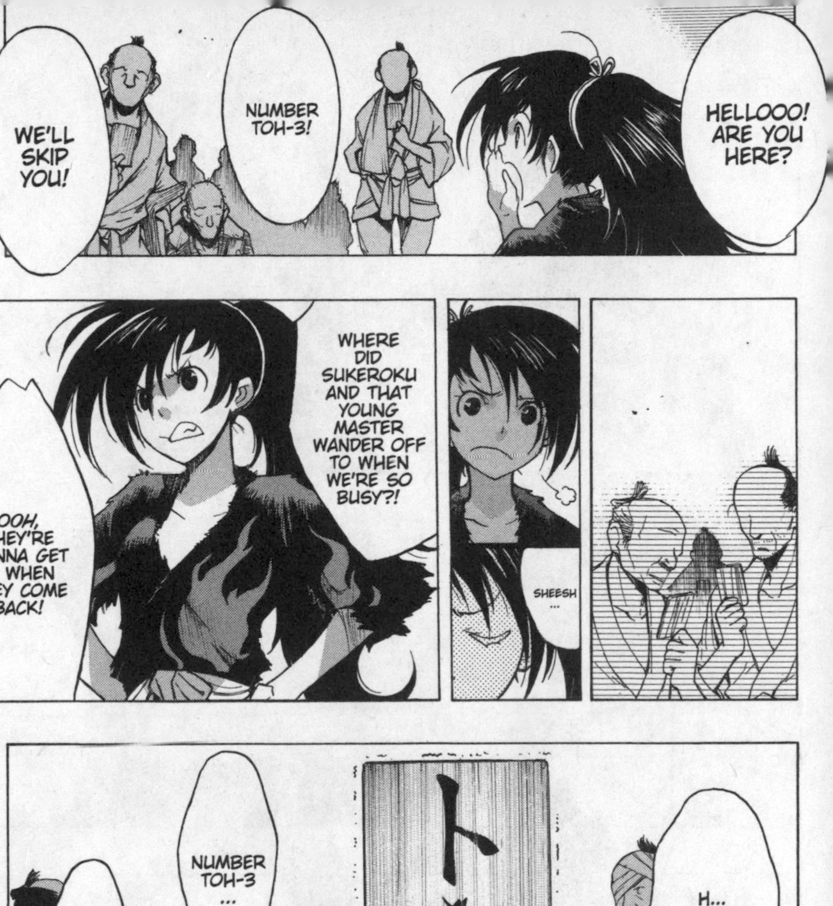
HELLOOO! ARE YOU HERE?
NUMBER TOH-3!
WE'LL SKIP YOU!
SHEESH...
WHERE DID SUKEROKU AND THAT YOUNG MASTER WANDER OFF TO WHEN WE'RE SO BUSY?!
OOH, THEY'RE GONNA GET IT WHEN THEY COME BACK!
H... HERE...
NUMBER TOH-3...
THAT'S ME...
Card: Toh-3.

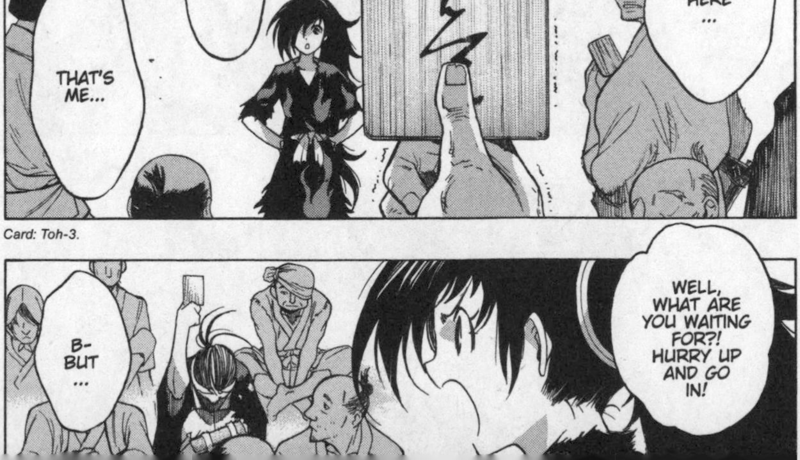
WELL, WHAT ARE YOU WAITING FOR?! HURRY UP AND GO IN!
B-BUT...

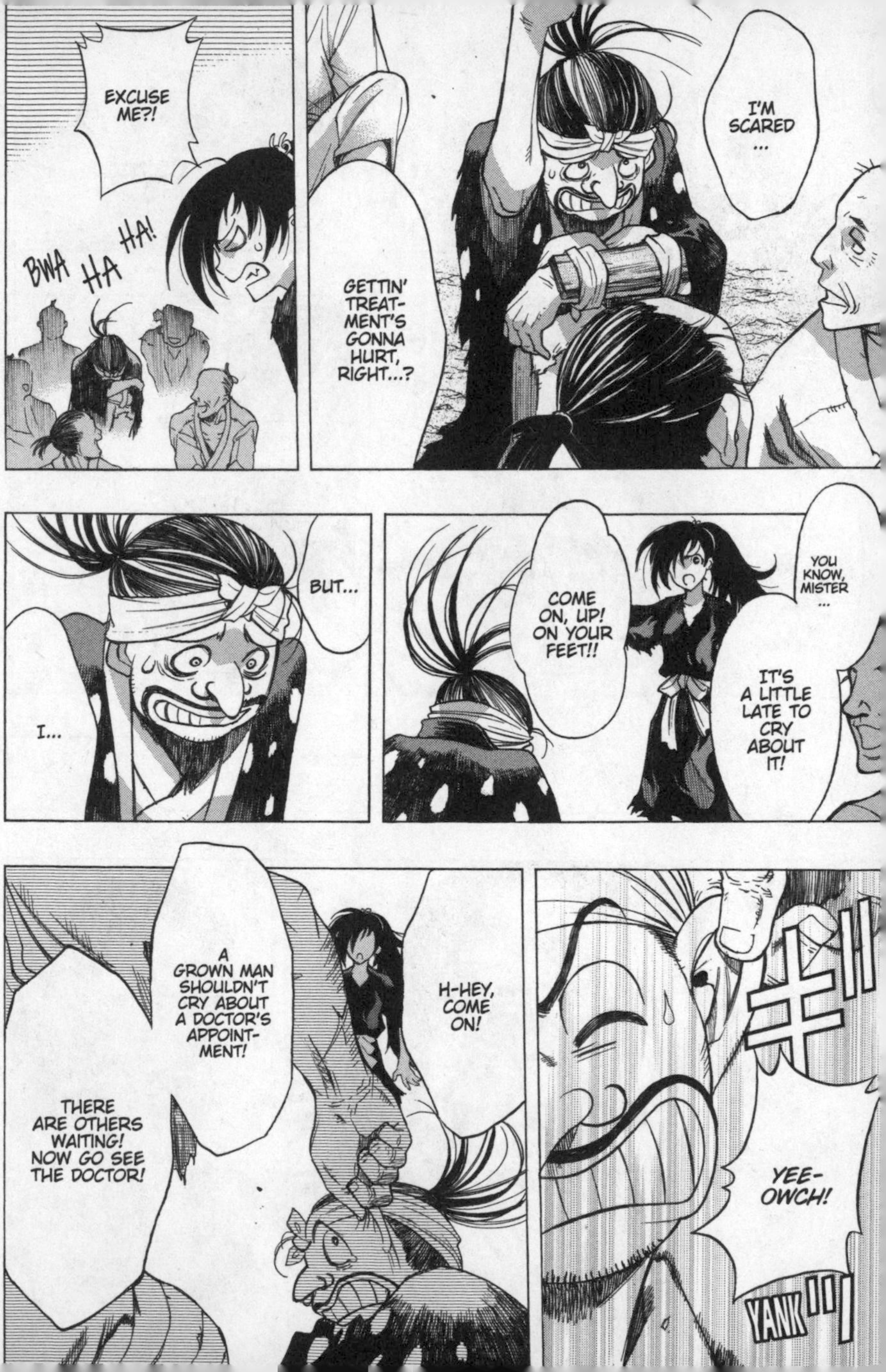
I'M SCARED ...
GETTIN' TREATMENT'S GONNA HURT, RIGHT...?
EXCUSE ME?!
BWA HA HA!
YOU KNOW, MISTER ...
IT'S A LITTLE LATE TO CRY ABOUT IT!
COME ON, UP! ON YOUR FEET!!
BUT...
I...
YEE-OWCH!
YANK
H-HEY, COME ON!
A GROWN MAN SHOULDN'T CRY ABOUT A DOCTOR'S APPOINTMENT!
THERE ARE OTHERS WAITING! NOW GO SEE THE DOCTOR!

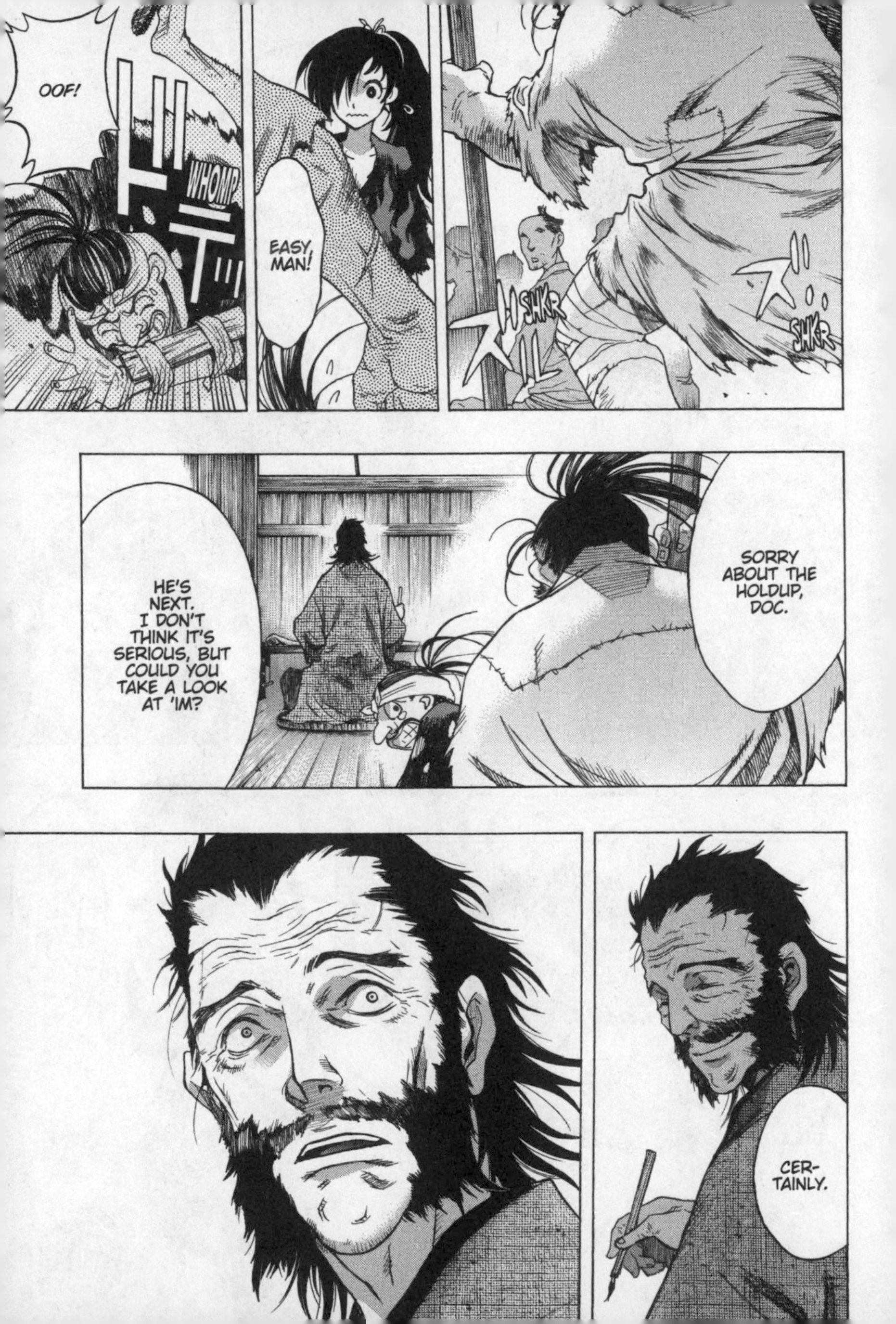
SHKR
SHKR
EASY MAN!
OOF!
WHOMP
SORRY ABOUT THE HOLDUP, DOC.
HE'S NEXT. I DON'T THINK IT'S SERIOUS, BUT COULD YOU TAKE A LOOK AT 'IM?
CER-TAINLY.

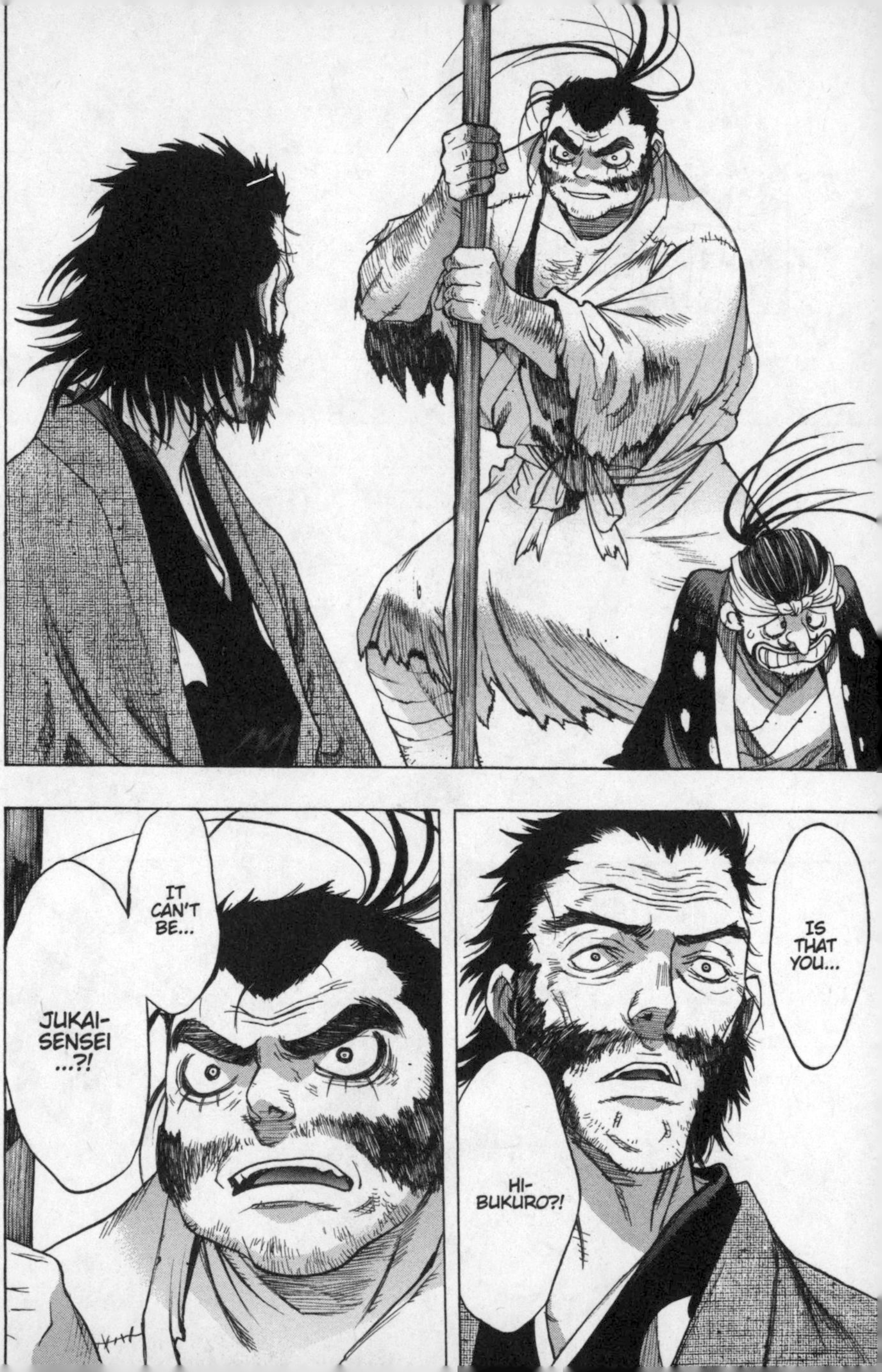
IS THAT YOU...
HI-BUKURO?!
IT CAN'T BE...
JUKAI-SENSEI ...?!

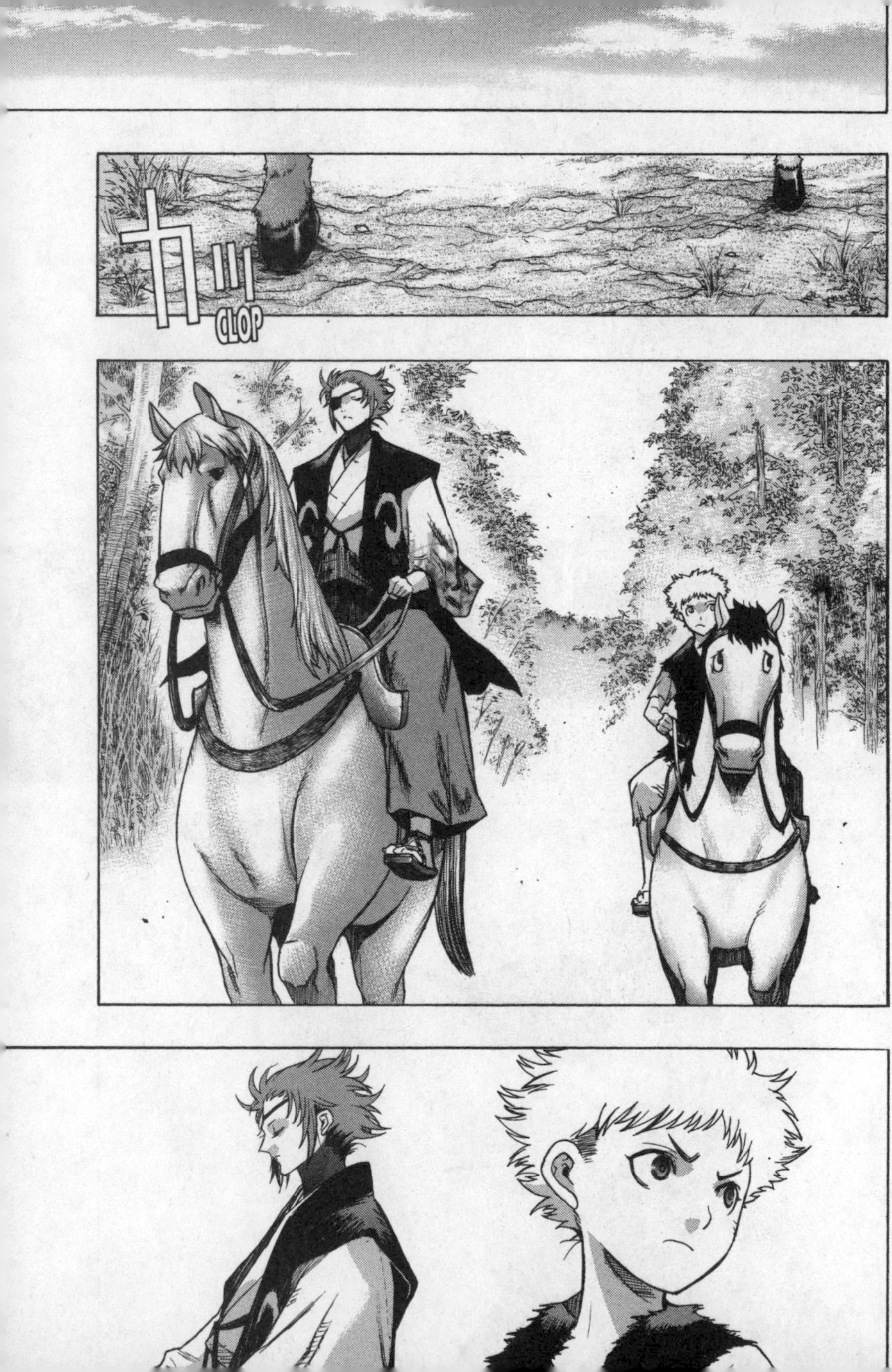
カッ
CLOP

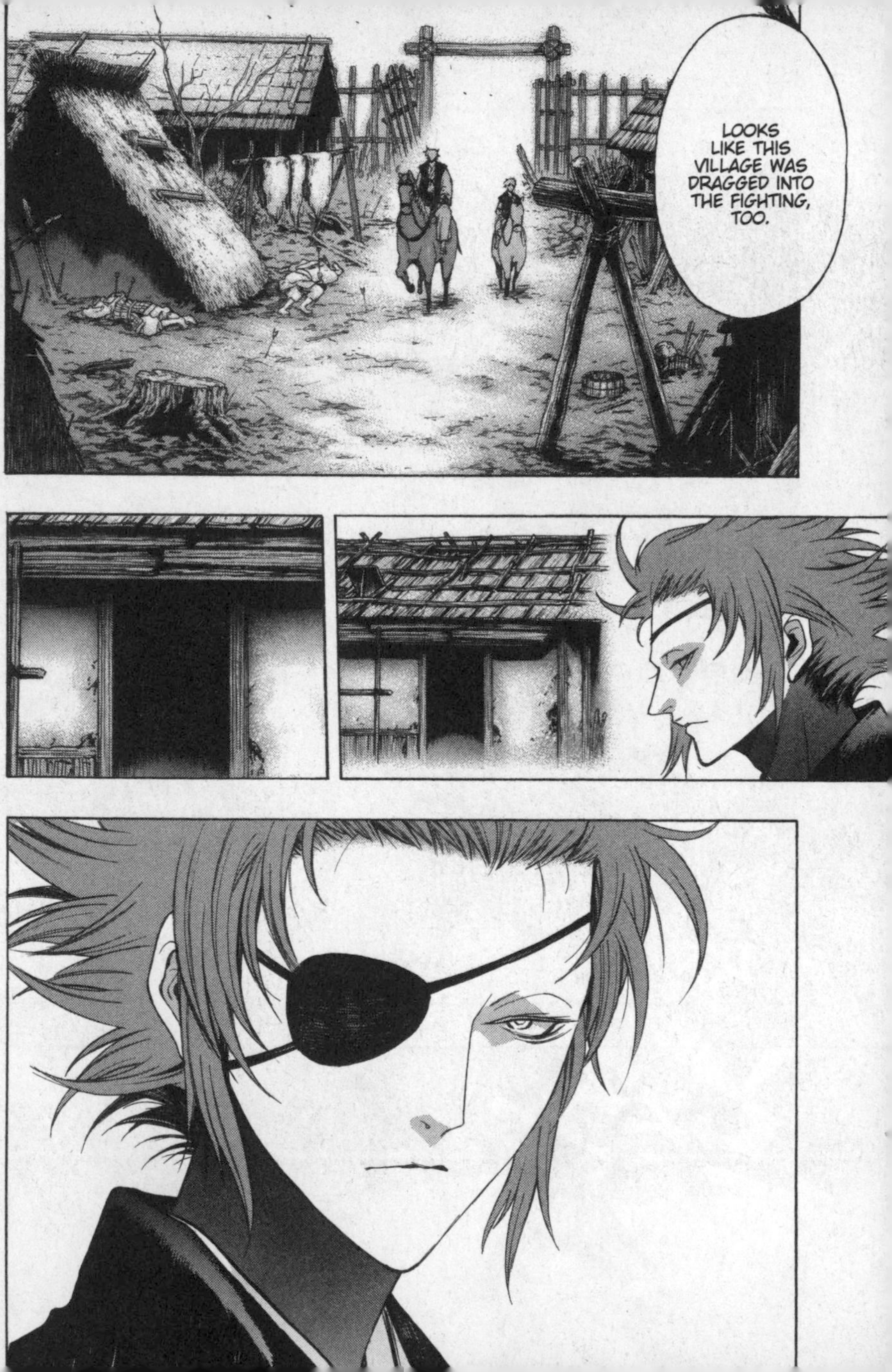
LOOKS LIKE THIS VILLAGE WAS DRAGGED INTO THE FIGHTING, TOO.

THE LEGEND OF
DORORO AND
HYAKKIMARU

どろろと
百鬼丸伝

THE LEGEND OF
DORORO AND **HYAKKIMARU**

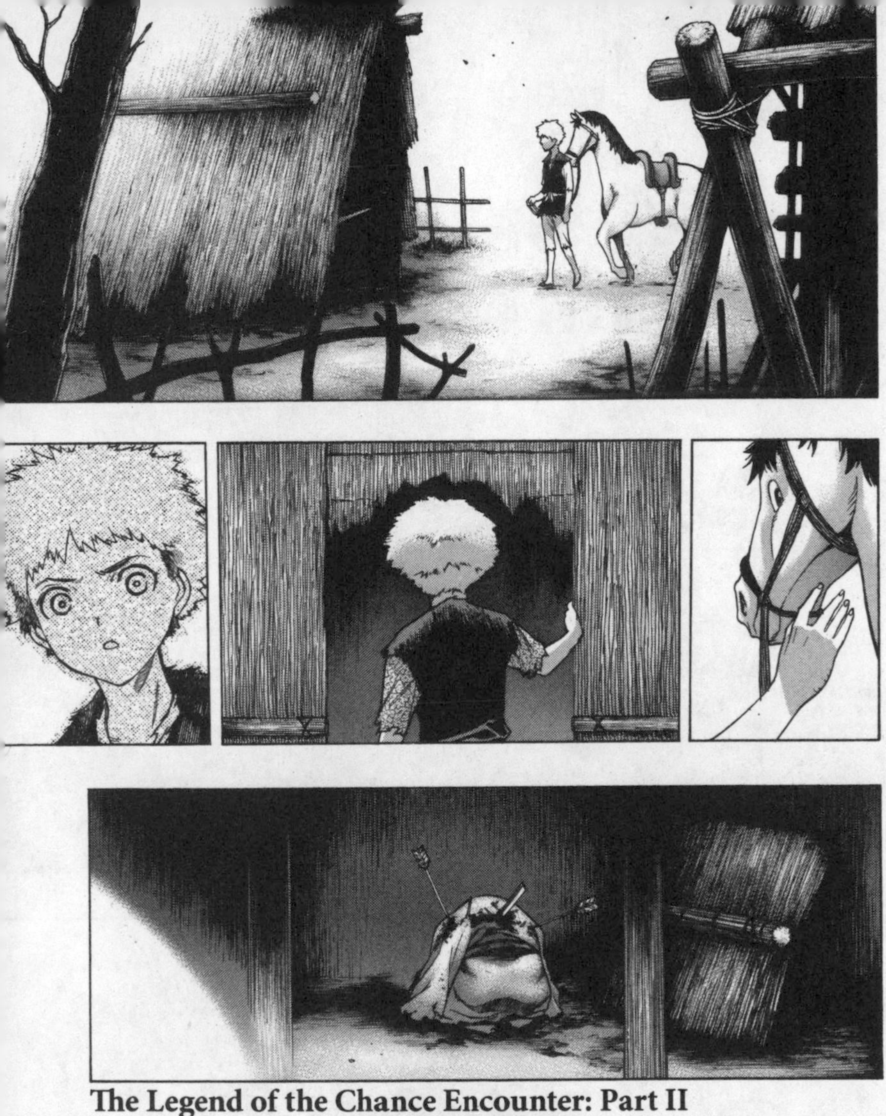

The Legend of the Chance Encounter: Part II

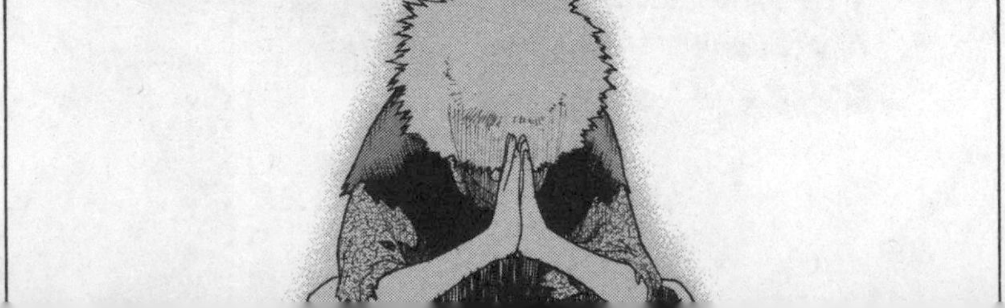

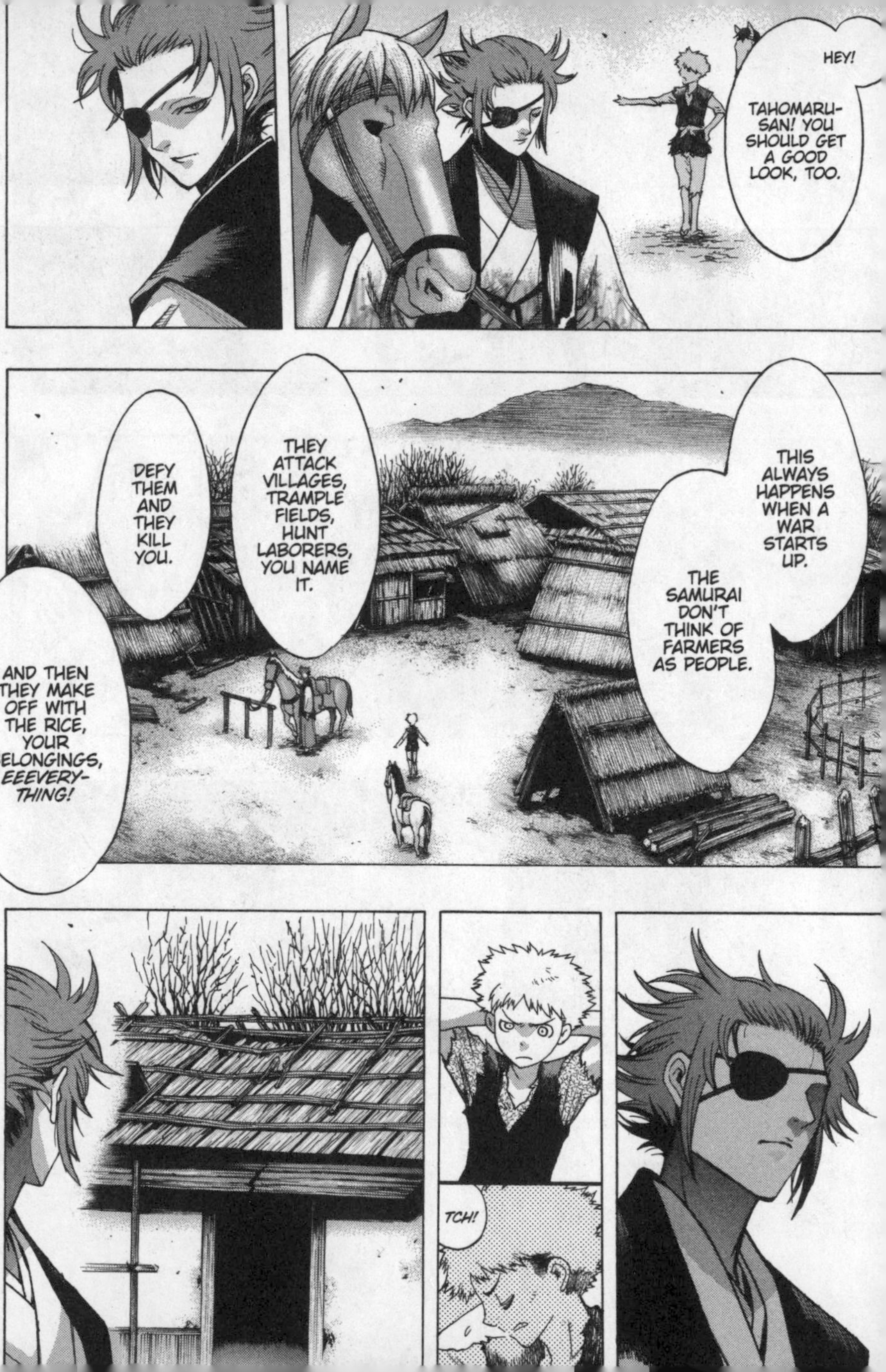
HEY!
TAHOMARU-SAN! YOU SHOULD GET A GOOD LOOK, TOO.
THIS ALWAYS HAPPENS WHEN A WAR STARTS UP.
THE SAMURAI DON'T THINK OF FARMERS AS PEOPLE.
THEY ATTACK VILLAGES, TRAMPLE FIELDS, HUNT LABORERS, YOU NAME IT.
DEFY THEM AND THEY KILL YOU.
AND THEN THEY MAKE OFF WITH THE RICE, YOUR BELONGINGS, *EEEVERY-THING!*
TCH!

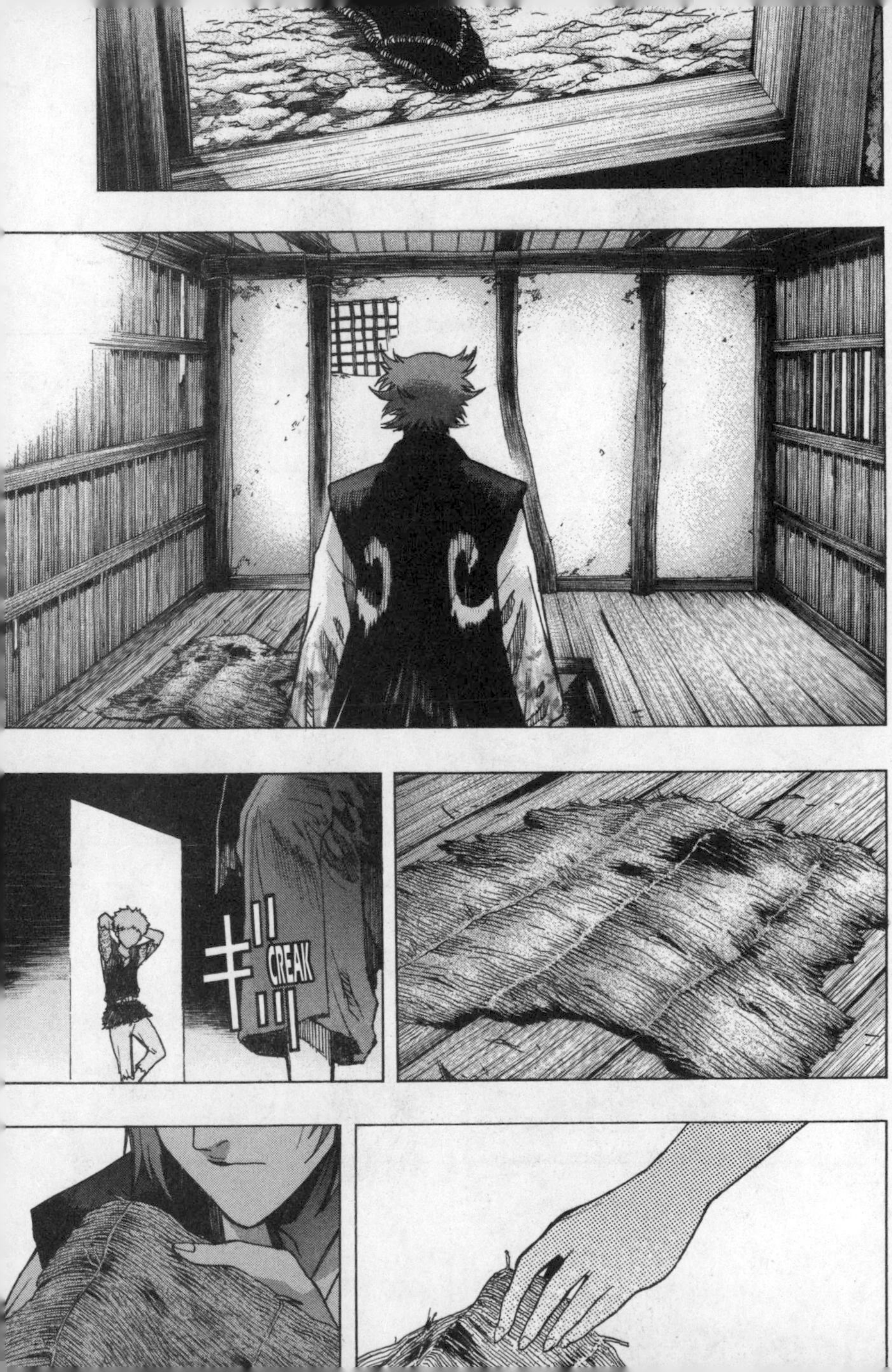
ギ
CREAK

HUH?

IN THIS AREA?

IF THERE WERE SURVIVORS, WHERE WOULD THEY BE TAKEN?

SUKE-ROKU.

HMMM.

LET'S SEE...

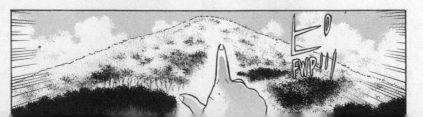

FWP!!!

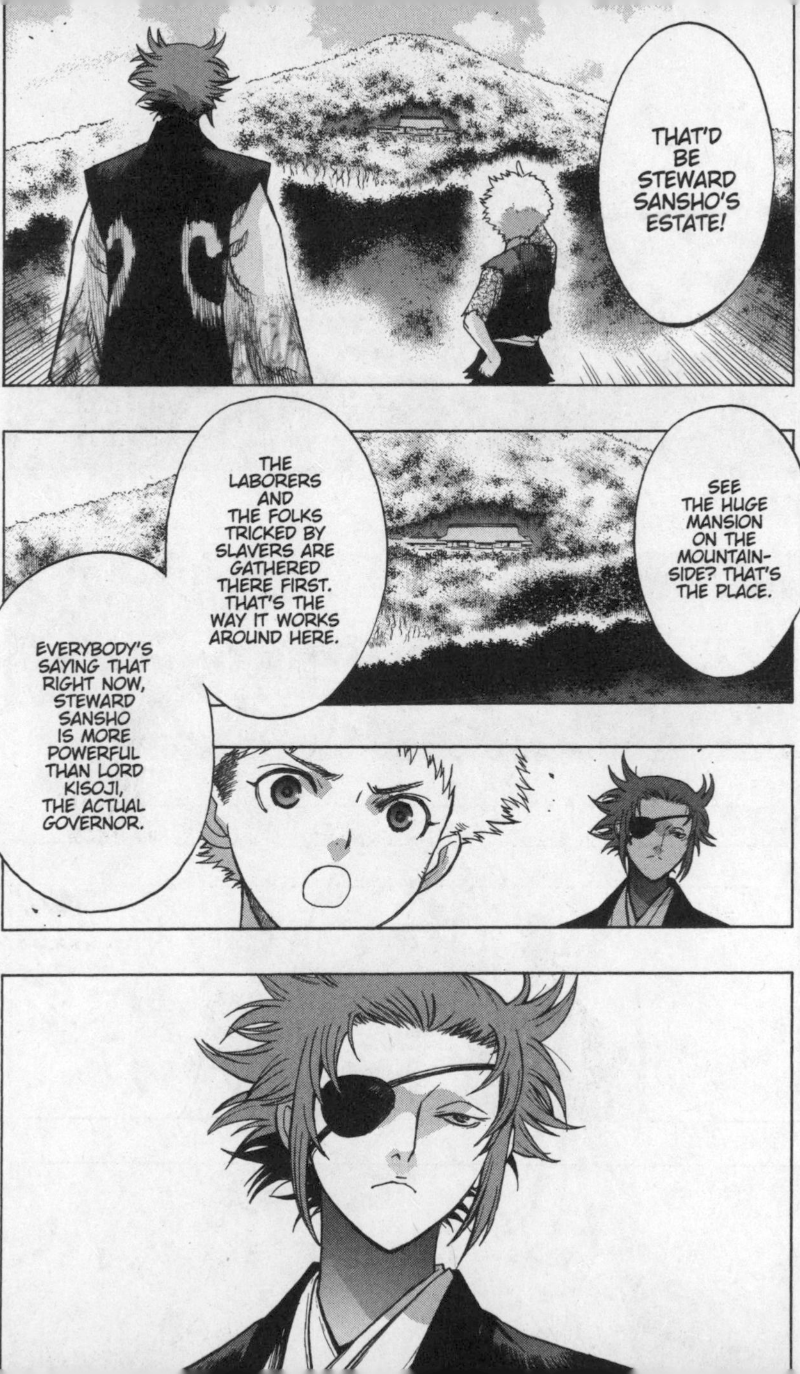
THAT'D BE STEWARD SANSHO'S ESTATE!
SEE THE HUGE MANSION ON THE MOUNTAIN-SIDE? THAT'S THE PLACE.
THE LABORERS AND THE FOLKS TRICKED BY SLAVERS ARE GATHERED THERE FIRST. THAT'S THE WAY IT WORKS AROUND HERE.
EVERYBODY'S SAYING THAT RIGHT NOW, STEWARD SANSHO IS MORE POWERFUL THAN LORD KISOJI, THE ACTUAL GOVERNOR.

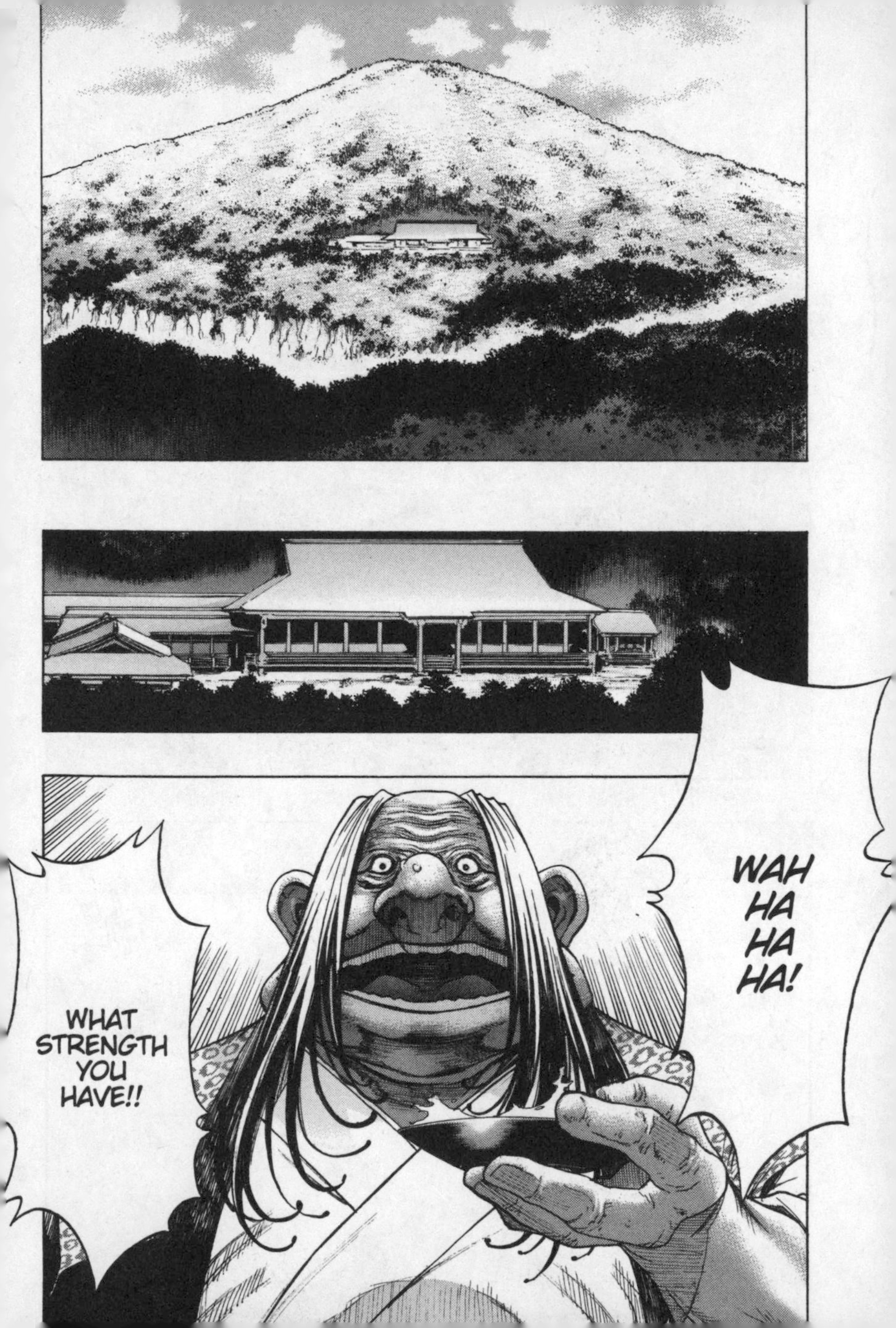
WAH HA HA HA!
WHAT STRENGTH YOU HAVE!!

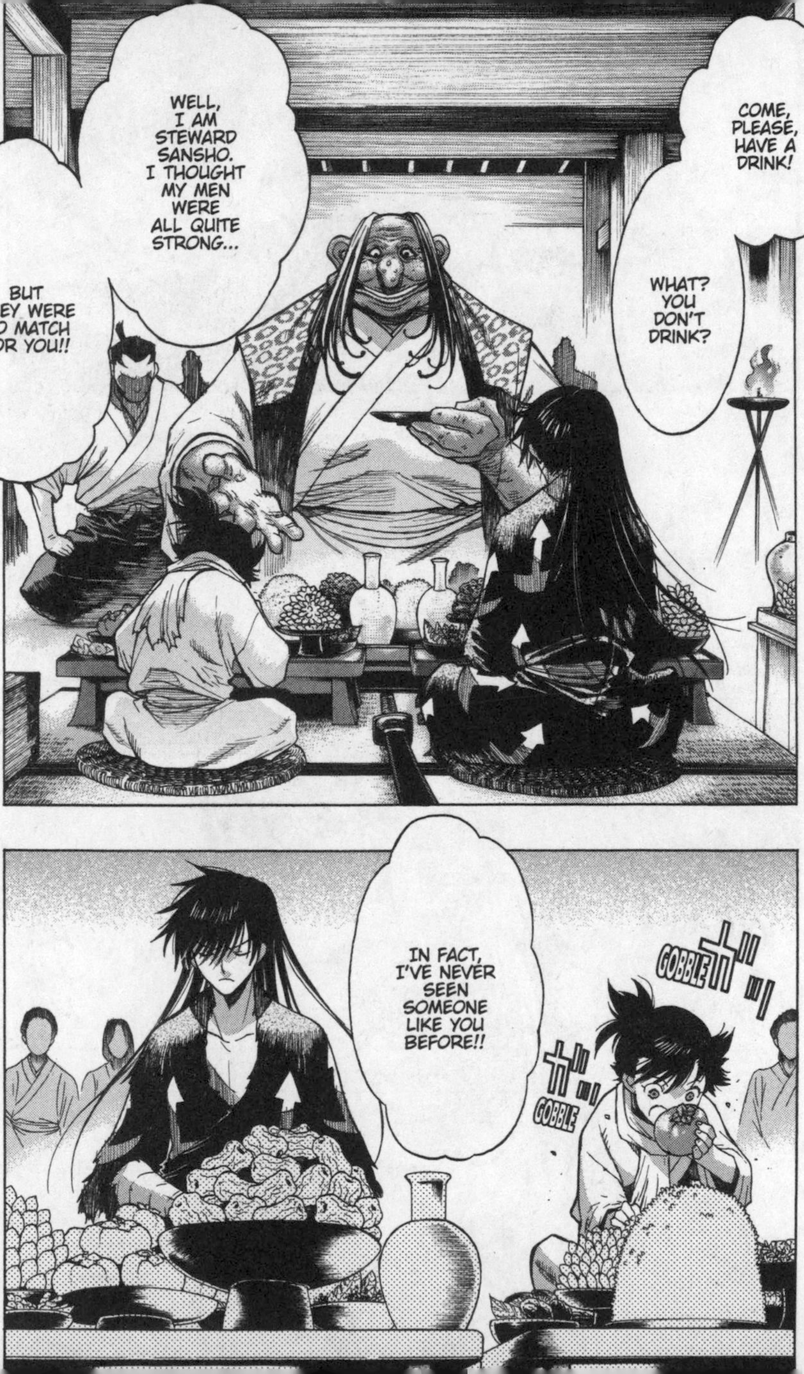
COME, PLEASE, HAVE A DRINK!
WHAT? YOU DON'T DRINK?
WELL, I AM STEWARD SANSHO. I THOUGHT MY MEN WERE ALL QUITE STRONG...
BUT THEY WERE NO MATCH FOR YOU!!
GOBBLE
IN FACT, I'VE NEVER SEEN SOMEONE LIKE YOU BEFORE!!
GOBBLE

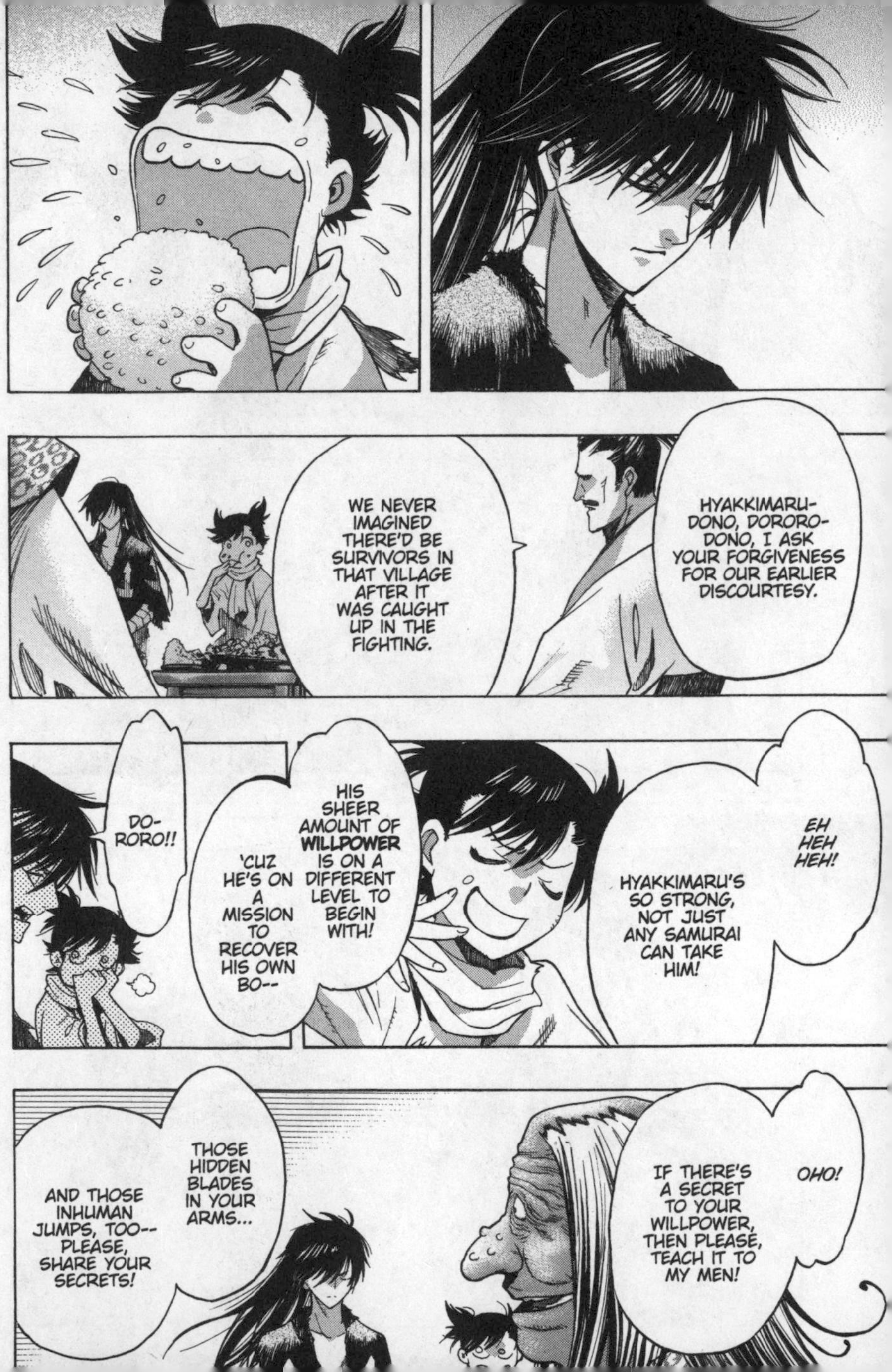
HYAKKIMARU-DONO, DORORO-DONO, I ASK YOUR FORGIVENESS FOR OUR EARLIER DISCOURTESY.
WE NEVER IMAGINED THERE'D BE SURVIVORS IN THAT VILLAGE AFTER IT WAS CAUGHT UP IN THE FIGHTING.
EH HEH HEH!
HYAKKIMARU'S SO STRONG, NOT JUST ANY SAMURAI CAN TAKE HIM!
HIS SHEER AMOUNT OF **WILLPOWER** IS ON A DIFFERENT LEVEL TO BEGIN WITH!
'CUZ HE'S ON A MISSION TO RECOVER HIS OWN BO--
DO-RORO!!
OHO!
IF THERE'S A SECRET TO YOUR WILLPOWER, THEN PLEASE, TEACH IT TO MY MEN!
THOSE HIDDEN BLADES IN YOUR ARMS...
AND THOSE INHUMAN JUMPS, TOO-- PLEASE, SHARE YOUR SECRETS!

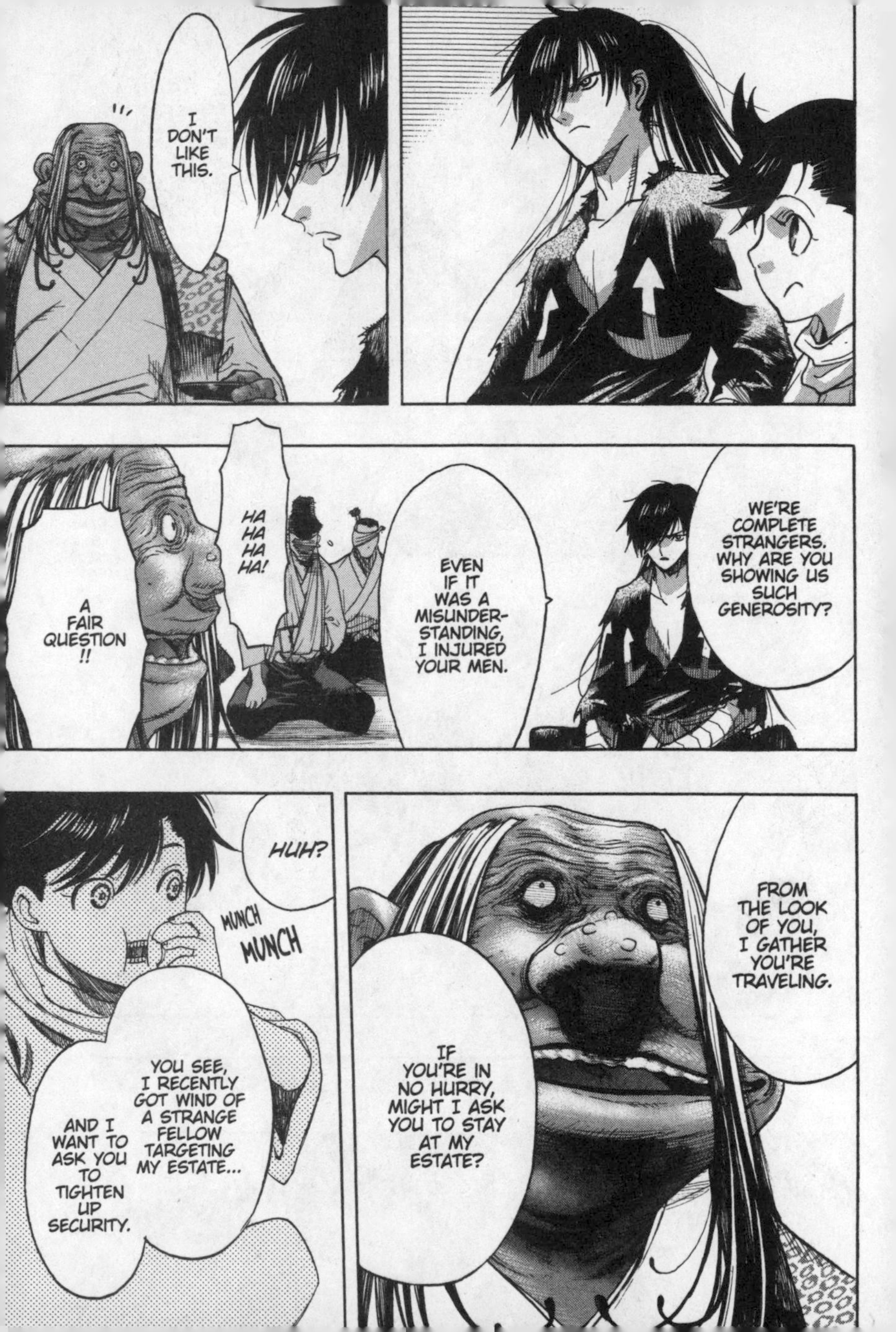
I DON'T LIKE THIS.
WE'RE COMPLETE STRANGERS. WHY ARE YOU SHOWING US SUCH GENEROSITY?
EVEN IF IT WAS A MISUNDERSTANDING, I INJURED YOUR MEN.
HA HA HA HA!
A FAIR QUESTION !!
FROM THE LOOK OF YOU, I GATHER YOU'RE TRAVELING.
IF YOU'RE IN NO HURRY, MIGHT I ASK YOU TO STAY AT MY ESTATE?
HUH?
MUNCH MUNCH
YOU SEE, I RECENTLY GOT WIND OF A STRANGE FELLOW TARGETING MY ESTATE...
AND I WANT TO ASK YOU TO TIGHTEN UP SECURITY.

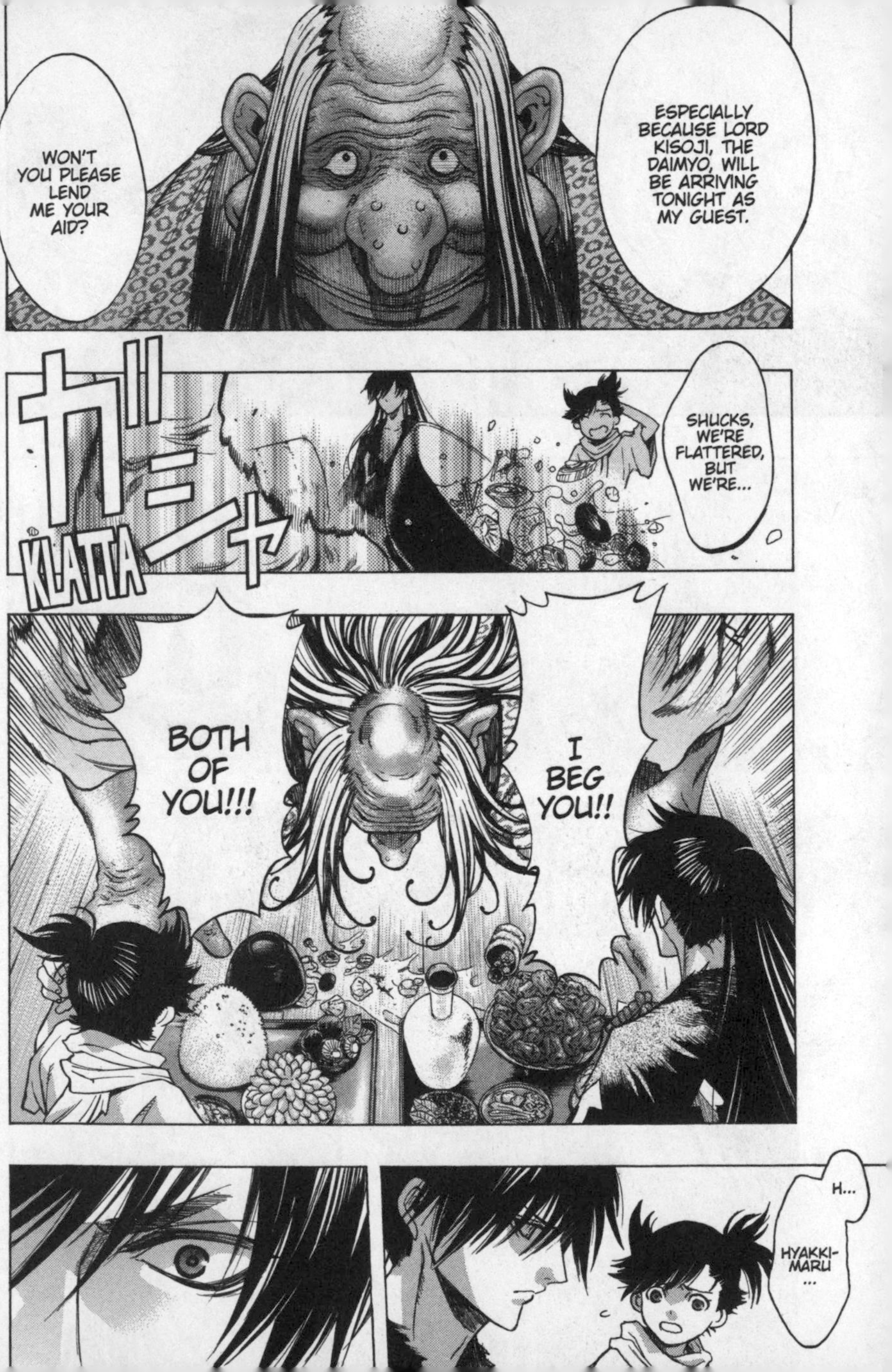
ESPECIALLY BECAUSE LORD KISOJI, THE DAIMYO, WILL BE ARRIVING TONIGHT AS MY GUEST.
WON'T YOU PLEASE LEND ME YOUR AID?
SHUCKS, WE'RE FLATTERED, BUT WE'RE...
KLATTA
I BEG YOU!!
BOTH OF YOU!!!
H...
HYAKKI-MARU ...

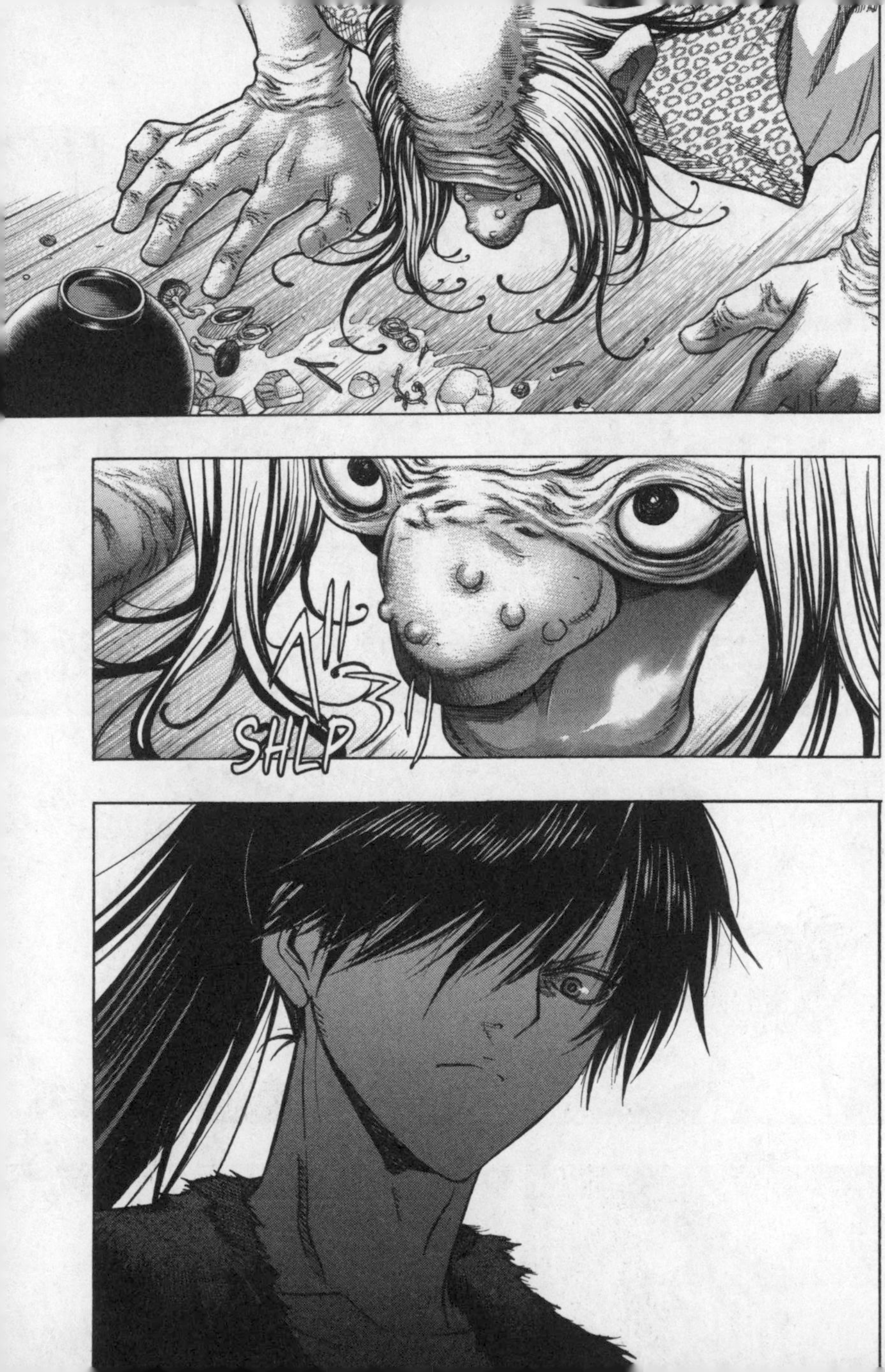
SHLP

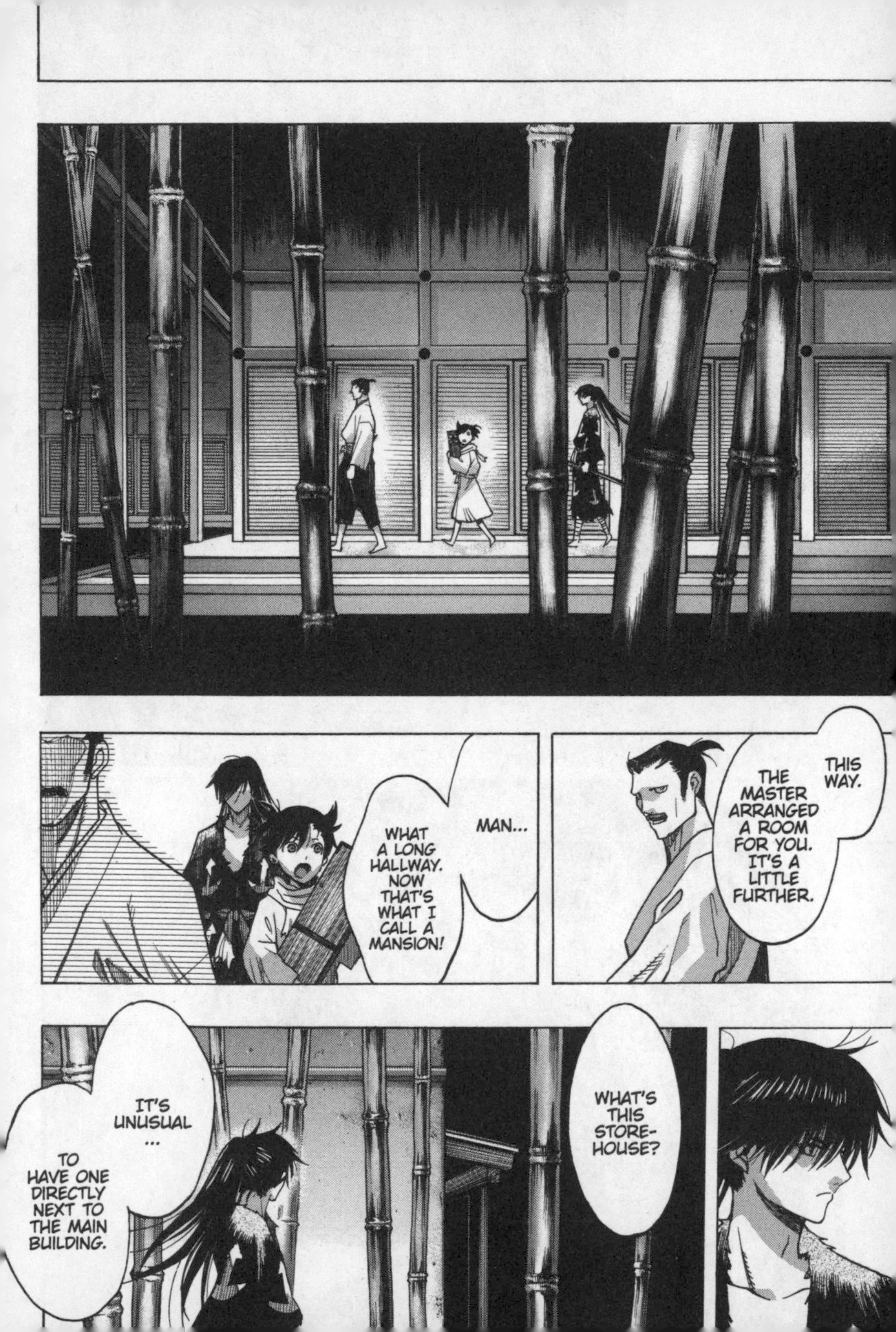
THIS WAY.
THE MASTER ARRANGED A ROOM FOR YOU. IT'S A LITTLE FURTHER.
MAN...
WHAT A LONG HALLWAY. NOW THAT'S WHAT I CALL A MANSION!
WHAT'S THIS STORE-HOUSE?
IT'S UNUSUAL ...
TO HAVE ONE DIRECTLY NEXT TO THE MAIN BUILDING.

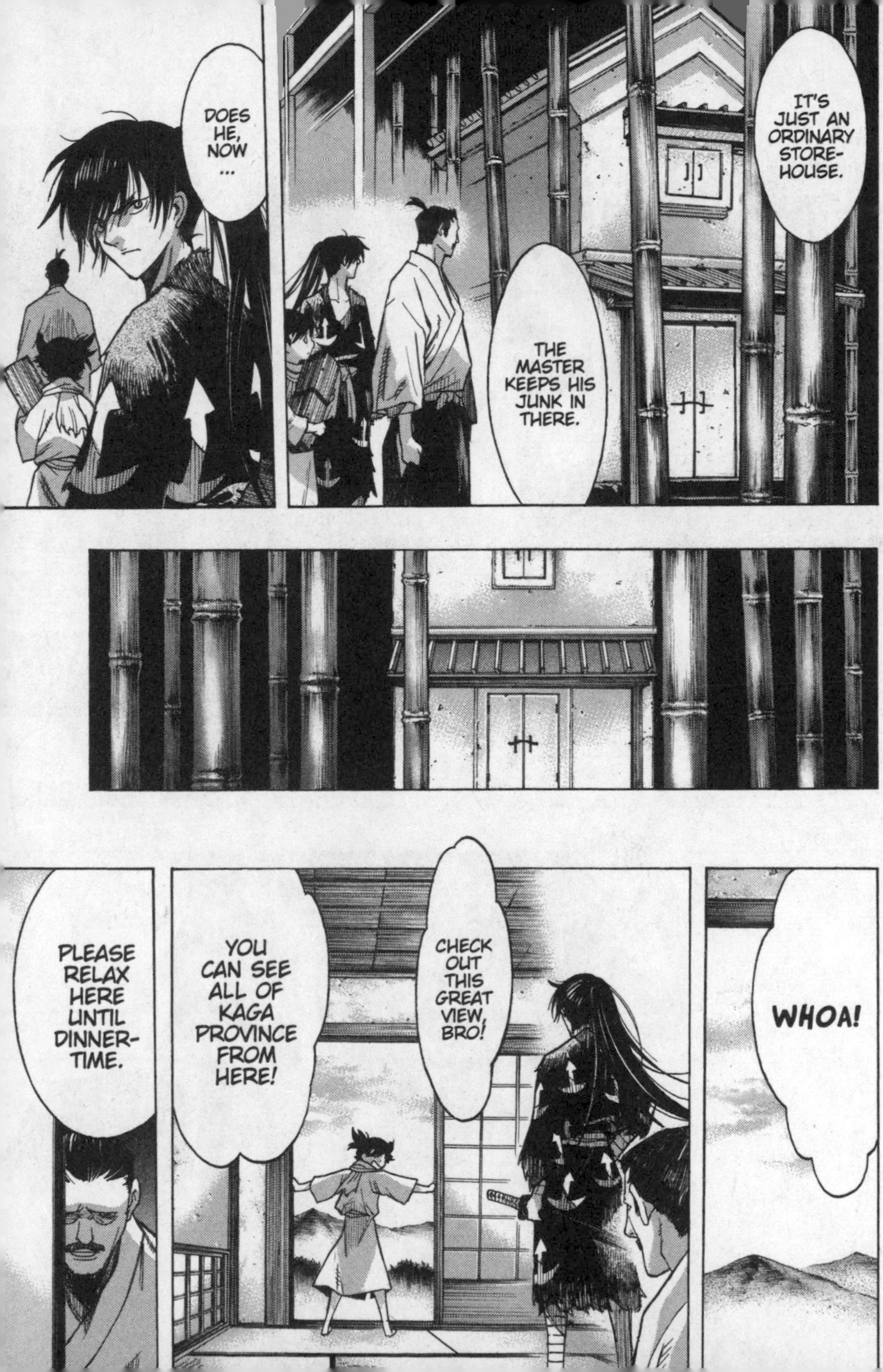
IT'S JUST AN ORDINARY STORE-HOUSE.
THE MASTER KEEPS HIS JUNK IN THERE.
DOES HE, NOW ...
WHOA!
CHECK OUT THIS GREAT VIEW, BRO!
YOU CAN SEE ALL OF KAGA PROVINCE FROM HERE!
PLEASE RELAX HERE UNTIL DINNER-TIME.

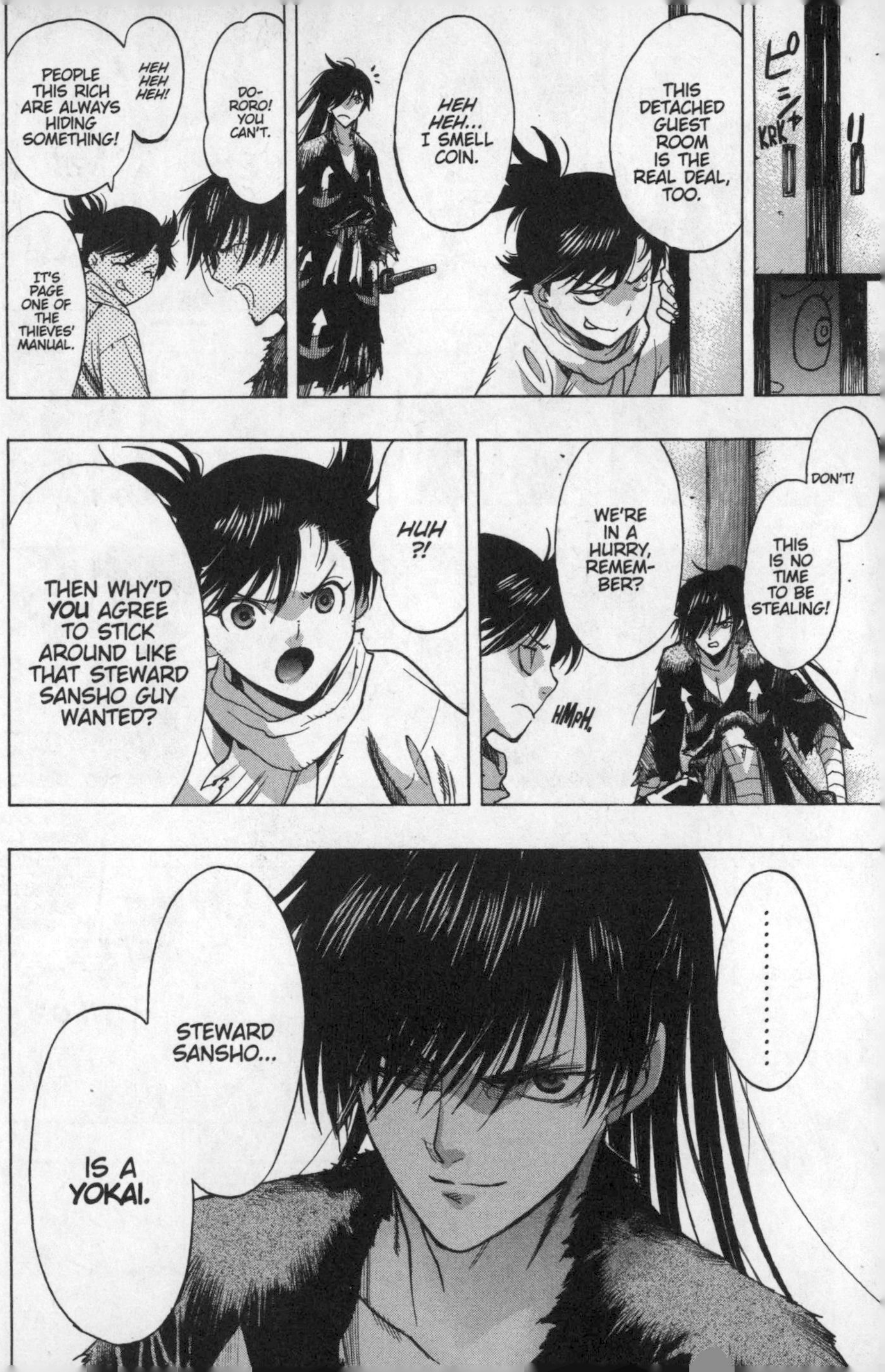
ピシャ
リ
KRK
THIS DETACHED GUEST ROOM IS THE REAL DEAL, TOO.
HEH HEH... I SMELL COIN.
DO-RORO! YOU CAN'T.
HEH HEH HEH!
PEOPLE THIS RICH ARE ALWAYS HIDING SOMETHING!
IT'S PAGE ONE OF THE THIEVES' MANUAL.
DON'T!
THIS IS NO TIME TO BE STEALING!
WE'RE IN A HURRY, REMEMBER?
HMPH.
HUH ?!
THEN WHY'D YOU AGREE TO STICK AROUND LIKE THAT STEWARD SANSHO GUY WANTED?
......
STEWARD SANSHO...
IS A YOKAI.

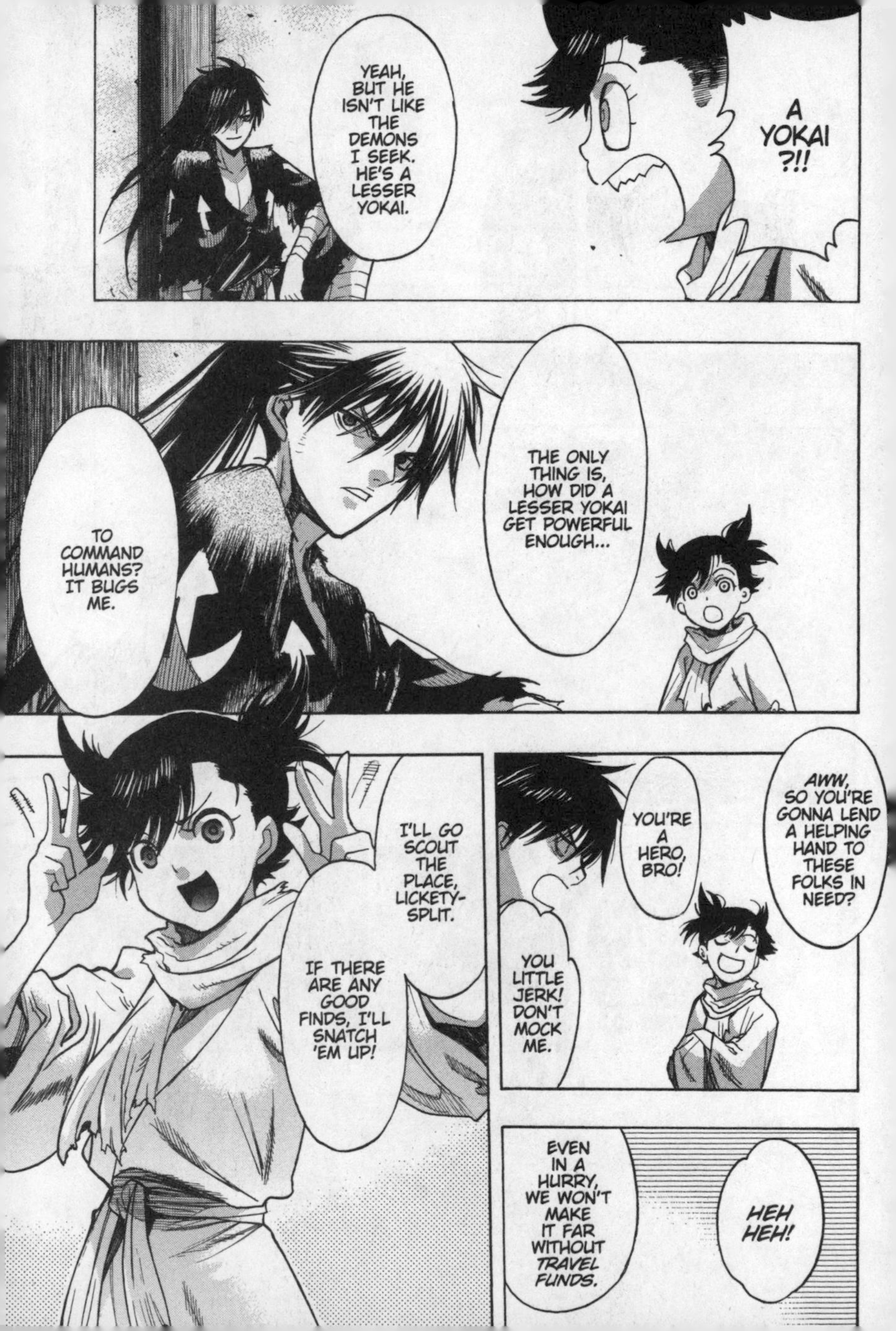
A YOKAI ?!!
YEAH, BUT HE ISN'T LIKE THE DEMONS I SEEK. HE'S A LESSER YOKAI.
THE ONLY THING IS, HOW DID A LESSER YOKAI GET POWERFUL ENOUGH...
TO COMMAND HUMANS? IT BUGS ME.
AWW, SO YOU'RE GONNA LEND A HELPING HAND TO THESE FOLKS IN NEED?
YOU'RE A HERO, BRO!
YOU LITTLE JERK! DON'T MOCK ME.
HEH HEH!
EVEN IN A HURRY, WE WON'T MAKE IT FAR WITHOUT *TRAVEL FUNDS.*
I'LL GO SCOUT THE PLACE, LICKETY-SPLIT.
IF THERE ARE ANY GOOD FINDS, I'LL SNATCH 'EM UP!

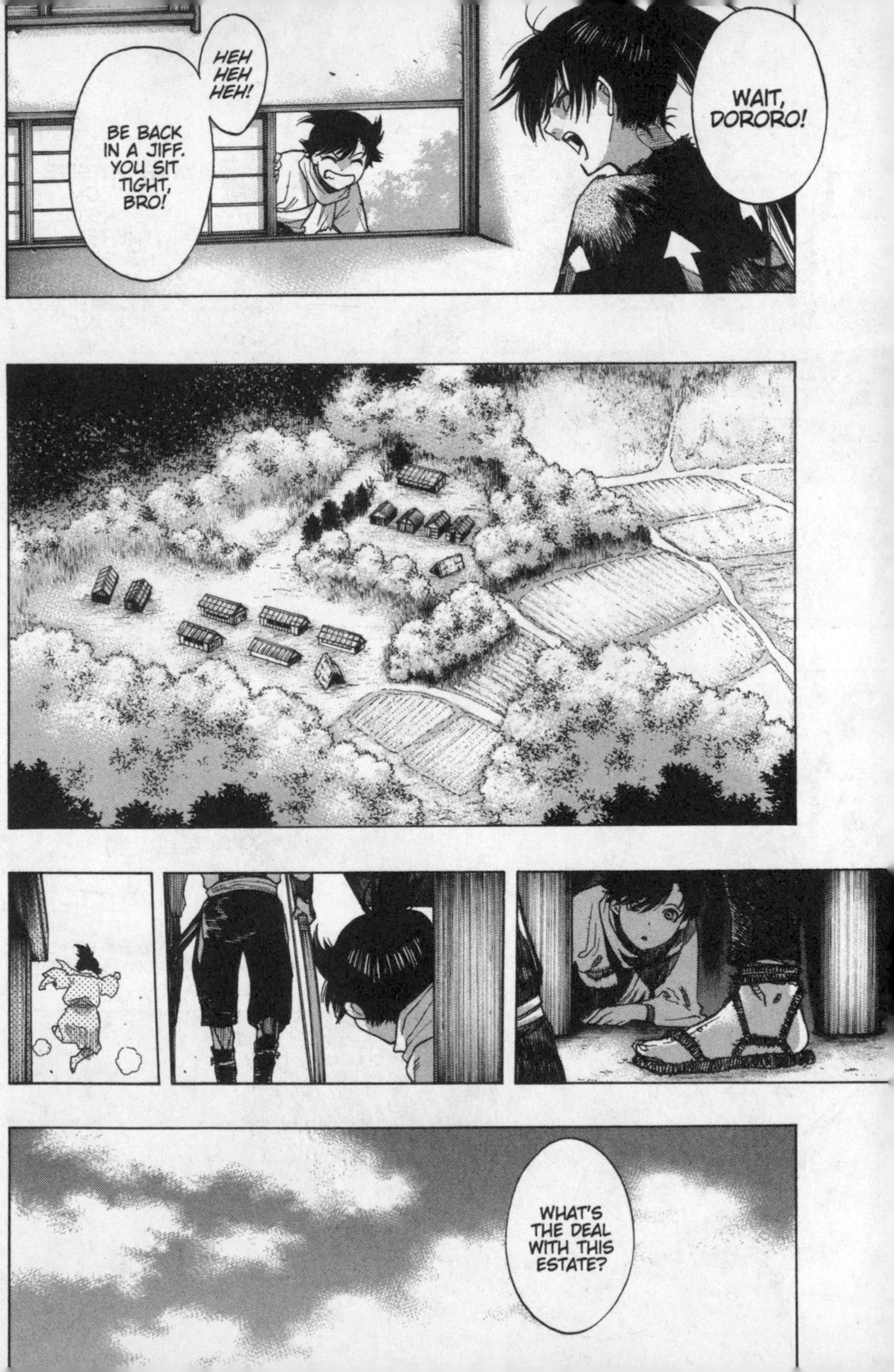
WAIT, DORORO!
HEH HEH HEH!
BE BACK IN A JIFF. YOU SIT TIGHT, BRO!
WHAT'S THE DEAL WITH THIS ESTATE?

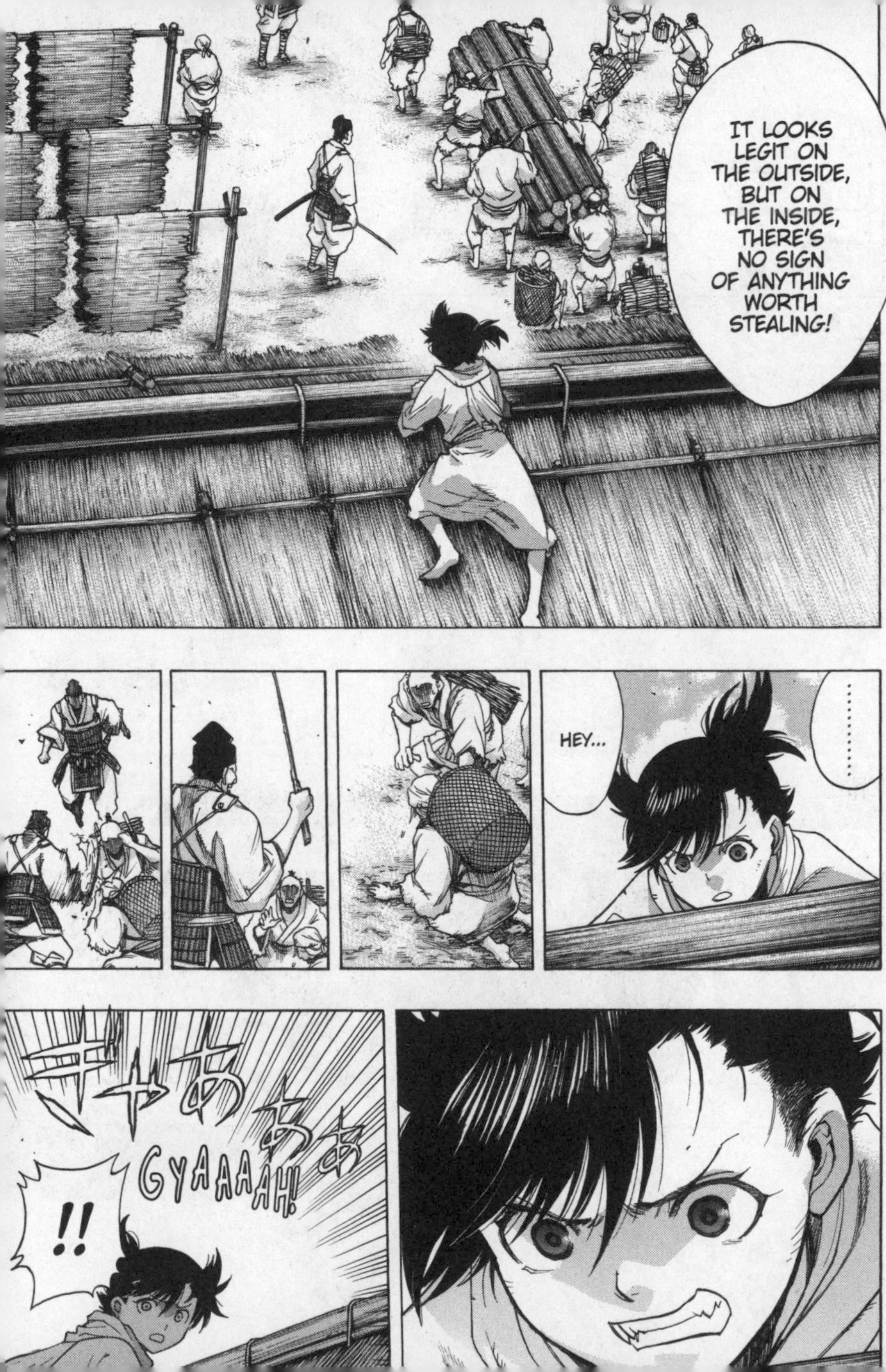
IT LOOKS LEGIT ON THE OUTSIDE, BUT ON THE INSIDE, THERE'S NO SIGN OF ANYTHING WORTH STEALING!
......
HEY...
GYAAAAH!
!!

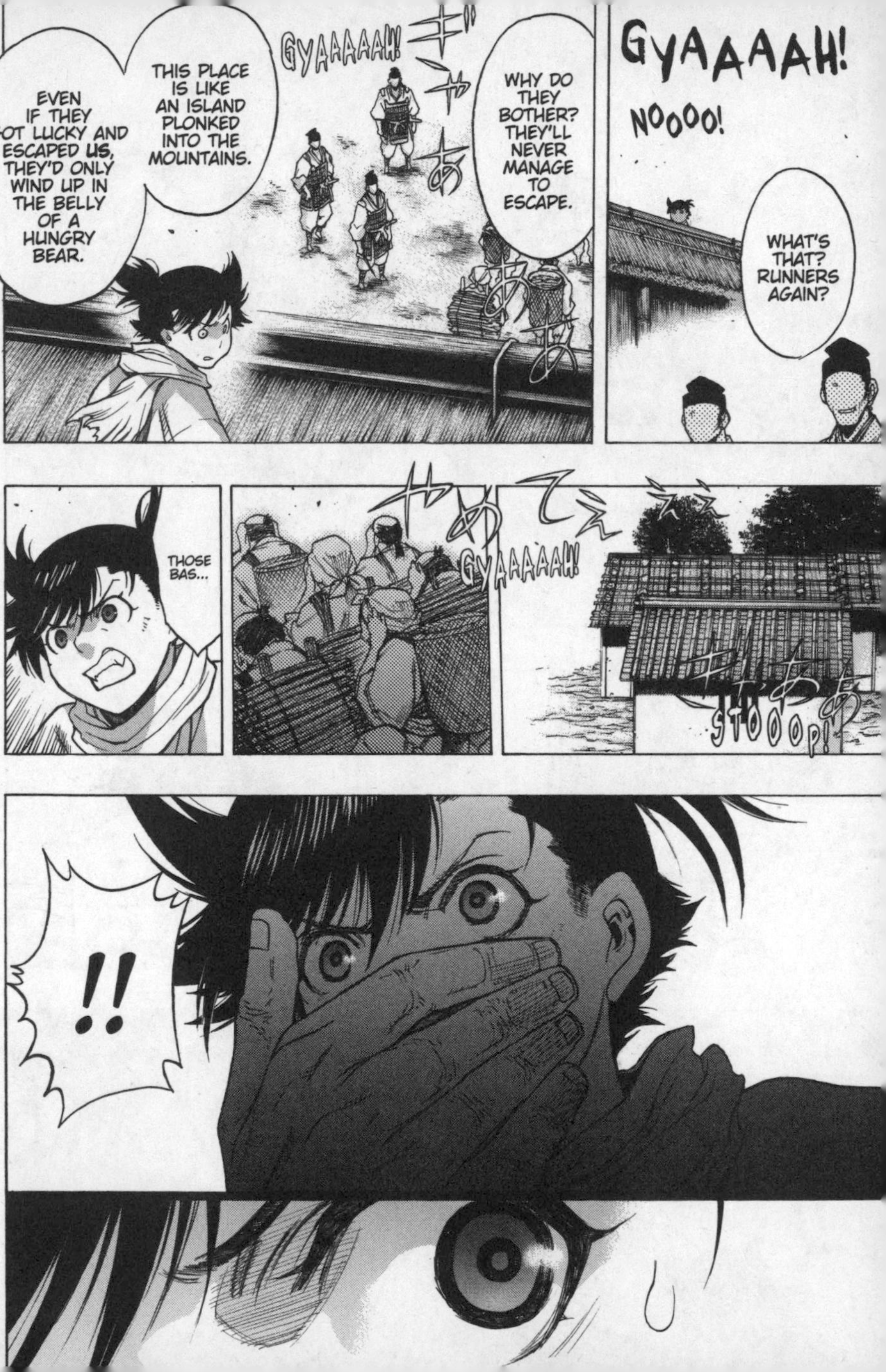
GYAAAAH!
NOOOO!
WHAT'S THAT? RUNNERS AGAIN?
GYAAAAAH!
WHY DO THEY BOTHER? THEY'LL NEVER MANAGE TO ESCAPE.
THIS PLACE IS LIKE AN ISLAND PLONKED INTO THE MOUNTAINS.
EVEN IF THEY GOT LUCKY AND ESCAPED US, THEY'D ONLY WIND UP IN THE BELLY OF A HUNGRY BEAR.
STOOOP!
GYAAAAAH!
THOSE BAS...
!!

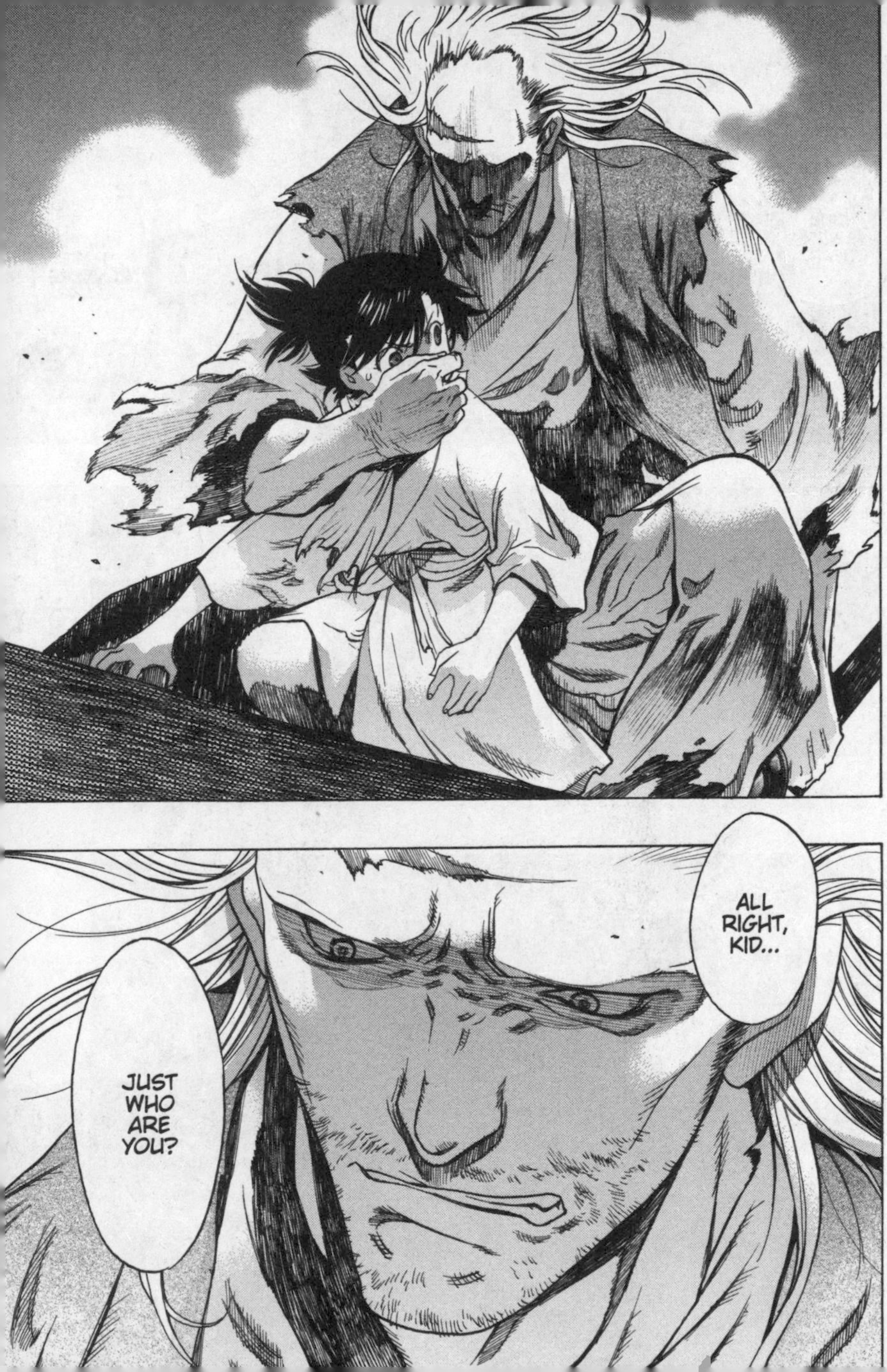
ALL RIGHT, KID...
JUST WHO ARE YOU?

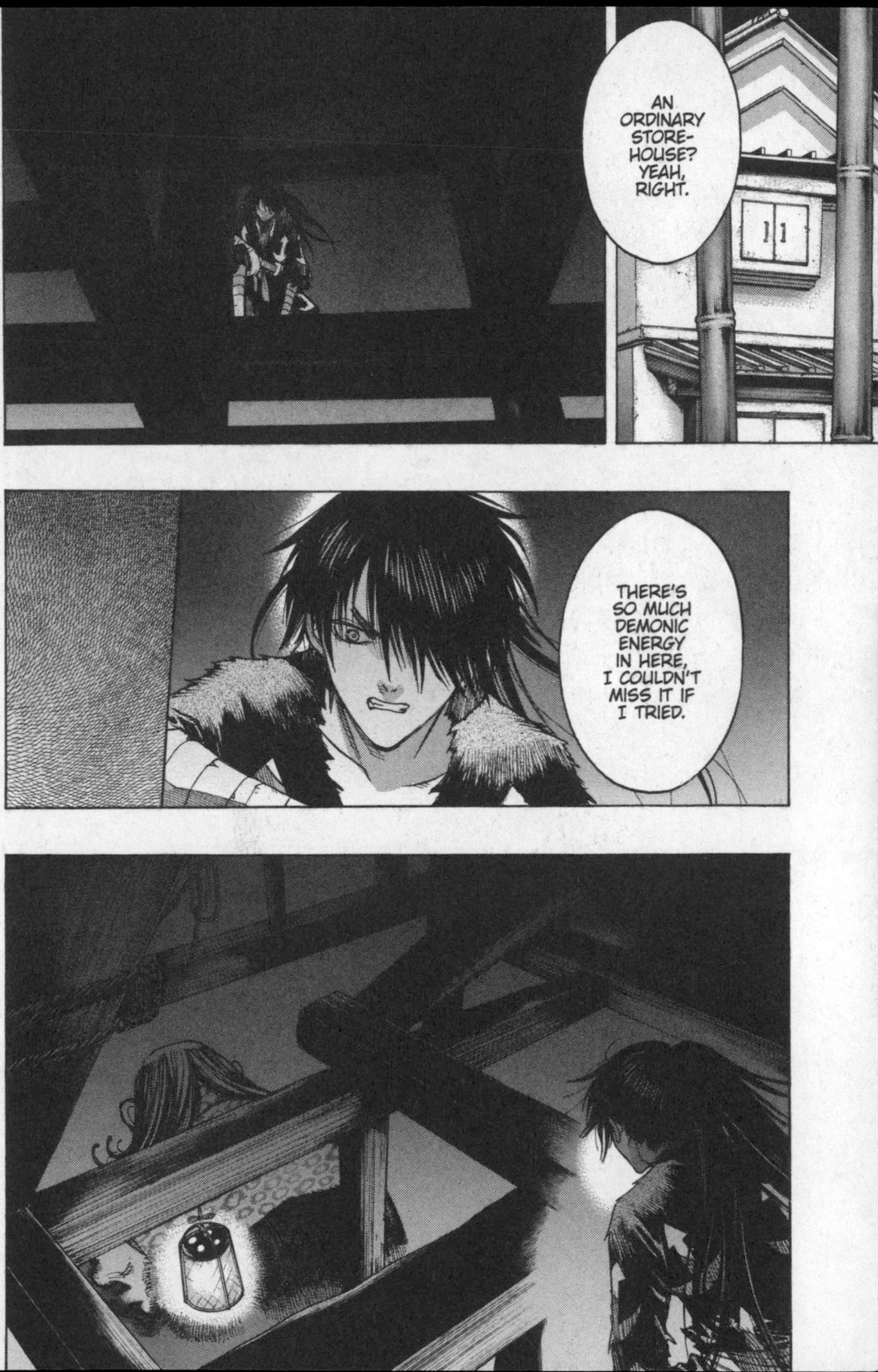
AN ORDINARY STORE-HOUSE? YEAH, RIGHT.
THERE'S SO MUCH DEMONIC ENERGY IN HERE, I COULDN'T MISS IT IF I TRIED.

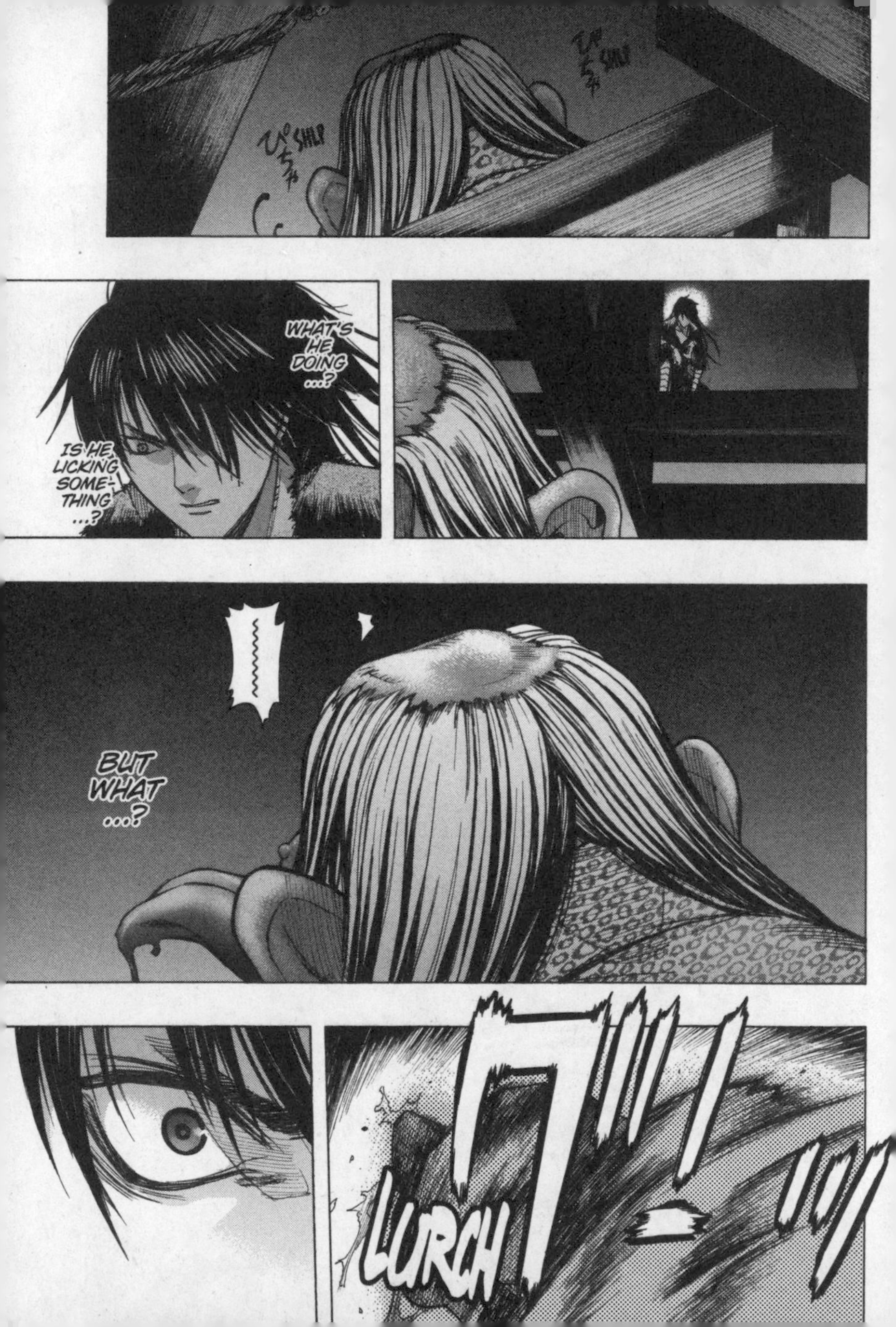
ぴちゃ SHLP
ぴちゃ SHLP
WHAT'S HE DOING ...?
IS HE LICKING SOME-THING ...?
!
BUT WHAT ...?
LURCH

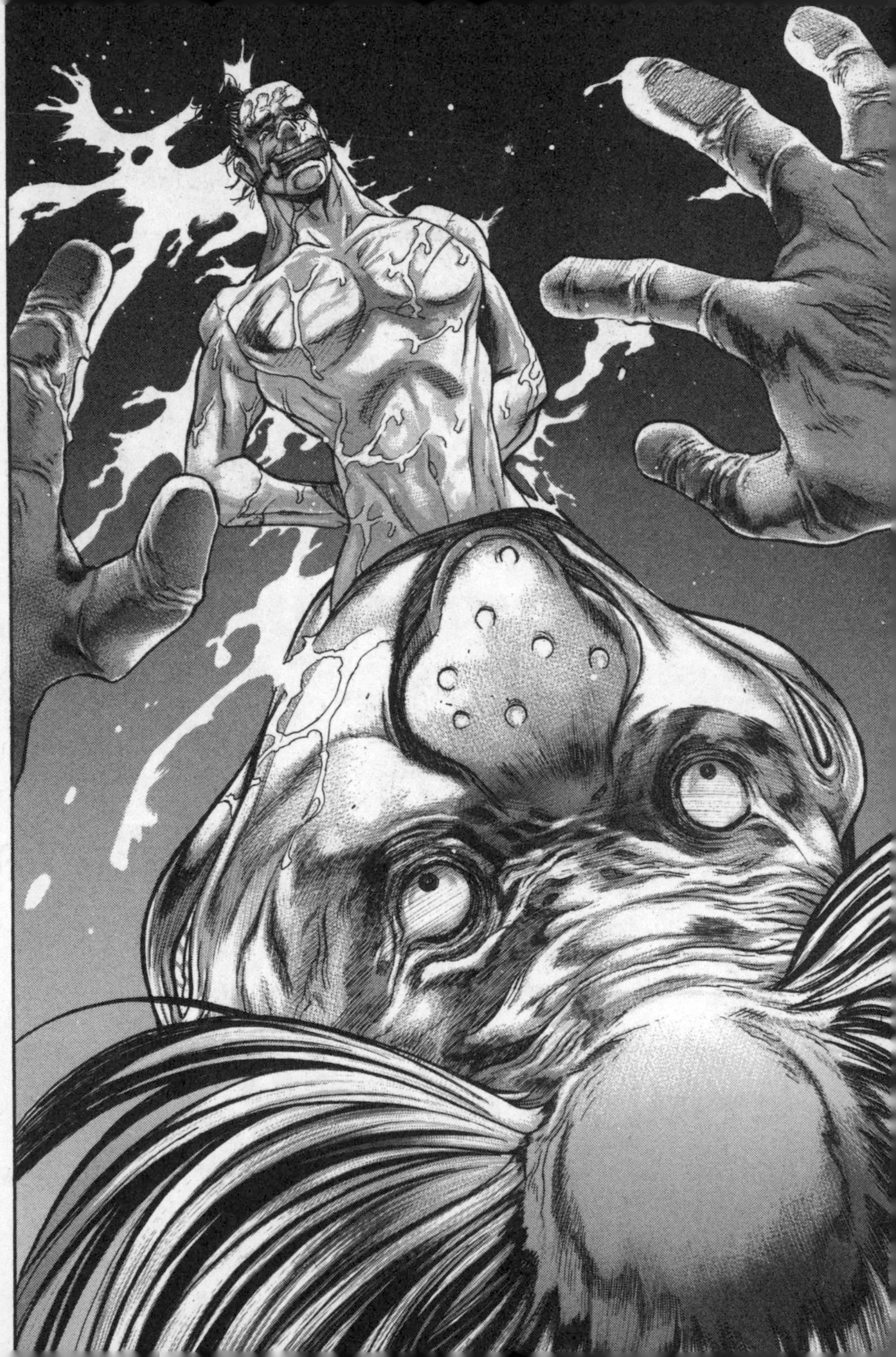

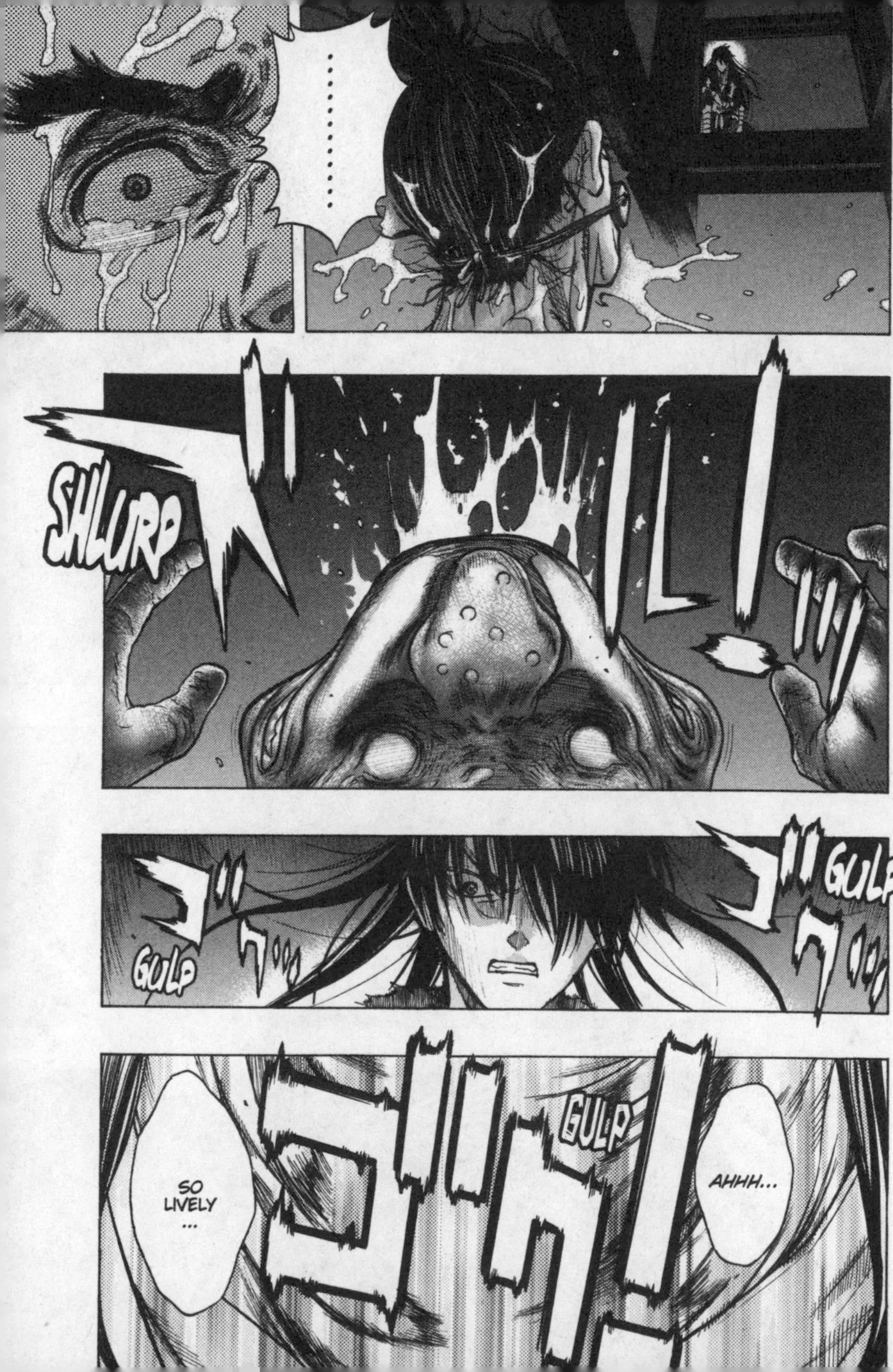
……
SHLURP
GULP
GULP
AHHH...
GULP
SO LIVELY ...

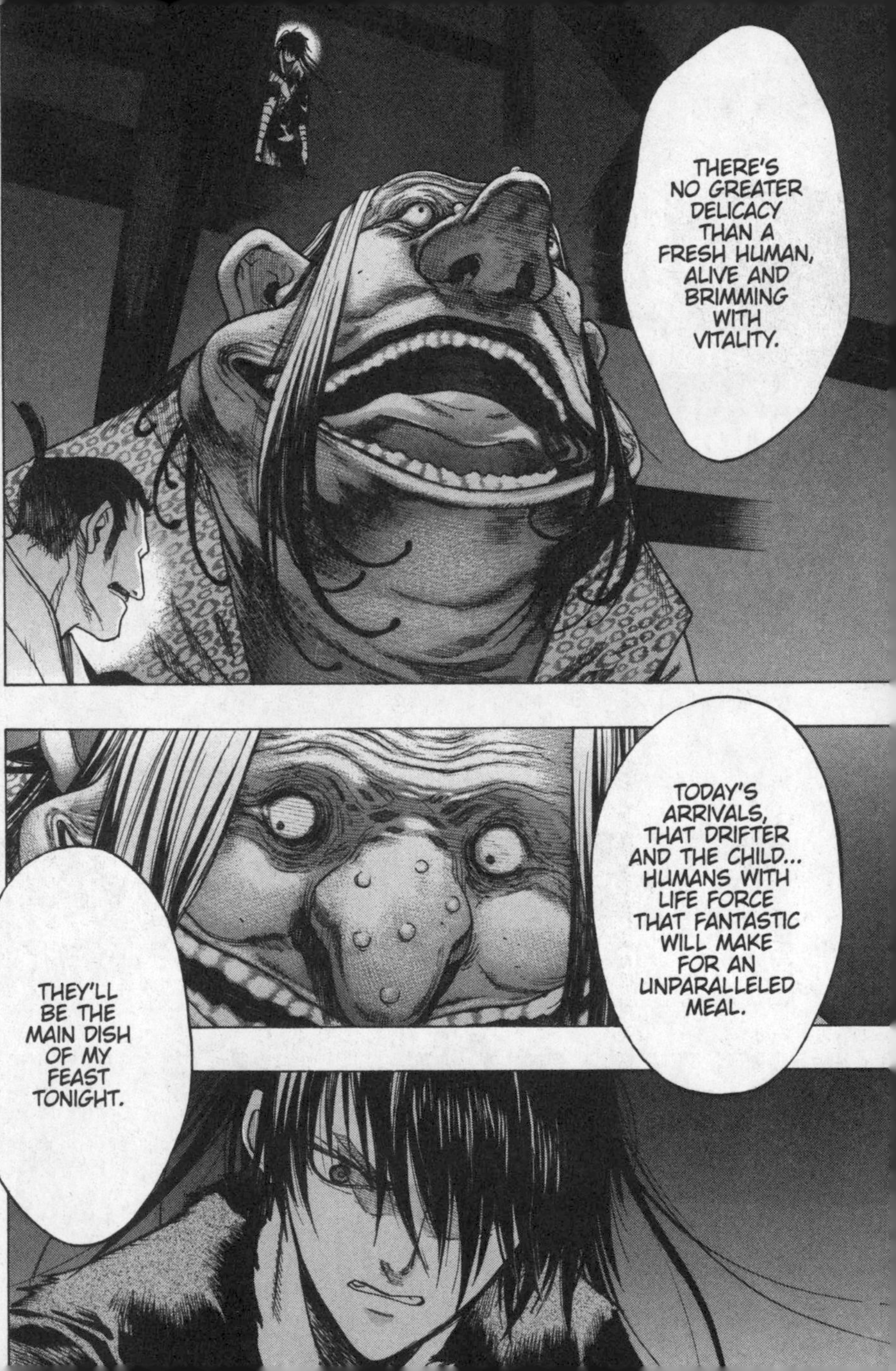
THERE'S NO GREATER DELICACY THAN A FRESH HUMAN, ALIVE AND BRIMMING WITH VITALITY.
TODAY'S ARRIVALS, THAT DRIFTER AND THE CHILD... HUMANS WITH LIFE FORCE THAT FANTASTIC WILL MAKE FOR AN UNPARALLELED MEAL.
THEY'LL BE THE MAIN DISH OF MY FEAST TONIGHT.

THE LEGEND OF
DORORO AND
HYAKKIMARU

どろろと百鬼丸伝

THE LEGEND OF
DORORO AND **HYAKKIMARU**

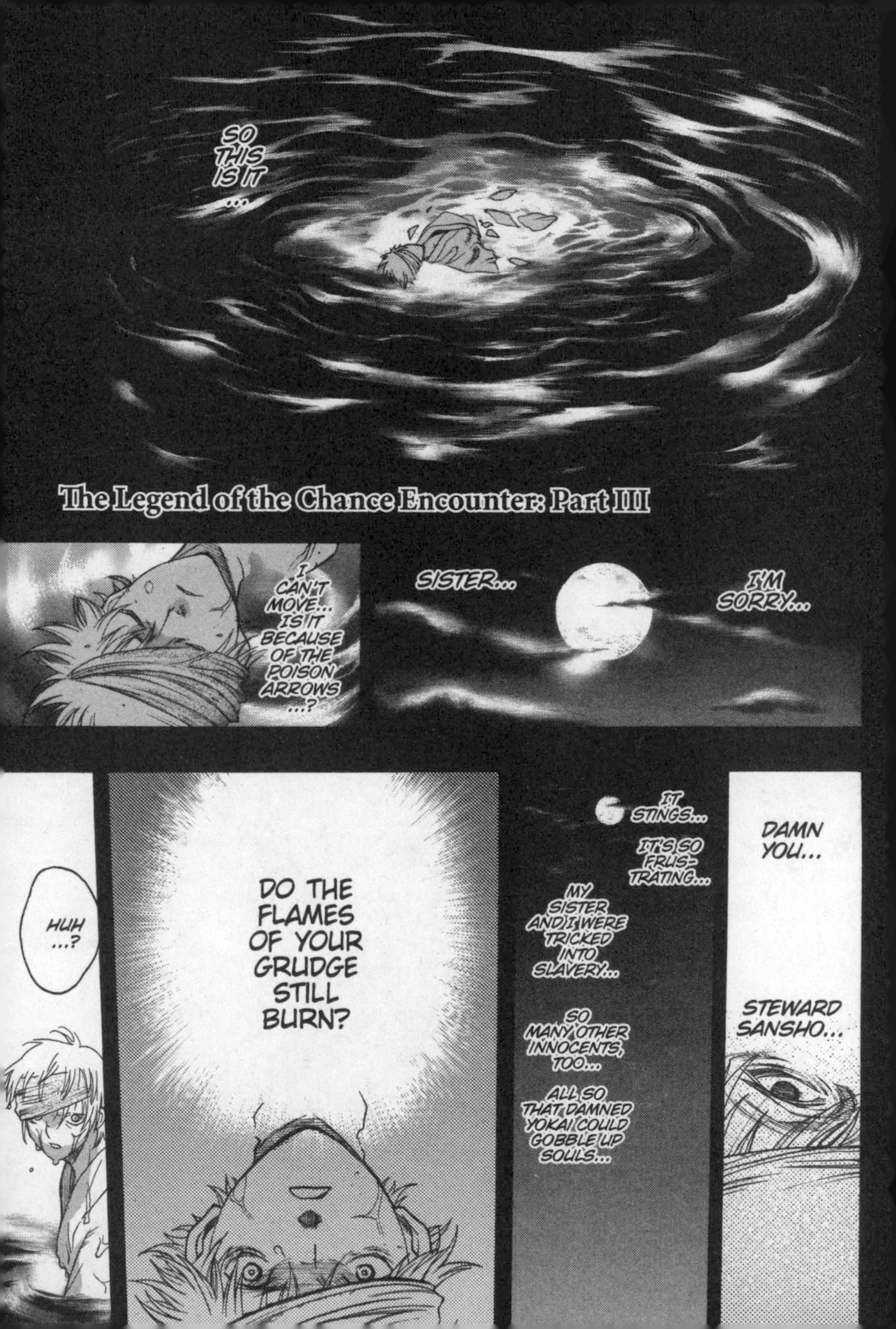
SO THIS IS IT ...
The Legend of the Chance Encounter: Part III
I'M SORRY...
SISTER...
I CAN'T MOVE... IS IT BECAUSE OF THE POISON ARROWS ...?
DAMN YOU...
STEWARD SANSHO...
IT STINGS...
IT'S SO FRUS-TRATING...
MY SISTER AND I WERE TRICKED INTO SLAVERY...
SO MANY OTHER INNOCENTS, TOO...
ALL SO THAT DAMNED YOKAI COULD GOBBLE UP SOULS...
DO THE FLAMES OF YOUR GRUDGE STILL BURN?
HUH ...?

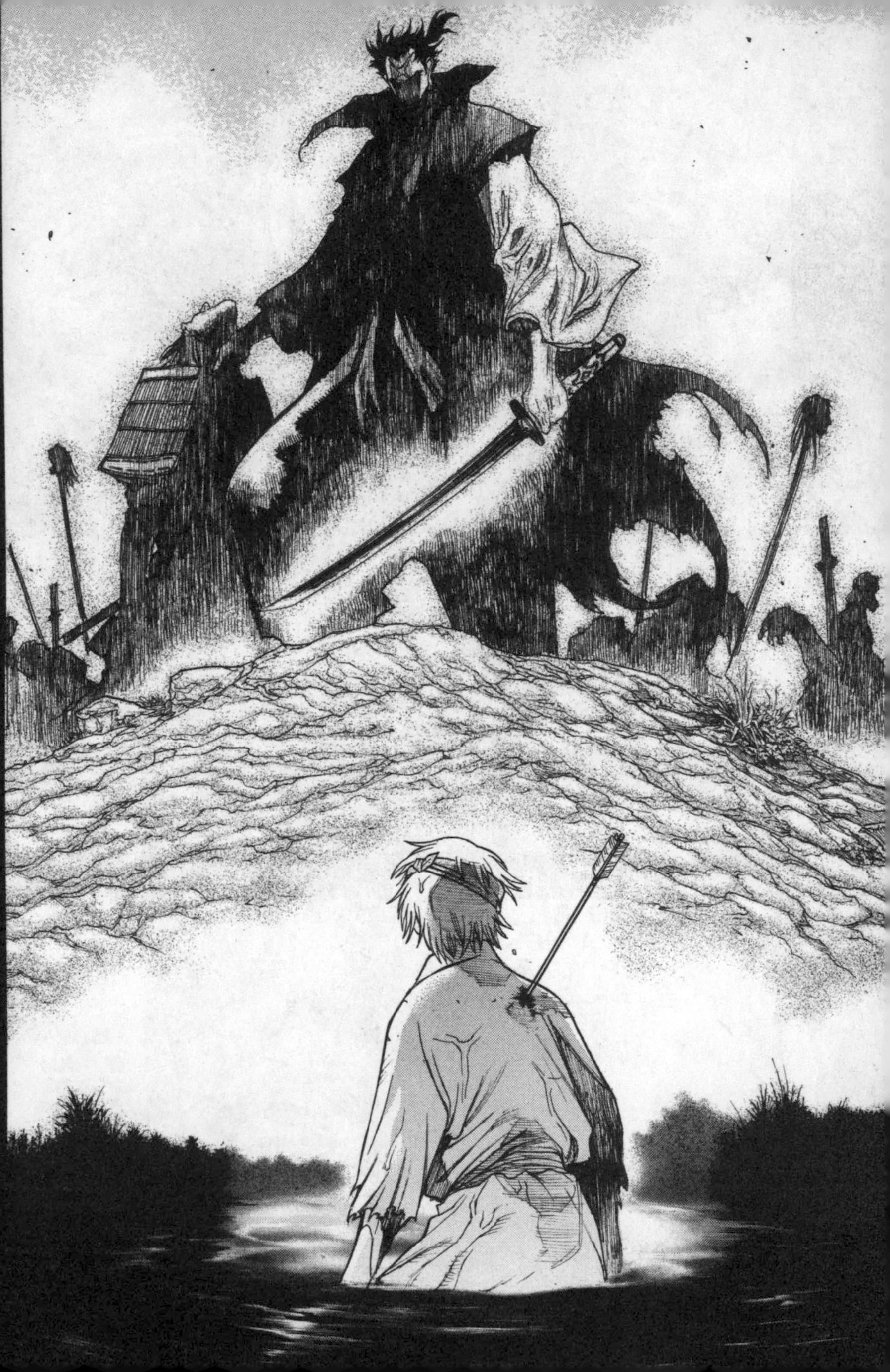

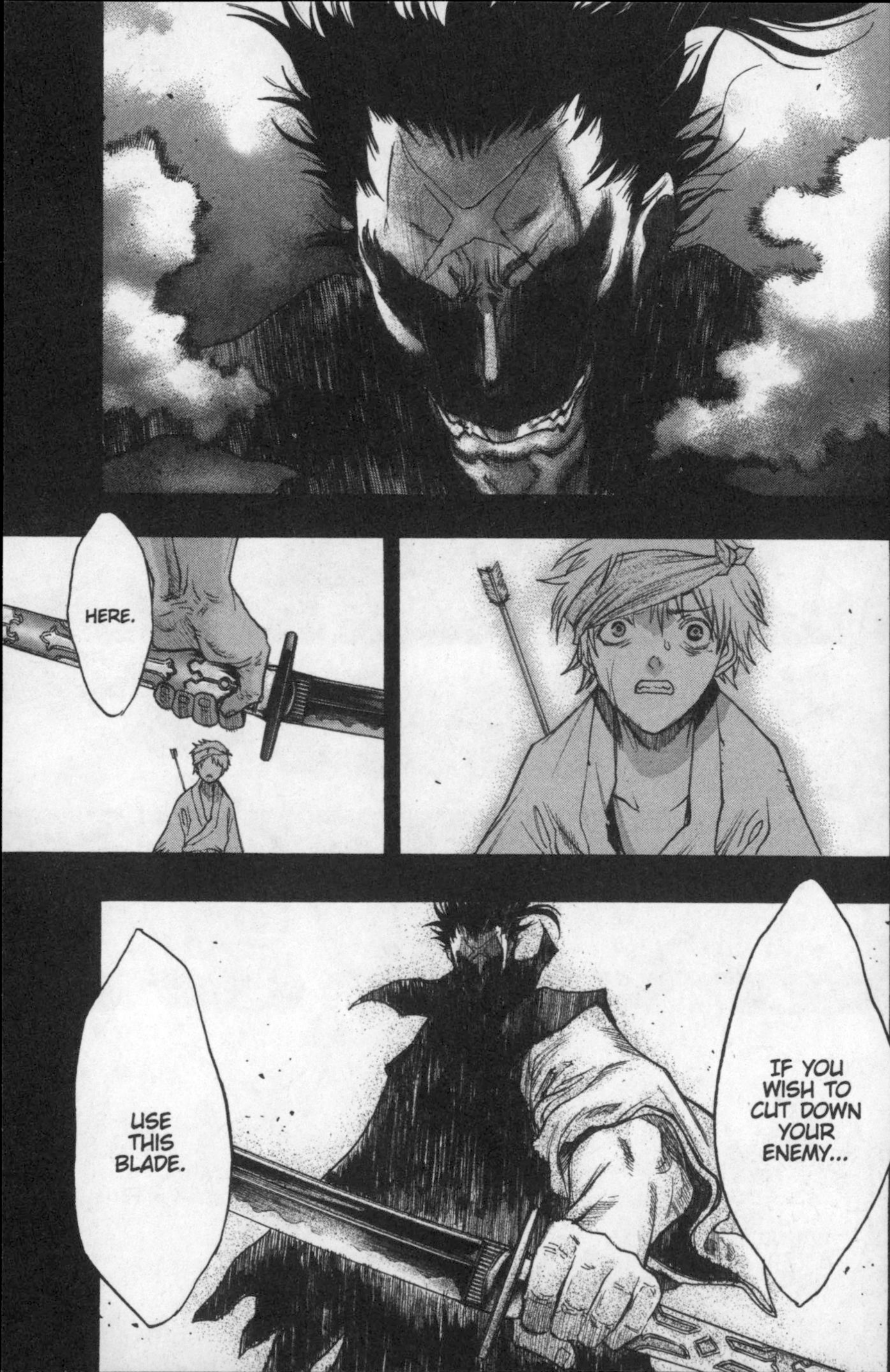
HERE.
IF YOU WISH TO CUT DOWN YOUR ENEMY...
USE THIS BLADE.

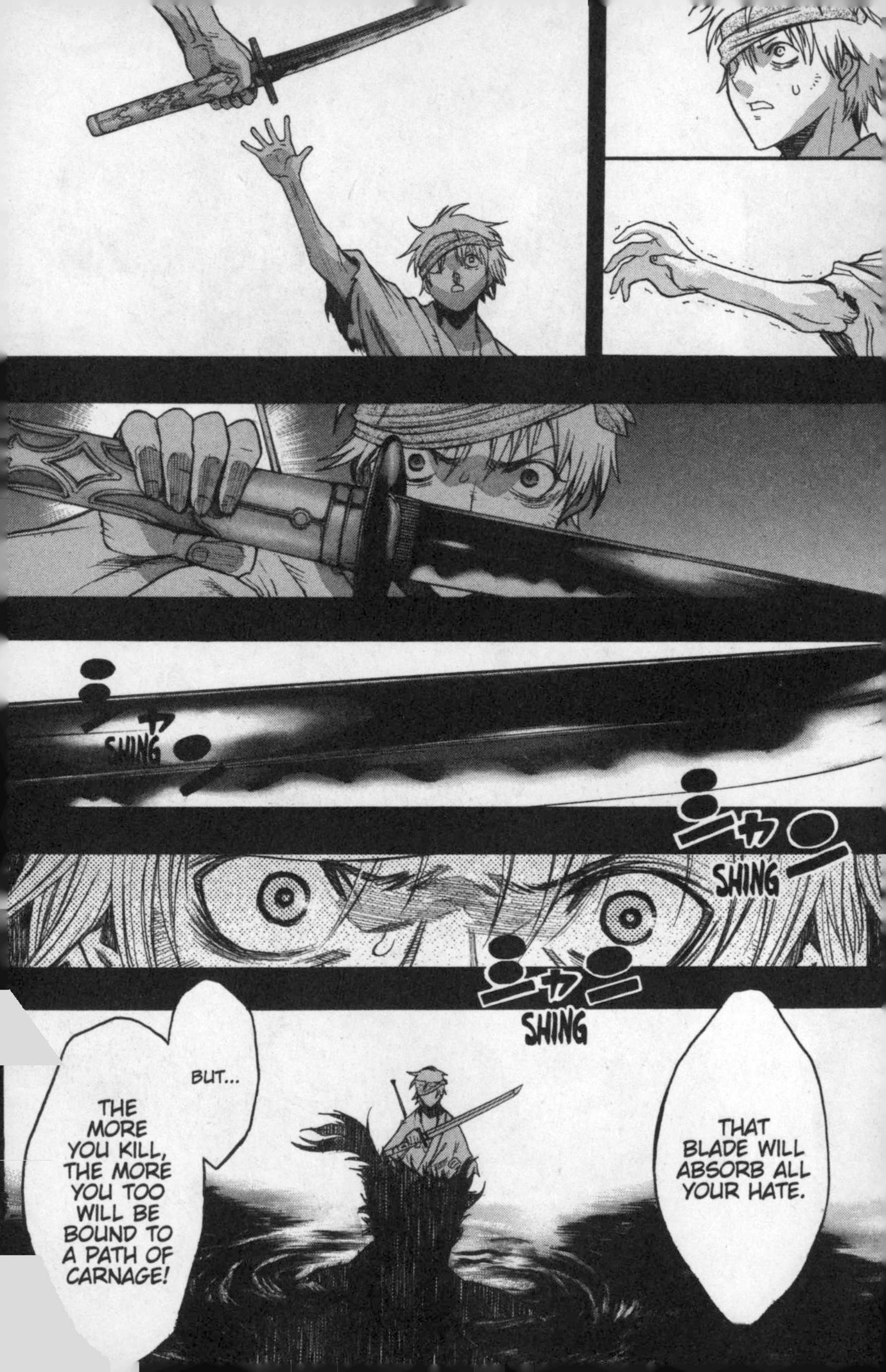
SHING
SHING
SHING
THAT BLADE WILL ABSORB ALL YOUR HATE.
BUT...
THE MORE YOU KILL, THE MORE YOU TOO WILL BE BOUND TO A PATH OF CARNAGE!

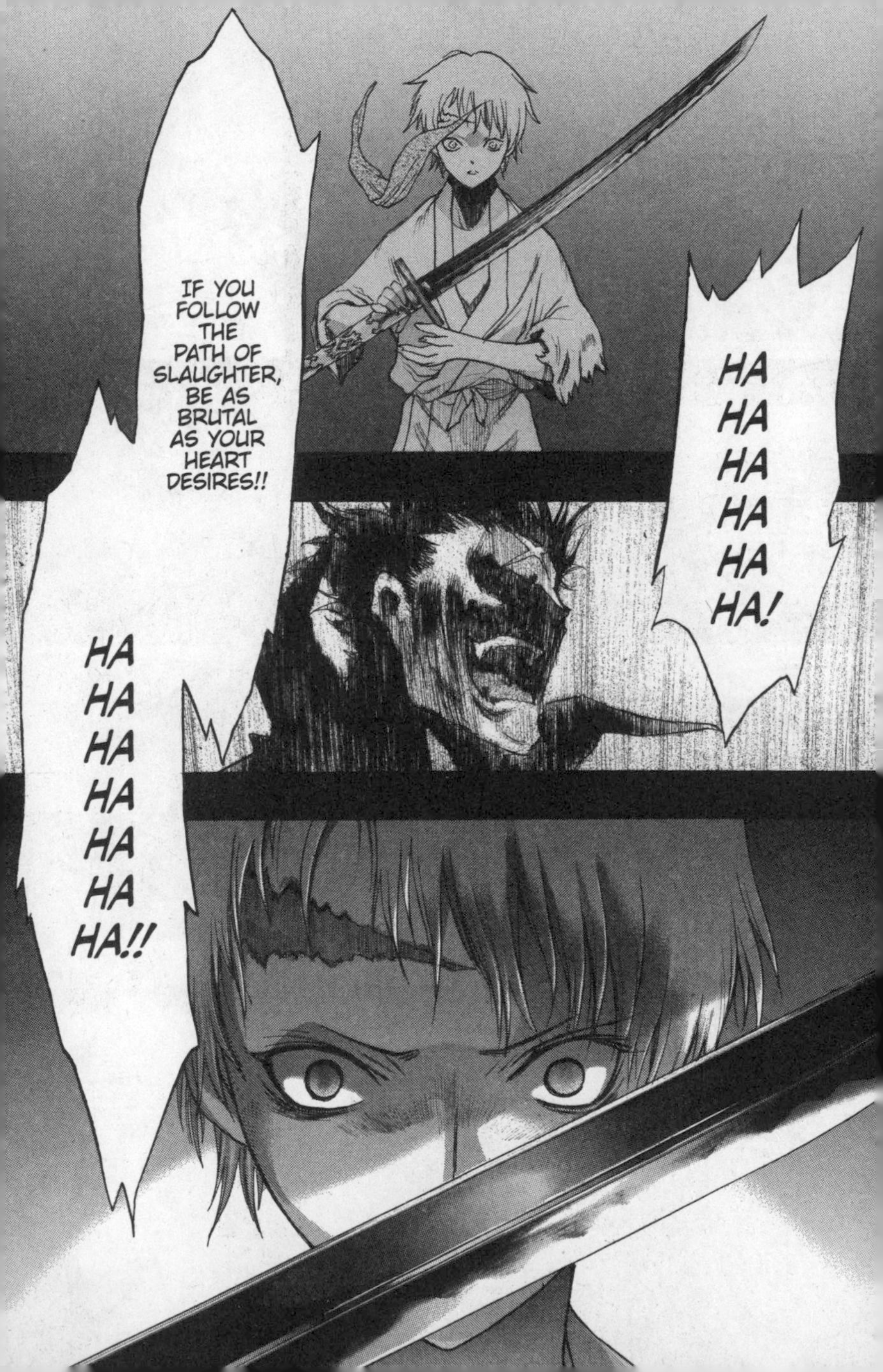
IF YOU FOLLOW THE PATH OF SLAUGHTER, BE AS BRUTAL AS YOUR HEART DESIRES!!
HA HA HA HA HA HA!
HA HA HA HA HA HA HA!!

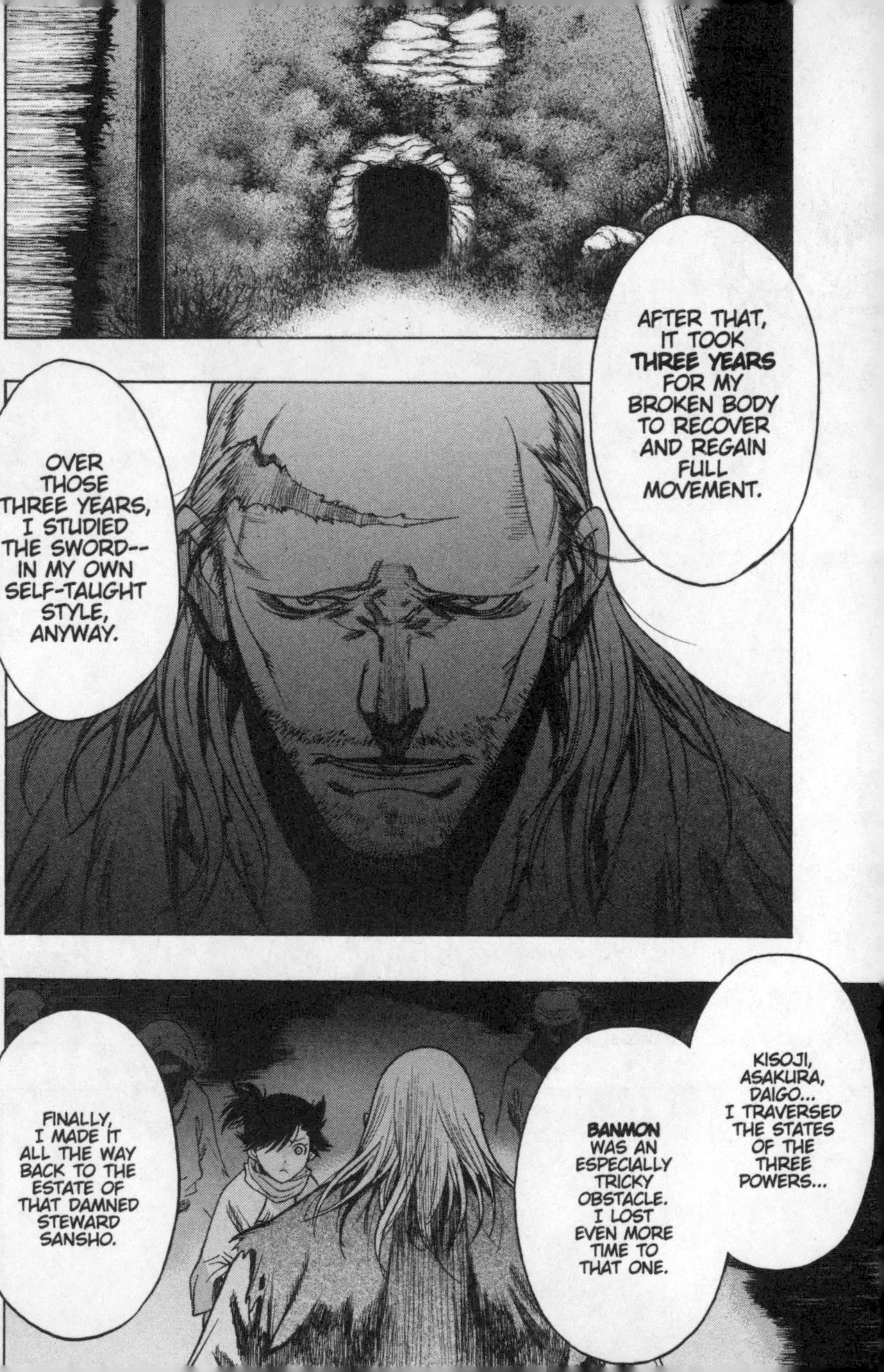
AFTER THAT, IT TOOK THREE YEARS FOR MY BROKEN BODY TO RECOVER AND REGAIN FULL MOVEMENT.
OVER THOSE THREE YEARS, I STUDIED THE SWORD-- IN MY OWN SELF-TAUGHT STYLE, ANYWAY.
KISOJI, ASAKURA, DAIGO... I TRAVERSED THE STATES OF THE THREE POWERS...
BANMON WAS AN ESPECIALLY TRICKY OBSTACLE. I LOST EVEN MORE TIME TO THAT ONE.
FINALLY, I MADE IT ALL THE WAY BACK TO THE ESTATE OF THAT DAMNED STEWARD SANSHO.

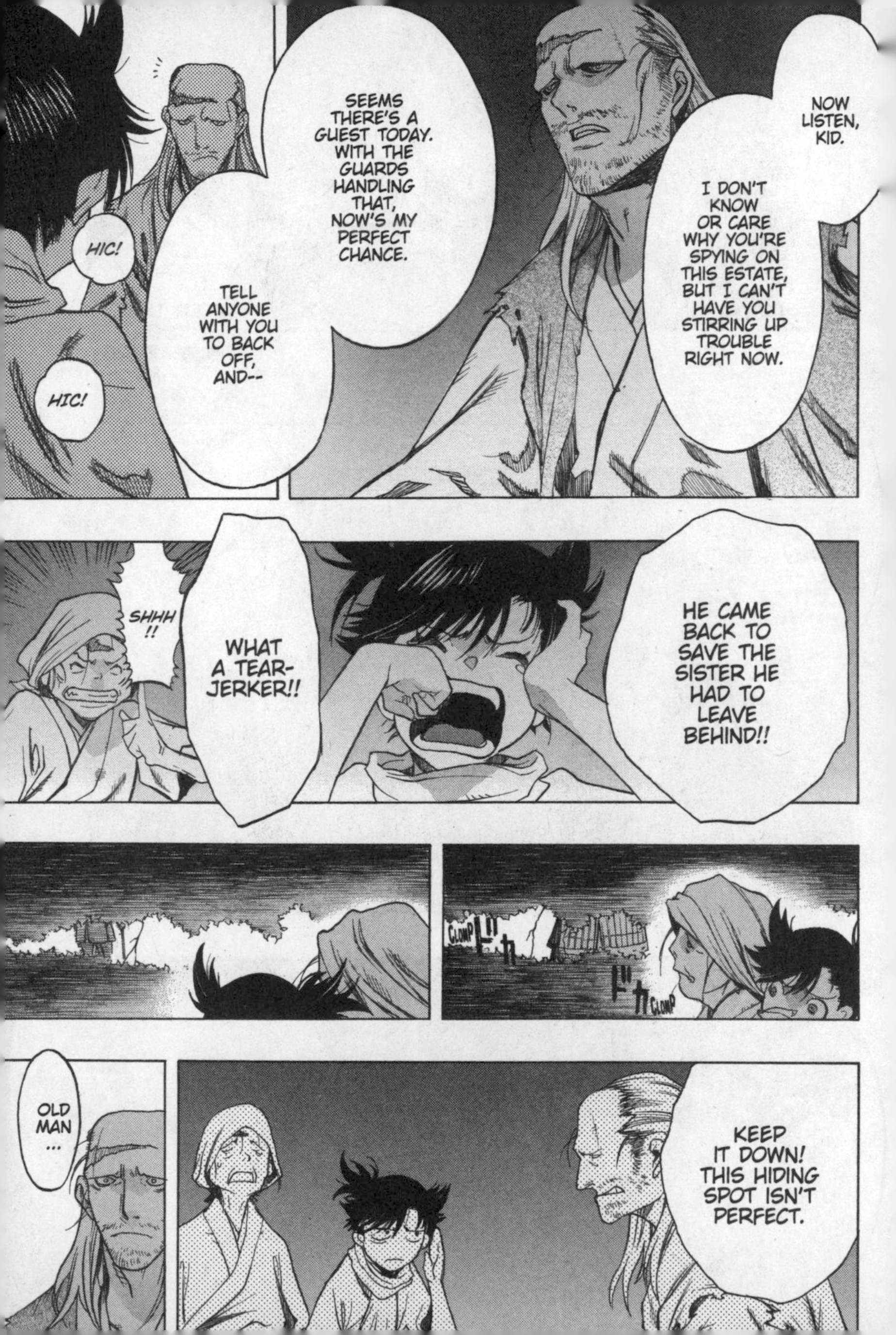
NOW LISTEN, KID.
I DON'T KNOW OR CARE WHY YOU'RE SPYING ON THIS ESTATE, BUT I CAN'T HAVE YOU STIRRING UP TROUBLE RIGHT NOW.
SEEMS THERE'S A GUEST TODAY. WITH THE GUARDS HANDLING THAT, NOW'S MY PERFECT CHANCE.
TELL ANYONE WITH YOU TO BACK OFF, AND--
HIC!
HIC!
HE CAME BACK TO SAVE THE SISTER HE HAD TO LEAVE BEHIND!!
WHAT A TEAR-JERKER!!
SHHH !!
CLOMP
CLOMP
KEEP IT DOWN! THIS HIDING SPOT ISN'T PERFECT.
OLD MAN ...

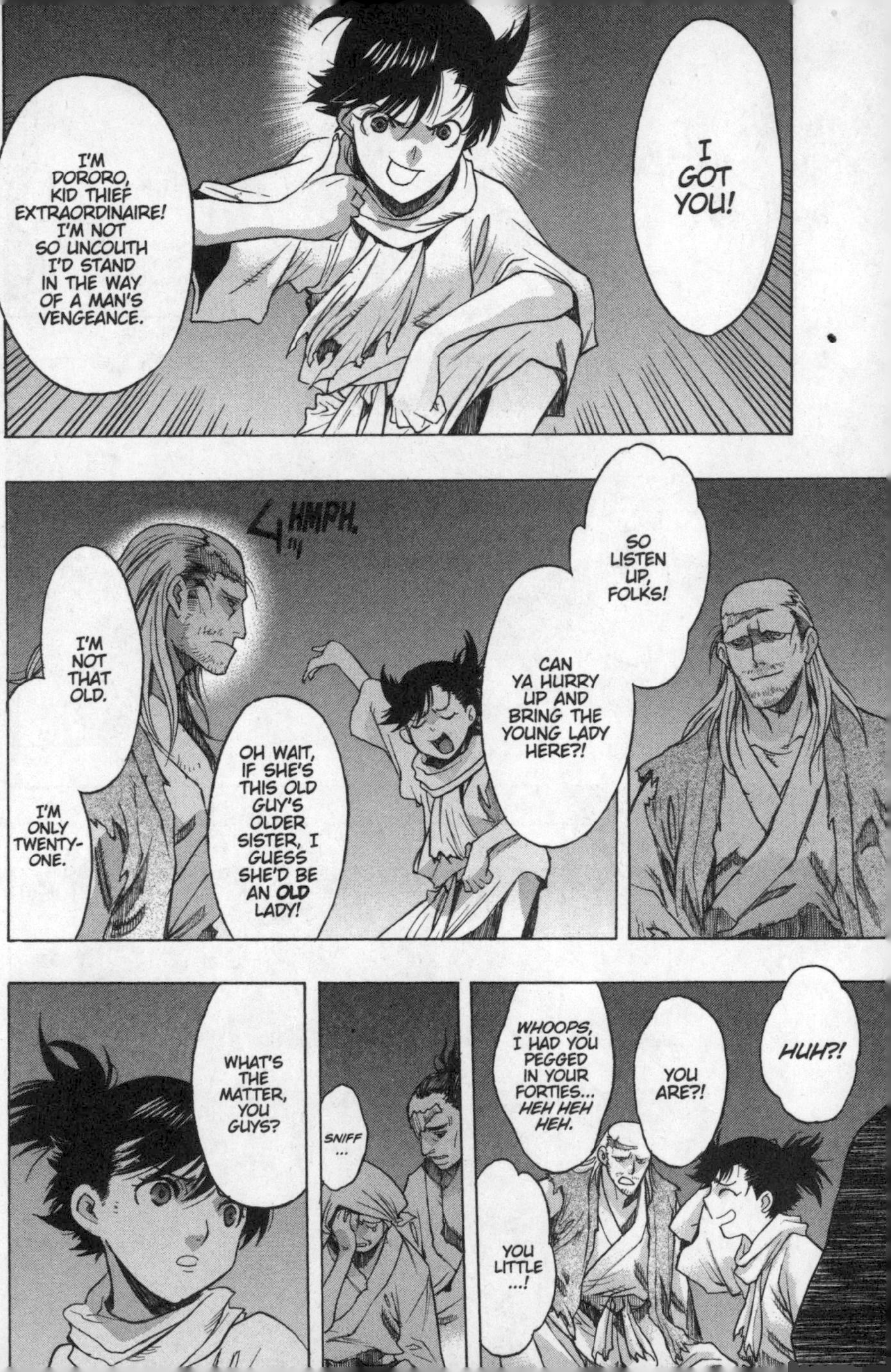
I GOT YOU!
I'M DORORO, KID THIEF EXTRAORDINAIRE! I'M NOT SO UNCOUTH I'D STAND IN THE WAY OF A MAN'S VENGEANCE.
SO LISTEN UP, FOLKS!
CAN YA HURRY UP AND BRING THE YOUNG LADY HERE?!
OH WAIT, IF SHE'S THIS OLD GUY'S OLDER SISTER, I GUESS SHE'D BE AN **OLD** LADY!
HMPH.
I'M NOT THAT OLD.
I'M ONLY TWENTY-ONE.
HUH?!
YOU ARE?!
WHOOPS, I HAD YOU PEGGED IN YOUR FORTIES... *HEH HEH HEH.*
YOU LITTLE ...!
SNIFF ...
WHAT'S THE MATTER, YOU GUYS?

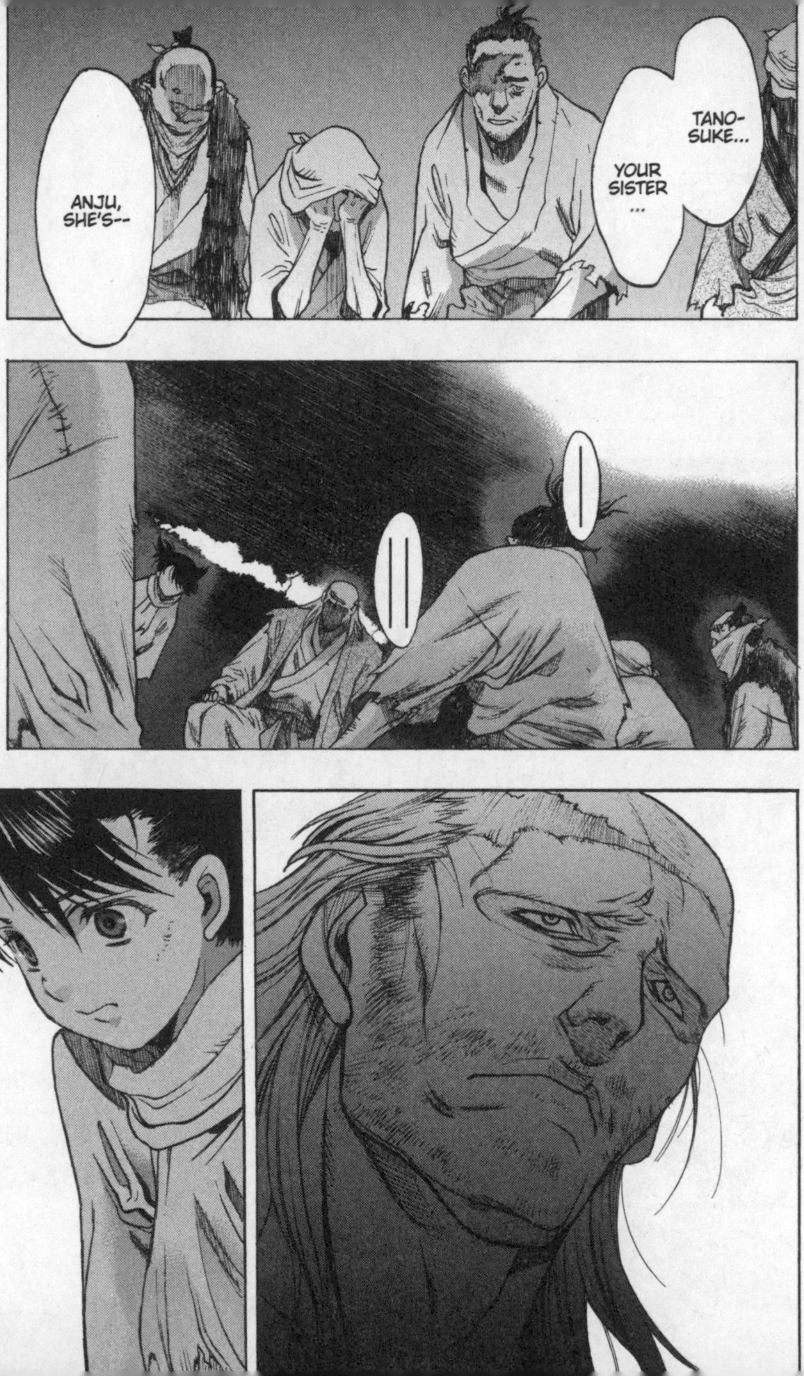
TANO-SUKE... YOUR SISTER ...
ANJU, SHE'S--

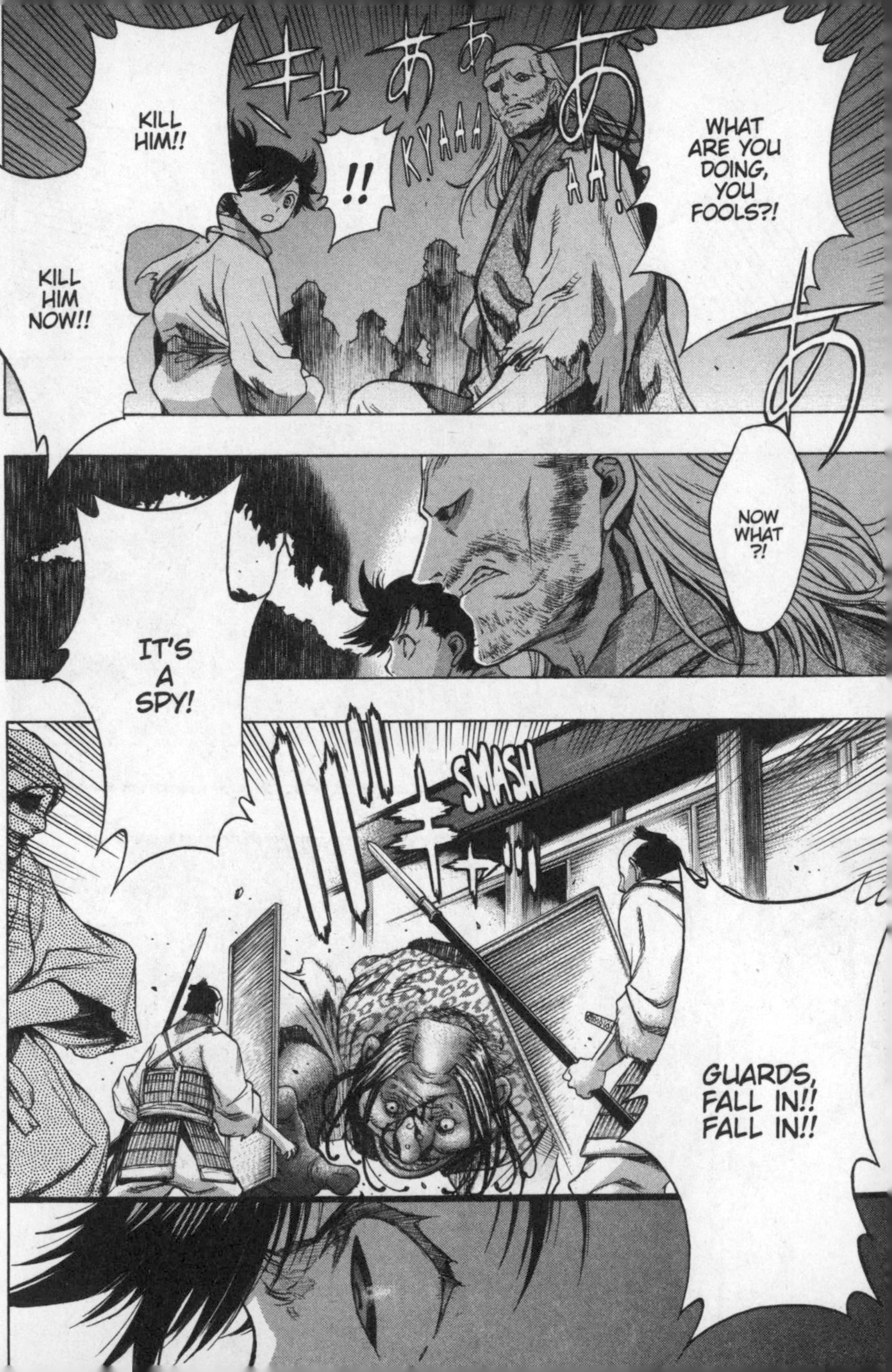
WHAT ARE YOU DOING, YOU FOOLS?!
KYAAAA AA!
!!
KILL HIM!!
KILL HIM NOW!!
NOW WHAT ?!
IT'S A SPY!
GUARDS, FALL IN!! FALL IN!!
SMASH

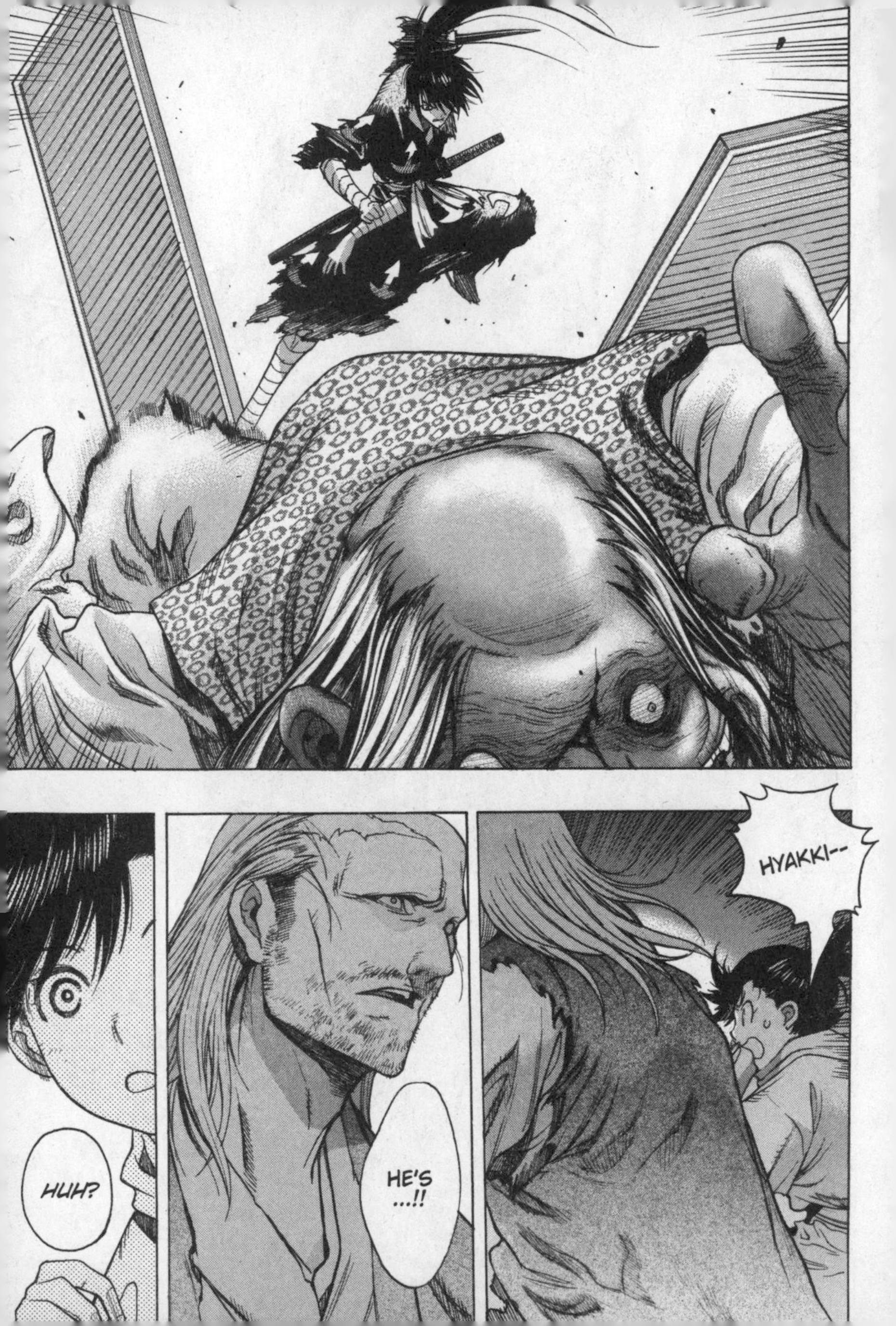
HYAKKI--
HE'S ....!!
HUH?

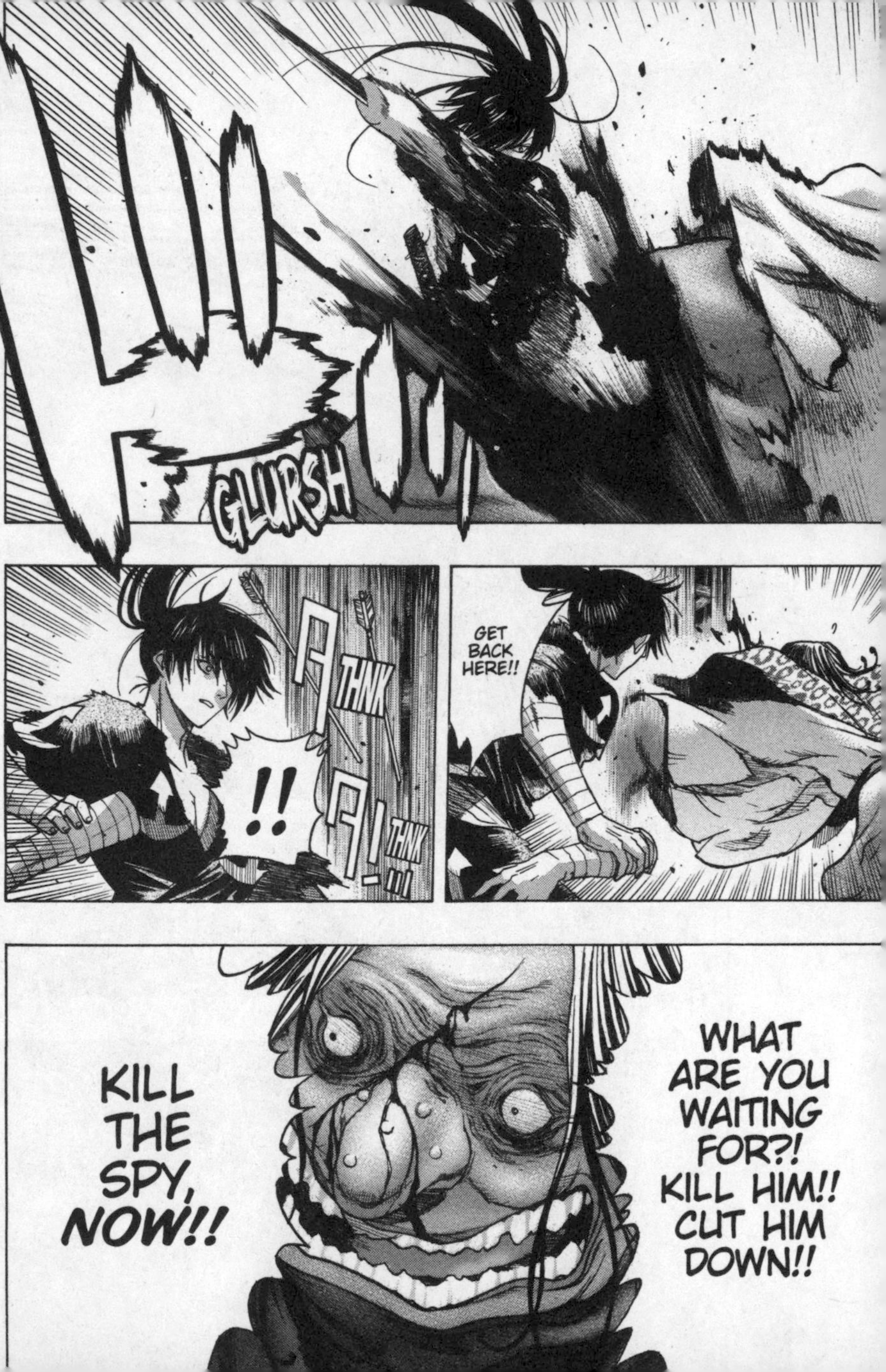
GLURSH
GET BACK HERE!!
THNK
!!
THNK
WHAT ARE YOU WAITING FOR?! KILL HIM!! CUT HIM DOWN!!
KILL THE SPY, NOW!!

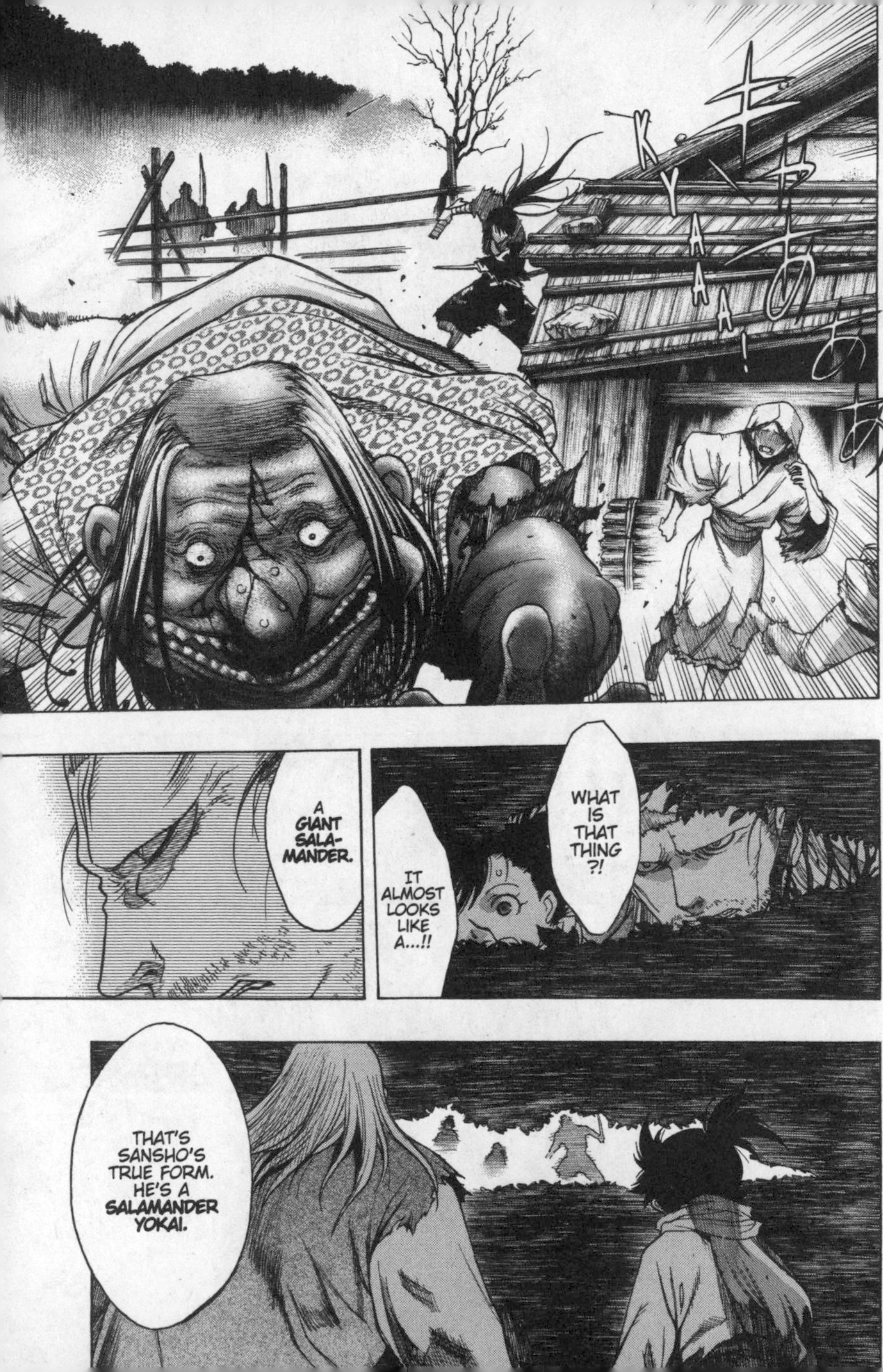
KYAAA!
WHAT IS THAT THING?!
IT ALMOST LOOKS LIKE A...!!
A GIANT SALAMANDER.
THAT'S SANSHO'S TRUE FORM. HE'S A SALAMANDER YOKAI.

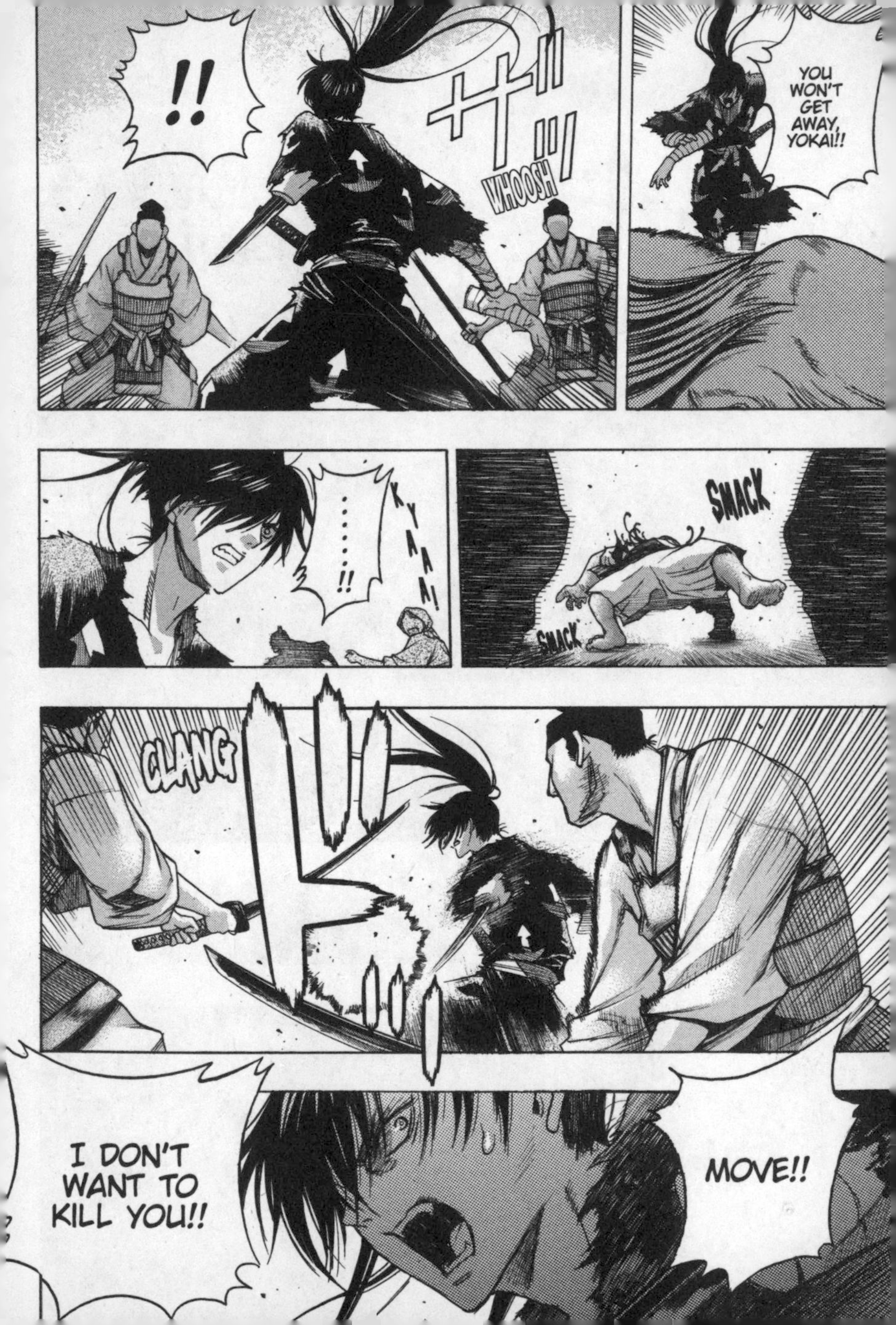
YOU WON'T GET AWAY, YOKAI!!
!!
WHOOSH
SMACK
SMACK
KYAAAA!
......!!
CLANG
MOVE!!
I DON'T WANT TO KILL YOU!!

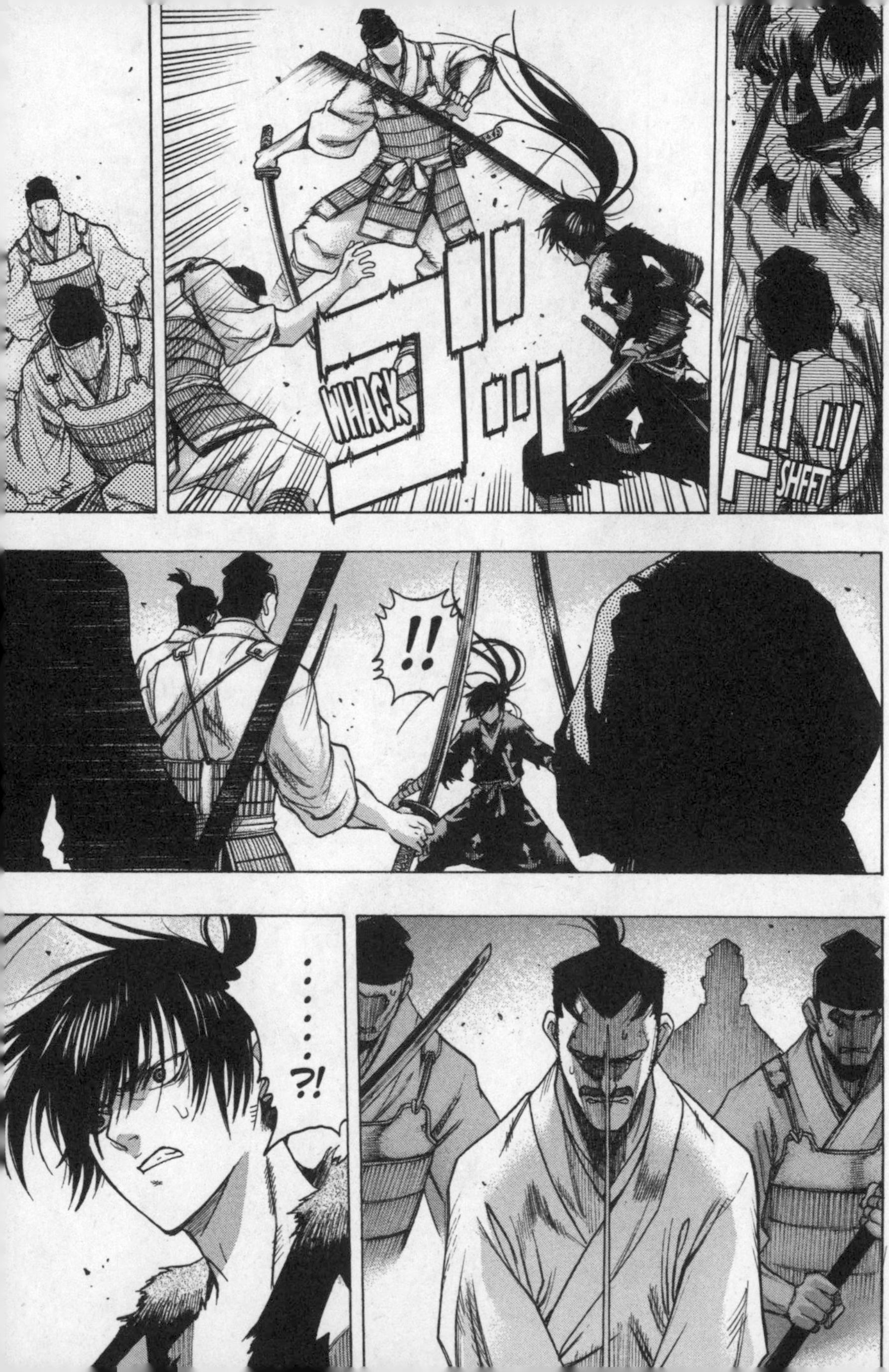
SHFFT
WHACK
!!
......
?!

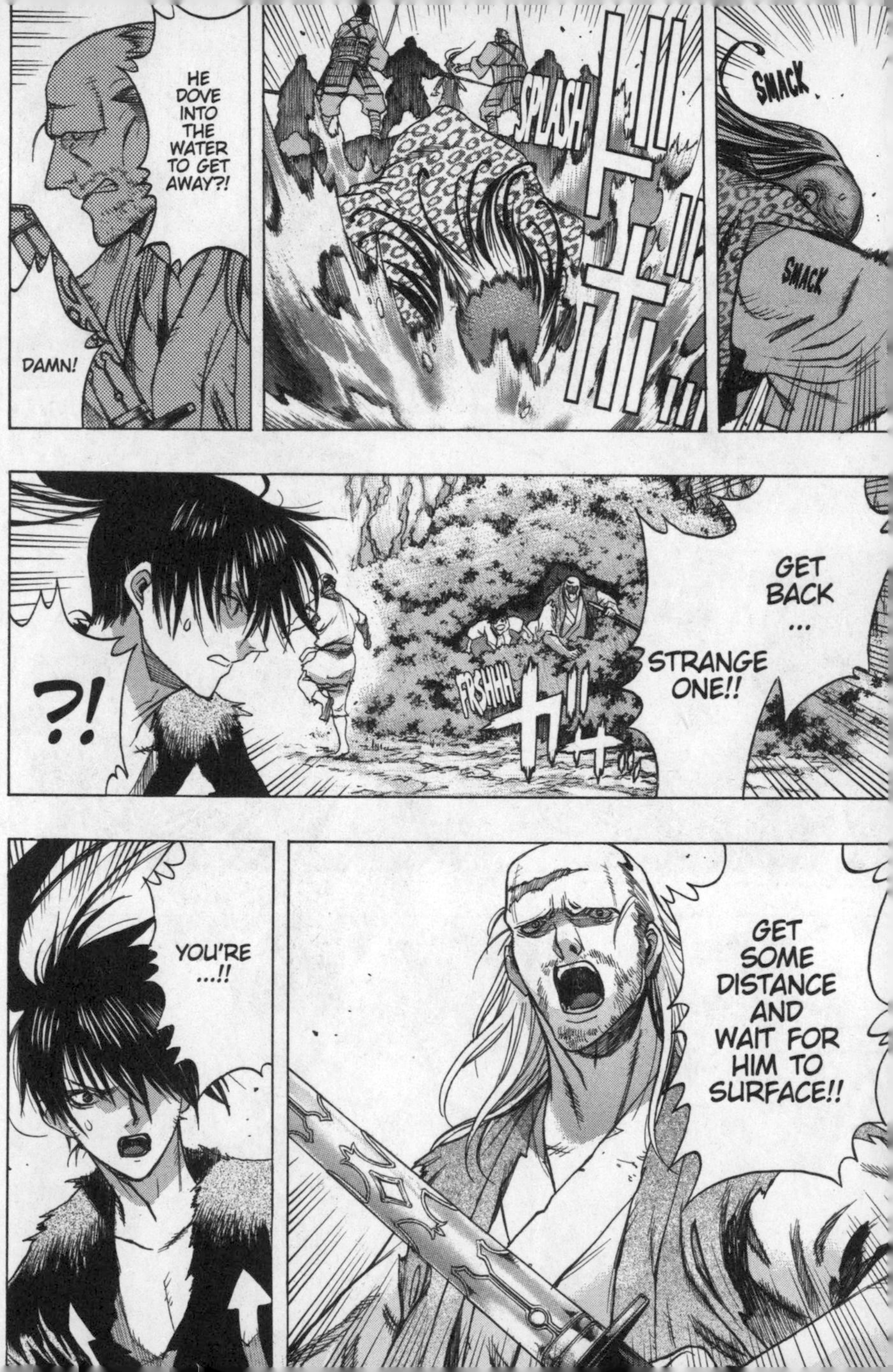
SMACK
SMACK
SPLASH
HE DOVE INTO THE WATER TO GET AWAY?!
DAMN!
GET BACK ...
STRANGE ONE!!
FRSHHH
?!
GET SOME DISTANCE AND WAIT FOR HIM TO SURFACE!!
YOU'RE ...!!

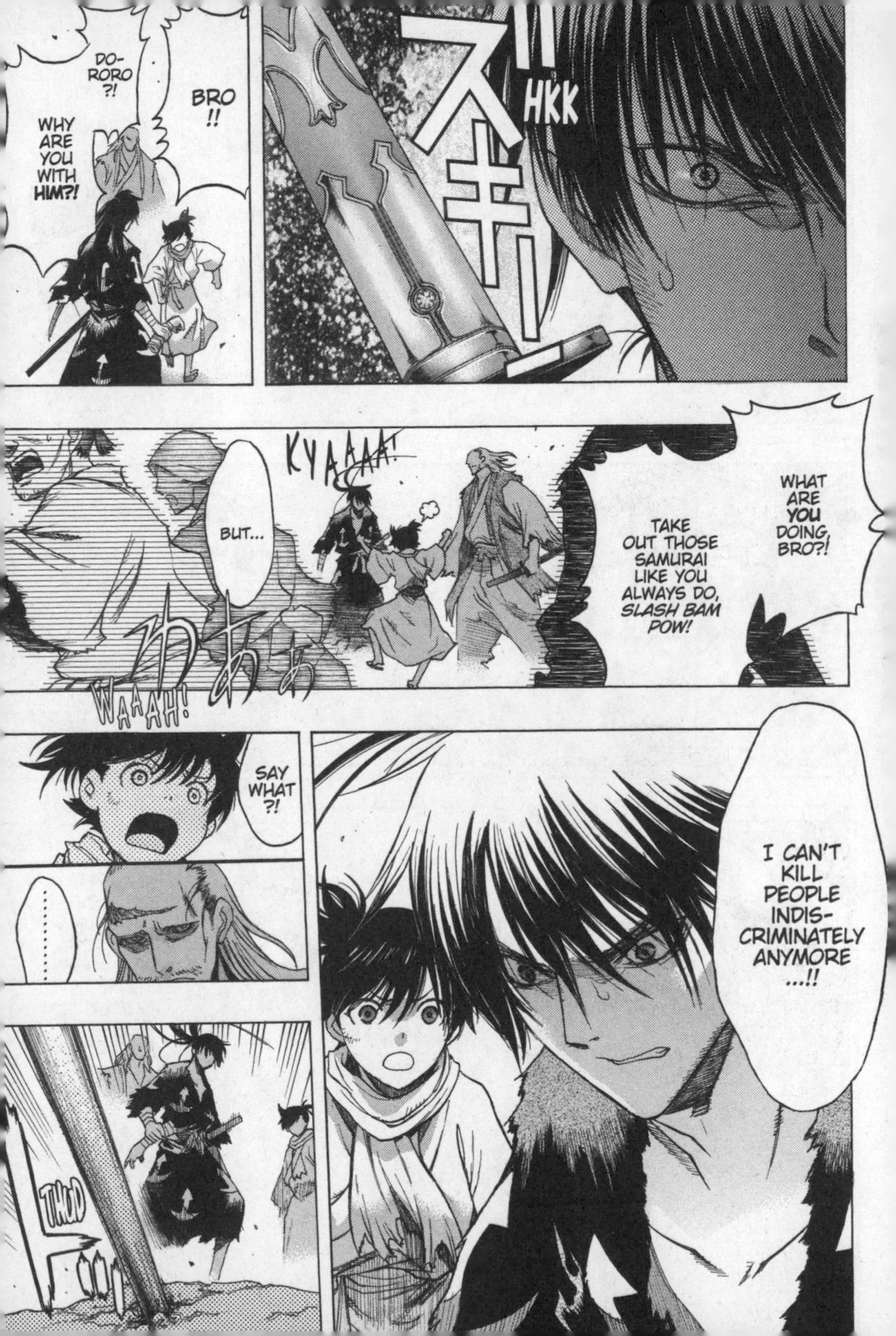

スキー
HKK
BRO!!
DO-RORO?!
WHY ARE YOU WITH HIM?!
WHAT ARE YOU DOING, BRO?!
TAKE OUT THOSE SAMURAI LIKE YOU ALWAYS DO, SLASH BAM POW!
KYAAAA!
BUT...
わあぁ
WAAAH!
I CAN'T KILL PEOPLE INDIS-CRIMINATELY ANYMORE ...!!
SAY WHAT?!
...
THUD

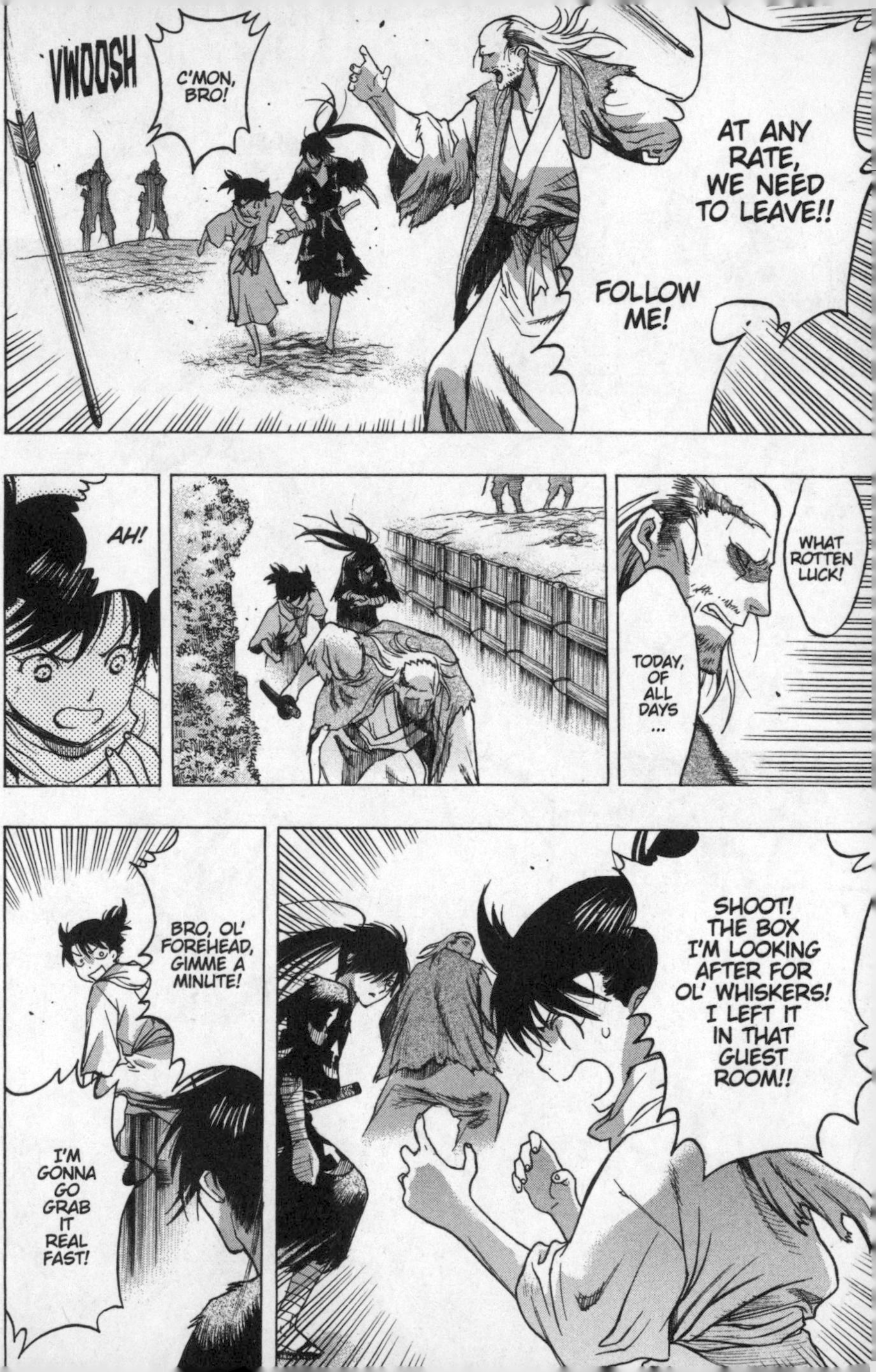
AT ANY RATE, WE NEED TO LEAVE!!
FOLLOW ME!
VWOOSH
C'MON, BRO!
WHAT ROTTEN LUCK!
TODAY, OF ALL DAYS ...
AH!
SHOOT! THE BOX I'M LOOKING AFTER FOR OL' WHISKERS! I LEFT IT IN THAT GUEST ROOM!!
BRO, OL' FOREHEAD, GIMME A MINUTE!
I'M GONNA GO GRAB IT REAL FAST!

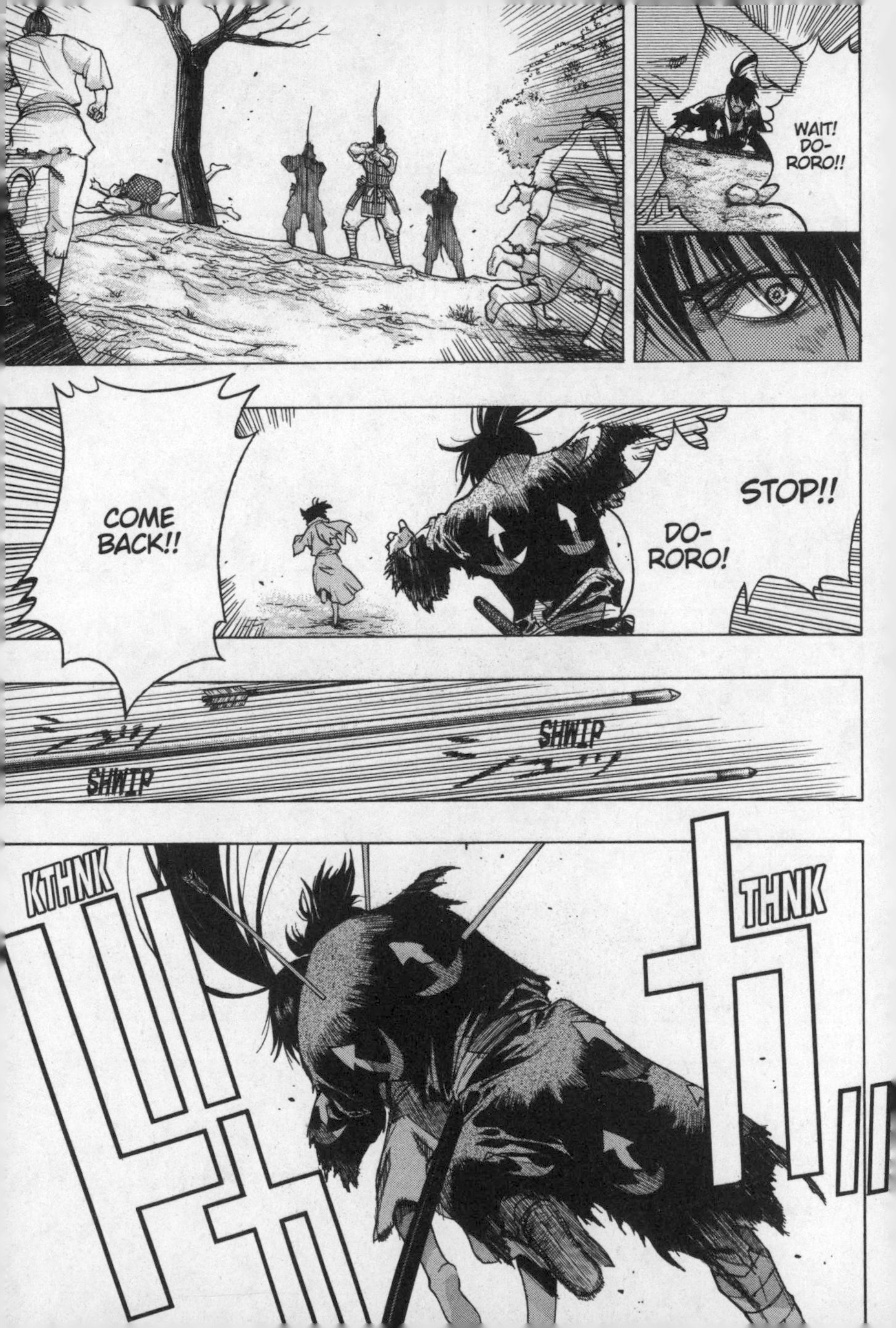
WAIT! DO-RORO!!
STOP!!
DO-RORO!
COME BACK!!
SHWIP
SHWIP
THNK
KTHNK

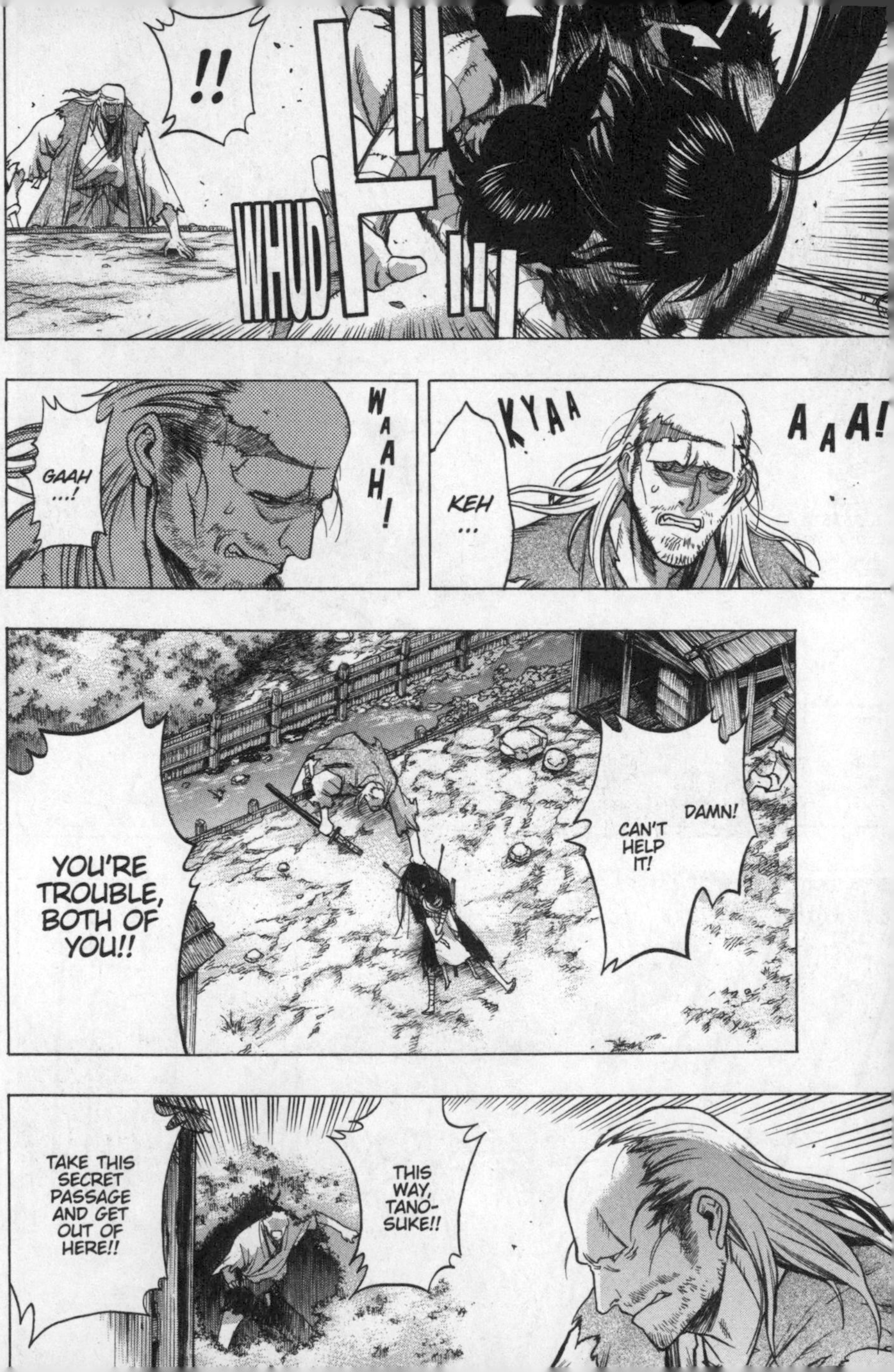
WHUD
!!
KYAA AAA!
KEH...
WAAAH!
GAAH...!
DAMN!
CAN'T HELP IT!
YOU'RE TROUBLE, BOTH OF YOU!!
THIS WAY, TANO-SUKE!!
TAKE THIS SECRET PASSAGE AND GET OUT OF HERE!!

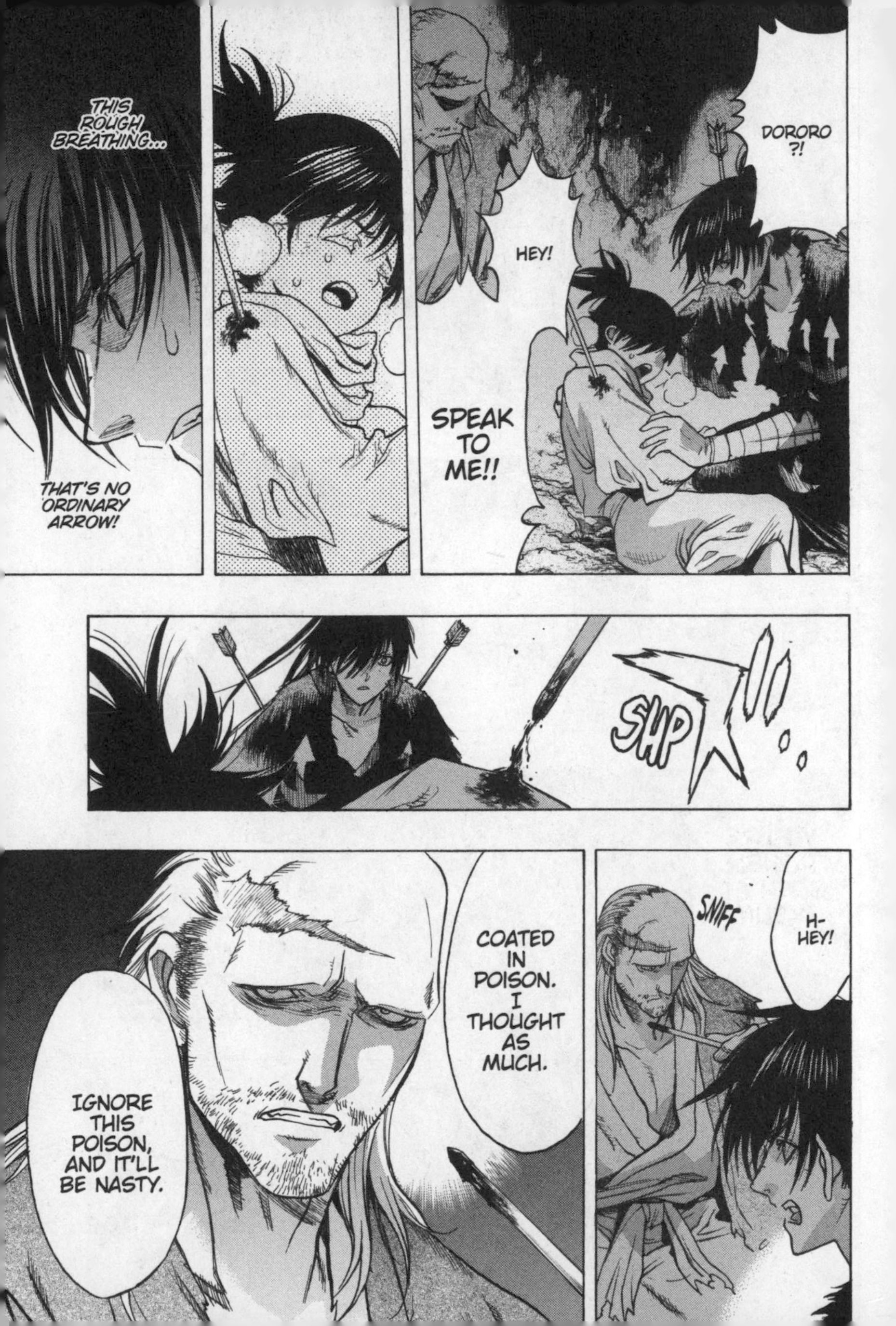
DORORO ?!
HEY!
SPEAK TO ME!!
THIS ROUGH BREATHING...
THAT'S NO ORDINARY ARROW!
SHP
H- HEY!
SNIFF
COATED IN POISON. I THOUGHT AS MUCH.
IGNORE THIS POISON, AND IT'LL BE NASTY.

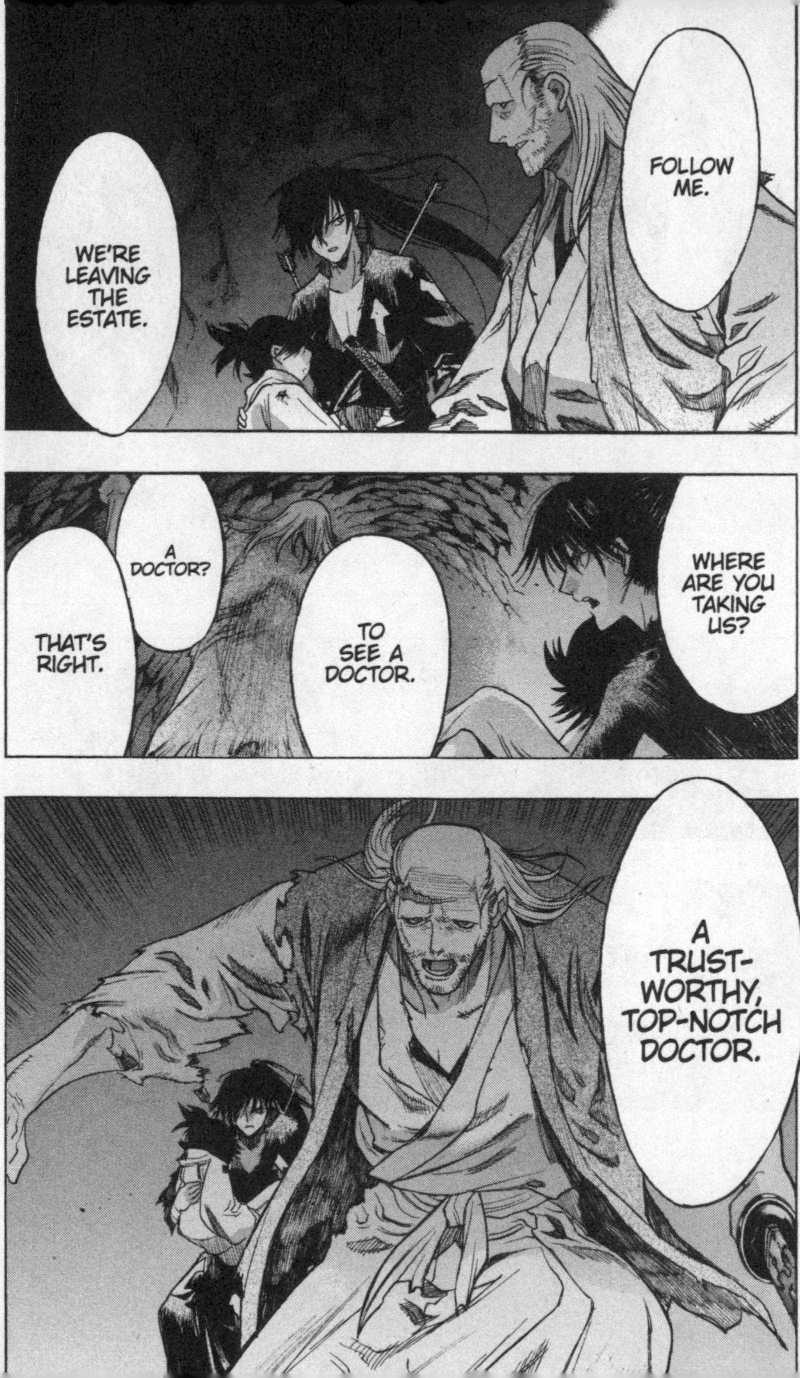
FOLLOW ME.
WE'RE LEAVING THE ESTATE.
WHERE ARE YOU TAKING US?
TO SEE A DOCTOR.
A DOCTOR?
THAT'S RIGHT.
A TRUST-WORTHY, TOP-NOTCH DOCTOR.

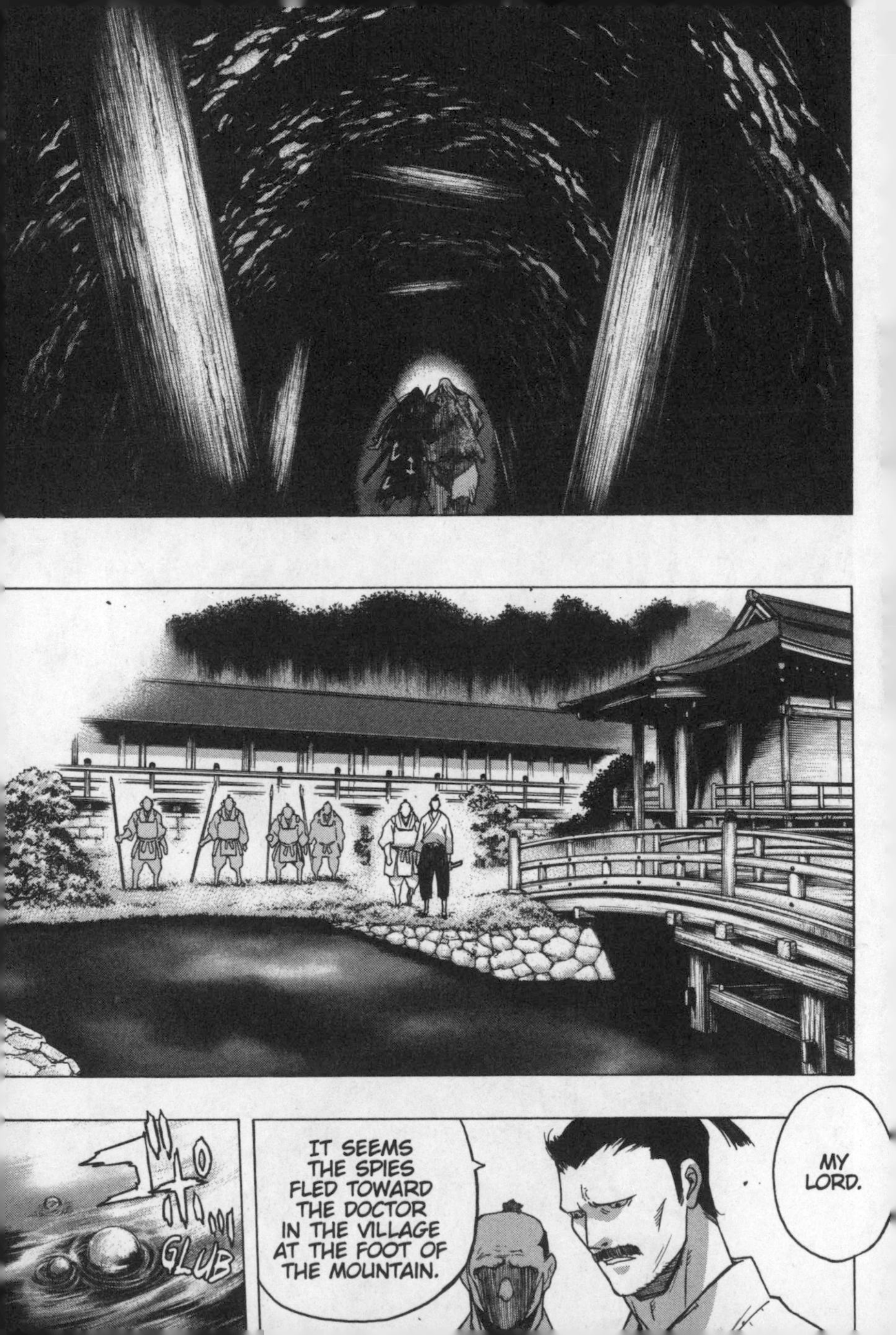
MY LORD.
IT SEEMS THE SPIES FLED TOWARD THE DOCTOR IN THE VILLAGE AT THE FOOT OF THE MOUNTAIN.
GLUB

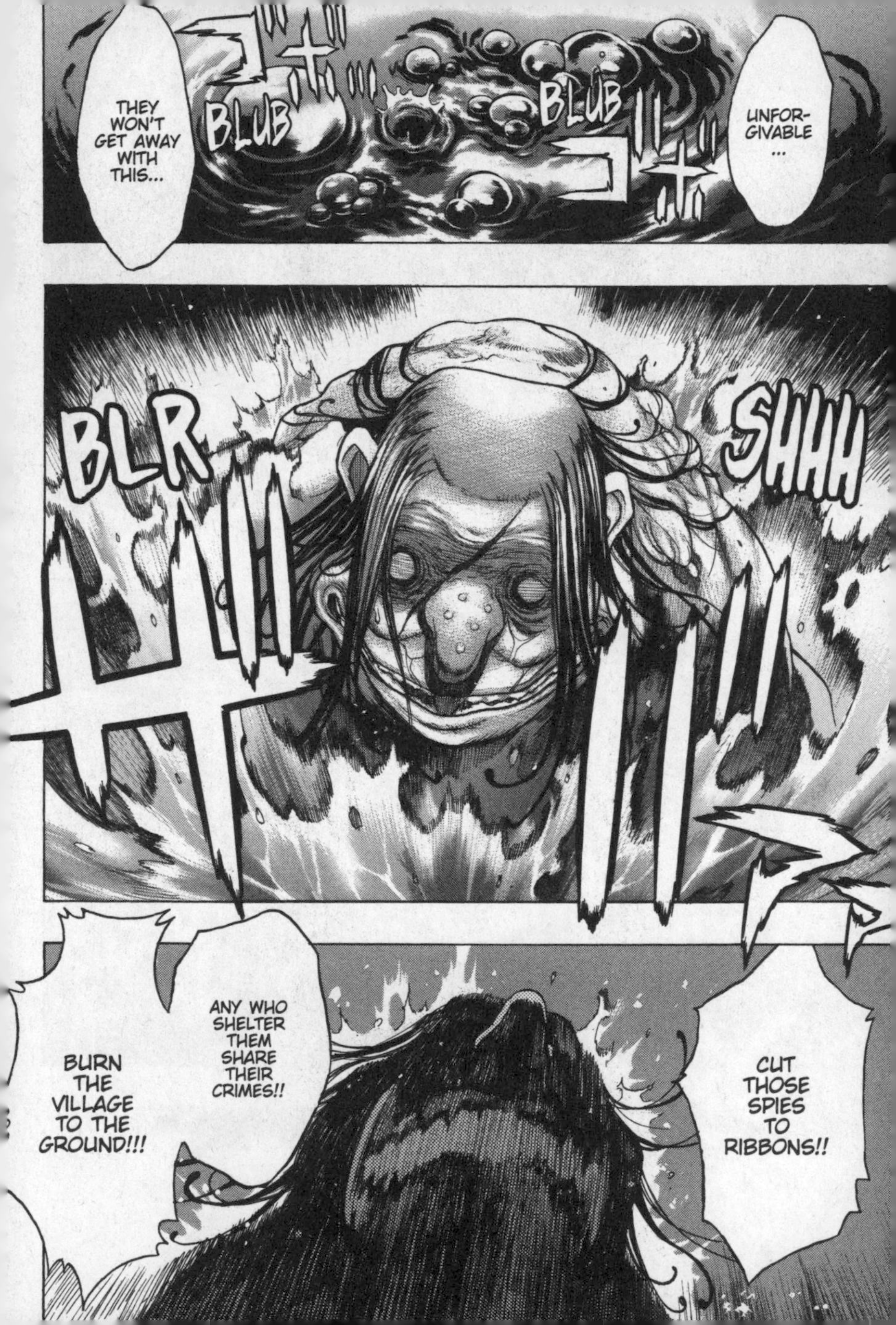
UNFOR-GIVABLE...
BLUB
BLUB
THEY WON'T GET AWAY WITH THIS...
SHHH
BLR
CUT THOSE SPIES TO RIBBONS!!
ANY WHO SHELTER THEM SHARE THEIR CRIMES!!
BURN THE VILLAGE TO THE GROUND!!!

THE LEGEND OF
DORORO AND
HYAKKIMARU

どろろと
百鬼丸伝

THE LEGEND OF
DORORO AND **HYAKKIMARU**

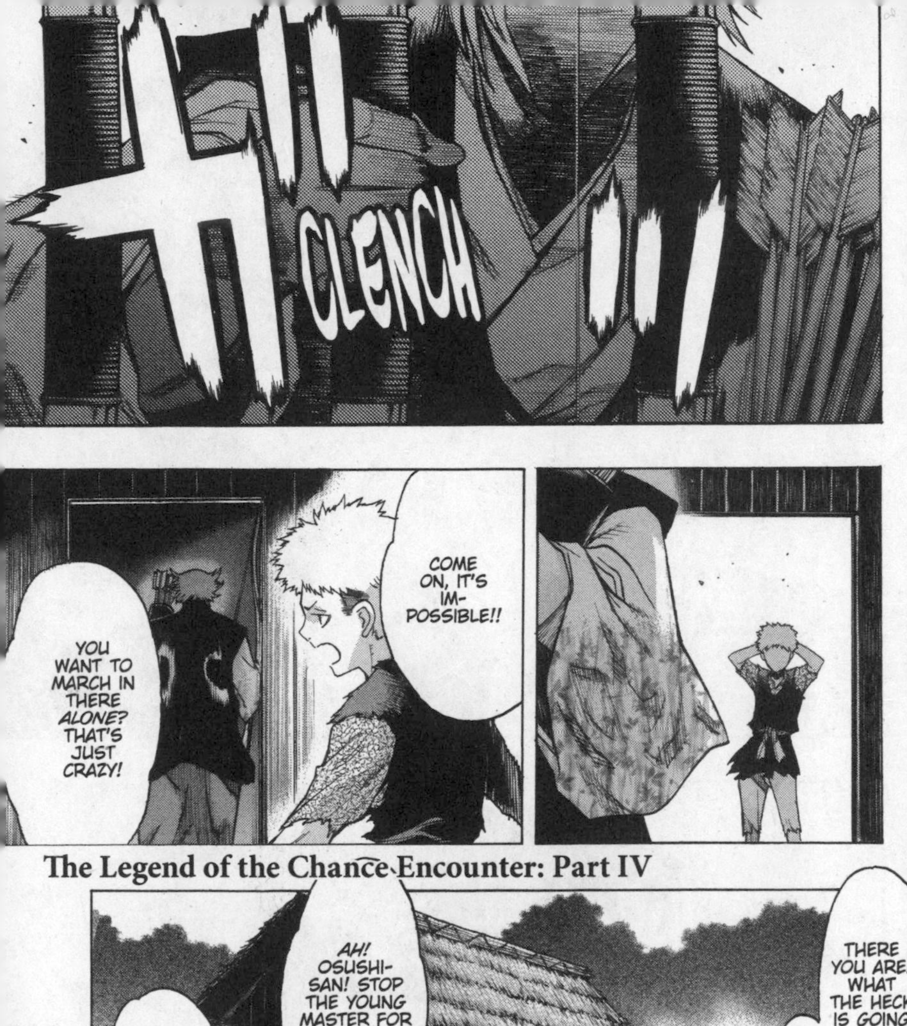
CLENCH
COME ON, IT'S IM-POSSIBLE!!
YOU WANT TO MARCH IN THERE *ALONE*? THAT'S JUST CRAZY!

The Legend of the Chance Encounter: Part IV

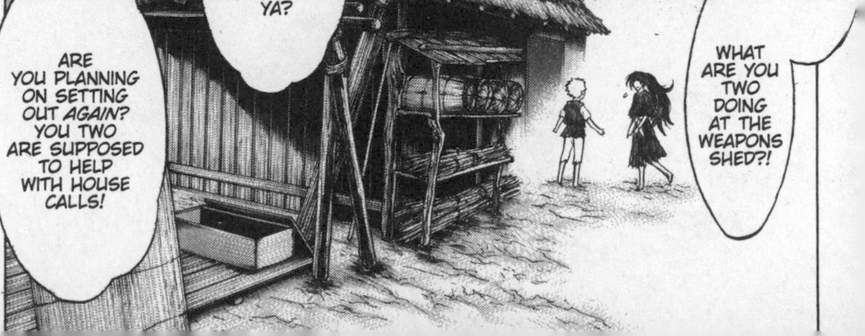
THERE YOU ARE! WHAT THE HECK IS GOING ON?
WHAT ARE YOU TWO DOING AT THE WEAPONS SHED?!
AH! OSUSHI-SAN! STOP THE YOUNG MASTER FOR ME, WILL YA?
ARE YOU PLANNING ON SETTING OUT *AGAIN*? YOU TWO ARE SUPPOSED TO HELP WITH HOUSE CALLS!

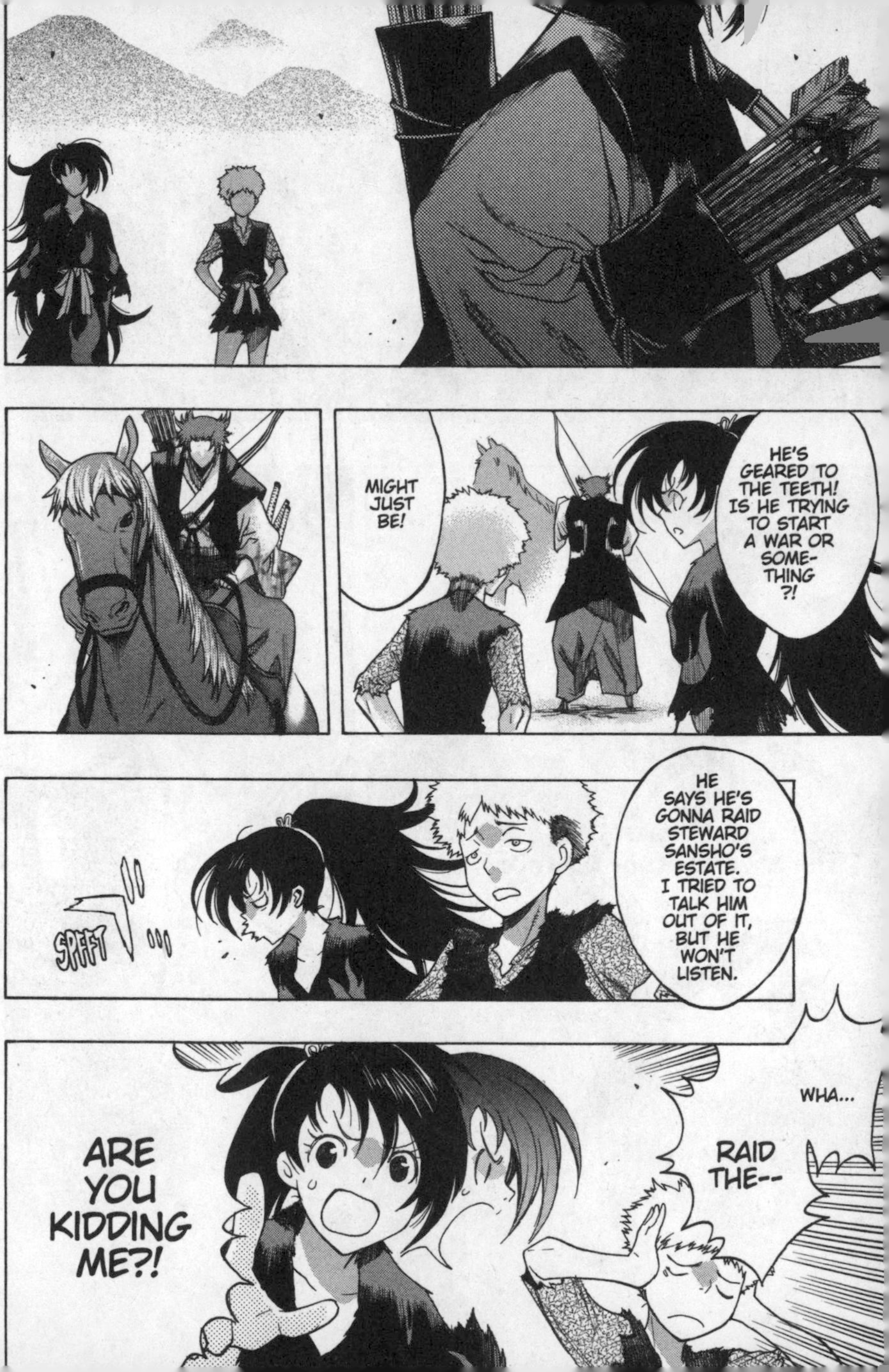
HE'S GEARED TO THE TEETH! IS HE TRYING TO START A WAR OR SOME-THING?!
MIGHT JUST BE!
HE SAYS HE'S GONNA RAID STEWARD SANSHO'S ESTATE. I TRIED TO TALK HIM OUT OF IT, BUT HE WON'T LISTEN.
SPFFT
WHA...
RAID THE--
ARE YOU KIDDING ME?!

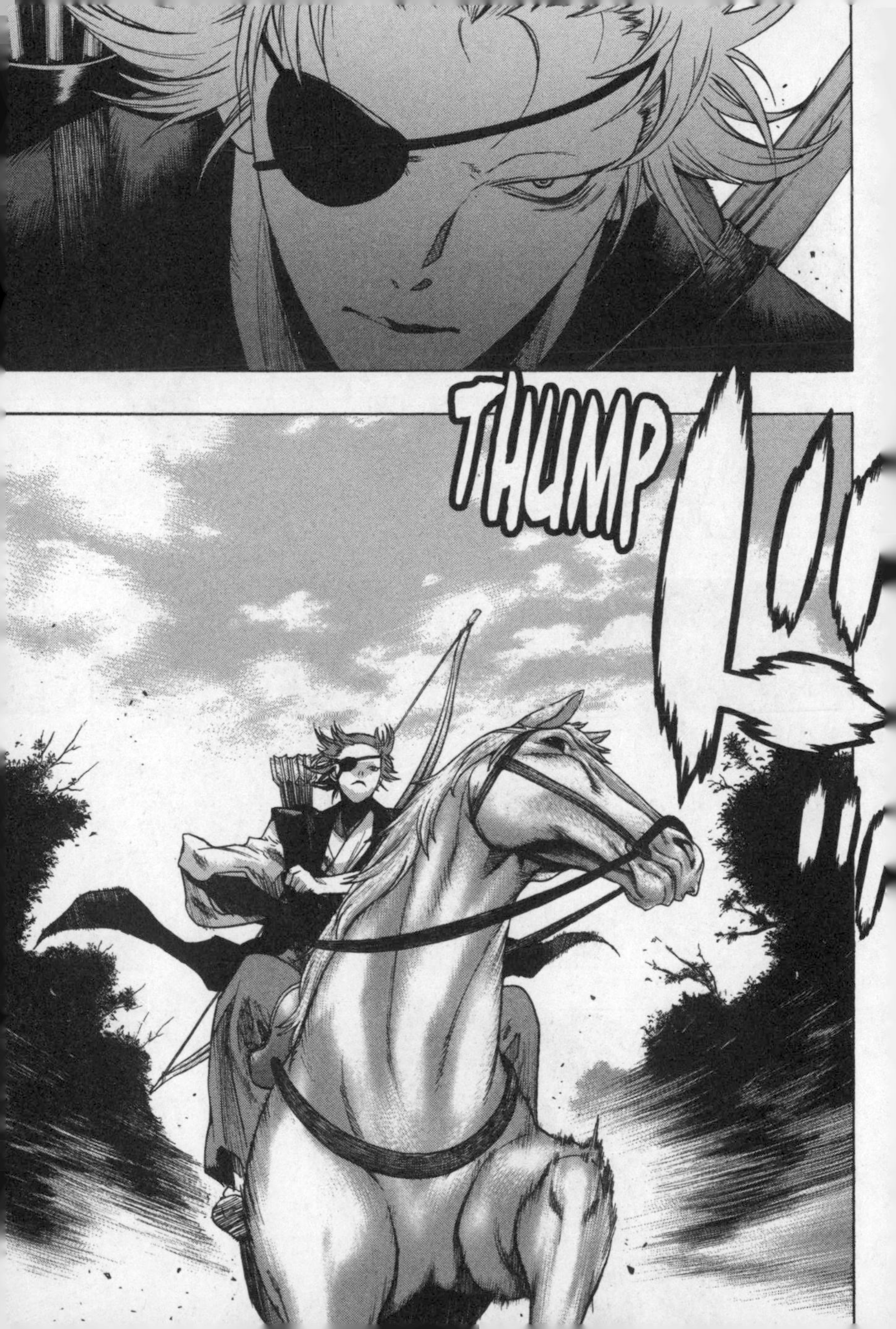
THUMP

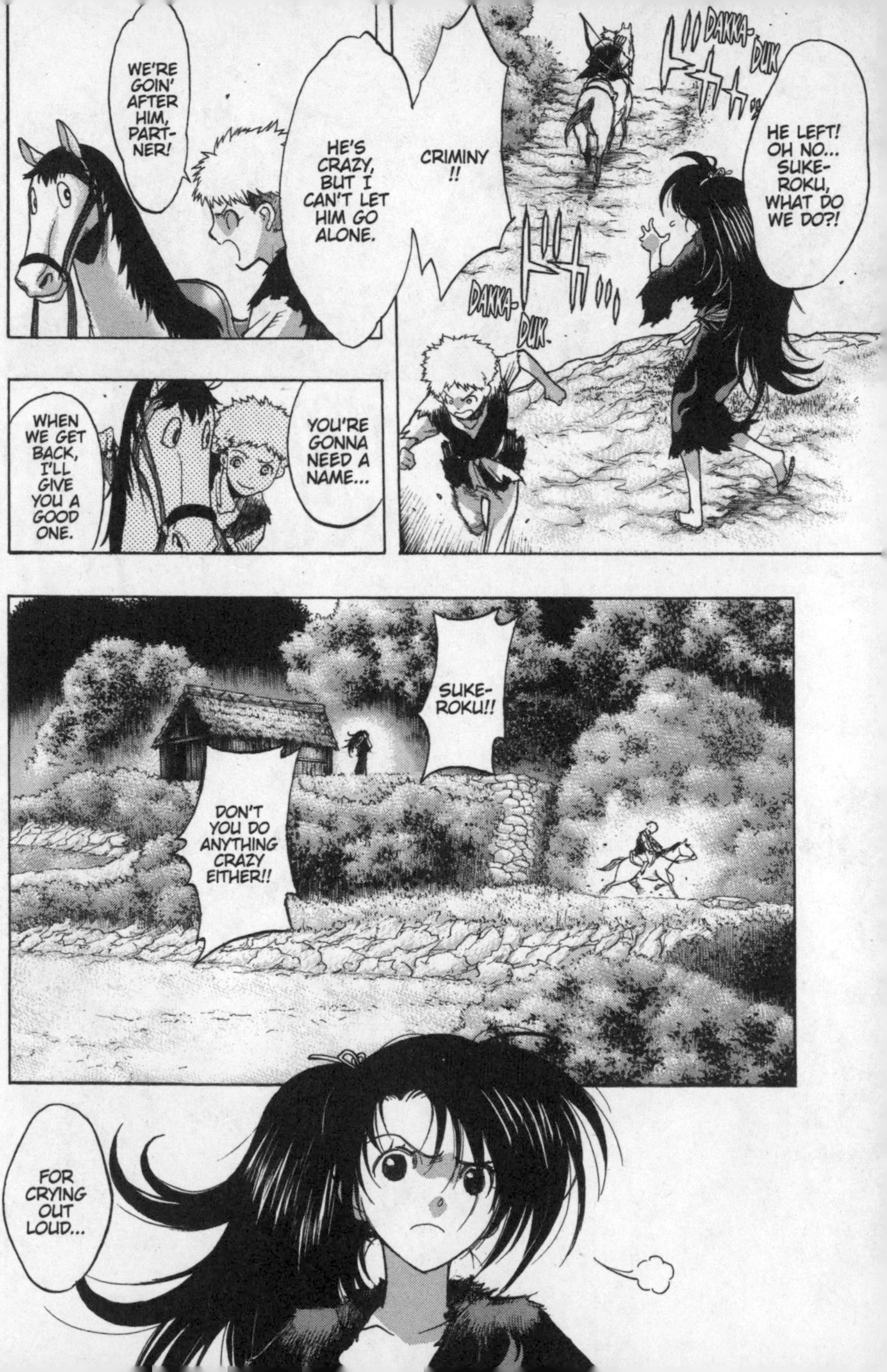
DAKKA-DUK
HE LEFT! OH NO... SUKE-ROKU, WHAT DO WE DO?!
CRIMINY!!
HE'S CRAZY, BUT I CAN'T LET HIM GO ALONE.
DAKKA-DUK
WE'RE GOIN' AFTER HIM, PARTNER!
YOU'RE GONNA NEED A NAME...
WHEN WE GET BACK, I'LL GIVE YOU A GOOD ONE.
SUKE-ROKU!!
DON'T YOU DO ANYTHING CRAZY EITHER!!
FOR CRYING OUT LOUD...

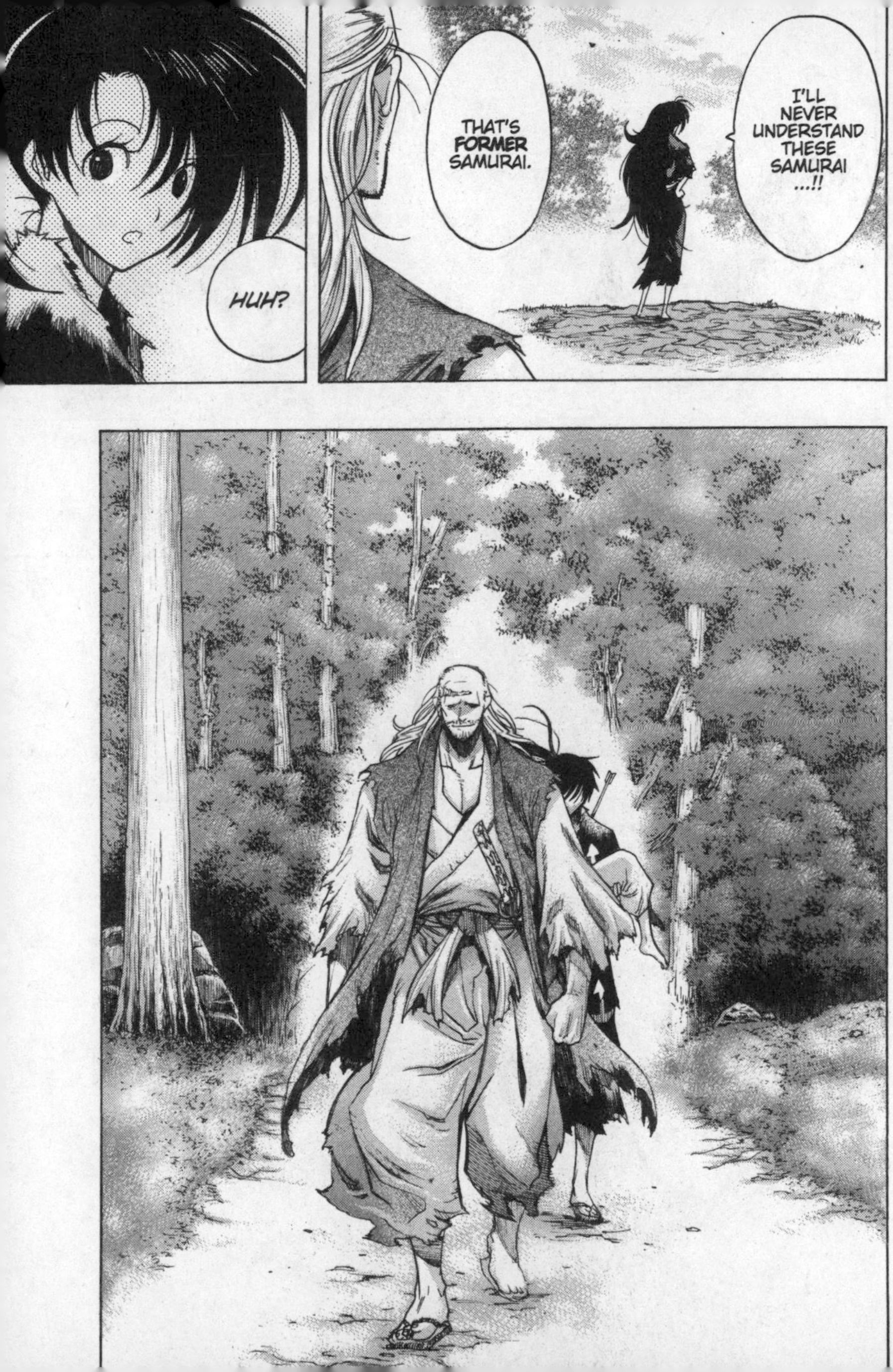
I'LL NEVER UNDERSTAND THESE SAMURAI ...!!
THAT'S FORMER SAMURAI.
HUH?

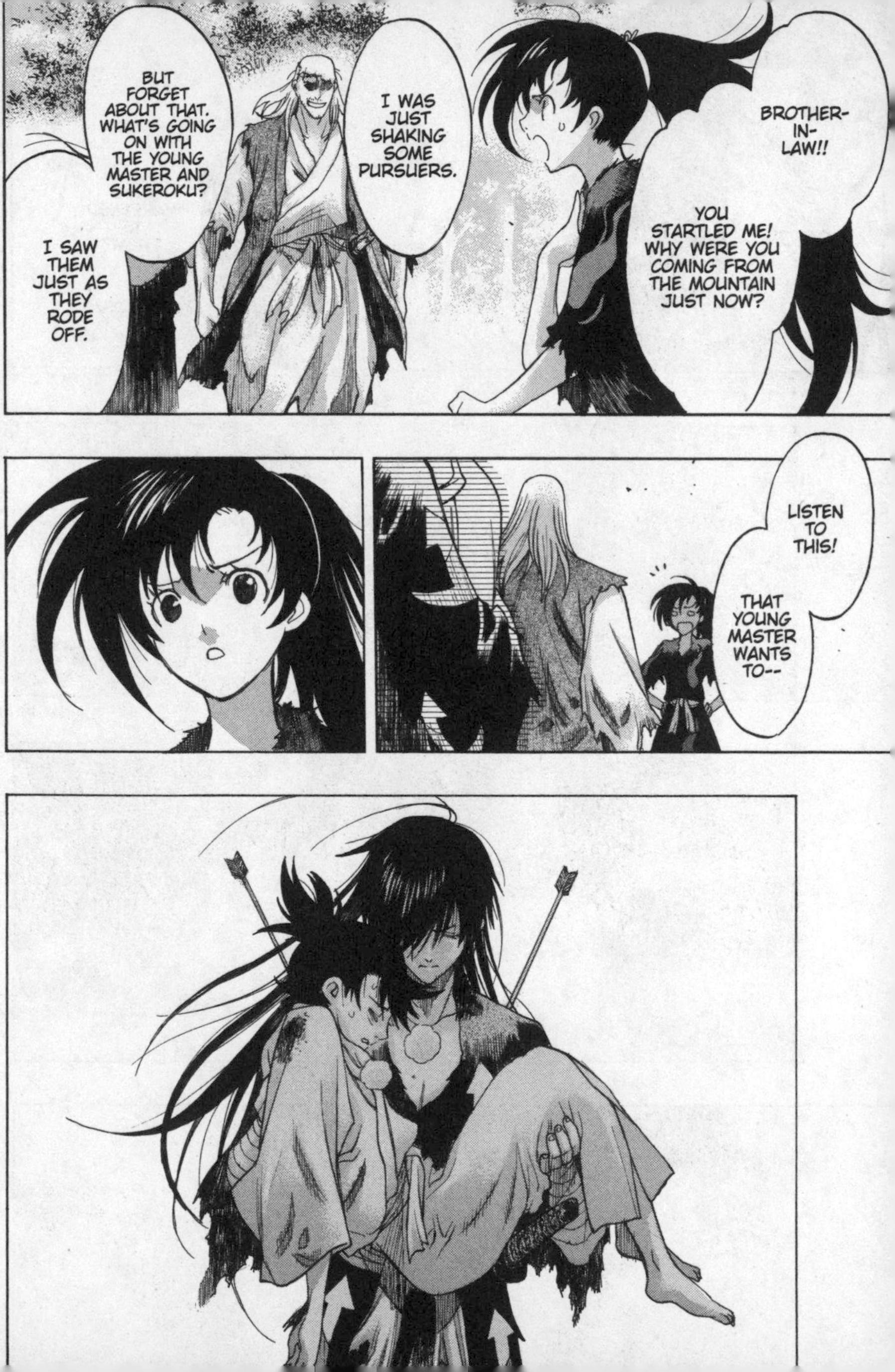
BROTHER-IN-LAW!!
YOU STARTLED ME! WHY WERE YOU COMING FROM THE MOUNTAIN JUST NOW?
I WAS JUST SHAKING SOME PURSUERS.
BUT FORGET ABOUT THAT. WHAT'S GOING ON WITH THE YOUNG MASTER AND SUKEROKU?
I SAW THEM JUST AS THEY RODE OFF.
LISTEN TO THIS!
THAT YOUNG MASTER WANTS TO--

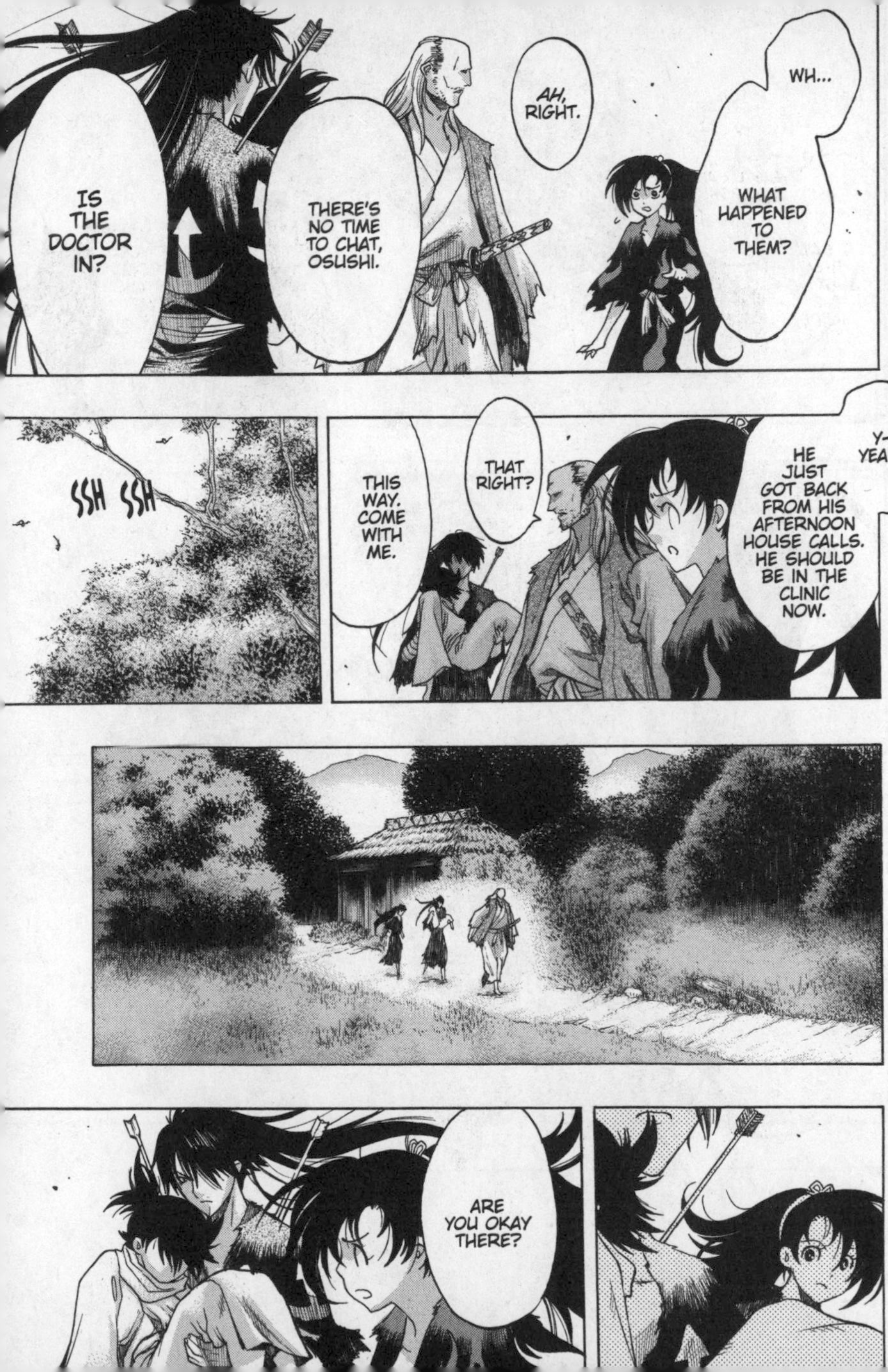
WH...
WHAT HAPPENED TO THEM?
AH, RIGHT.
THERE'S NO TIME TO CHAT, OSUSHI.
IS THE DOCTOR IN?
Y- YEAH.
HE JUST GOT BACK FROM HIS AFTERNOON HOUSE CALLS. HE SHOULD BE IN THE CLINIC NOW.
THAT RIGHT?
THIS WAY. COME WITH ME.
SSH SSH
ARE YOU OKAY THERE?

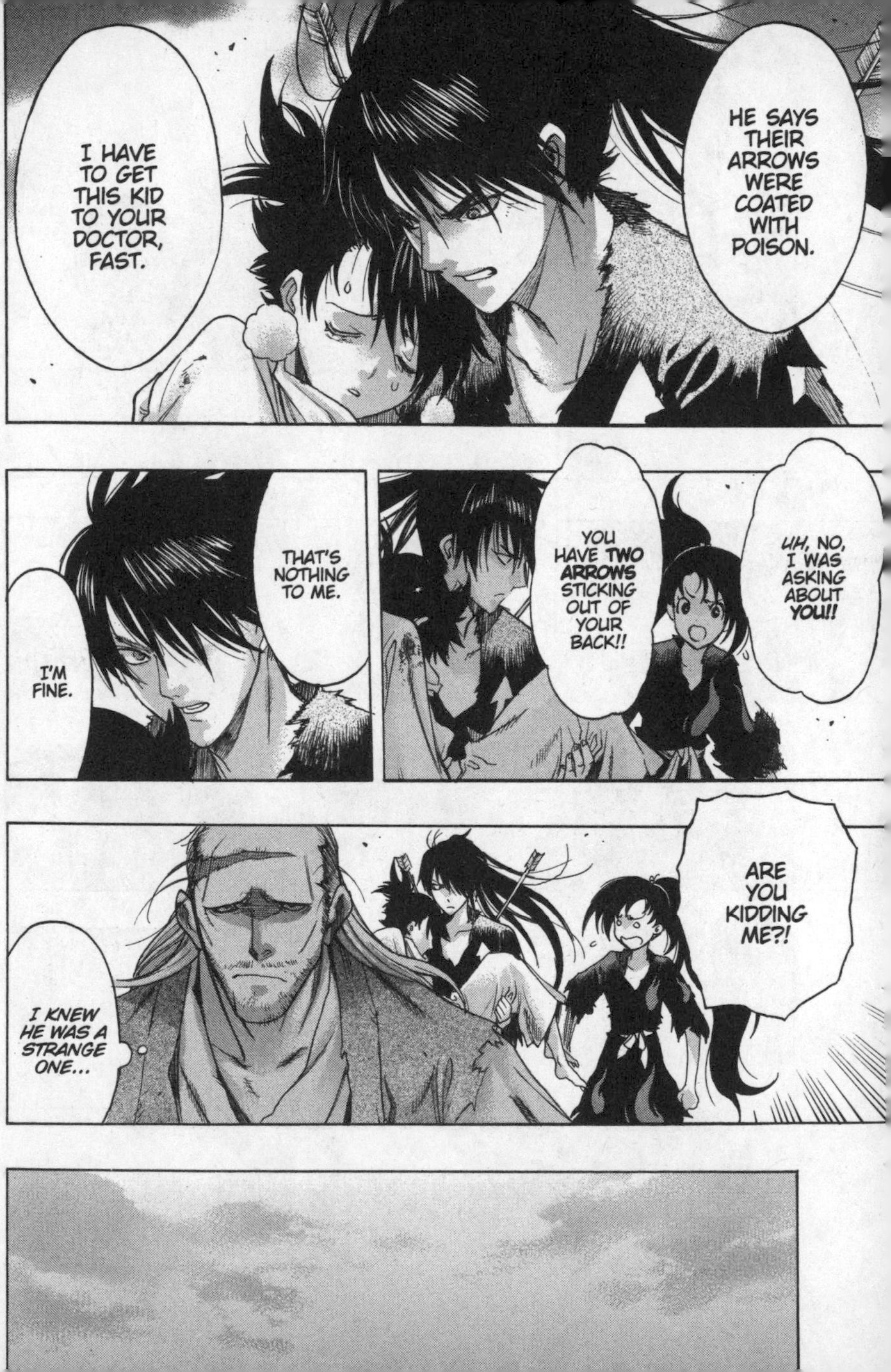
HE SAYS THEIR ARROWS WERE COATED WITH POISON.
I HAVE TO GET THIS KID TO YOUR DOCTOR, FAST.
UH, NO, I WAS ASKING ABOUT YOU!!
YOU HAVE TWO ARROWS STICKING OUT OF YOUR BACK!!
THAT'S NOTHING TO ME.
I'M FINE.
ARE YOU KIDDING ME?!
I KNEW HE WAS A STRANGE ONE...

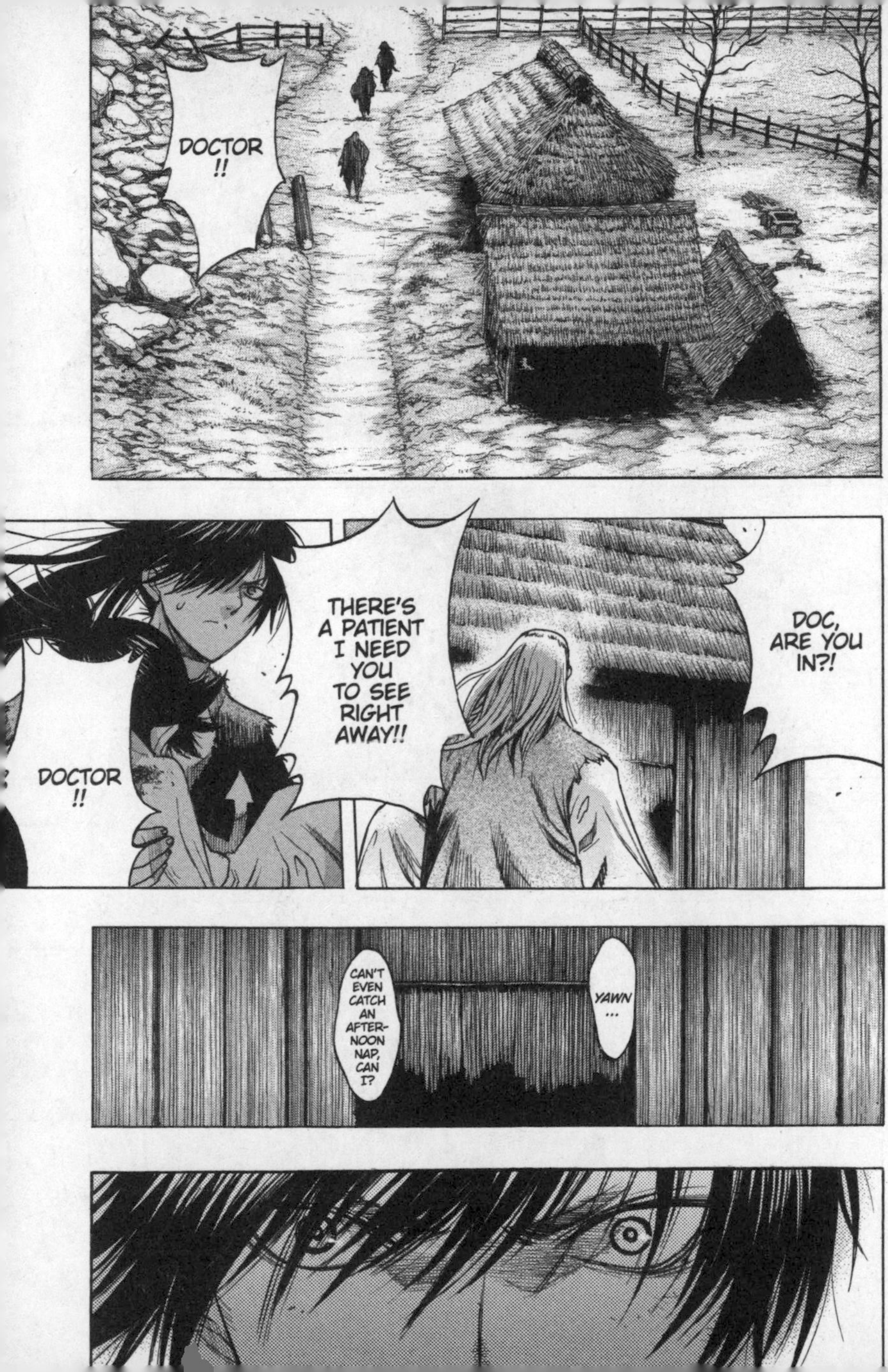
DOCTOR !!
DOC, ARE YOU IN?!
THERE'S A PATIENT I NEED YOU TO SEE RIGHT AWAY!!
DOCTOR !!
YAWN ...
CAN'T EVEN CATCH AN AFTER-NOON NAP, CAN I?

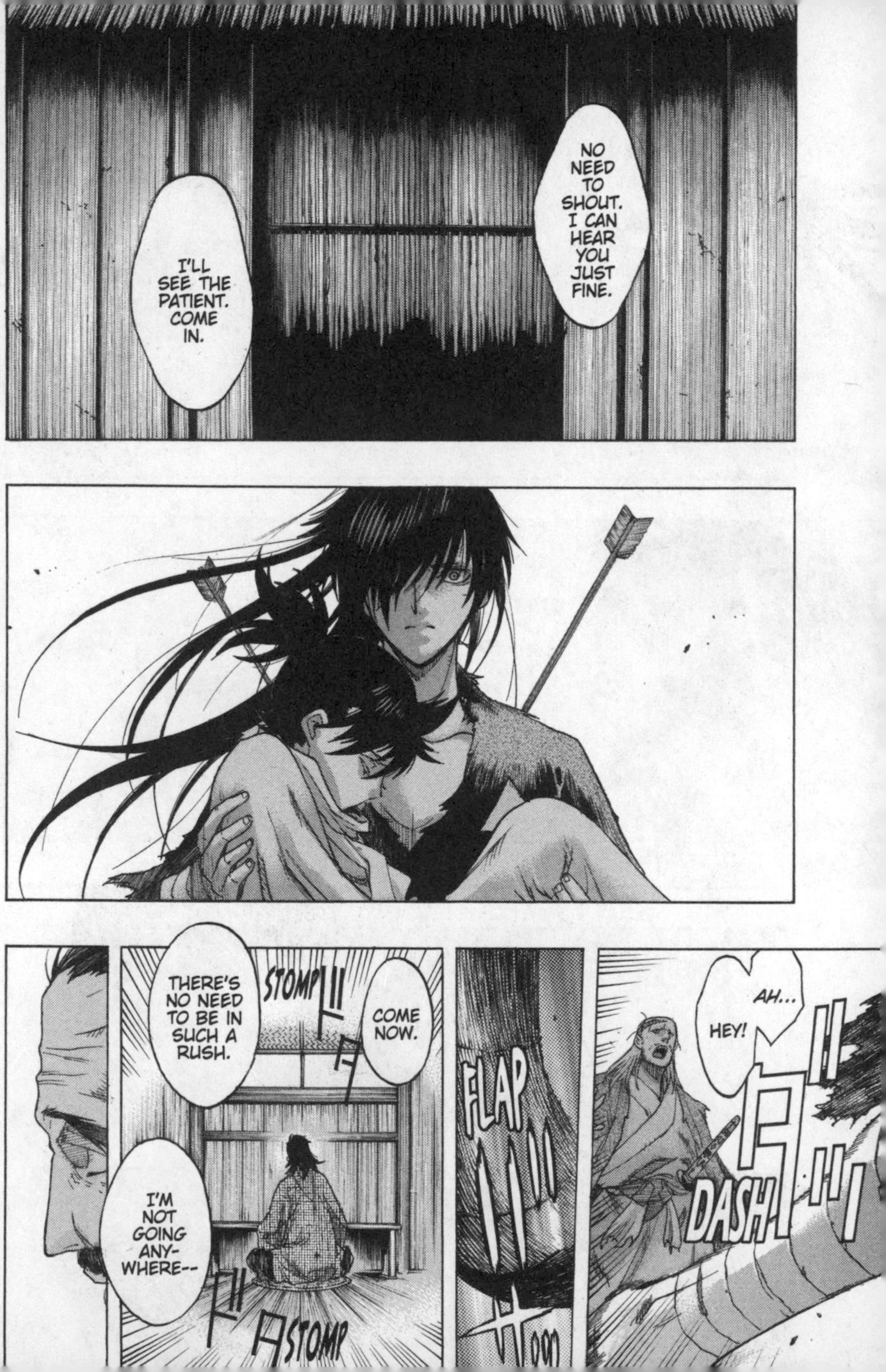
NO NEED TO SHOUT. I CAN HEAR YOU JUST FINE.
I'LL SEE THE PATIENT. COME IN.
AH... HEY!
DASH
FLAP
STOMP
COME NOW.
THERE'S NO NEED TO BE IN SUCH A RUSH.
STOMP
I'M NOT GOING ANY-WHERE--

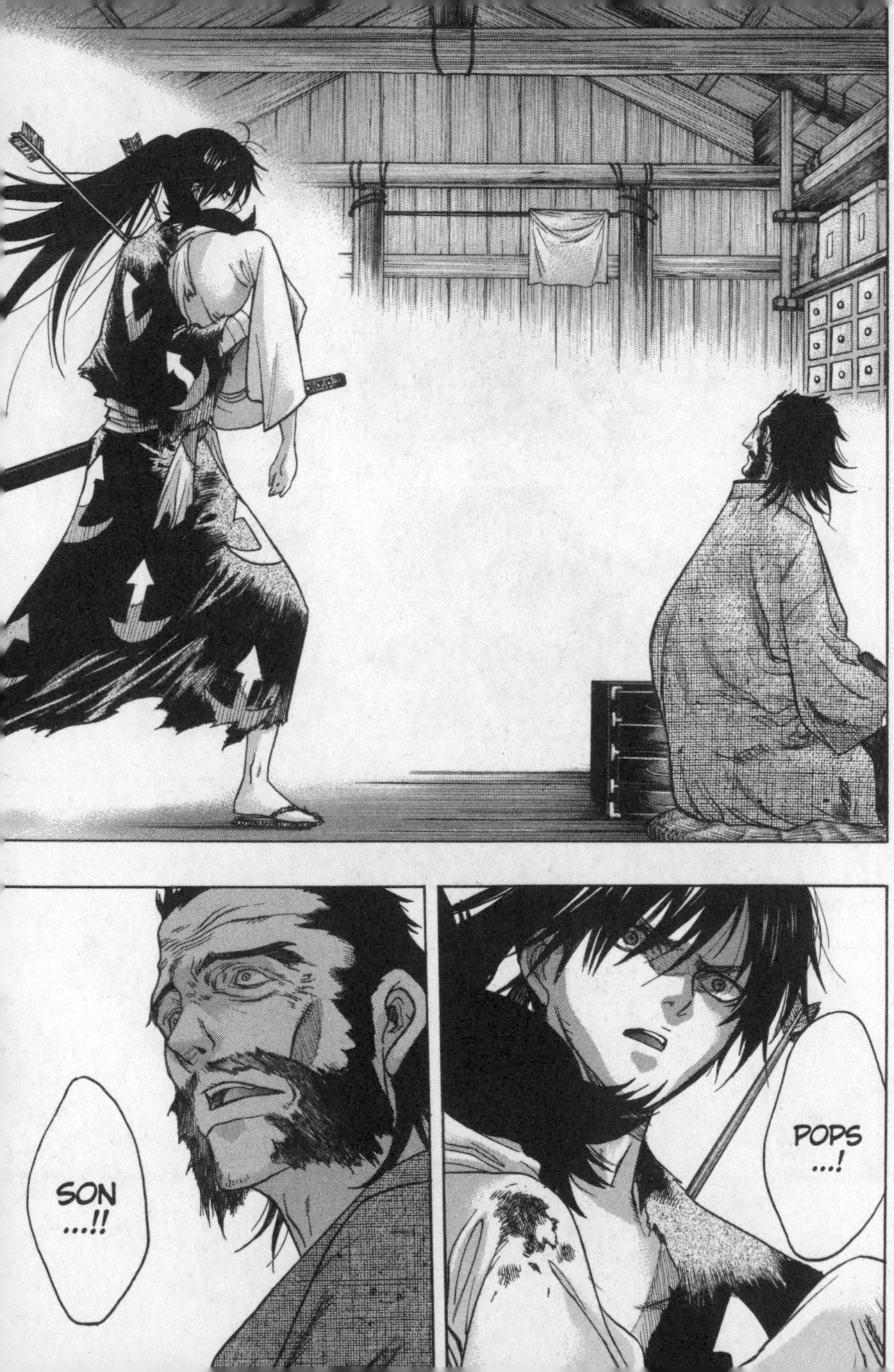
POPS ...!
SON ...!!

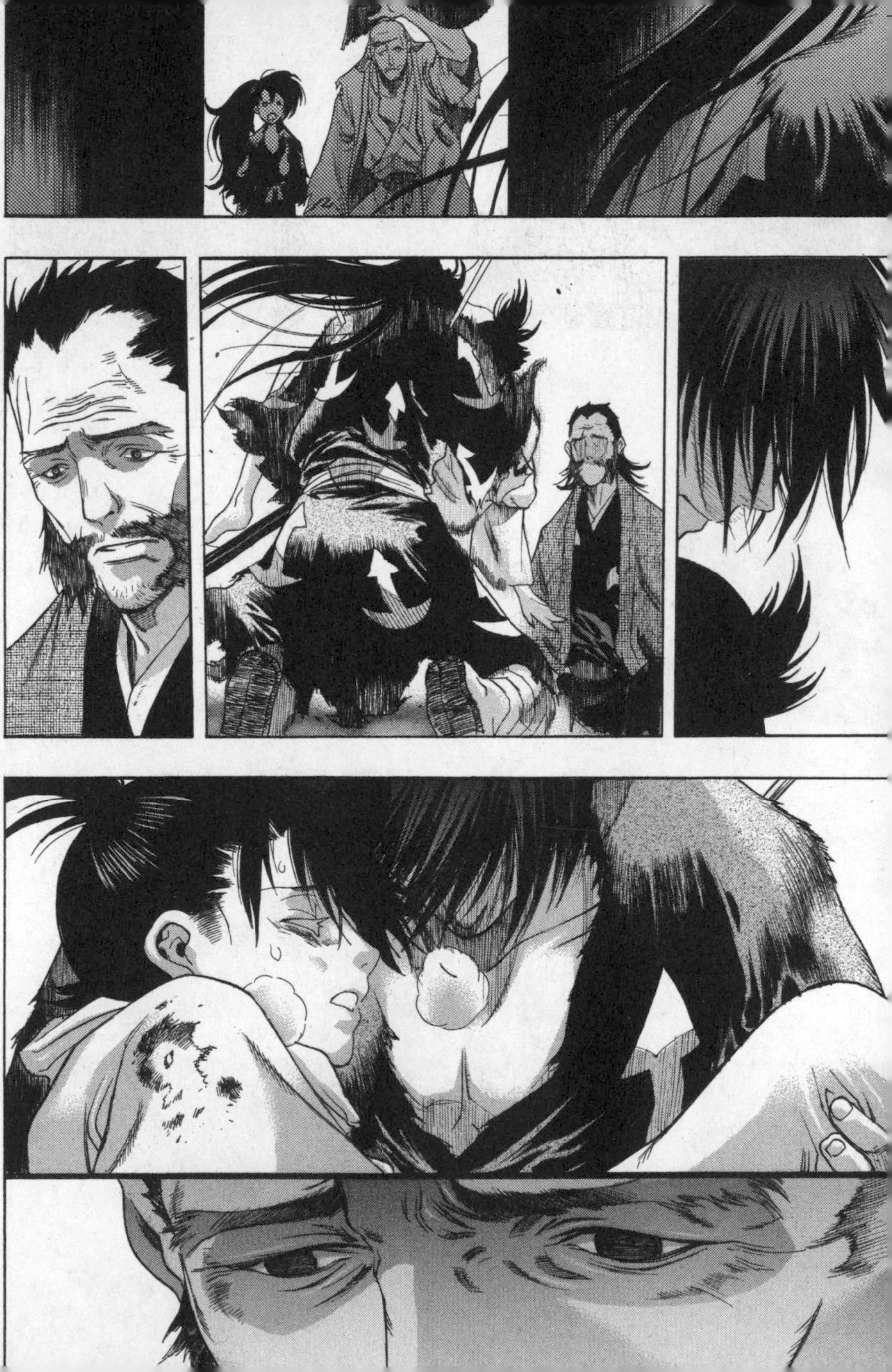

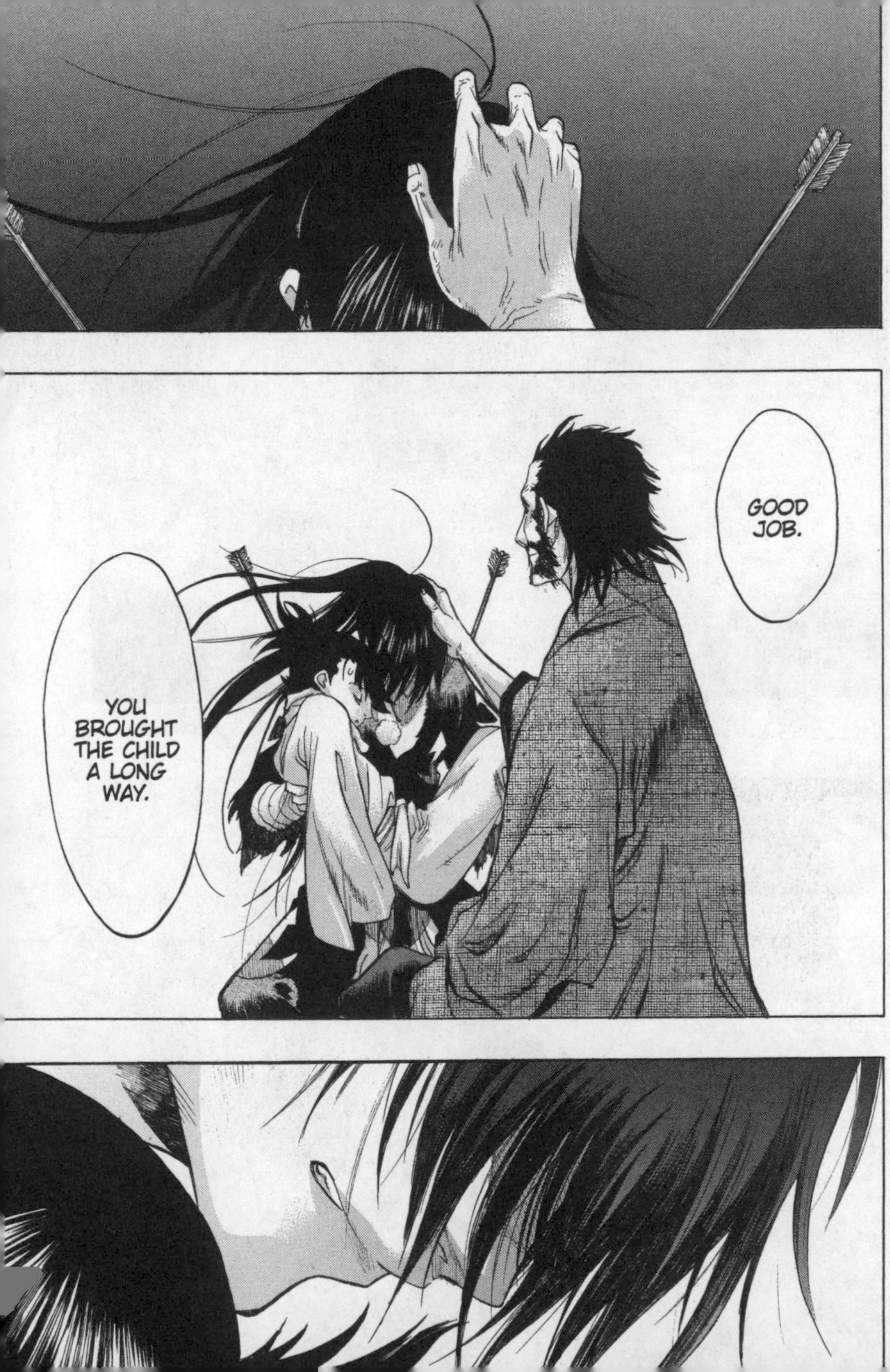
GOOD JOB.
YOU BROUGHT THE CHILD A LONG WAY.

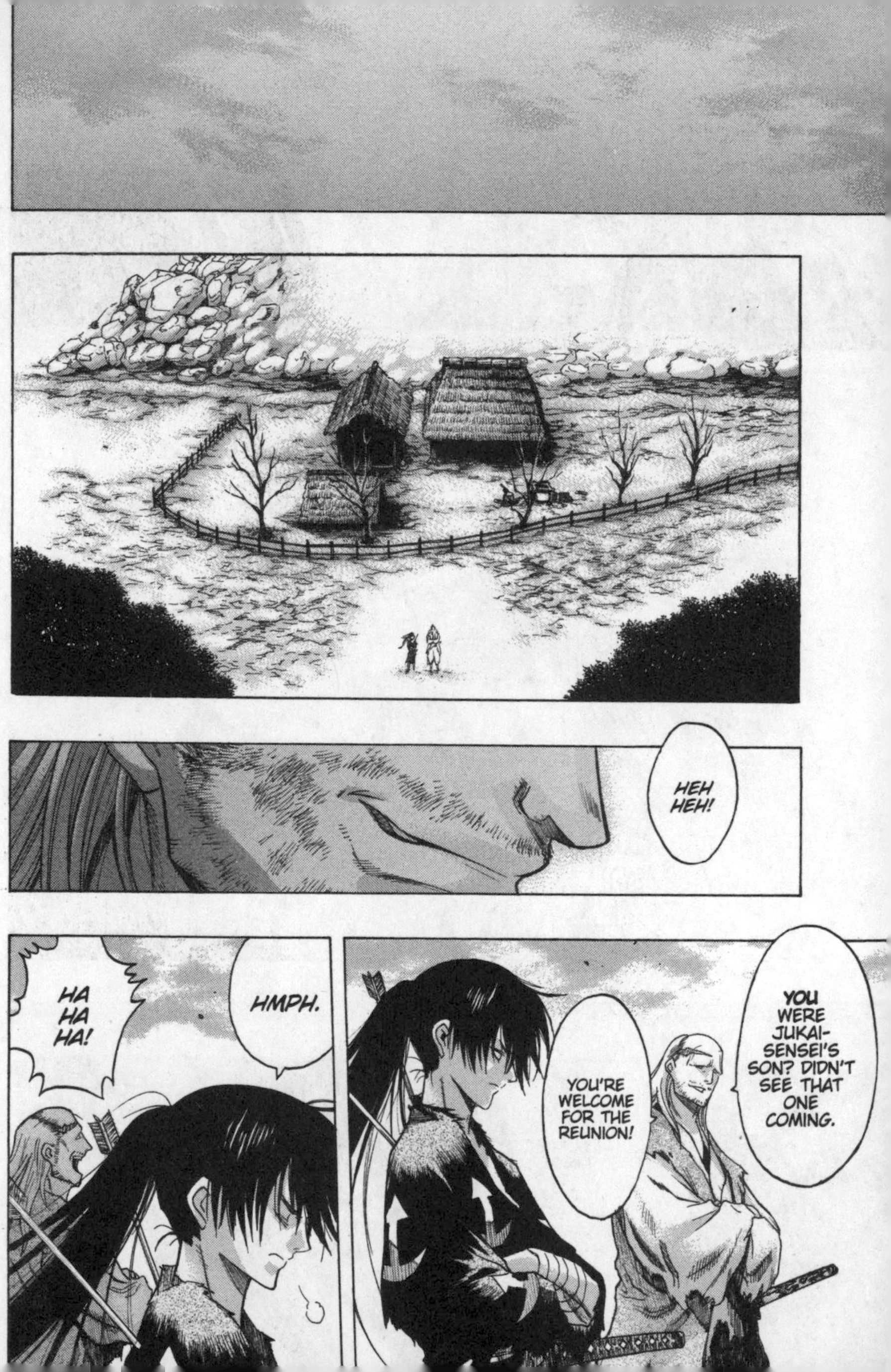
HEH HEH!
YOU WERE JUKAI-SENSEI'S SON? DIDN'T SEE THAT ONE COMING.
YOU'RE WELCOME FOR THE REUNION!
HMPH.
HA HA HA!

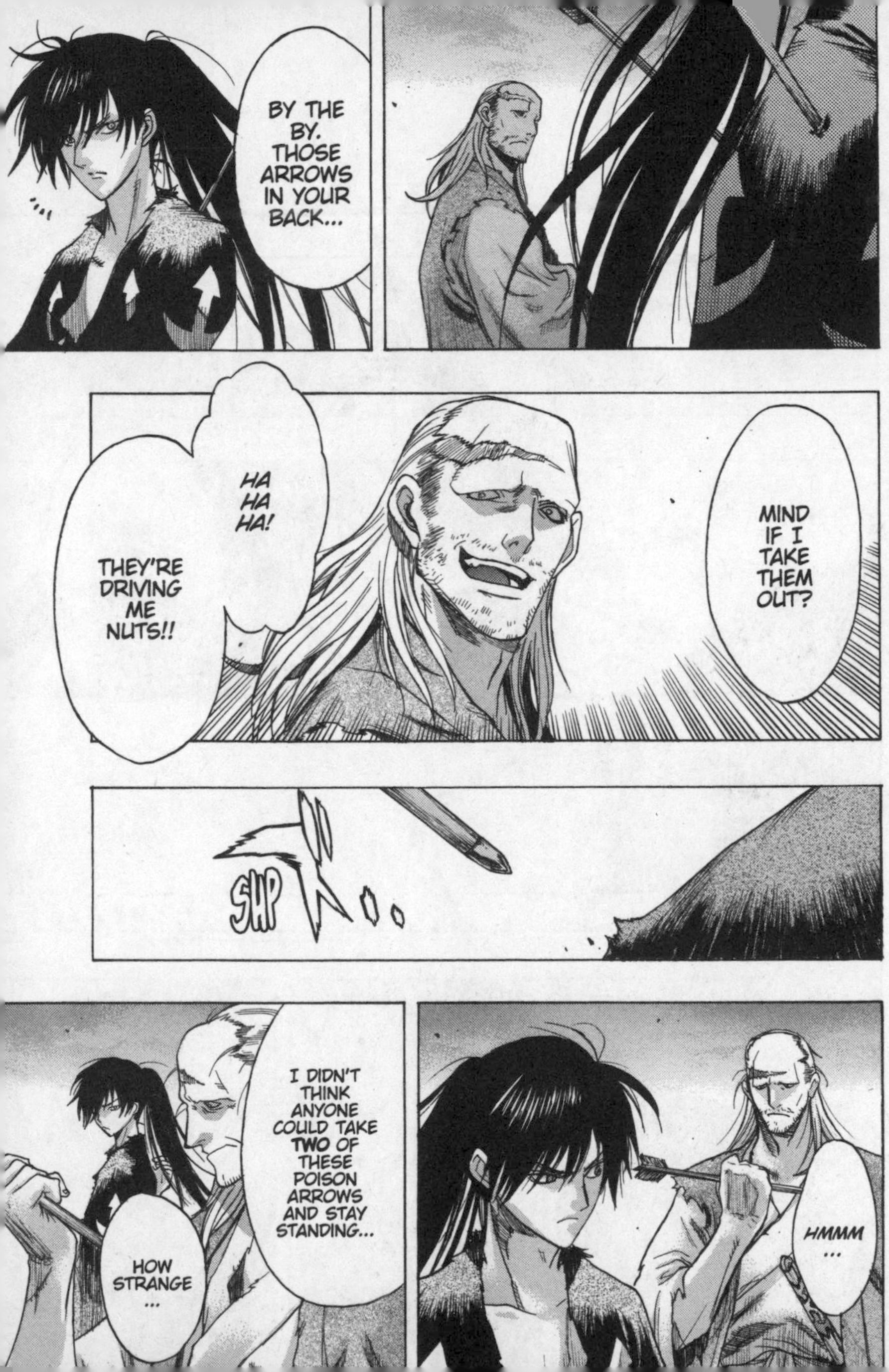
..!
BY THE BY. THOSE ARROWS IN YOUR BACK...
MIND IF I TAKE THEM OUT?
HA HA HA!
THEY'RE DRIVING ME NUTS!!
SHP
HMMM ...
I DIDN'T THINK ANYONE COULD TAKE TWO OF THESE POISON ARROWS AND STAY STANDING...
HOW STRANGE ...

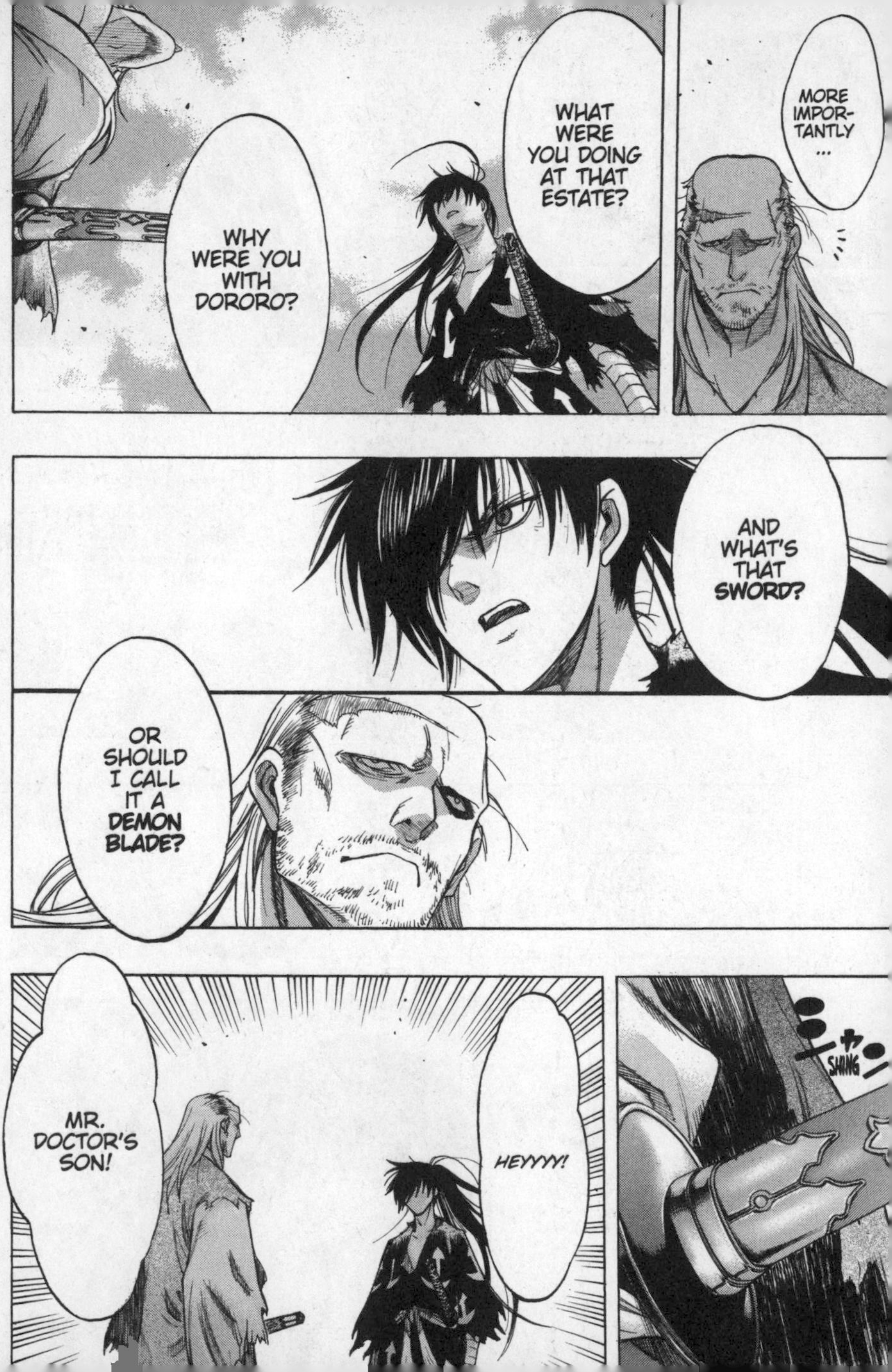
MORE IMPORTANTLY...
WHAT WERE YOU DOING AT THAT ESTATE?
WHY WERE YOU WITH DORORO?
AND WHAT'S THAT SWORD?
OR SHOULD I CALL IT A DEMON BLADE?
SHING
HEYYYY!
MR. DOCTOR'S SON!

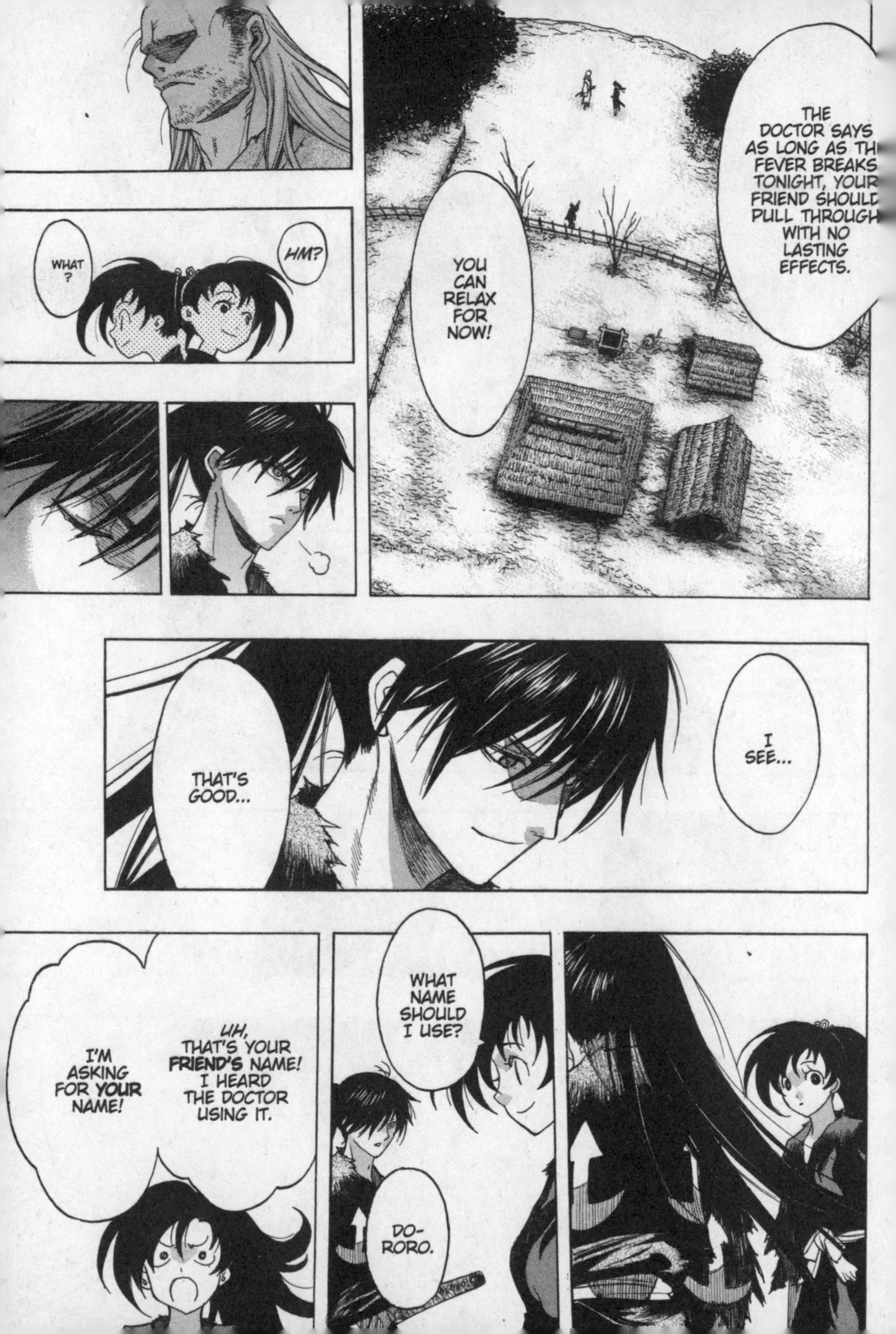
THE DOCTOR SAYS AS LONG AS TH FEVER BREAKS TONIGHT, YOUR FRIEND SHOULD PULL THROUGH WITH NO LASTING EFFECTS.
YOU CAN RELAX FOR NOW!
HM?
WHAT?
I SEE...
THAT'S GOOD...
WHAT NAME SHOULD I USE?
DO-RORO.
UH, THAT'S YOUR **FRIEND'S** NAME! I HEARD THE DOCTOR USING IT.
I'M ASKING FOR **YOUR** NAME!

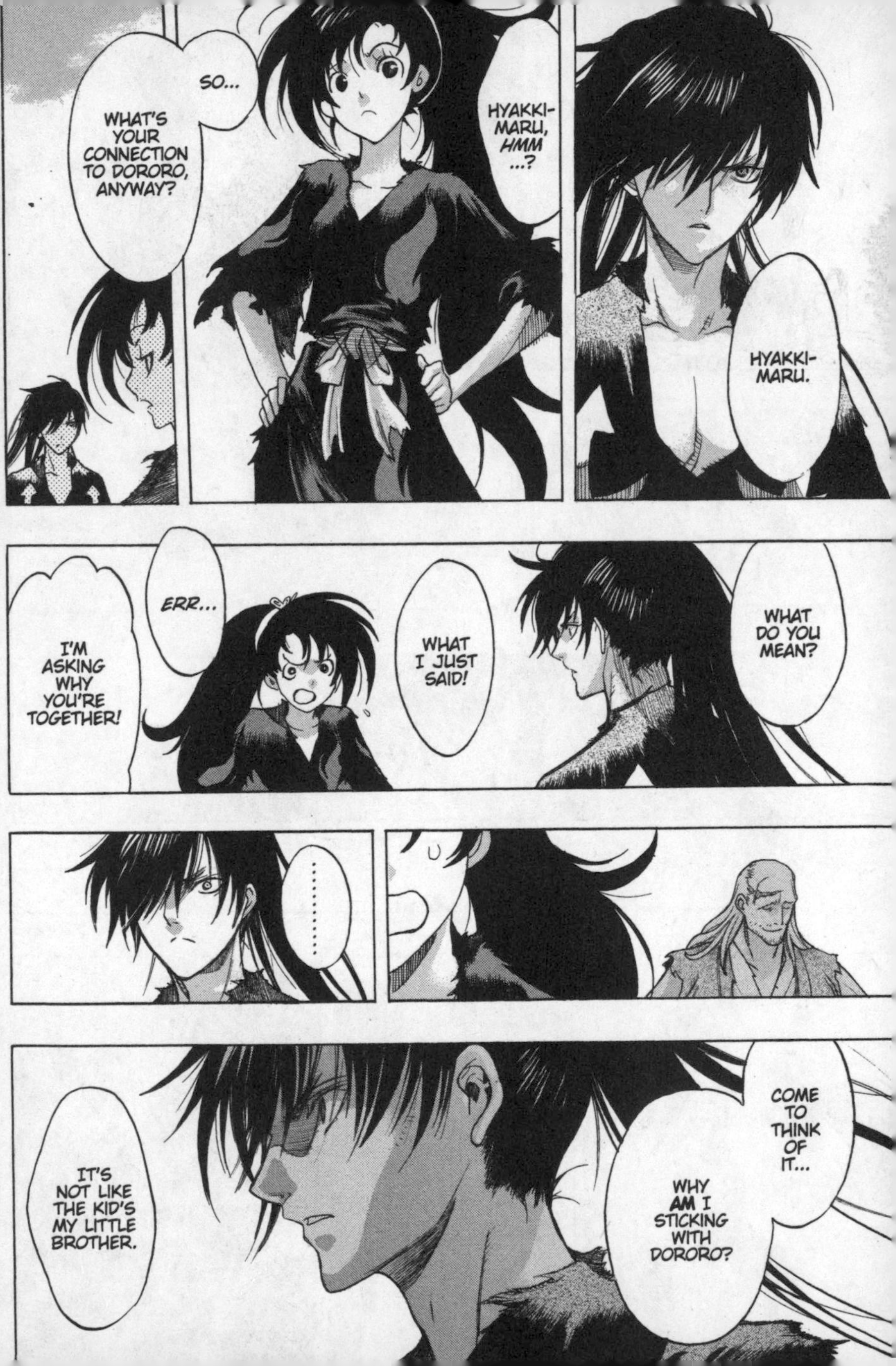
HYAKKIMARU.
HYAKKI-MARU, *HMM* ...?
SO...
WHAT'S YOUR CONNECTION TO DORORO, ANYWAY?
WHAT DO YOU MEAN?
WHAT I JUST SAID!
ERR...
I'M ASKING WHY YOU'RE TOGETHER!
......
COME TO THINK OF IT...
WHY **AM** I STICKING WITH DORORO?
IT'S NOT LIKE THE KID'S MY LITTLE BROTHER.

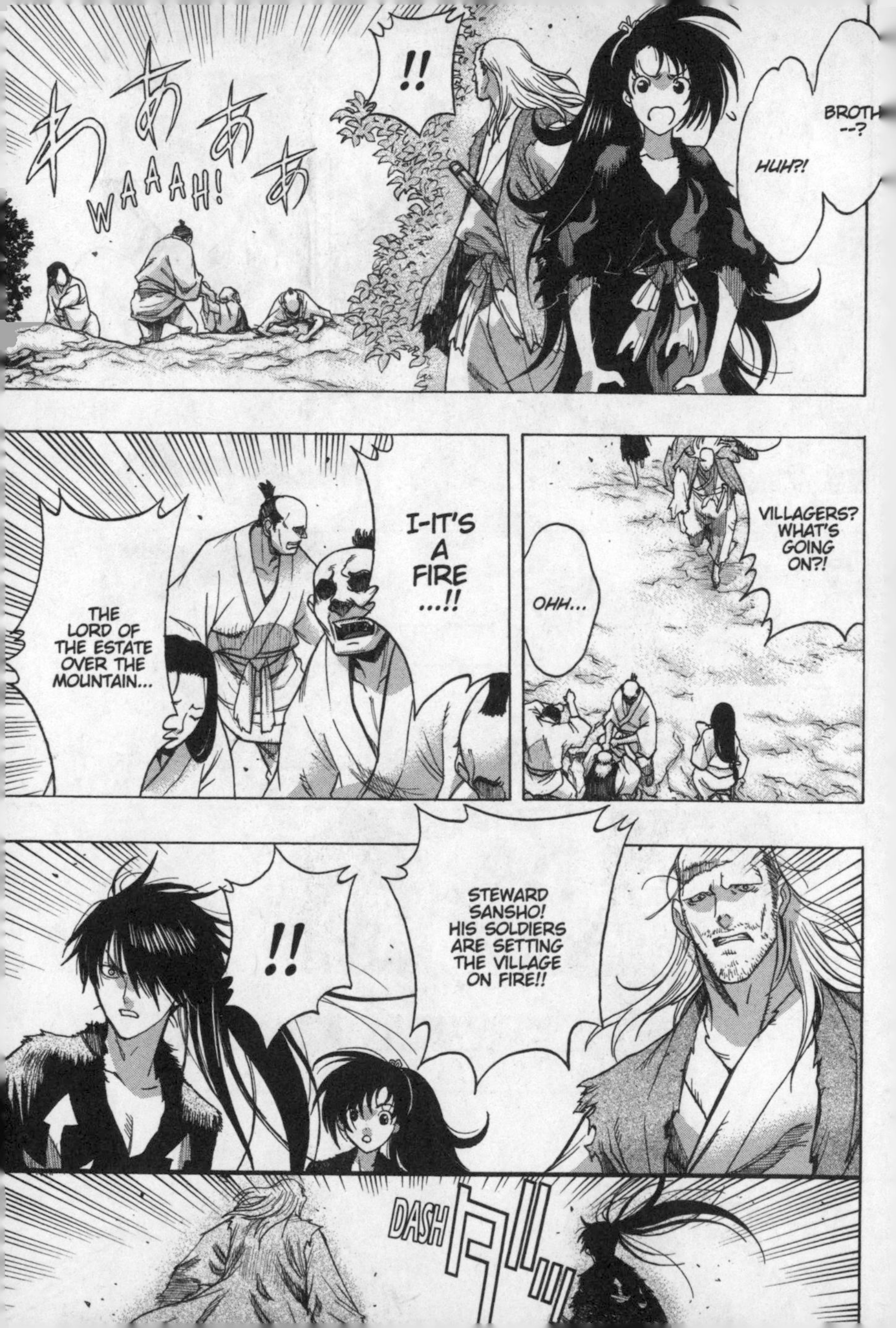
BROTH--?
HUH?!
!!
わあああ
WAAAH!
VILLAGERS? WHAT'S GOING ON?!
OHH...
I-IT'S A FIRE...!!
THE LORD OF THE ESTATE OVER THE MOUNTAIN...
STEWARD SANSHO! HIS SOLDIERS ARE SETTING THE VILLAGE ON FIRE!!
!!
DASH

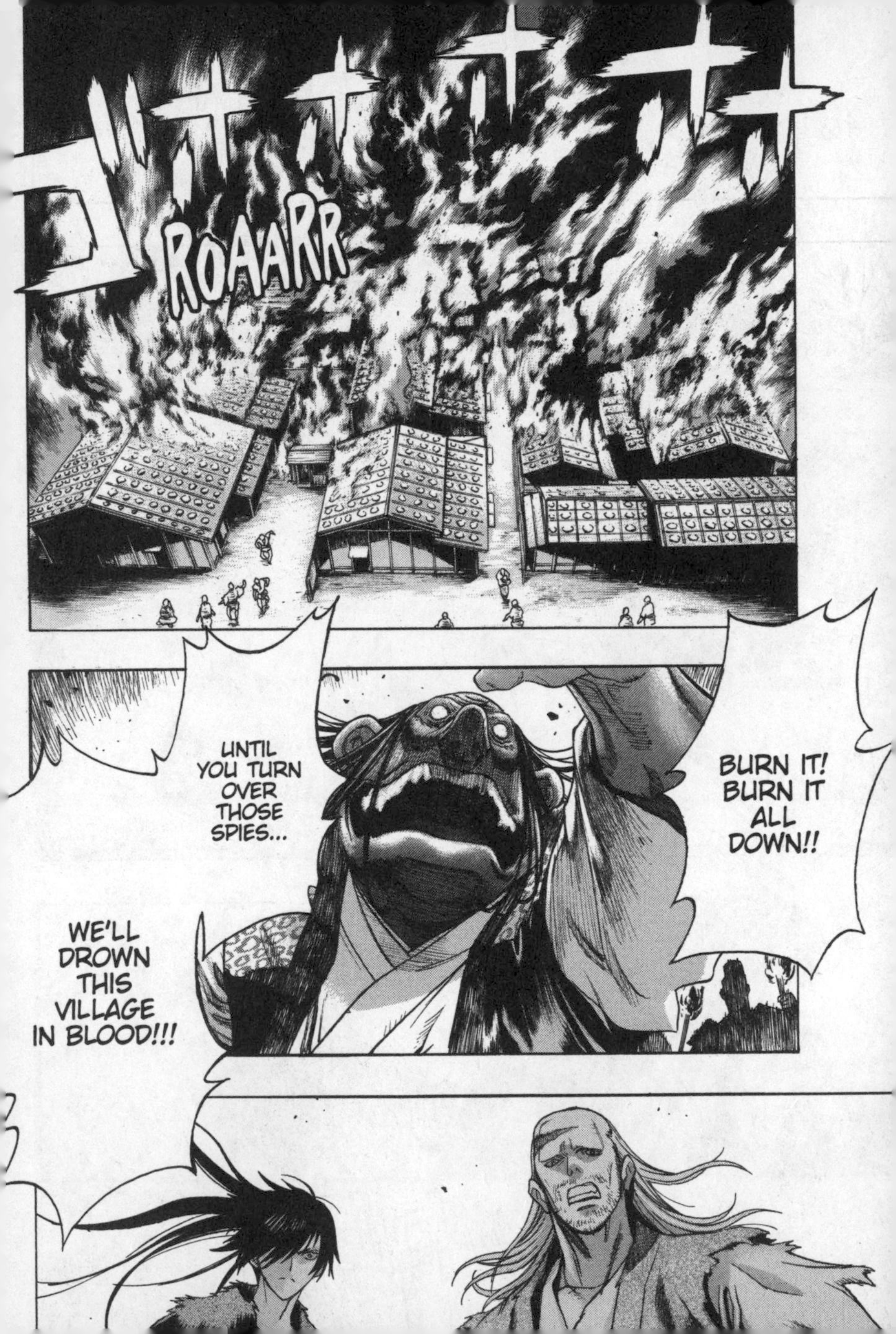
ROAARR
BURN IT! BURN IT ALL DOWN!!
UNTIL YOU TURN OVER THOSE SPIES...
WE'LL DROWN THIS VILLAGE IN BLOOD!!!

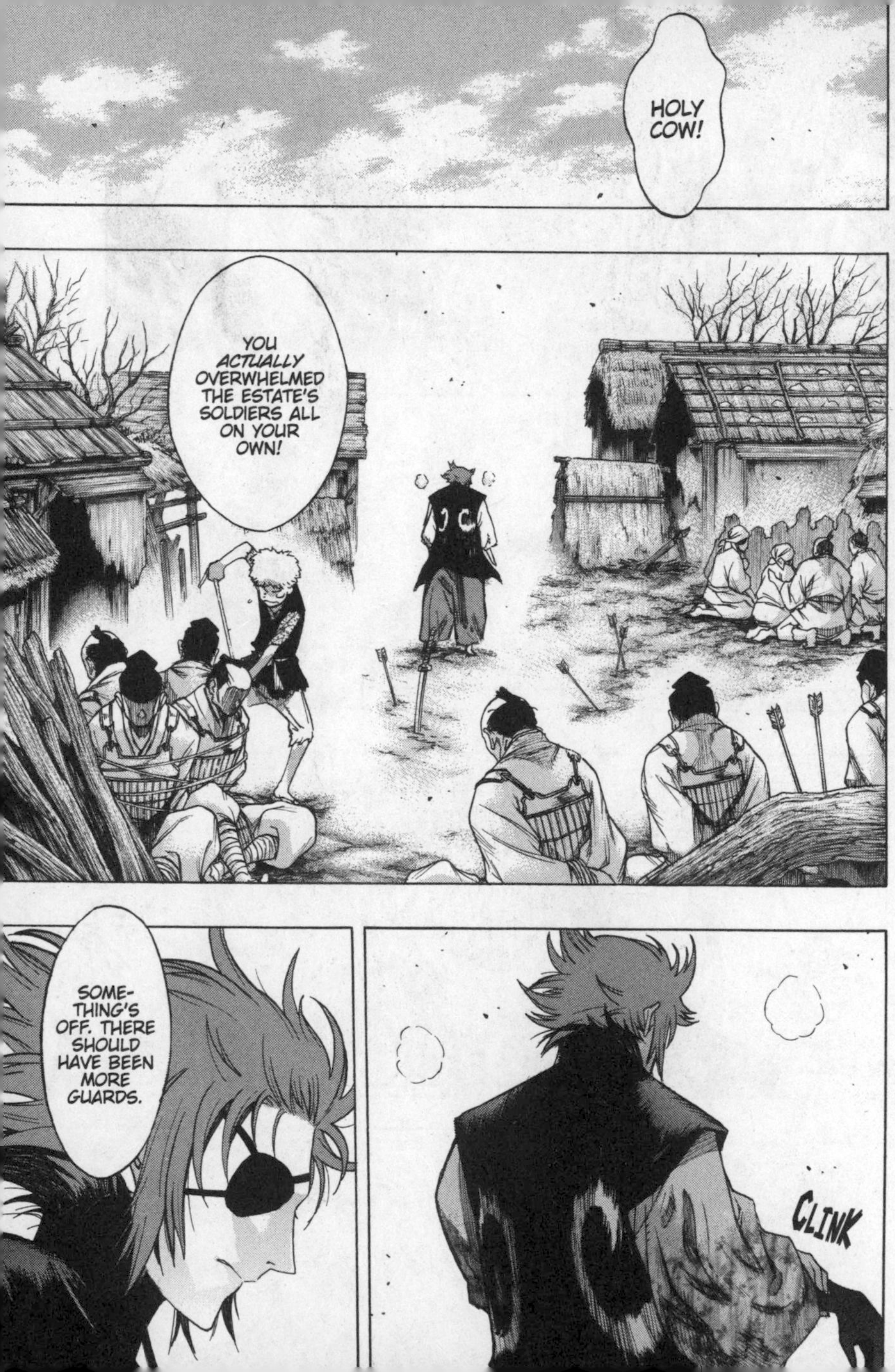
HOLY COW!
YOU ACTUALLY OVERWHELMED THE ESTATE'S SOLDIERS ALL ON YOUR OWN!
CLINK
SOME-THING'S OFF. THERE SHOULD HAVE BEEN MORE GUARDS.

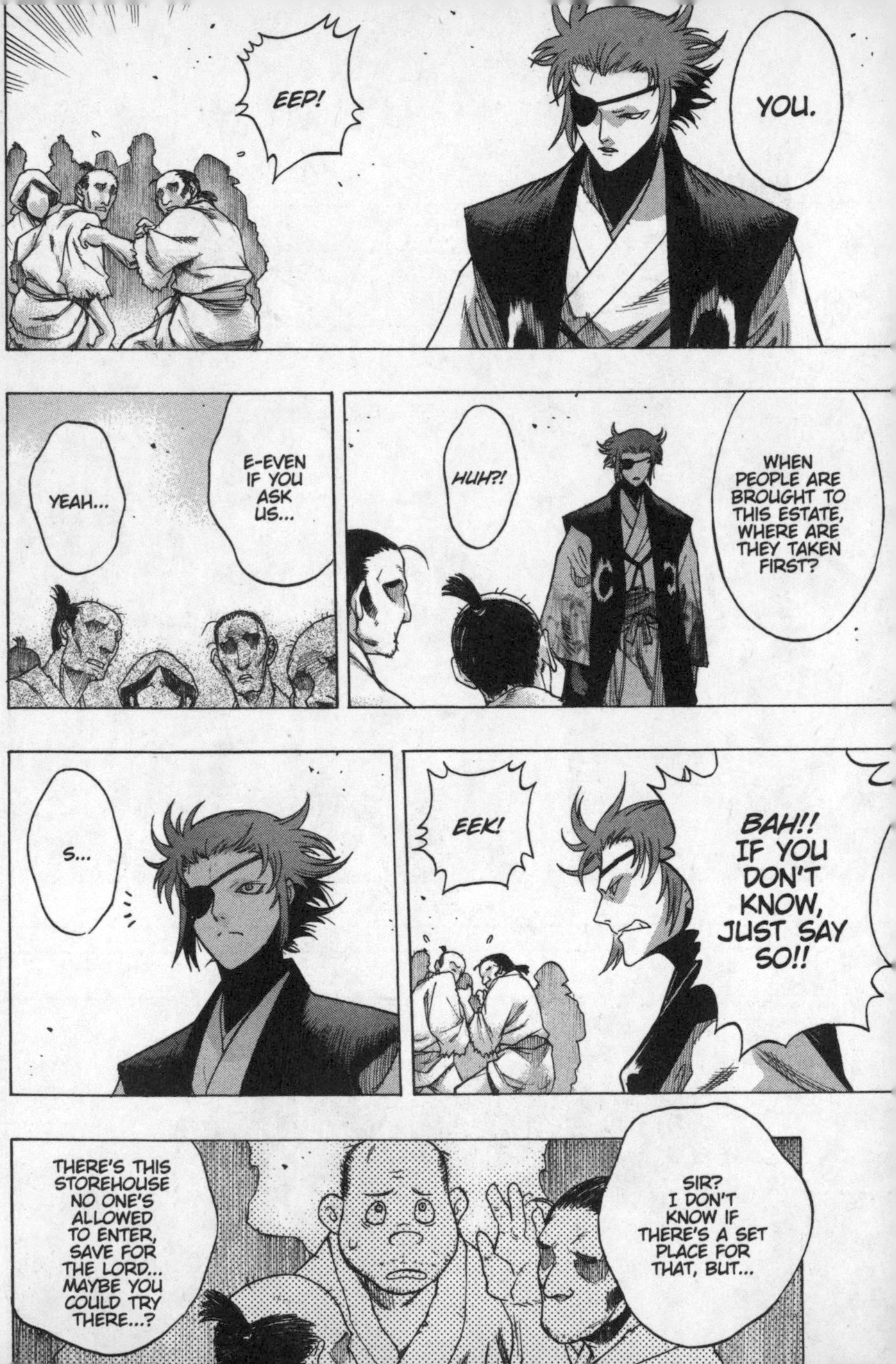
YOU.
EEP!
WHEN PEOPLE ARE BROUGHT TO THIS ESTATE, WHERE ARE THEY TAKEN FIRST?
HUH?!
E-EVEN IF YOU ASK US...
YEAH...
BAH!! IF YOU DON'T KNOW, JUST SAY SO!!
EEK!
S...
SIR? I DON'T KNOW IF THERE'S A SET PLACE FOR THAT, BUT...
THERE'S THIS STOREHOUSE NO ONE'S ALLOWED TO ENTER, SAVE FOR THE LORD... MAYBE YOU COULD TRY THERE...?

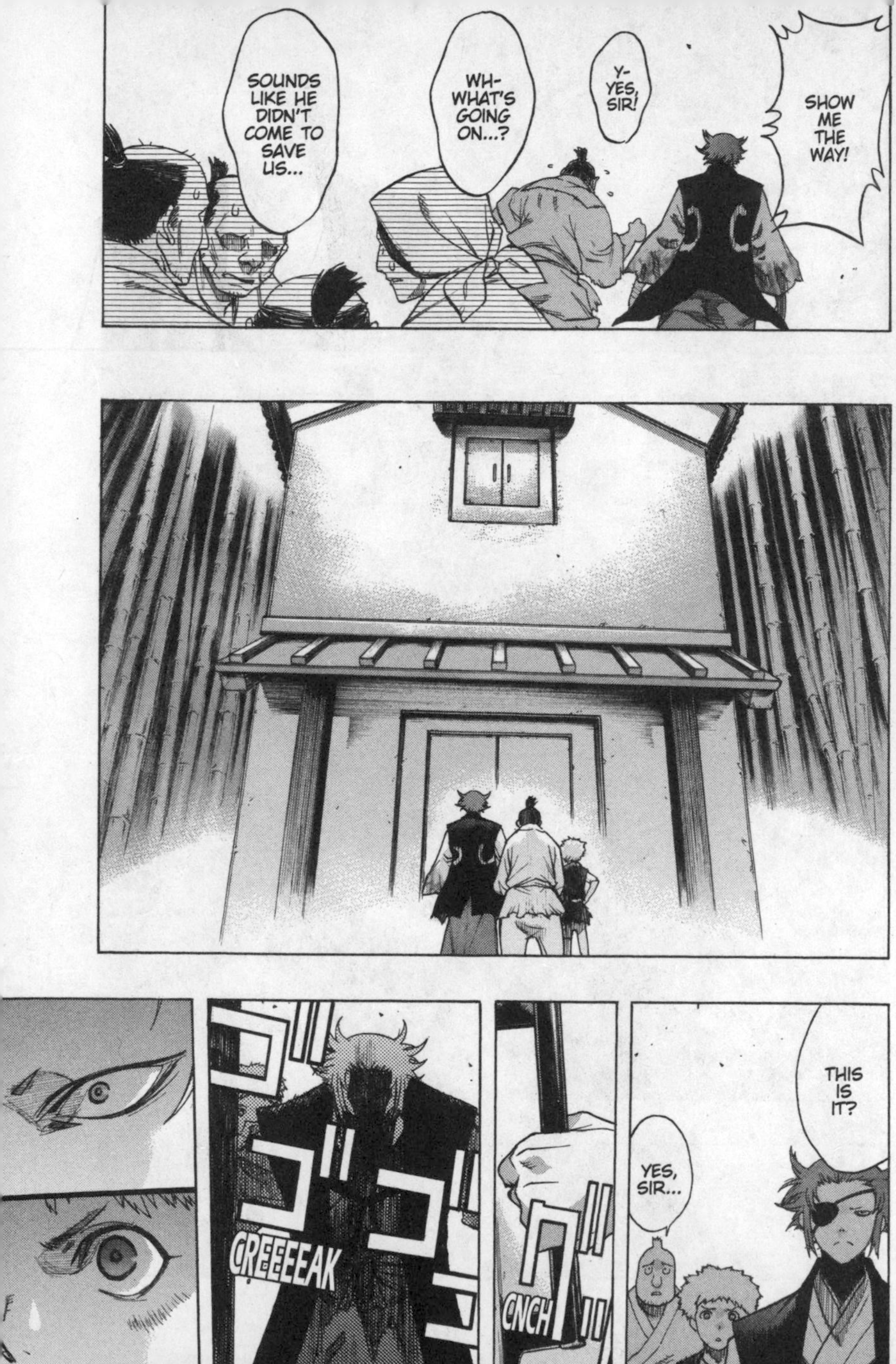
SHOW ME THE WAY!
Y-YES, SIR!
WH-WHAT'S GOING ON...?
SOUNDS LIKE HE DIDN'T COME TO SAVE US...
THIS IS IT?
YES, SIR...
CNCH
GREEEEAK

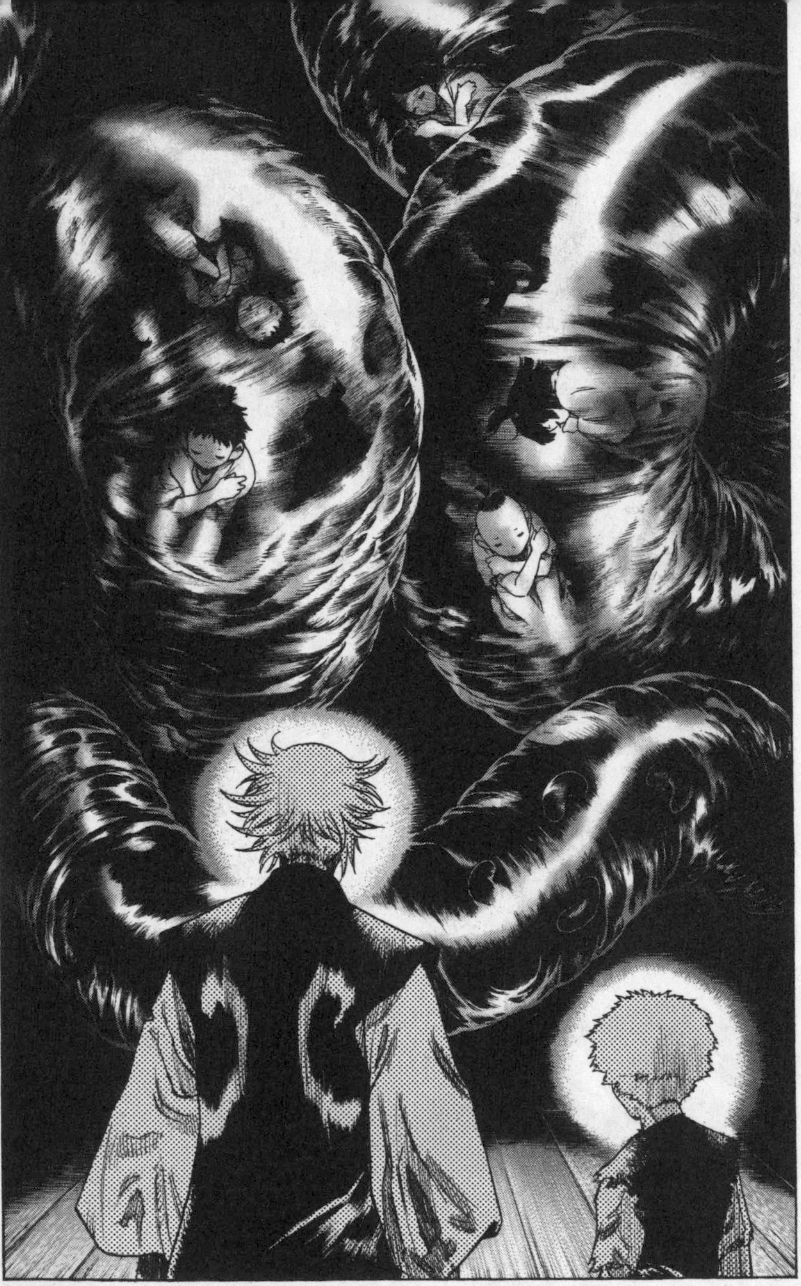

THE LEGEND OF
DORORO AND
HYAKKIMARU

どろろと
百鬼丸伝

THE LEGEND OF
DORORO AND **HYAKKIMARU**

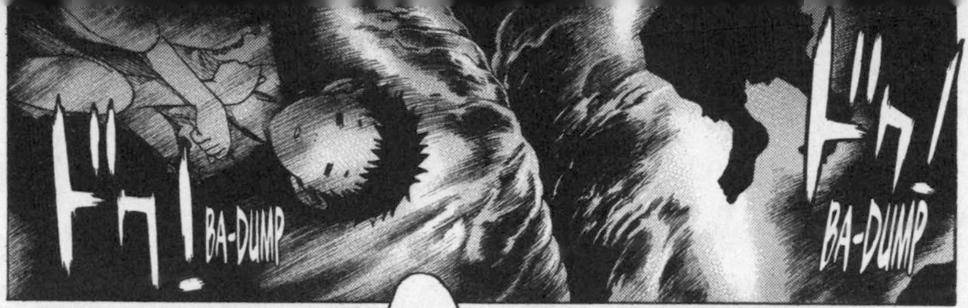
ドクン!
BA-DUMP
ドクン!
BA-DUMP

The Legend of the Chance Encounter: Part V

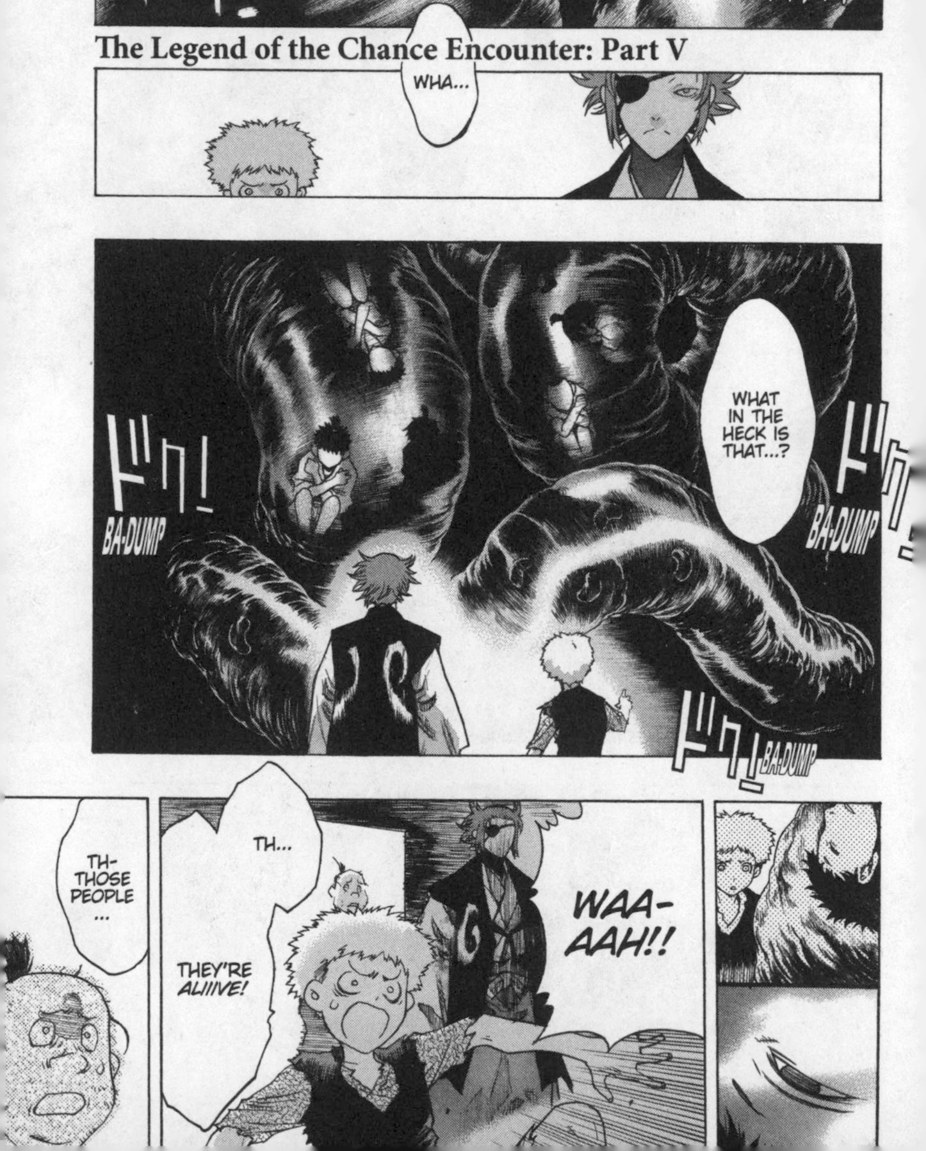
WHA...
WHAT IN THE HECK IS THAT...?
ドクン!
BA-DUMP
ドクン!
BA-DUMP
ドクン!
BA-DUMP
TH...
THEY'RE ALIIIVE!
WAA-AAH!!
TH- THOSE PEOPLE ...

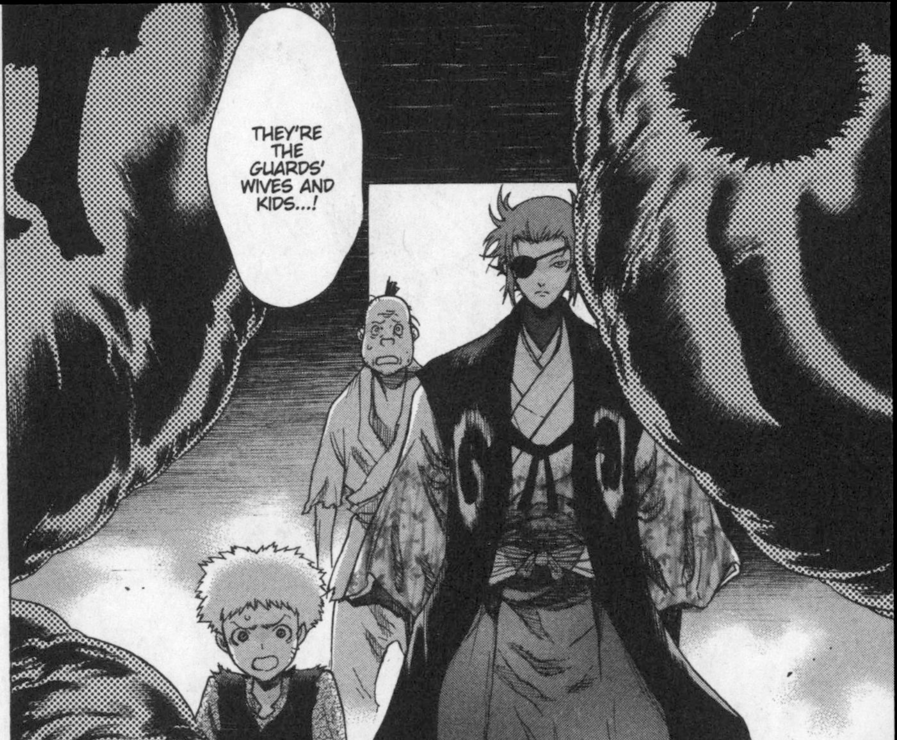
THEY'RE THE GUARDS' WIVES AND KIDS...!
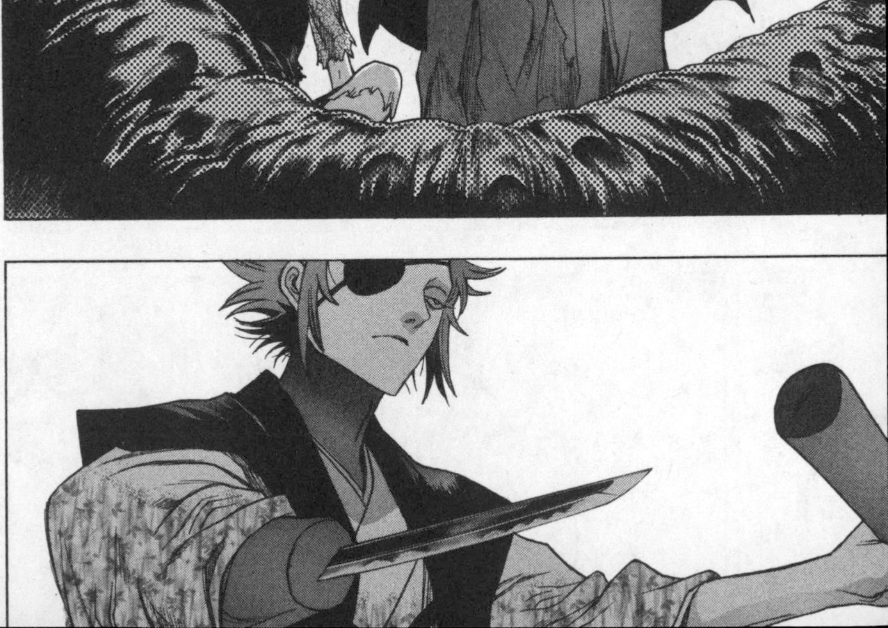

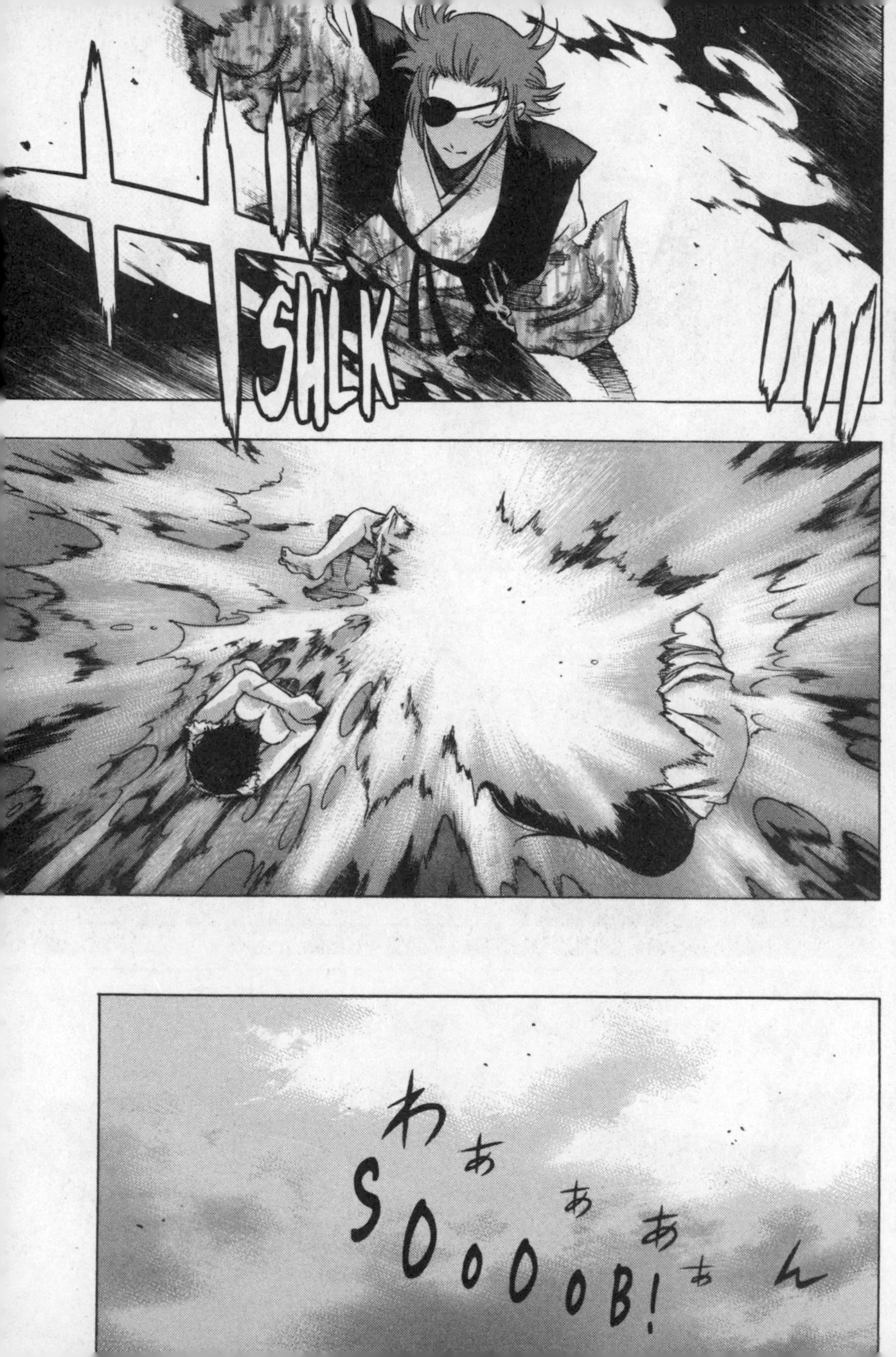
SHLK
わあああぁん
SOOOOB!

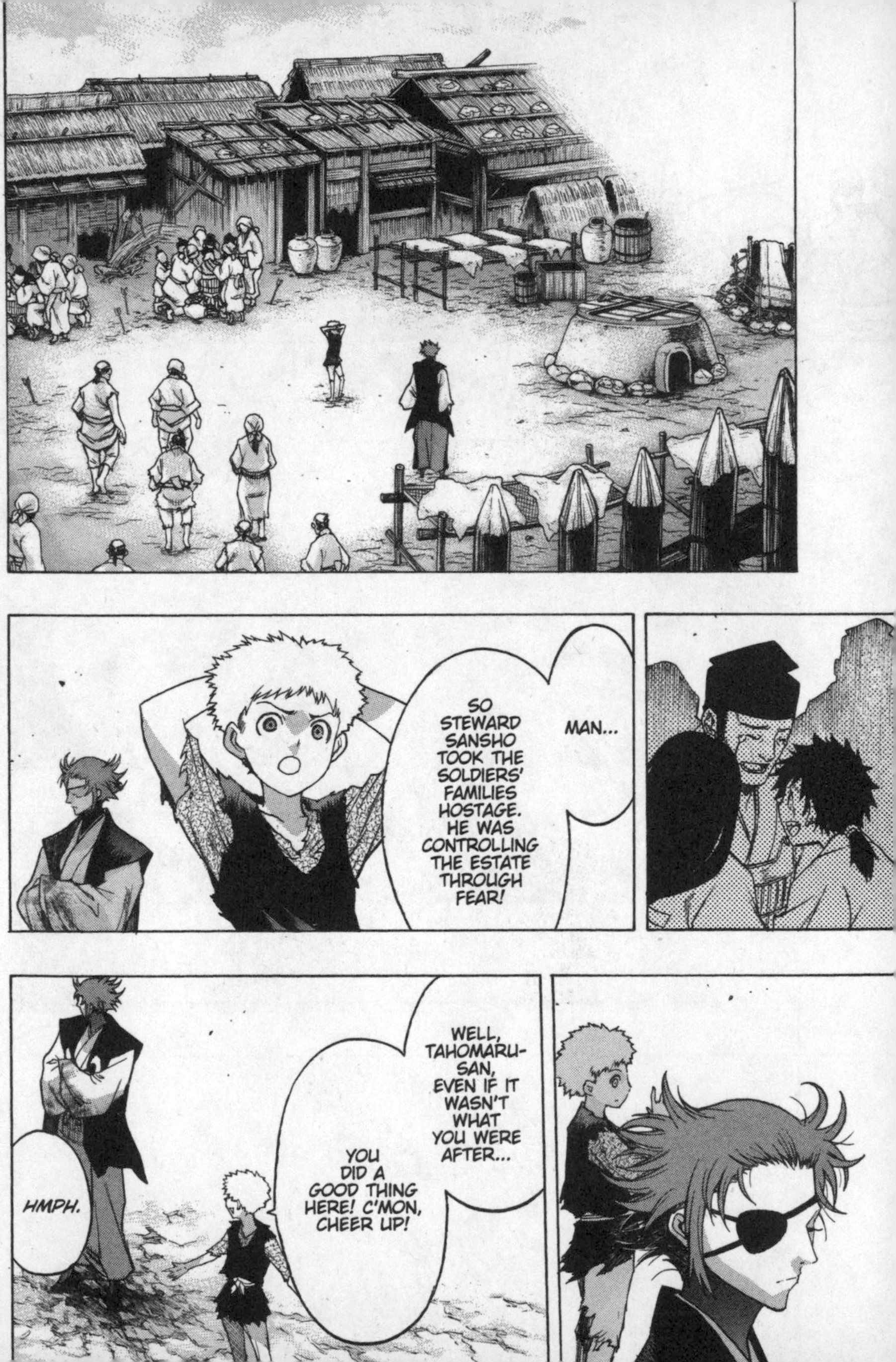
MAN...
SO STEWARD SANSHO TOOK THE SOLDIERS' FAMILIES HOSTAGE. HE WAS CONTROLLING THE ESTATE THROUGH FEAR!
WELL, TAHOMARU-SAN, EVEN IF IT WASN'T WHAT YOU WERE AFTER...
YOU DID A GOOD THING HERE! C'MON, CHEER UP!
HMPH.

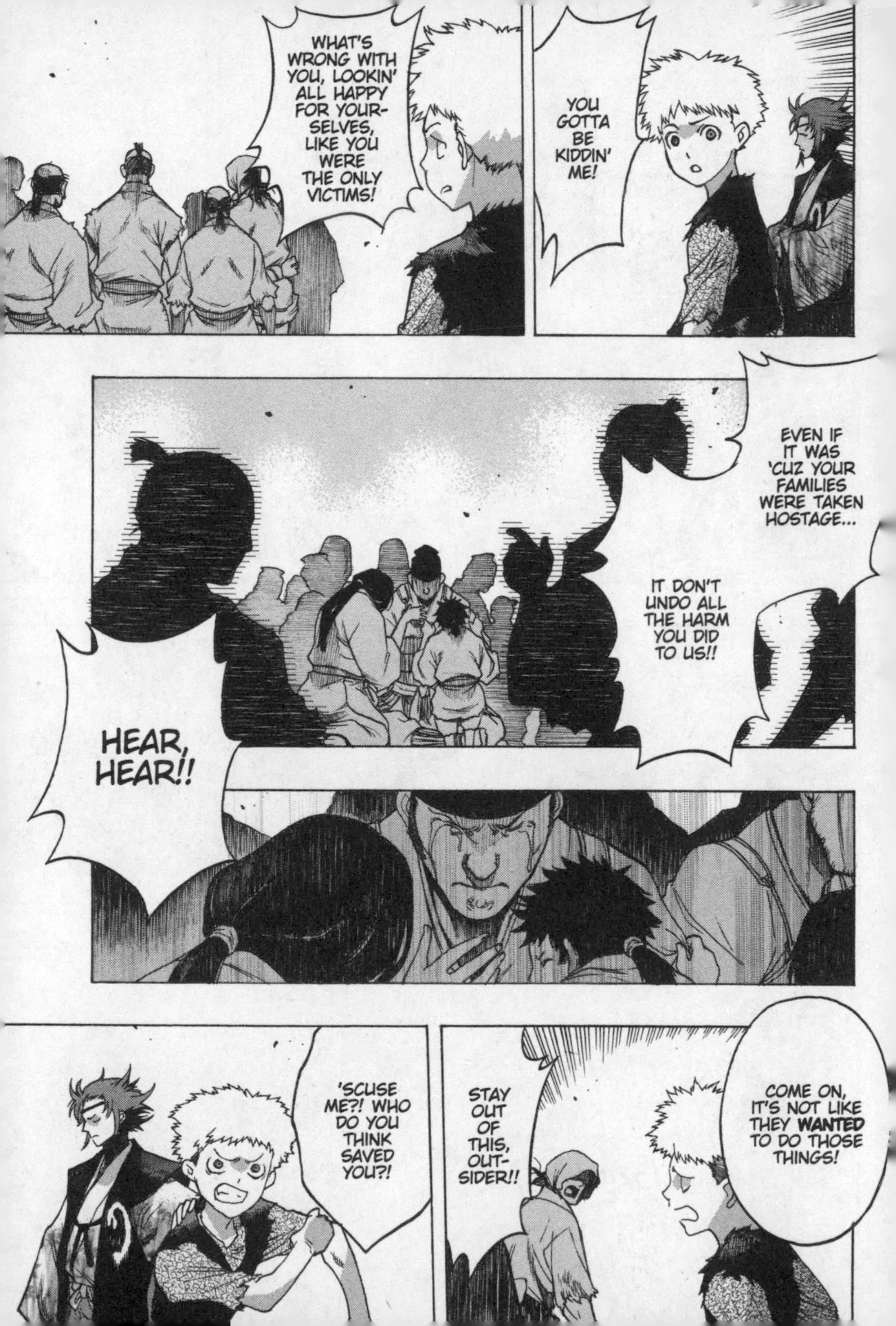
YOU GOTTA BE KIDDIN' ME!
WHAT'S WRONG WITH YOU, LOOKIN' ALL HAPPY FOR YOURSELVES, LIKE YOU WERE THE ONLY VICTIMS!
EVEN IF IT WAS 'CUZ YOUR FAMILIES WERE TAKEN HOSTAGE...
IT DON'T UNDO ALL THE HARM YOU DID TO US!!
HEAR, HEAR!!
COME ON, IT'S NOT LIKE THEY **WANTED** TO DO THOSE THINGS!
STAY OUT OF THIS, OUTSIDER!!
'SCUSE ME?! WHO DO YOU THINK SAVED YOU?!

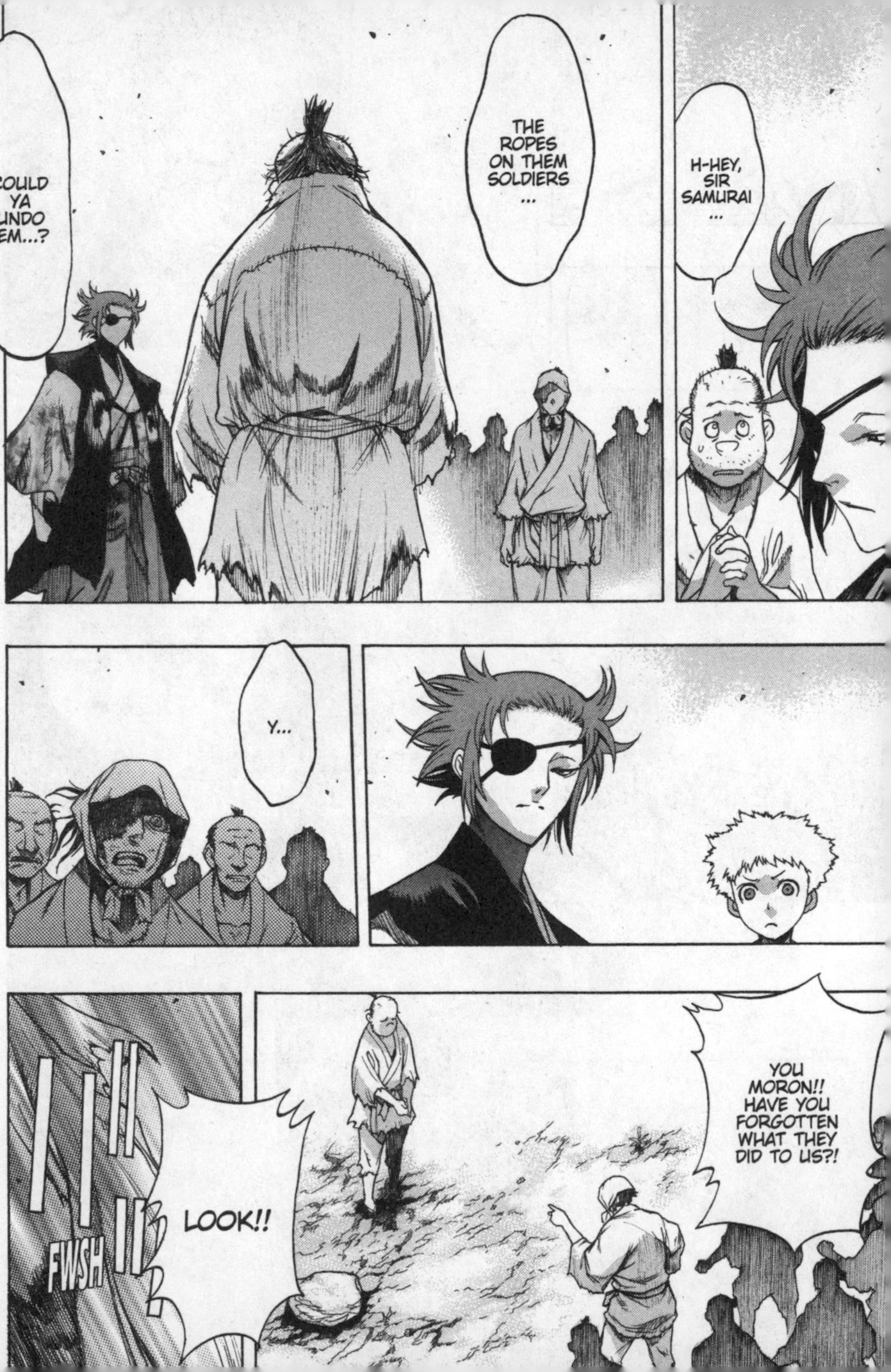
H-HEY, SIR SAMURAI ...
THE ROPES ON THEM SOLDIERS ...
COULD YA UNDO 'EM...?
Y...
YOU MORON!! HAVE YOU FORGOTTEN WHAT THEY DID TO US?!
LOOK!!
FWSH

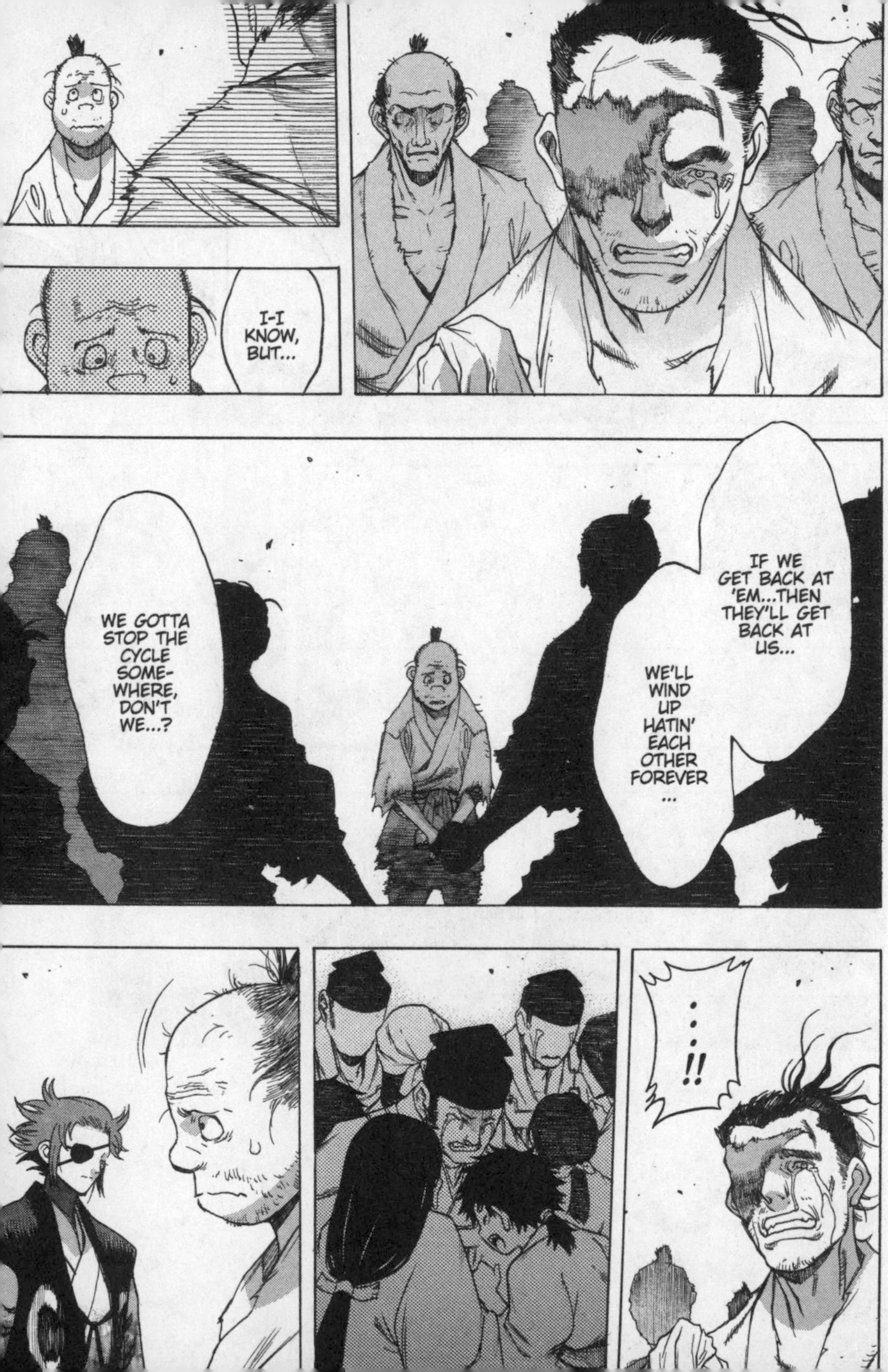
I-I KNOW, BUT...
IF WE GET BACK AT 'EM...THEN THEY'LL GET BACK AT US...
WE'LL WIND UP HATIN' EACH OTHER FOREVER...
WE GOTTA STOP THE CYCLE SOME-WHERE, DON'T WE...?
...!!

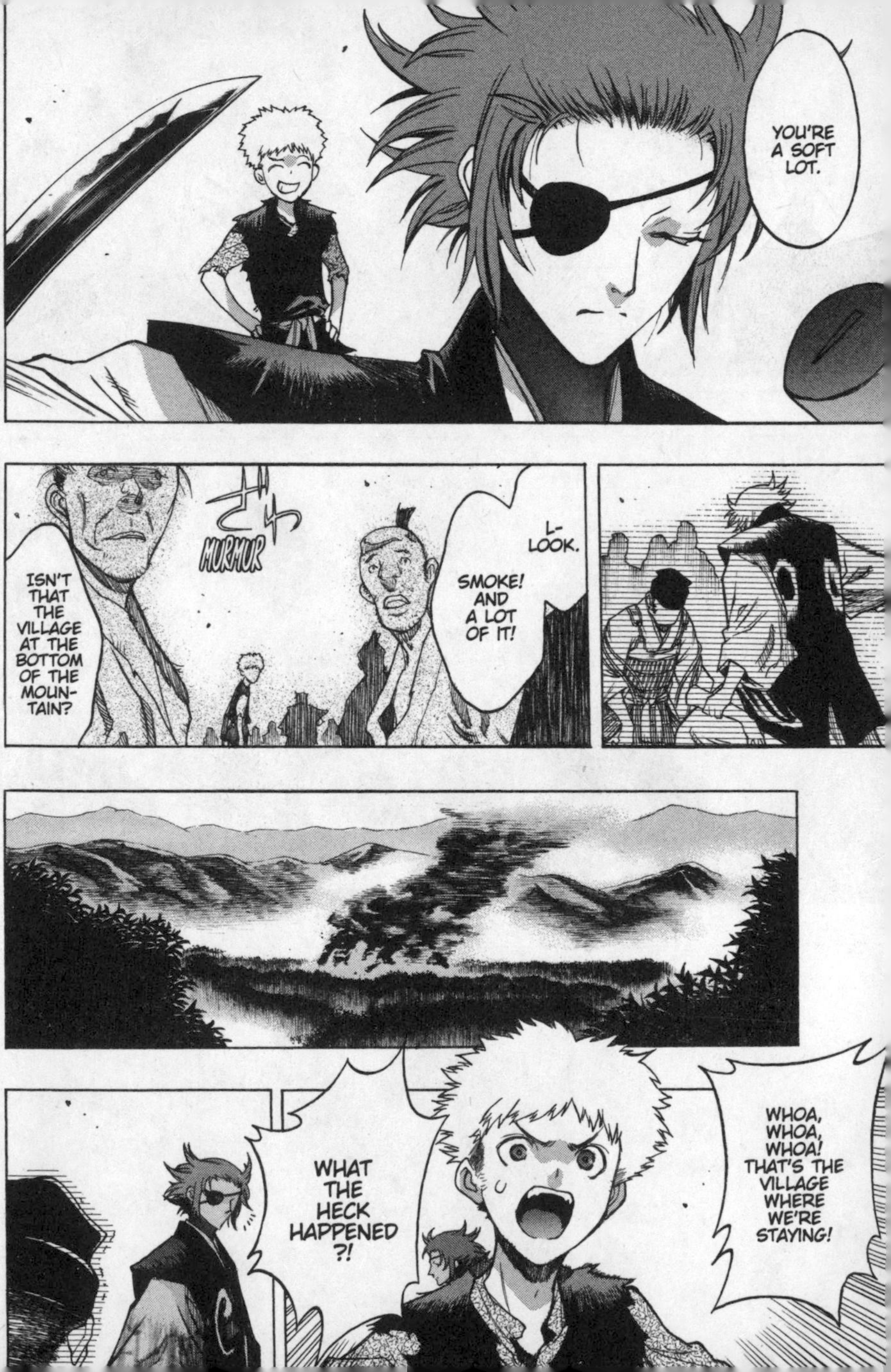
YOU'RE A SOFT LOT.
L-LOOK.
SMOKE! AND A LOT OF IT!
MURMUR
ISN'T THAT THE VILLAGE AT THE BOTTOM OF THE MOUNTAIN?
WHOA, WHOA, WHOA! THAT'S THE VILLAGE WHERE WE'RE STAYING!
WHAT THE HECK HAPPENED?!

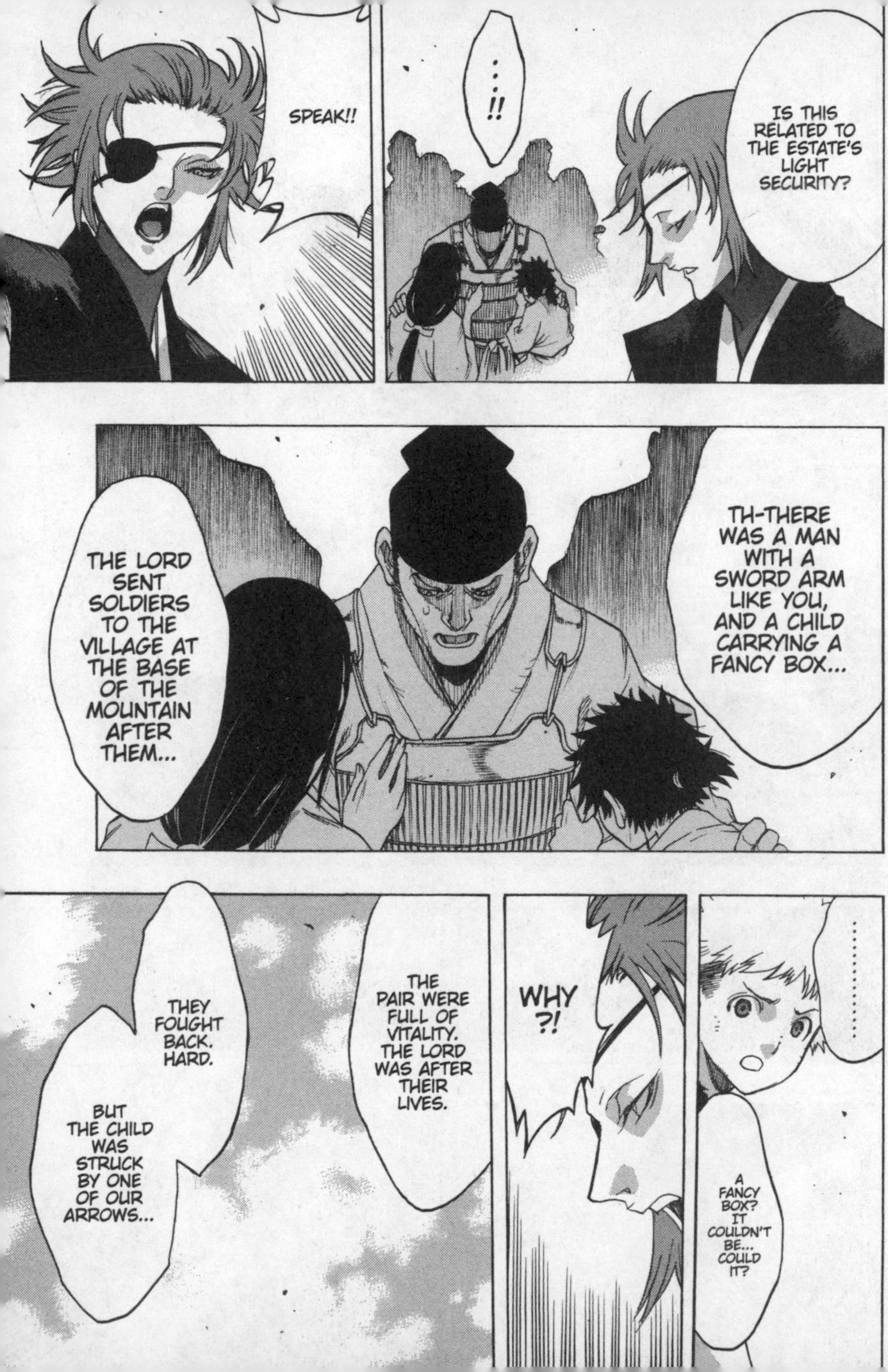
IS THIS RELATED TO THE ESTATE'S LIGHT SECURITY?
...!!
SPEAK!!
TH-THERE WAS A MAN WITH A SWORD ARM LIKE YOU, AND A CHILD CARRYING A FANCY BOX...
THE LORD SENT SOLDIERS TO THE VILLAGE AT THE BASE OF THE MOUNTAIN AFTER THEM...
......
A FANCY BOX? IT COULDN'T BE... COULD IT?
WHY?!
THE PAIR WERE FULL OF VITALITY. THE LORD WAS AFTER THEIR LIVES.
THEY FOUGHT BACK. HARD.
BUT THE CHILD WAS STRUCK BY ONE OF OUR ARROWS...

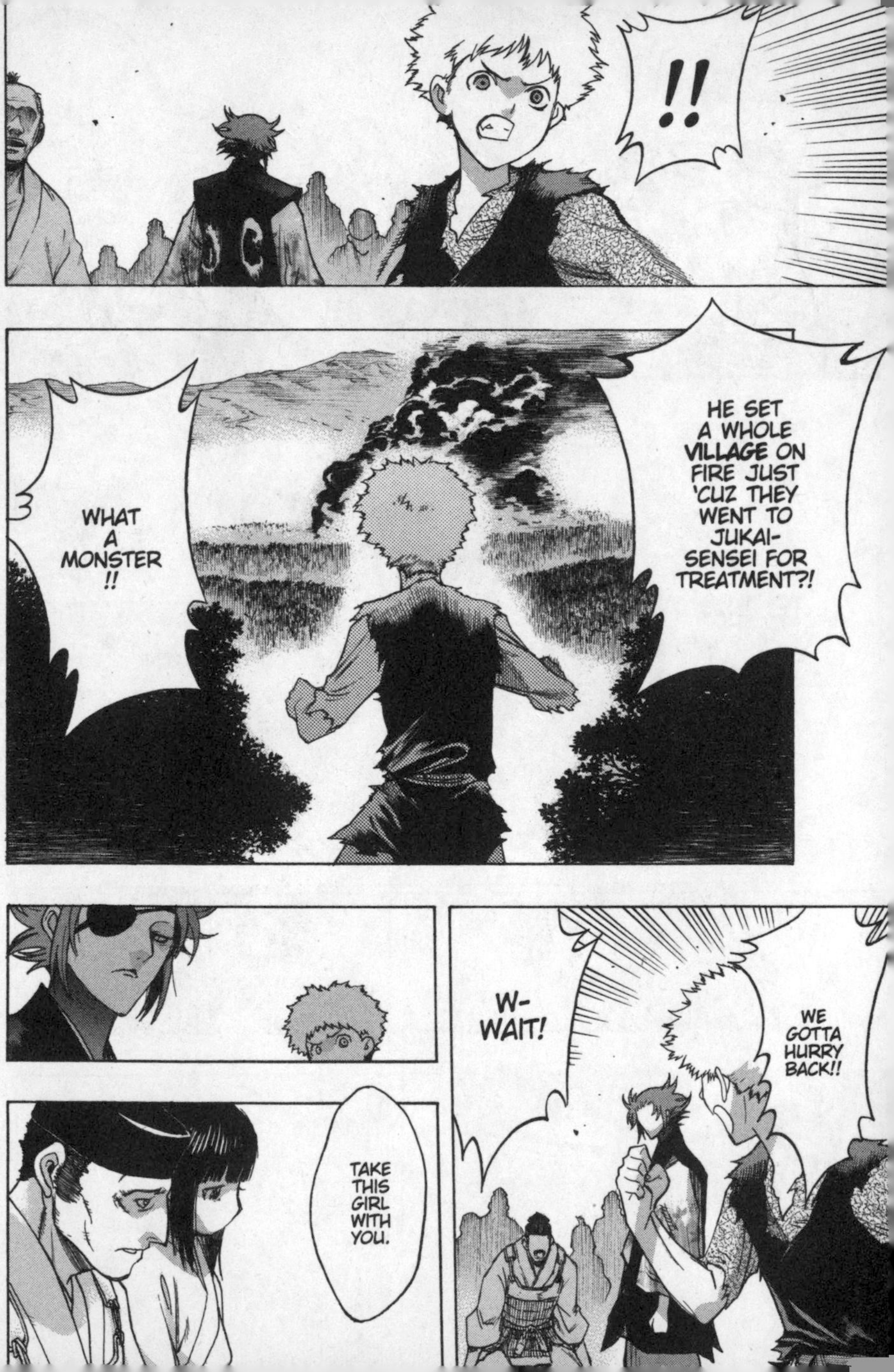
!!
HE SET A WHOLE VILLAGE ON FIRE JUST 'CUZ THEY WENT TO JUKAI-SENSEI FOR TREATMENT?!
WHAT A MONSTER!!
WE GOTTA HURRY BACK!!
W-WAIT!
TAKE THIS GIRL WITH YOU.

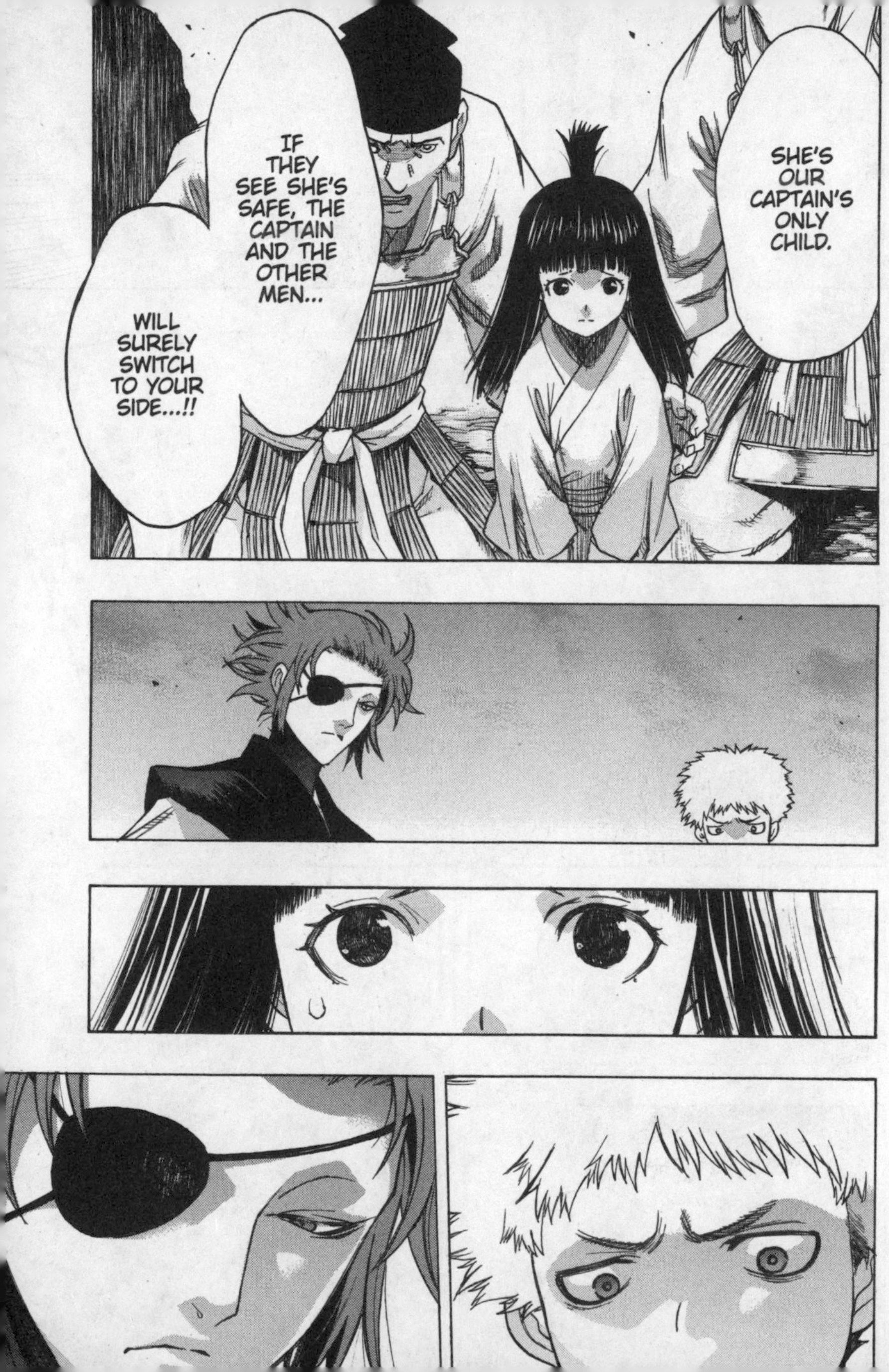
SHE'S OUR CAPTAIN'S ONLY CHILD.
IF THEY SEE SHE'S SAFE, THE CAPTAIN AND THE OTHER MEN...
WILL SURELY SWITCH TO YOUR SIDE...!!

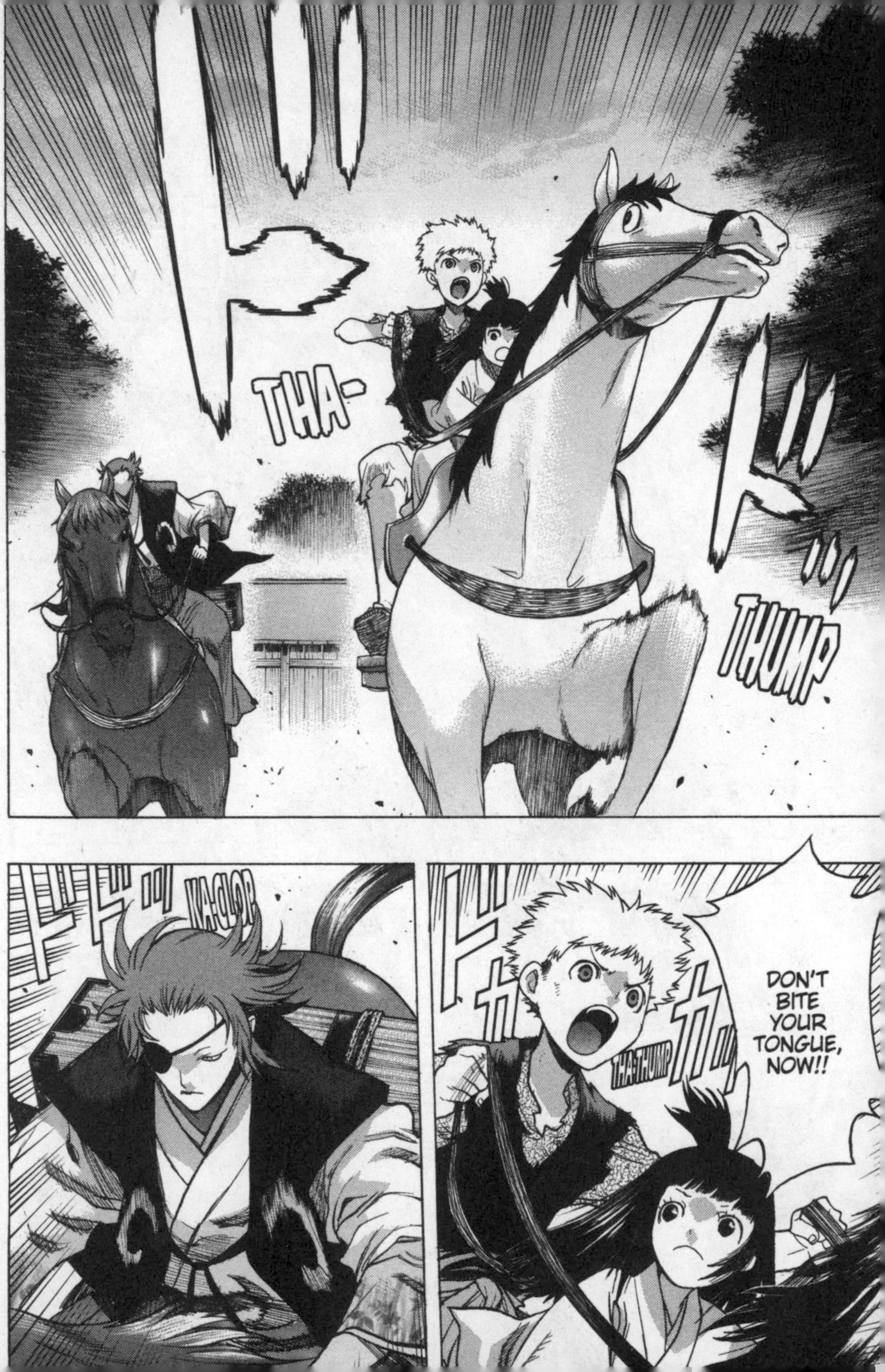
THA-
THUMP
DON'T BITE YOUR TONGUE, NOW!!
THA-THUMP
KA-CLOP

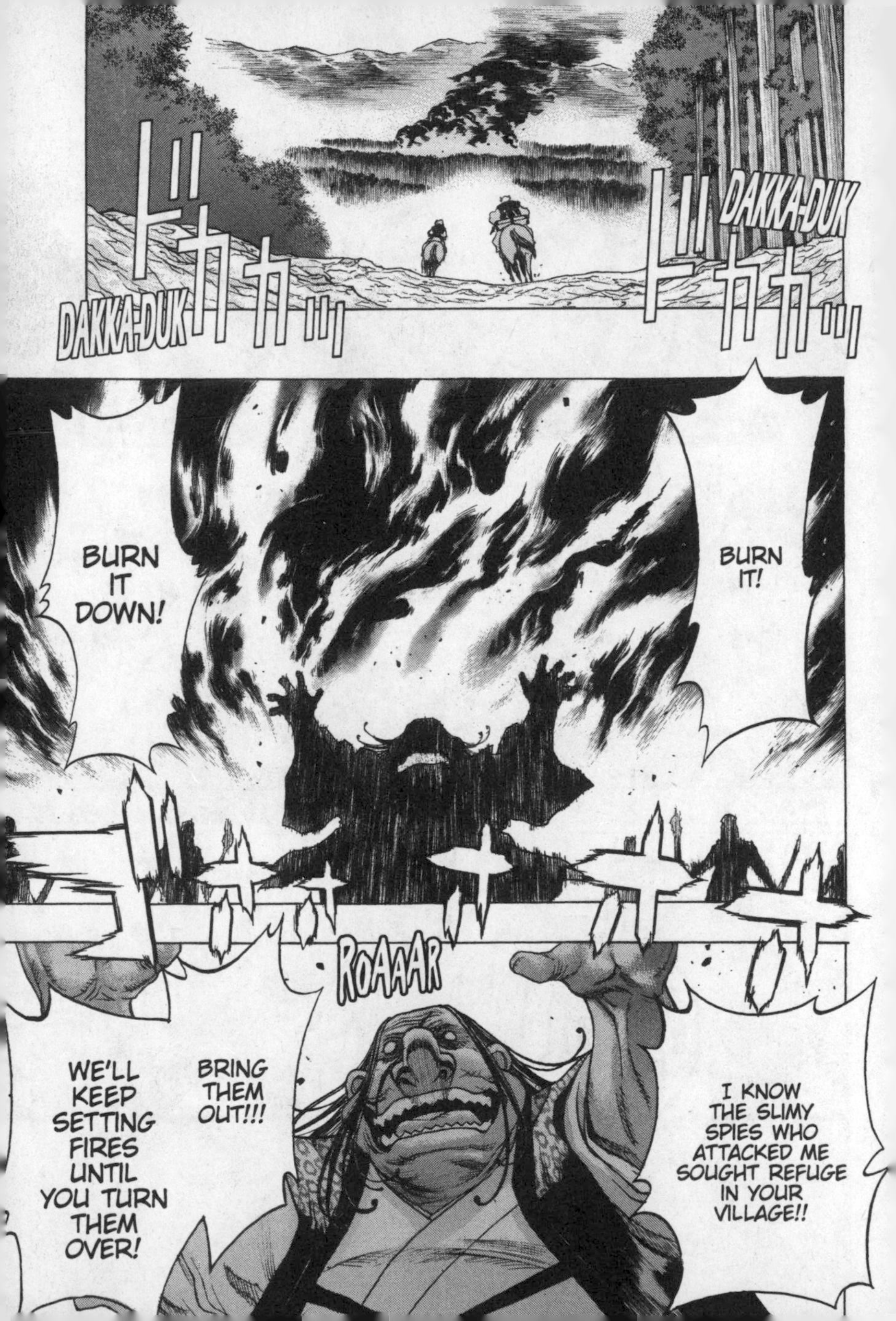
DAKKA-DUK
ドカカカ…
DAKKA-DUK
ドカカカ…
BURN IT!
BURN IT DOWN!
ROAAAR
I KNOW THE SLIMY SPIES WHO ATTACKED ME SOUGHT REFUGE IN YOUR VILLAGE!!
BRING THEM OUT!!!
WE'LL KEEP SETTING FIRES UNTIL YOU TURN THEM OVER!

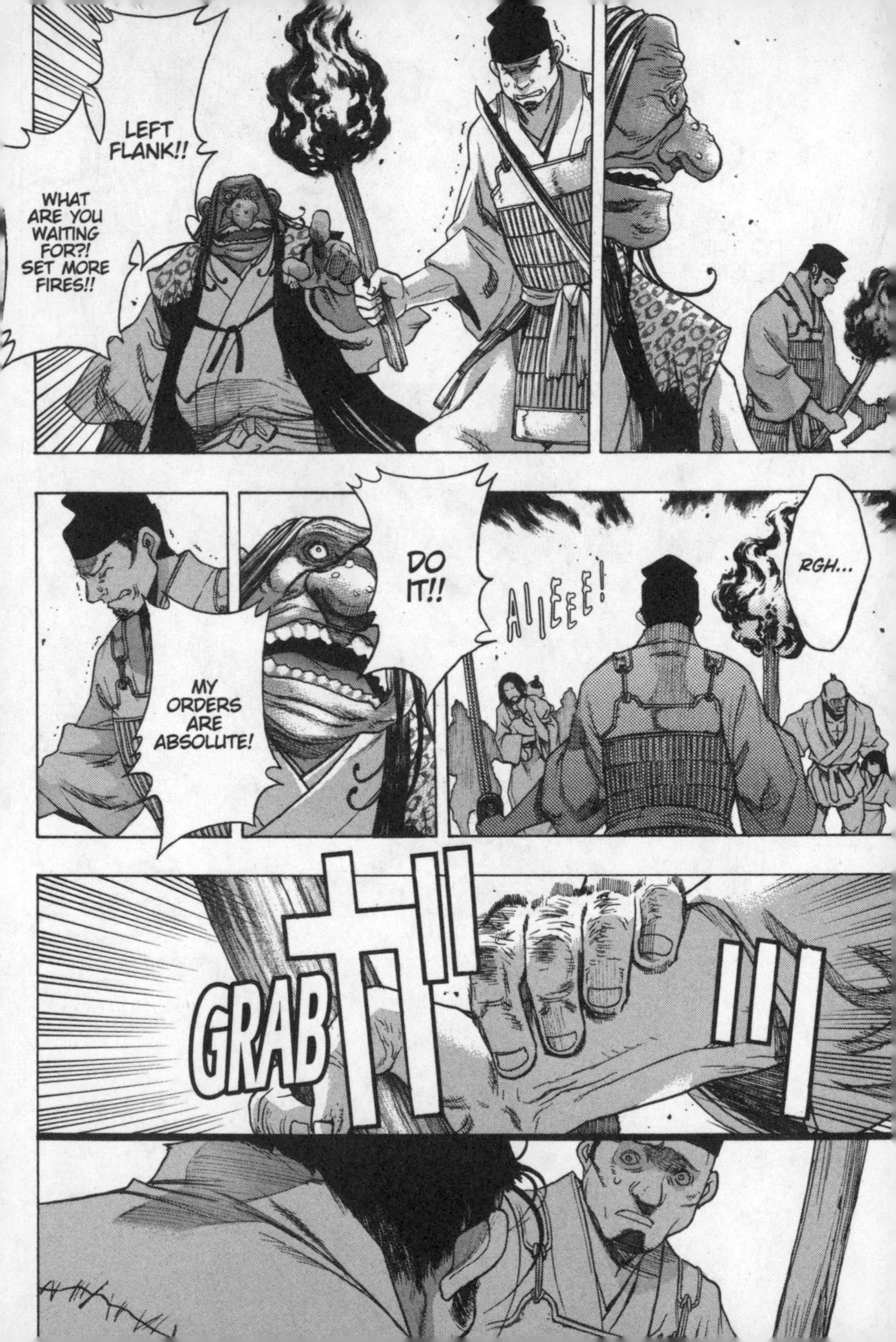
LEFT FLANK!!
WHAT ARE YOU WAITING FOR?! SET MORE FIRES!!
RGH...
AIIEEE!
DO IT!!
MY ORDERS ARE ABSOLUTE!
GRAB

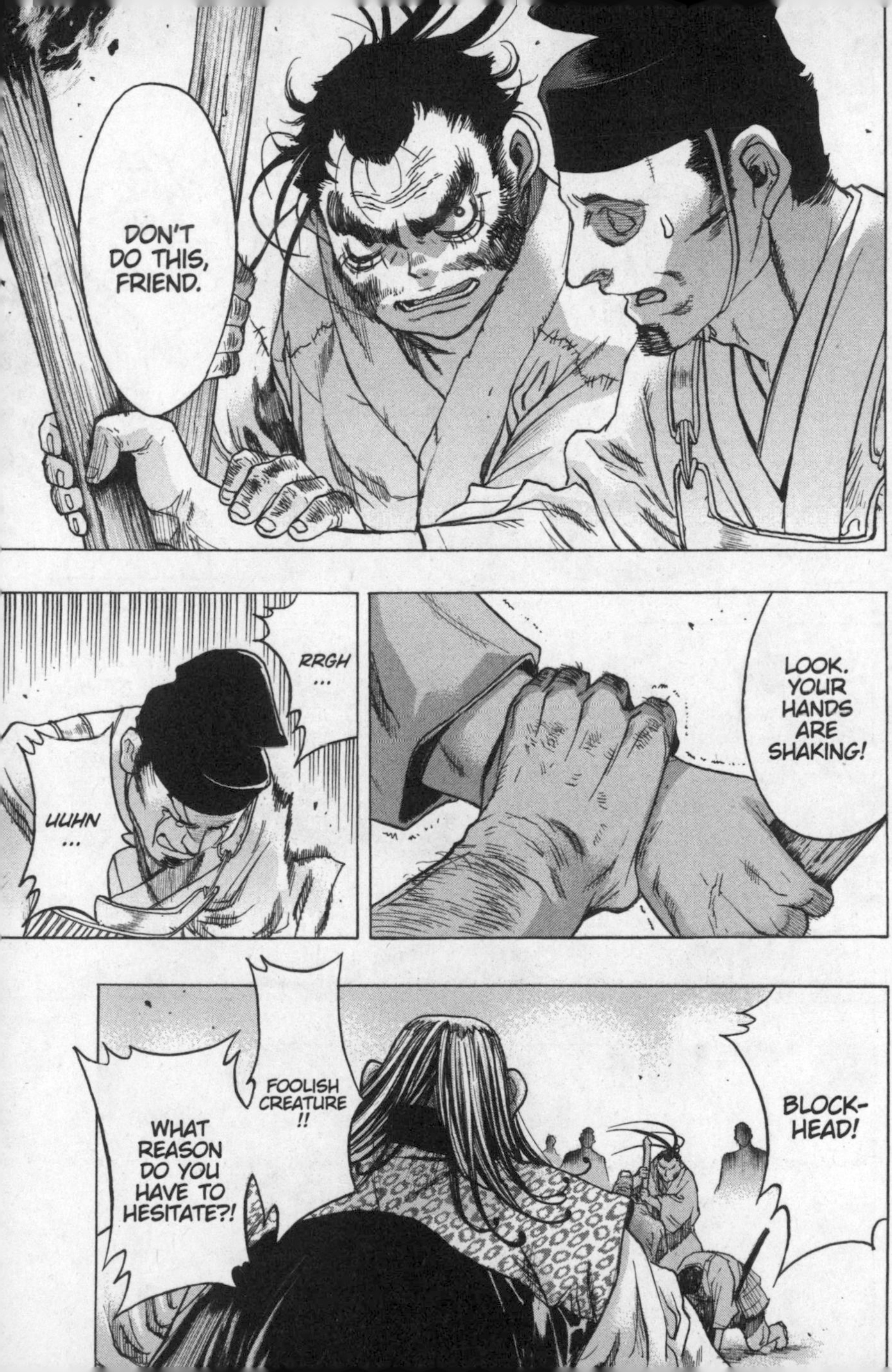
DON'T DO THIS, FRIEND.
LOOK. YOUR HANDS ARE SHAKING!
RRGH ...
UUHN ...
BLOCK-HEAD!
FOOLISH CREATURE !!
WHAT REASON DO YOU HAVE TO HESITATE?!

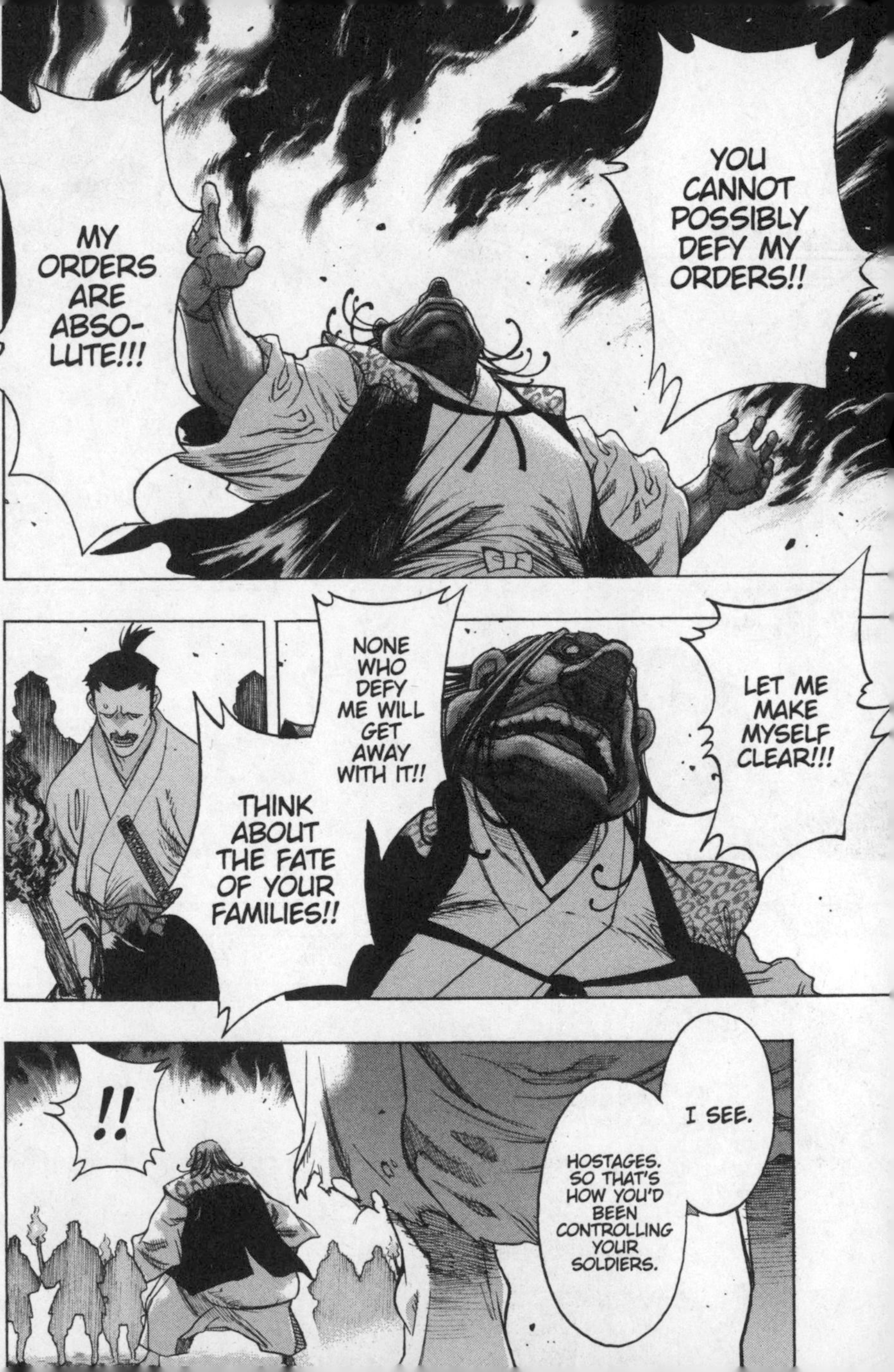
YOU CANNOT POSSIBLY DEFY MY ORDERS!!
MY ORDERS ARE ABSO-LUTE!!!
LET ME MAKE MYSELF CLEAR!!!
NONE WHO DEFY ME WILL GET AWAY WITH IT!!
THINK ABOUT THE FATE OF YOUR FAMILIES!!
I SEE.
HOSTAGES. SO THAT'S HOW YOU'D BEEN CONTROLLING YOUR SOLDIERS.
!!

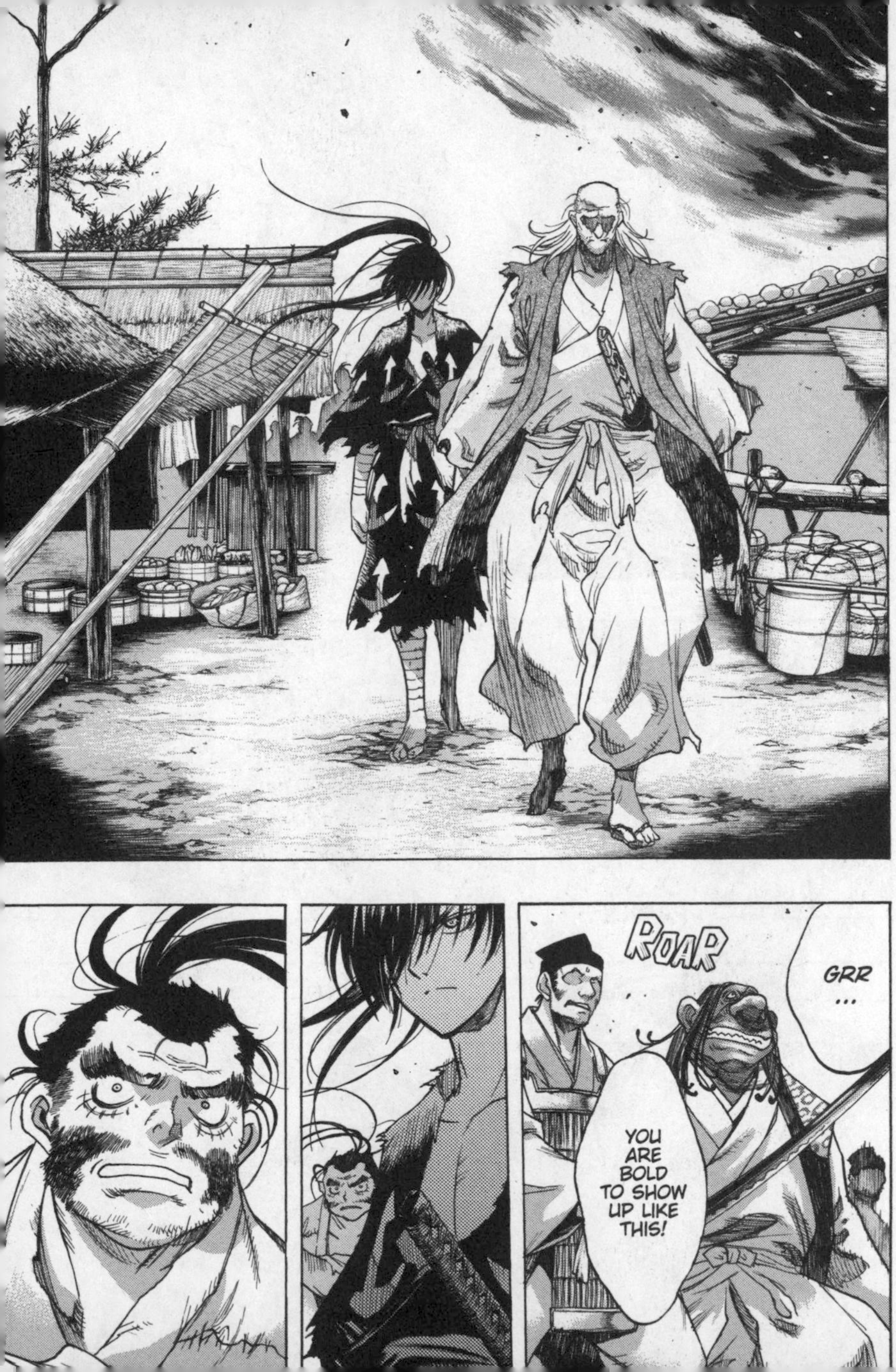
GRR ...
ROAR
YOU ARE BOLD TO SHOW UP LIKE THIS!

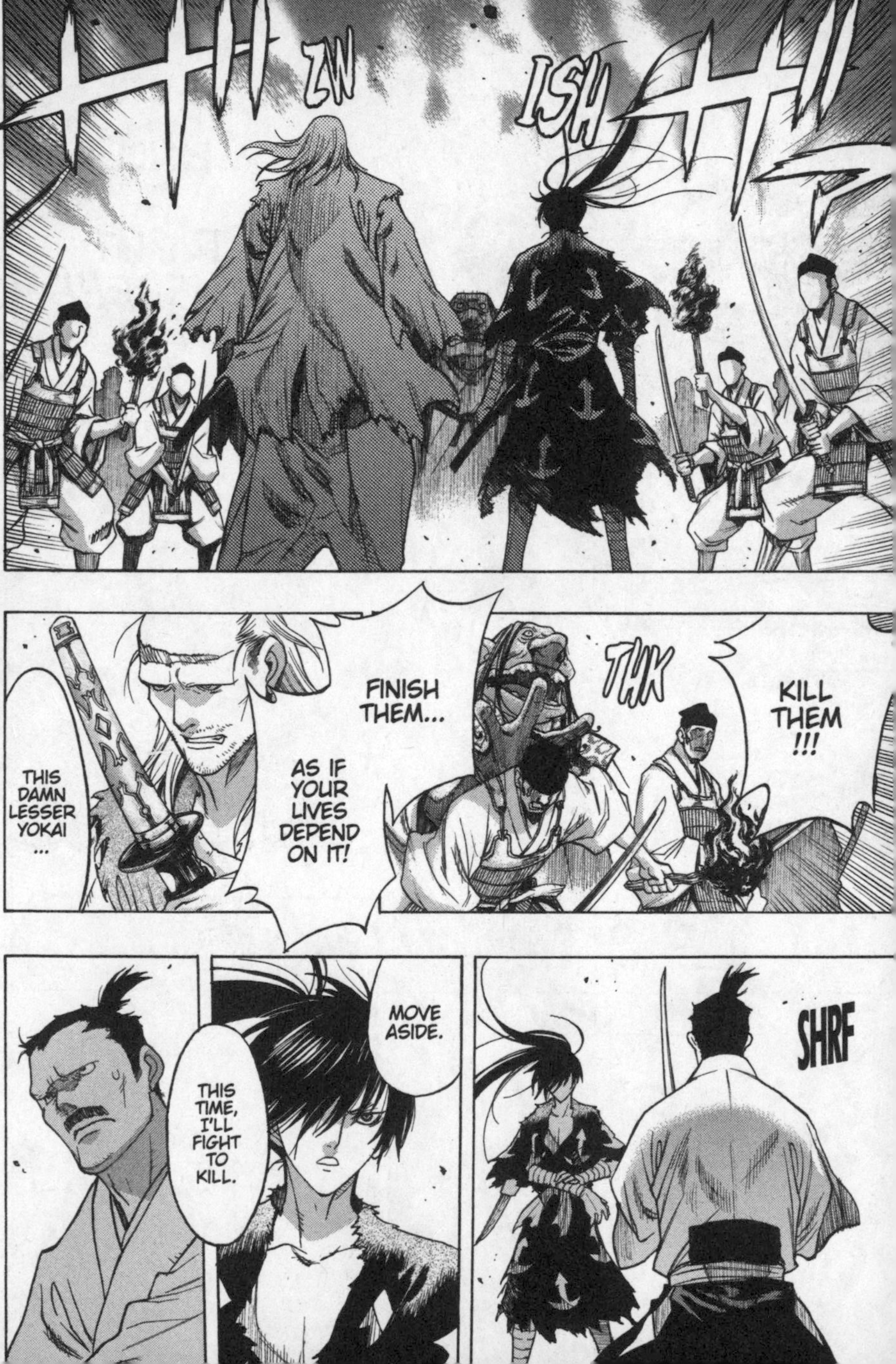
ISH
ZW
KILL THEM !!!
THK
FINISH THEM...
AS IF YOUR LIVES DEPEND ON IT!
THIS DAMN LESSER YOKAI ...
SHRF
MOVE ASIDE.
THIS TIME, I'LL FIGHT TO KILL.

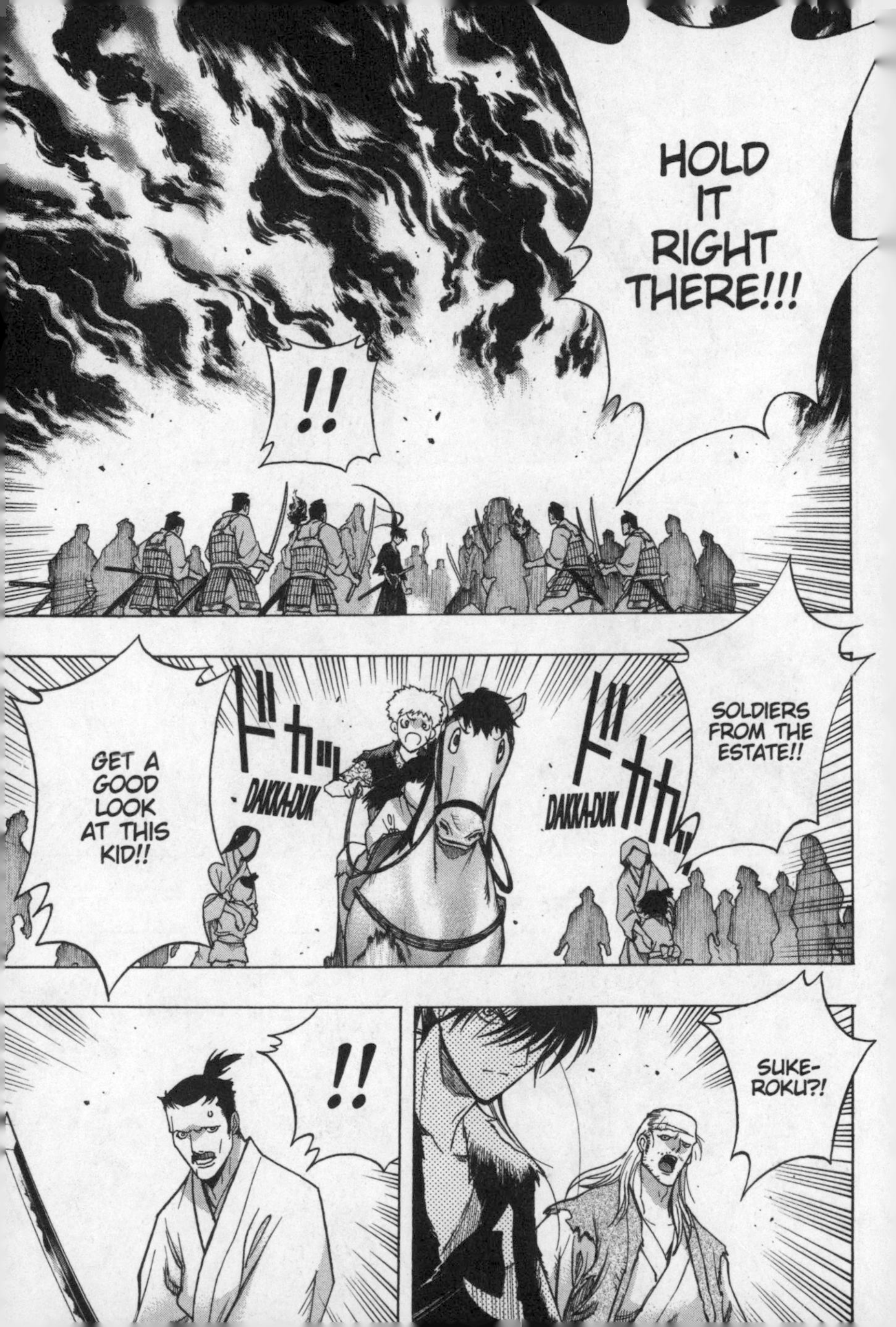
HOLD IT RIGHT THERE!!!
!!
SOLDIERS FROM THE ESTATE!!
DAKKA-DUK
DAKKA-DUK
GET A GOOD LOOK AT THIS KID!!
SUKE-ROKU?!
!!

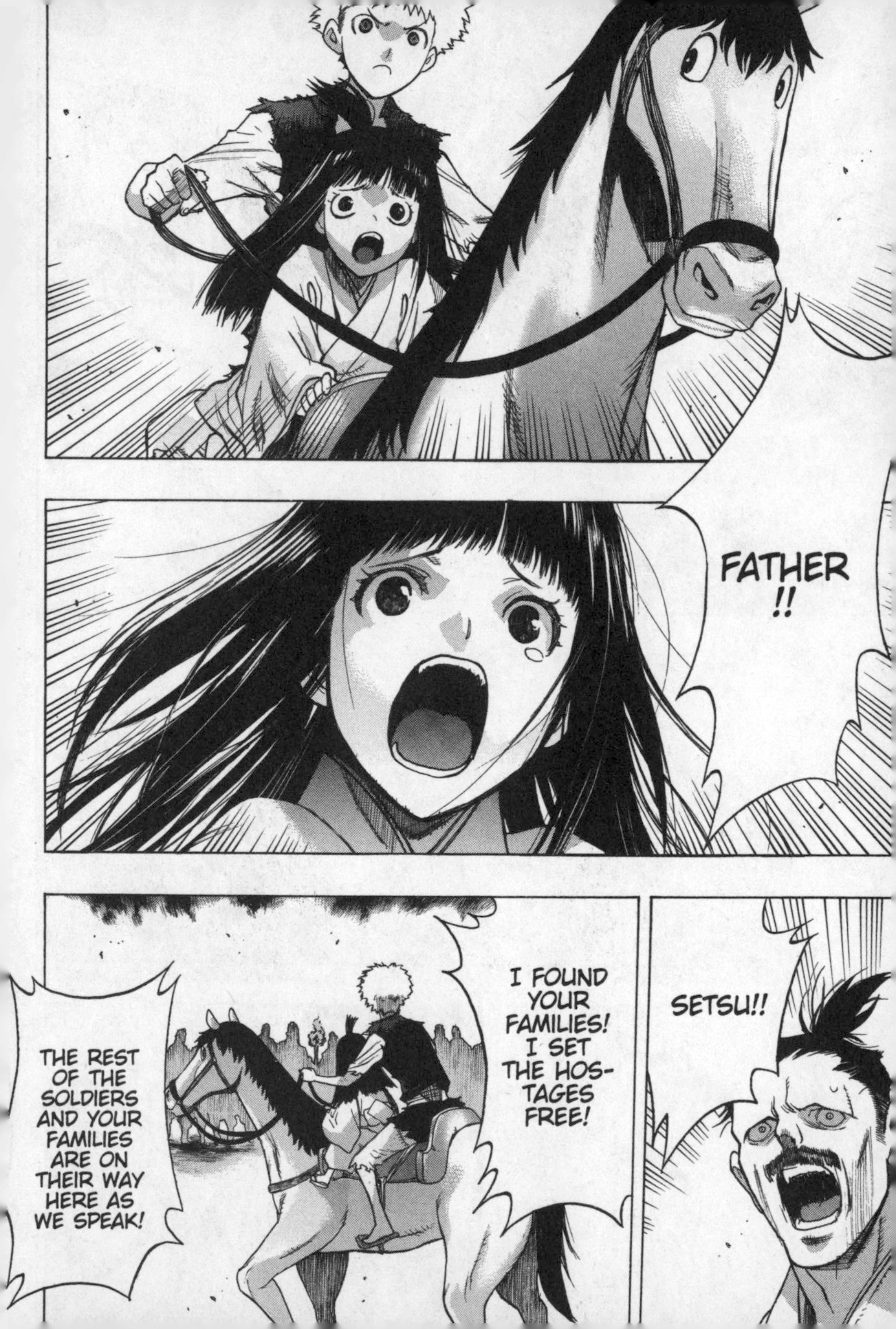
FATHER !!
SETSU!!
I FOUND YOUR FAMILIES! I SET THE HOS-TAGES FREE!
THE REST OF THE SOLDIERS AND YOUR FAMILIES ARE ON THEIR WAY HERE AS WE SPEAK!

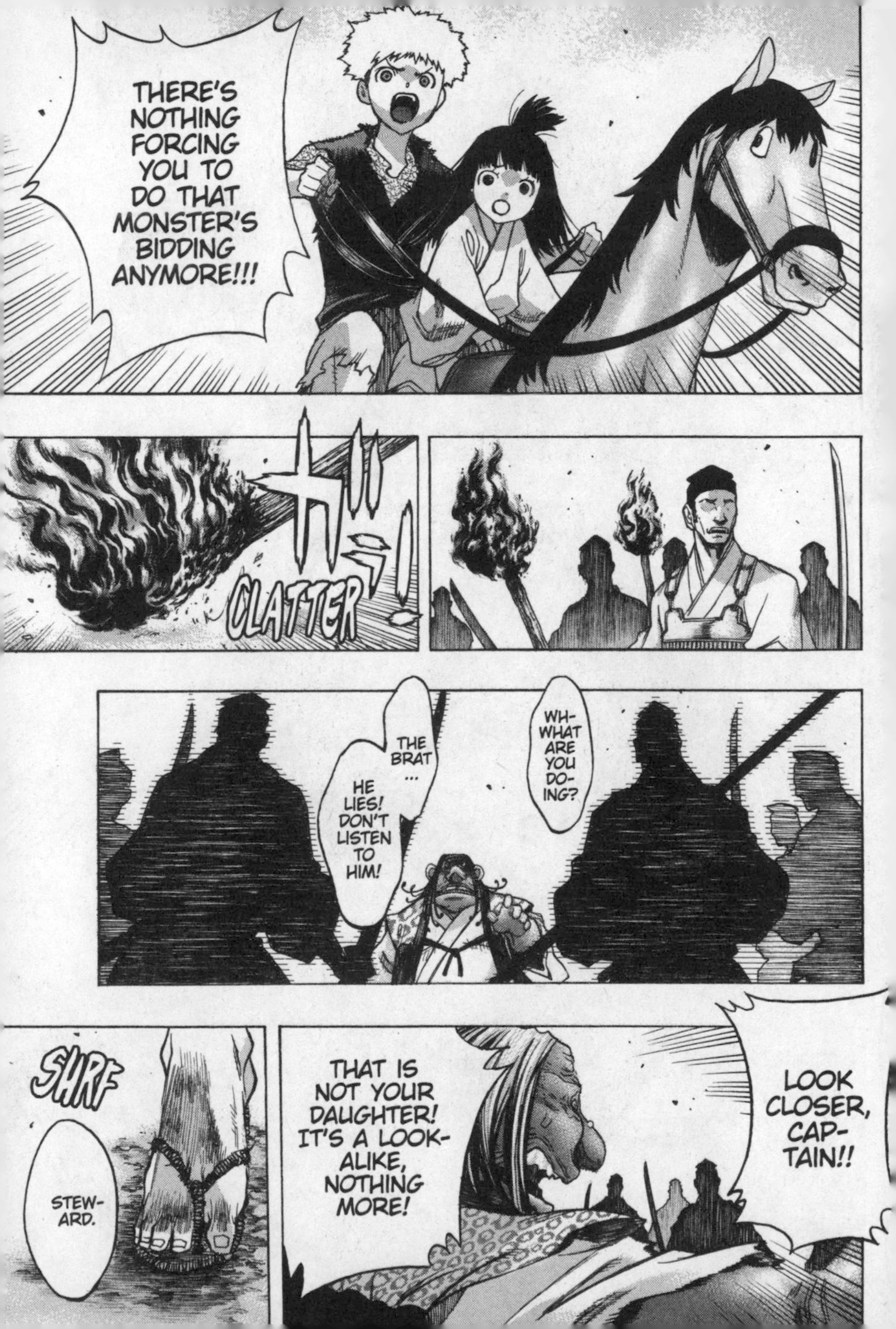
THERE'S NOTHING FORCING YOU TO DO THAT MONSTER'S BIDDING ANYMORE!!!
CLATTER
WH- WHAT ARE YOU DO- ING?
THE BRAT ...
HE LIES! DON'T LISTEN TO HIM!
LOOK CLOSER, CAP- TAIN!!
THAT IS NOT YOUR DAUGHTER! IT'S A LOOK- ALIKE, NOTHING MORE!
SHRF
STEW- ARD.

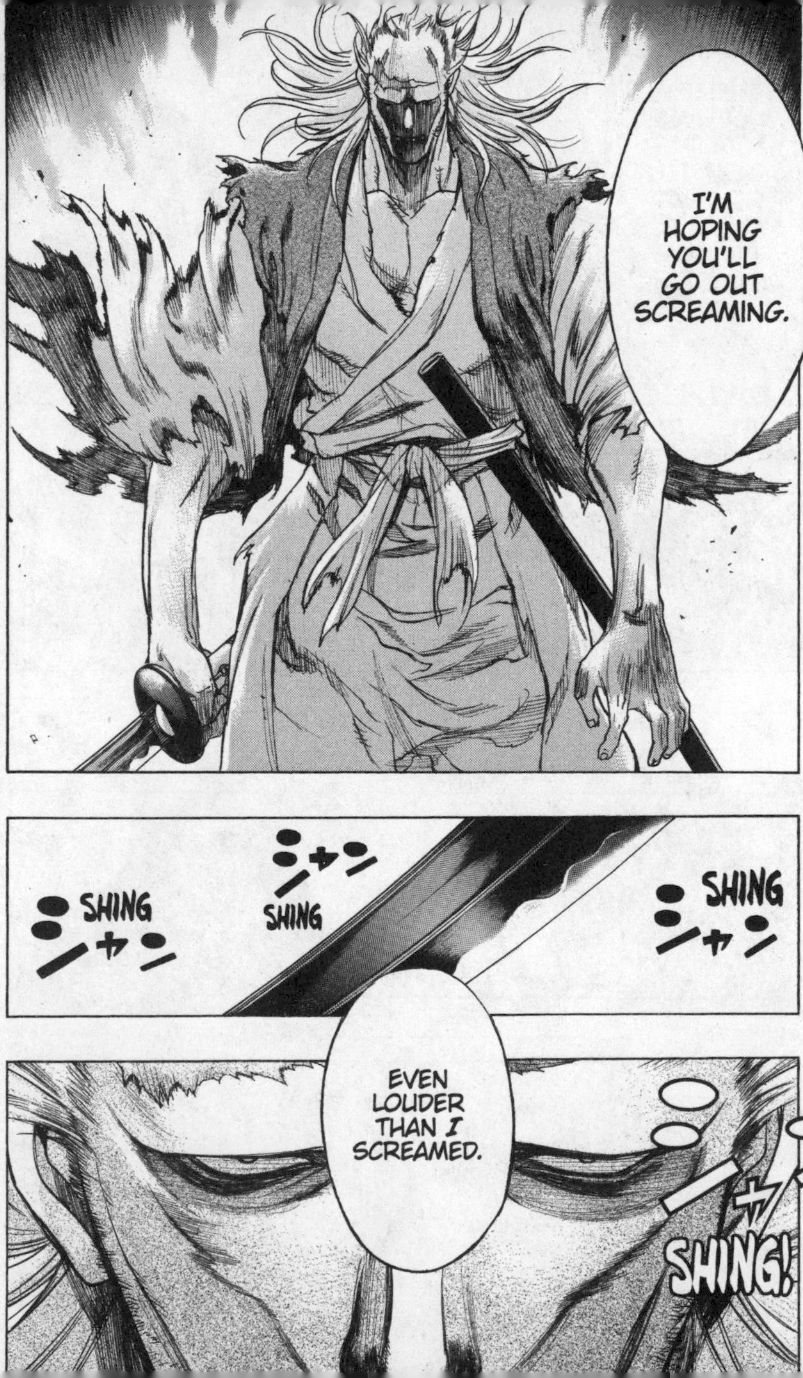
I'M HOPING YOU'LL GO OUT SCREAMING.
シャン
SHING
シャン
SHING
シャン
SHING
EVEN LOUDER THAN *I* SCREAMED.
シャン
SHING!

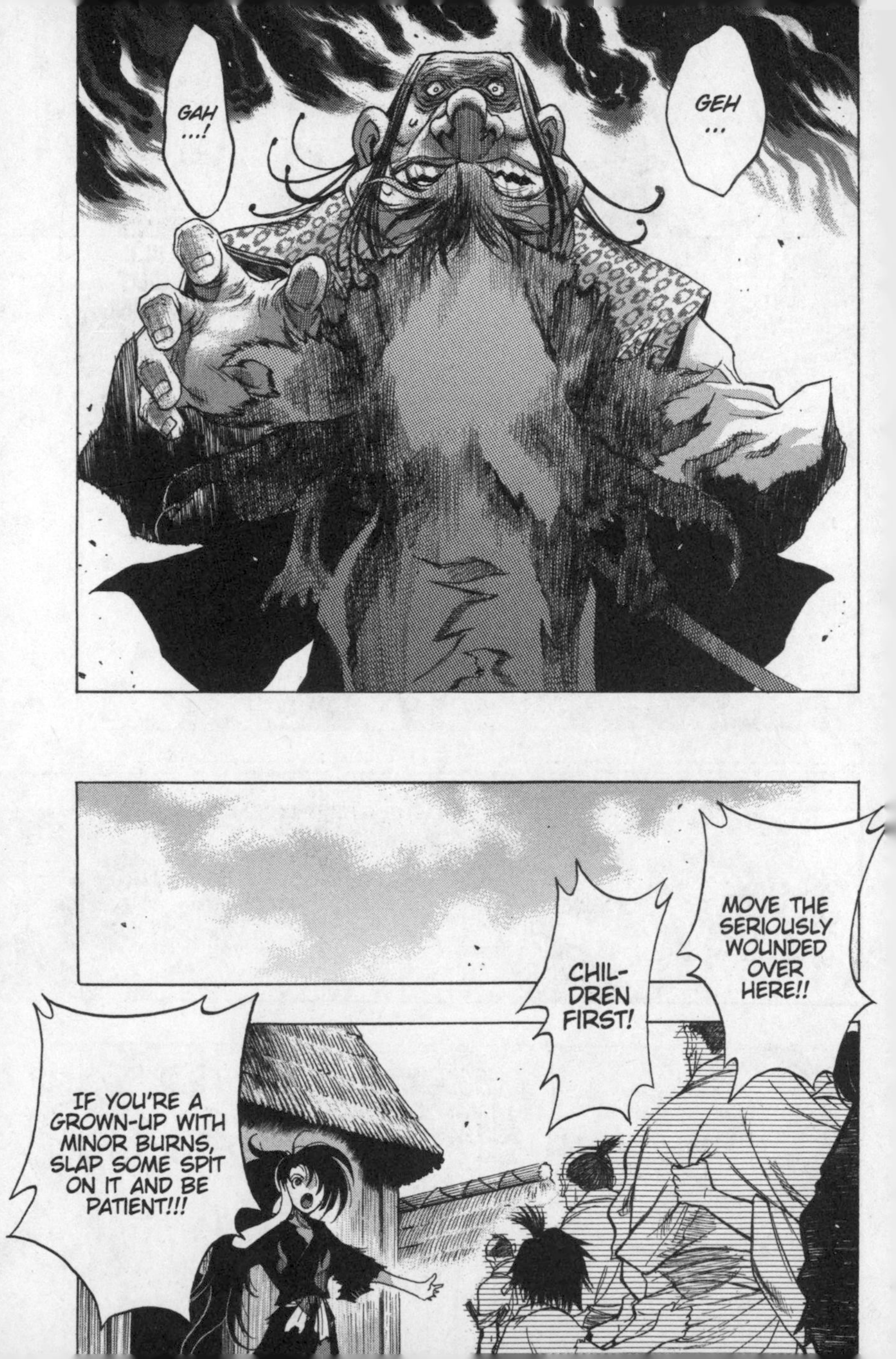
GEH ...
GAH ...!
MOVE THE SERIOUSLY WOUNDED OVER HERE!!
CHIL-DREN FIRST!
IF YOU'RE A GROWN-UP WITH MINOR BURNS, SLAP SOME SPIT ON IT AND BE PATIENT!!!

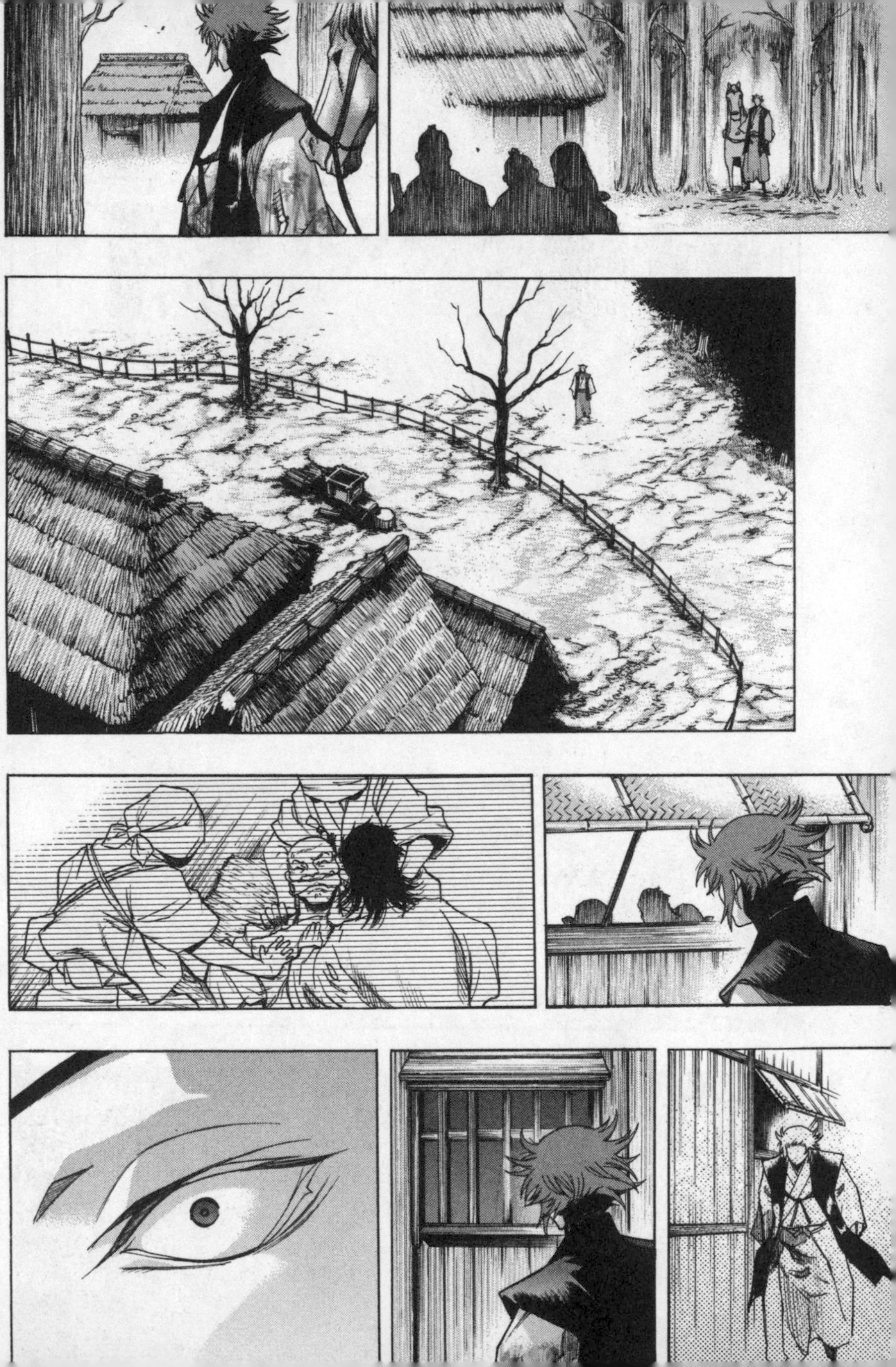

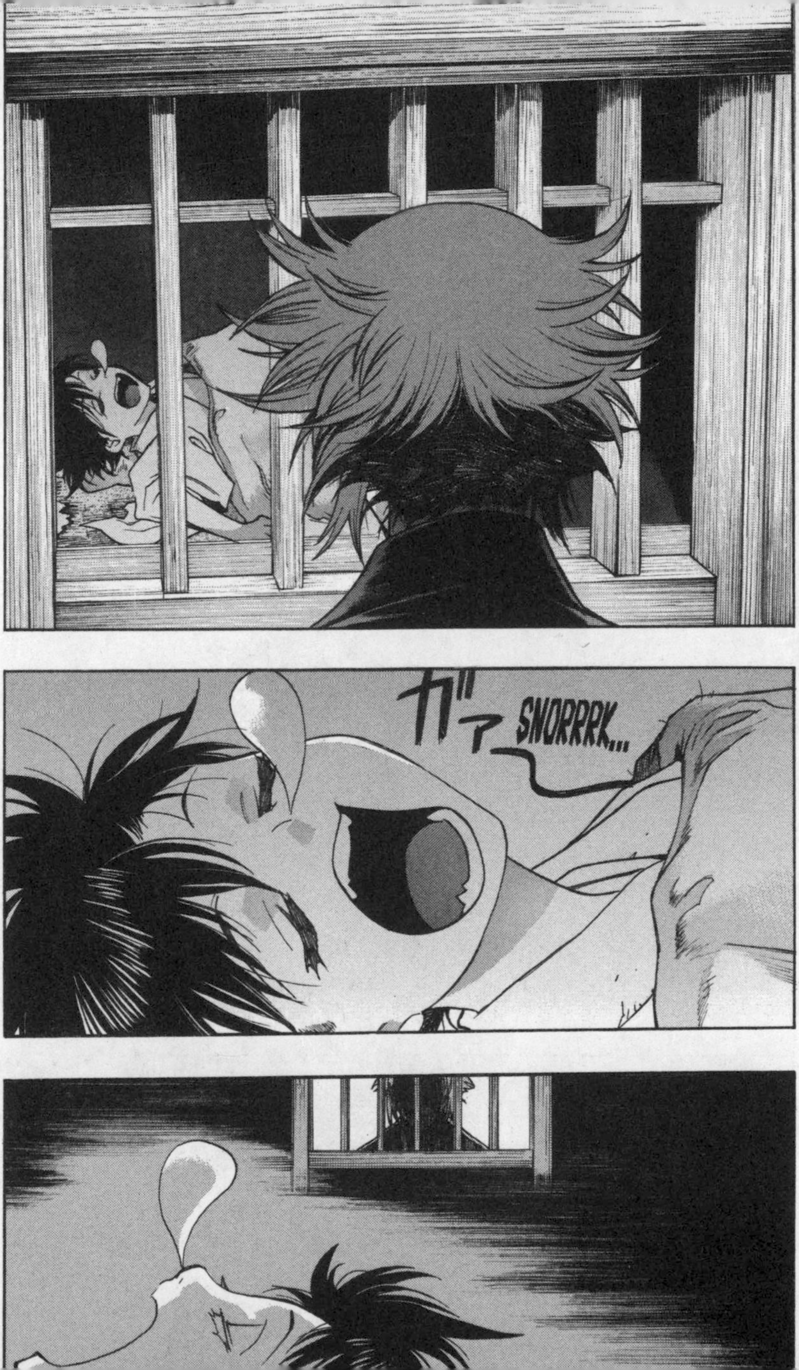
ガァ
SNORRRK...

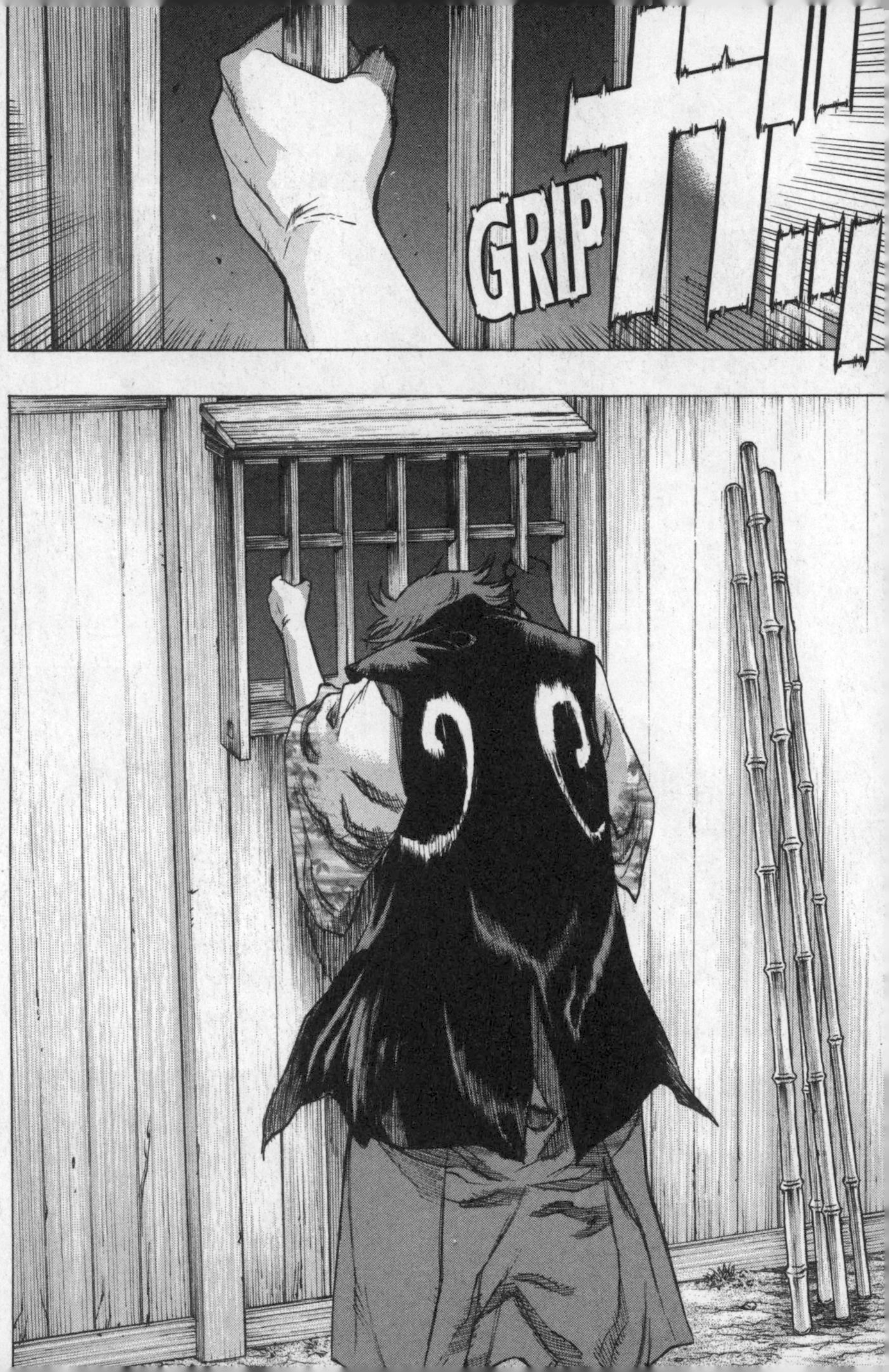
GRIP

THE LEGEND OF
DORORO AND
HYAKKIMARU

どろろと
百鬼丸伝

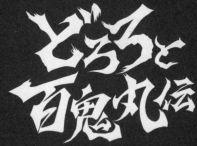

THE LEGEND OF
DORORO AND HYAKKIMARU

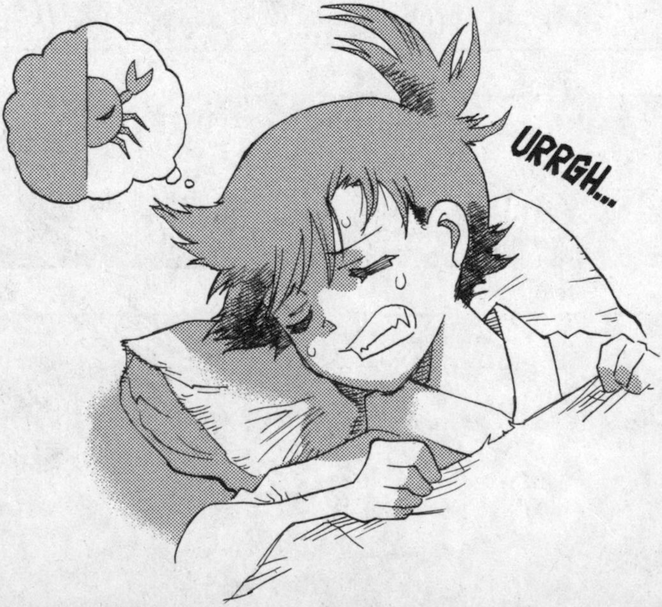
URRGH...

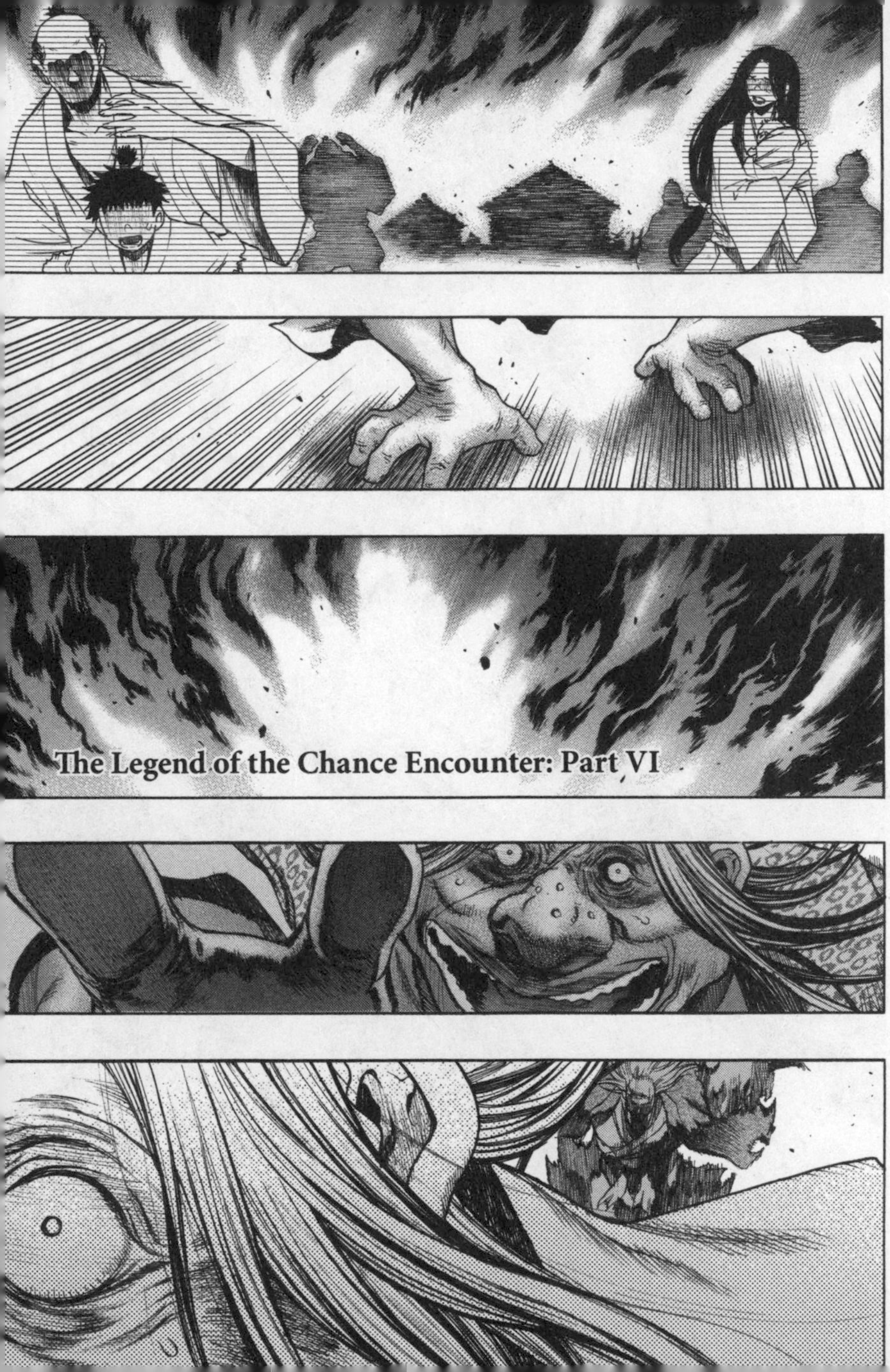
The Legend of the Chance Encounter: Part VI

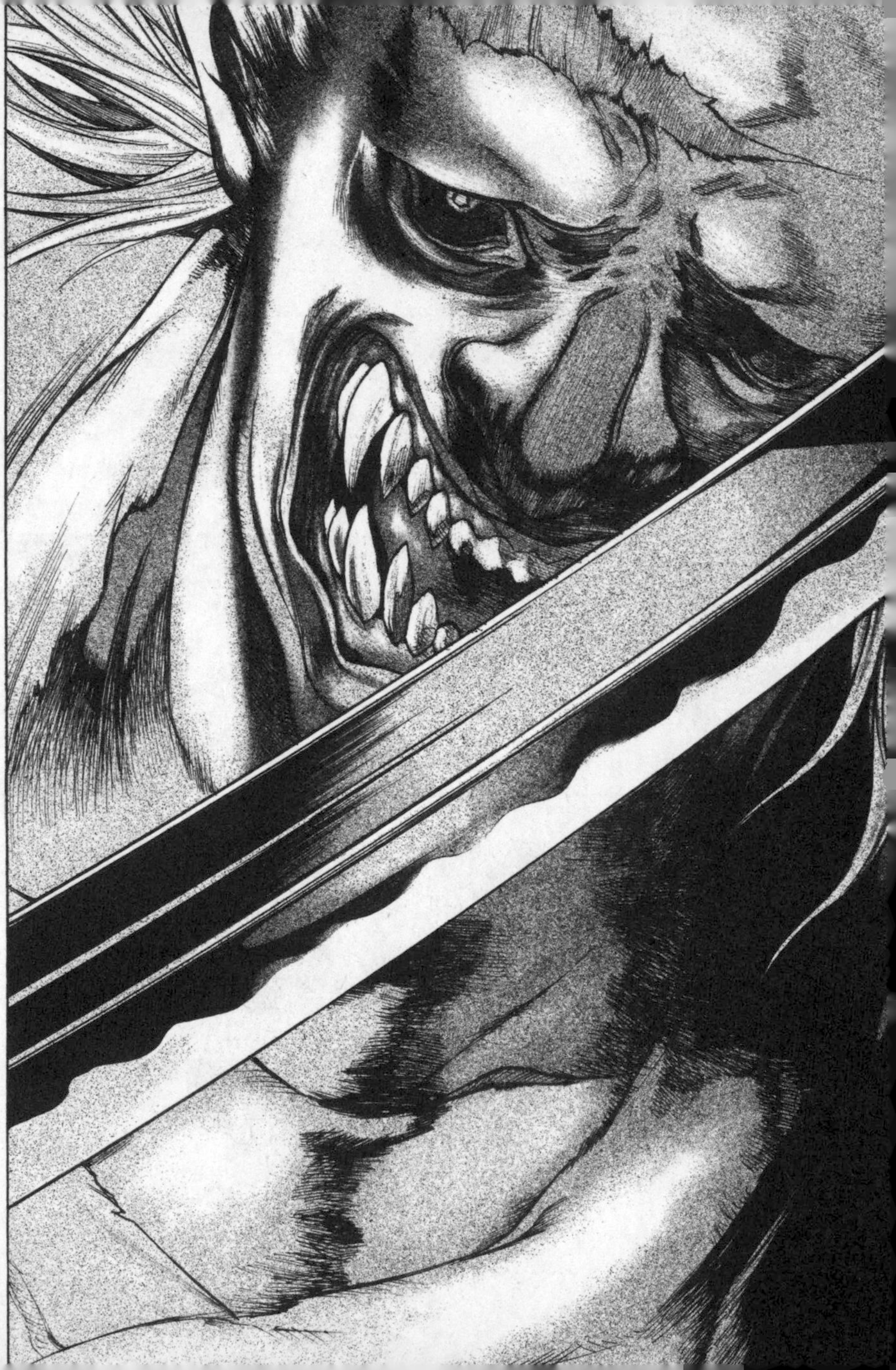

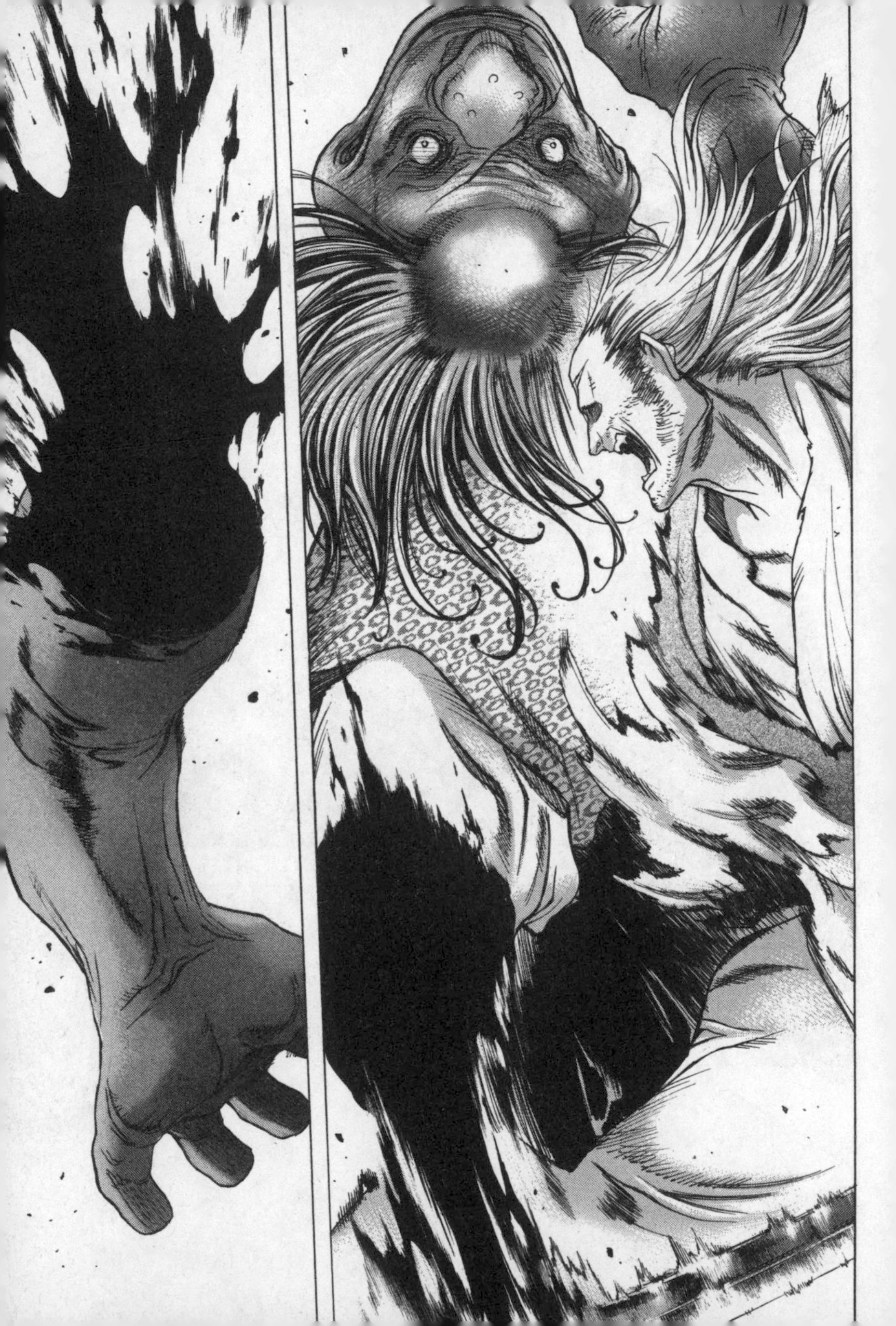

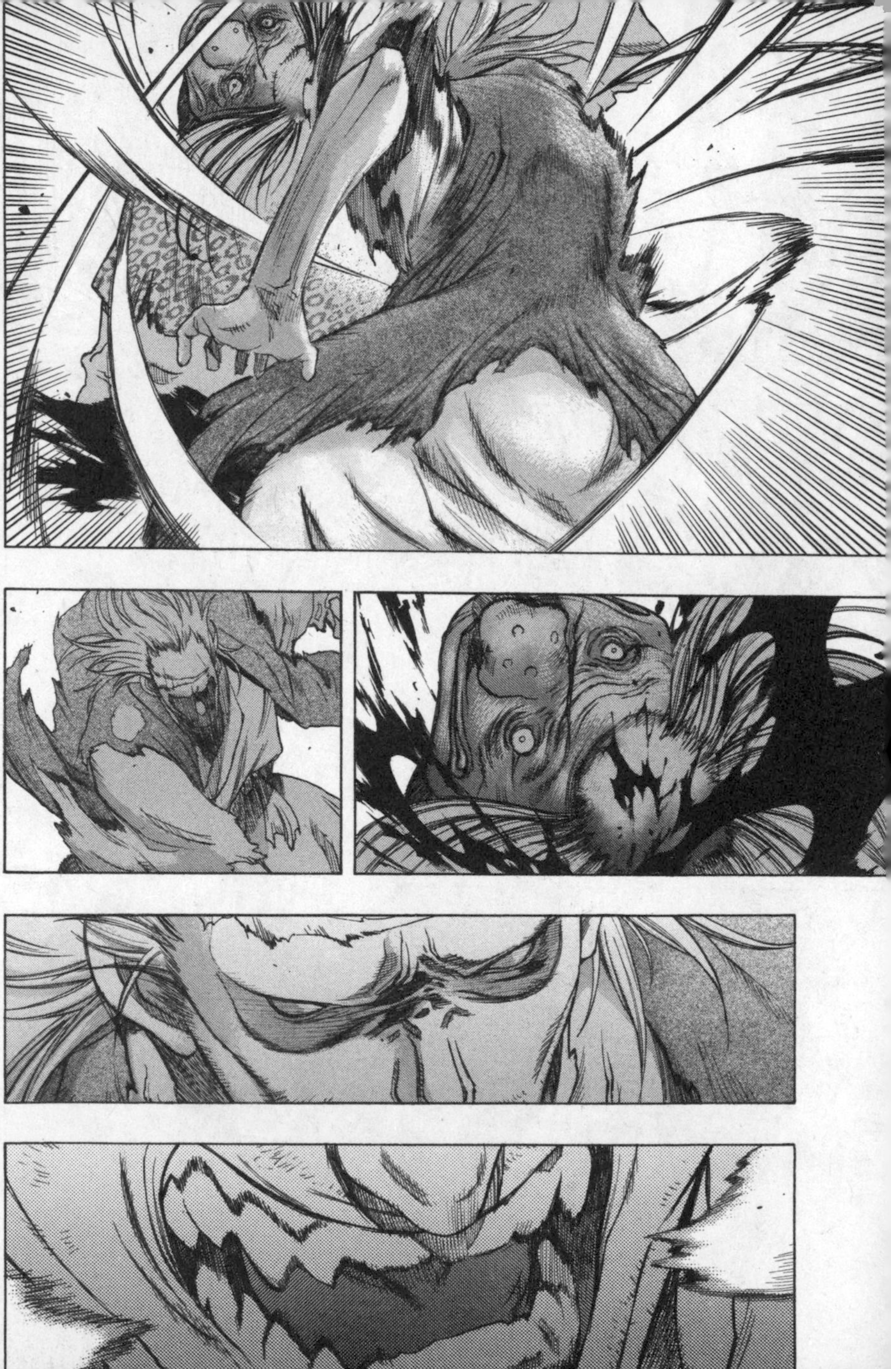

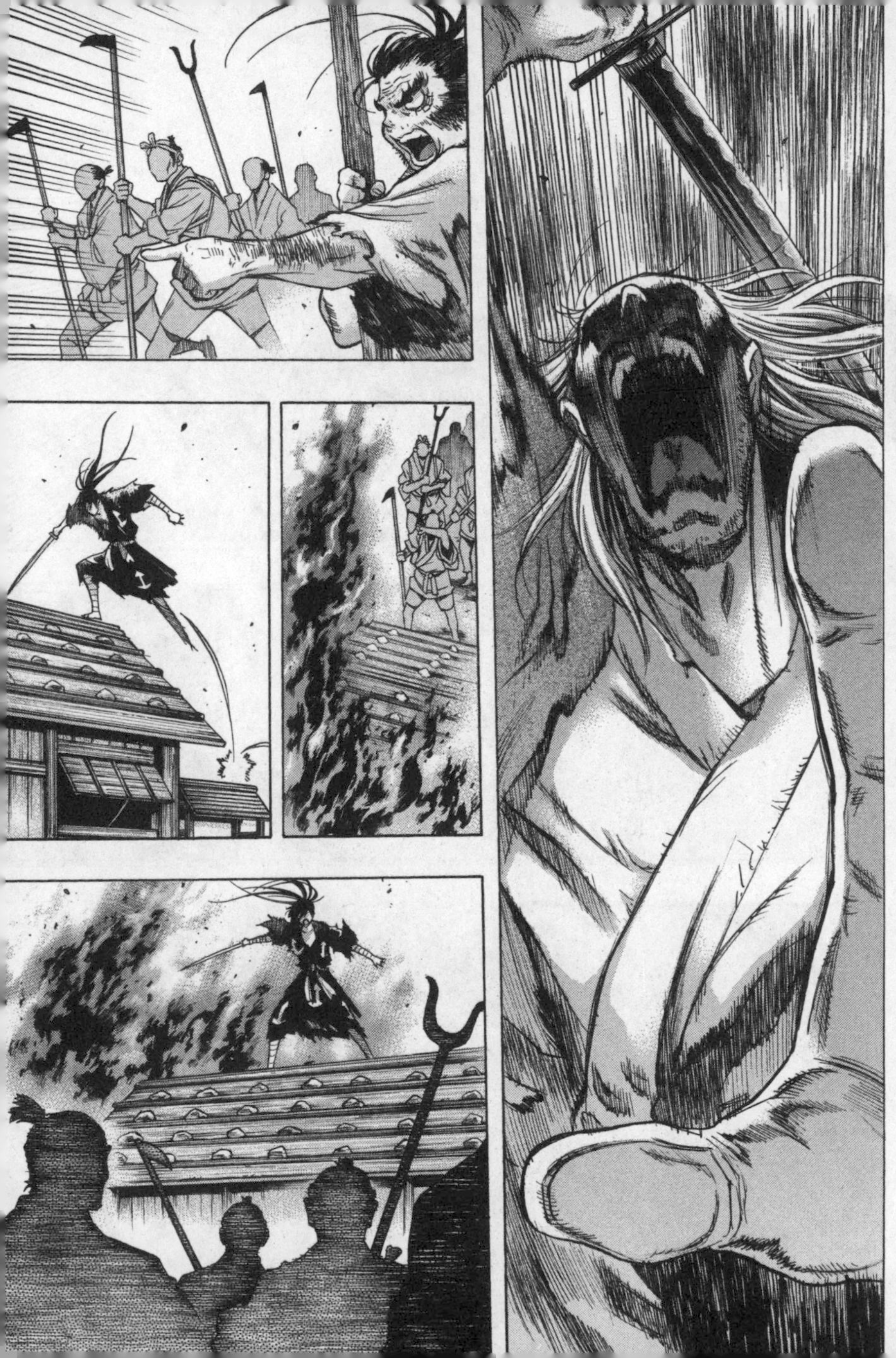

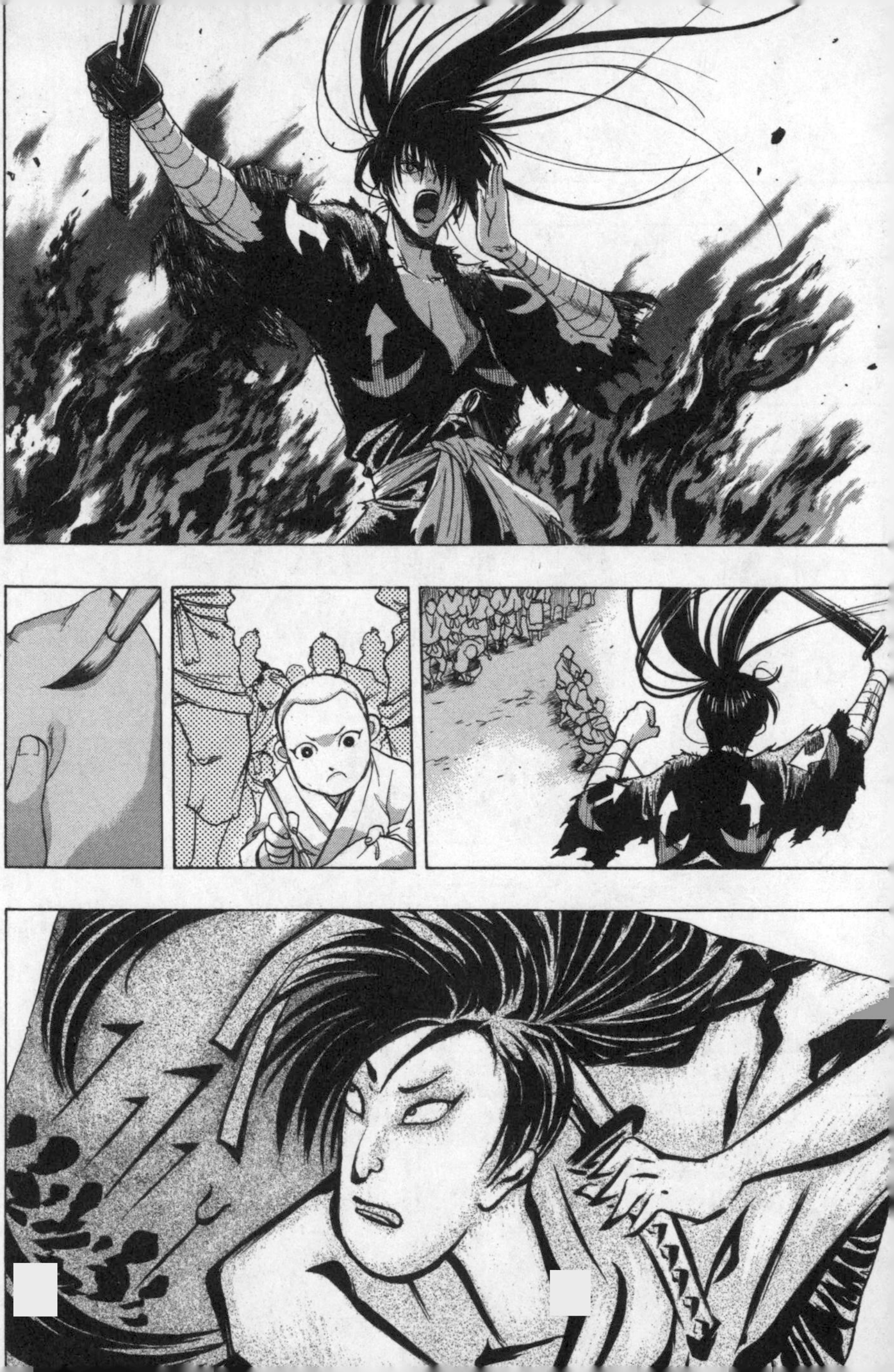

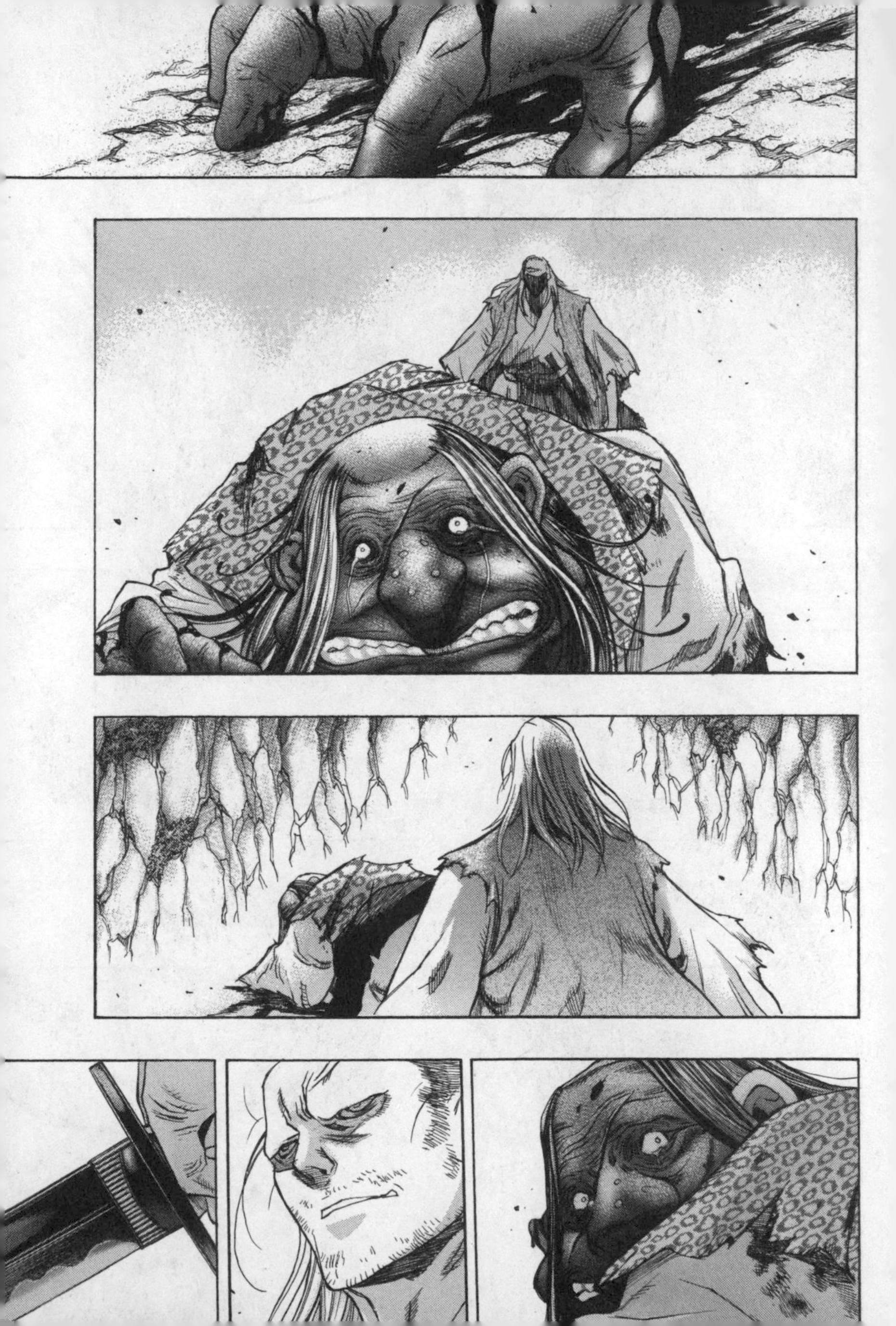

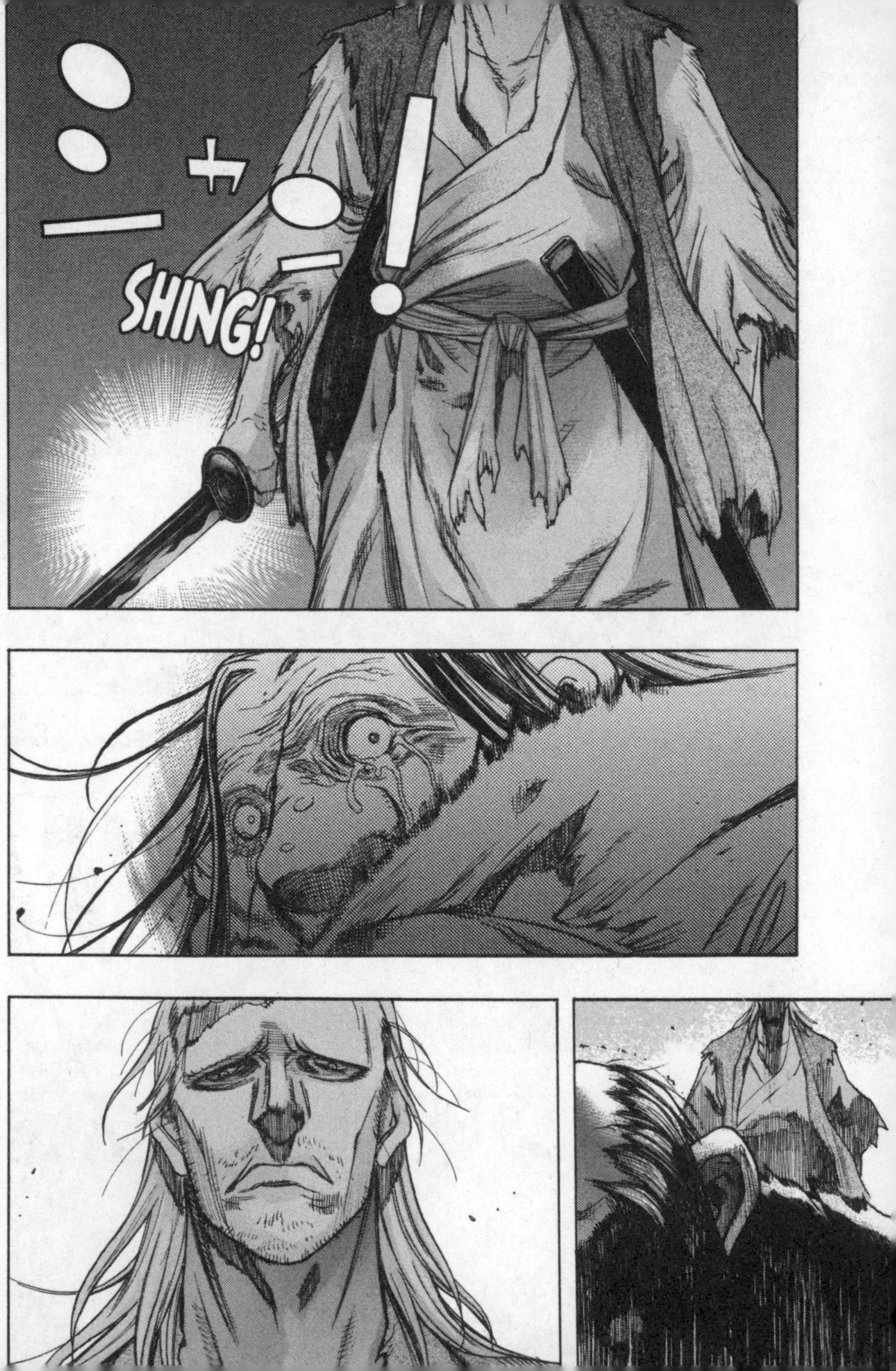
SHING!

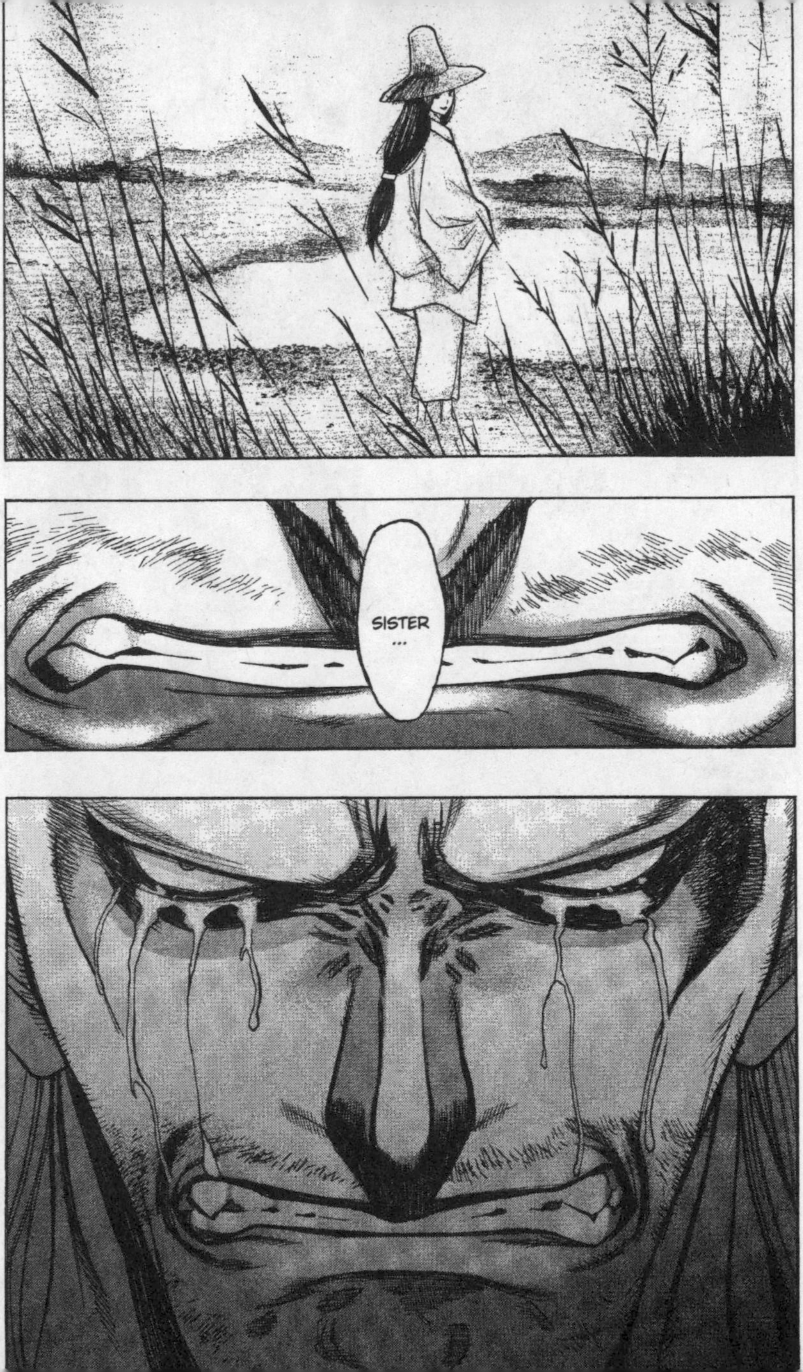
SISTER ...

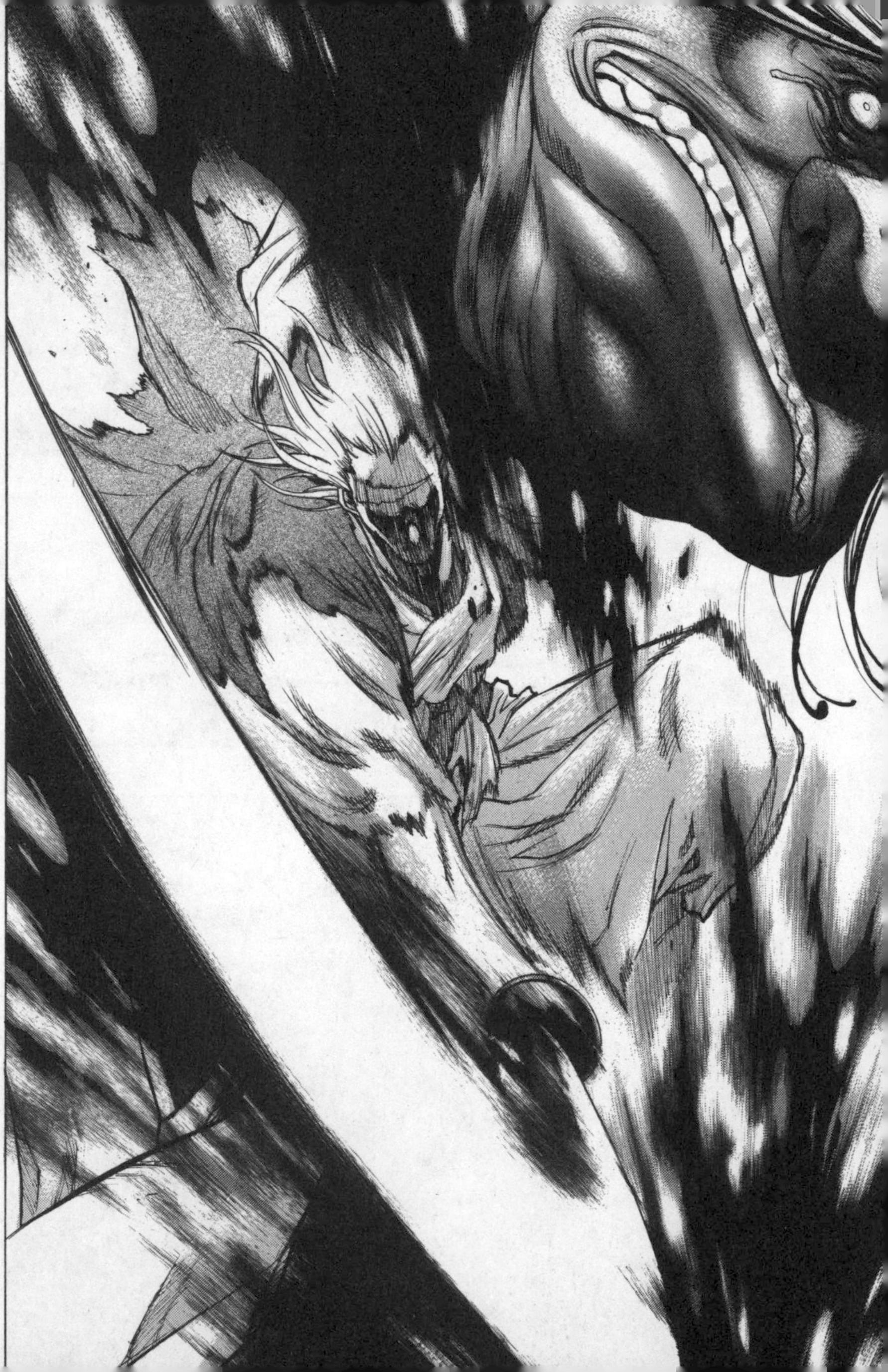

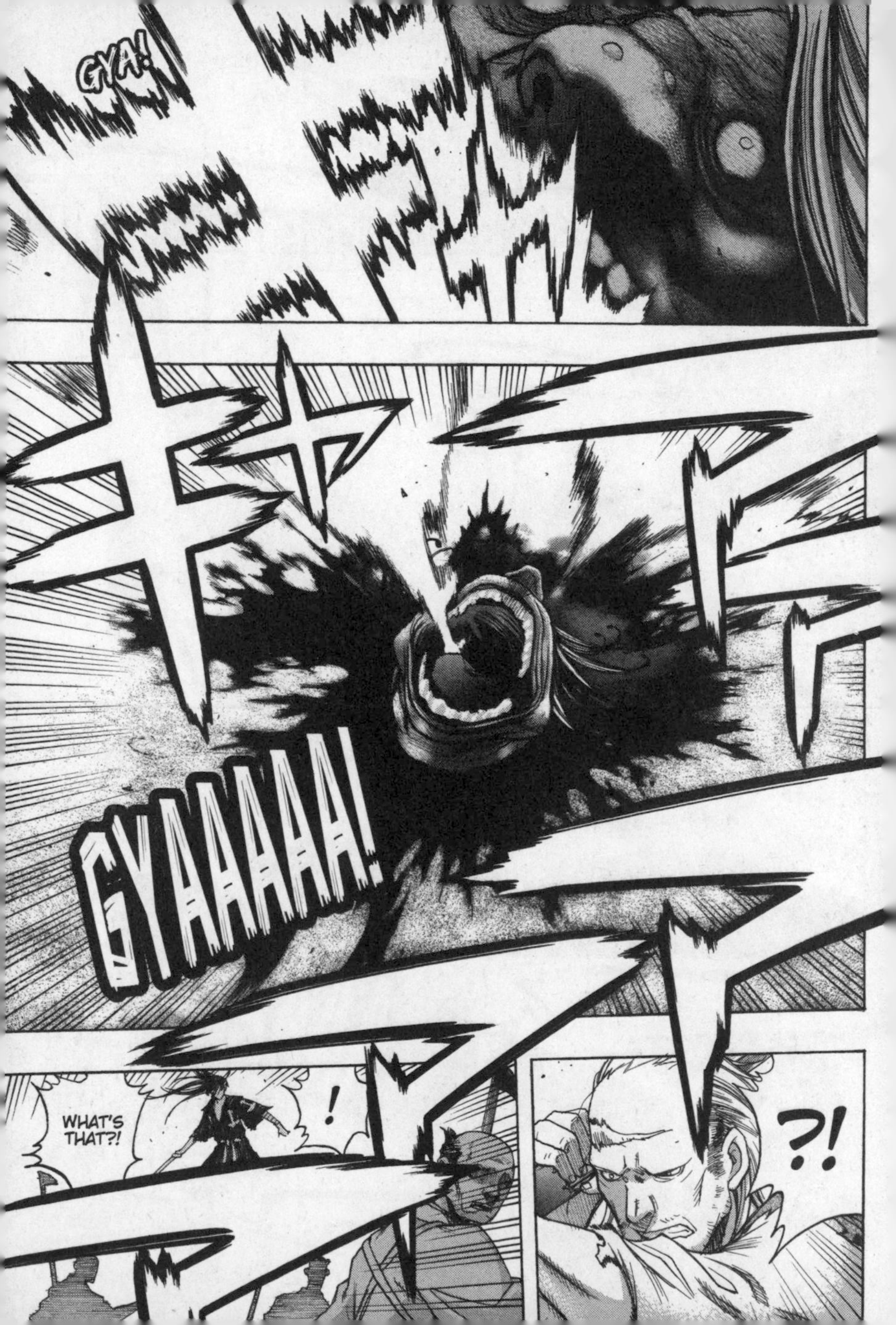
GYA!
GYAAAAA!
?!
!
WHAT'S THAT?!

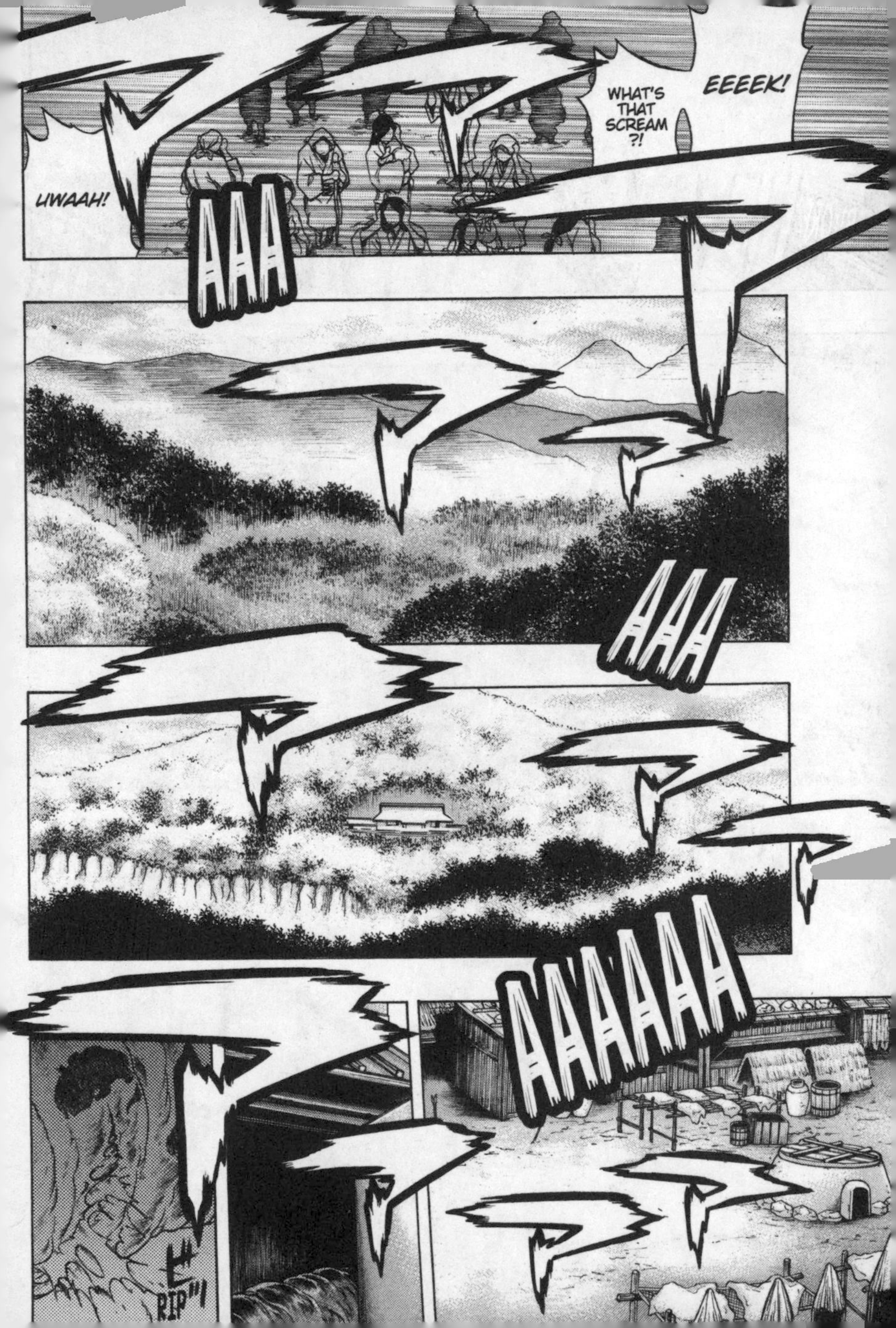
EEEEK!
WHAT'S THAT SCREAM ?!
UWAAH!
AAA
AAA
AAAAAA
RIP

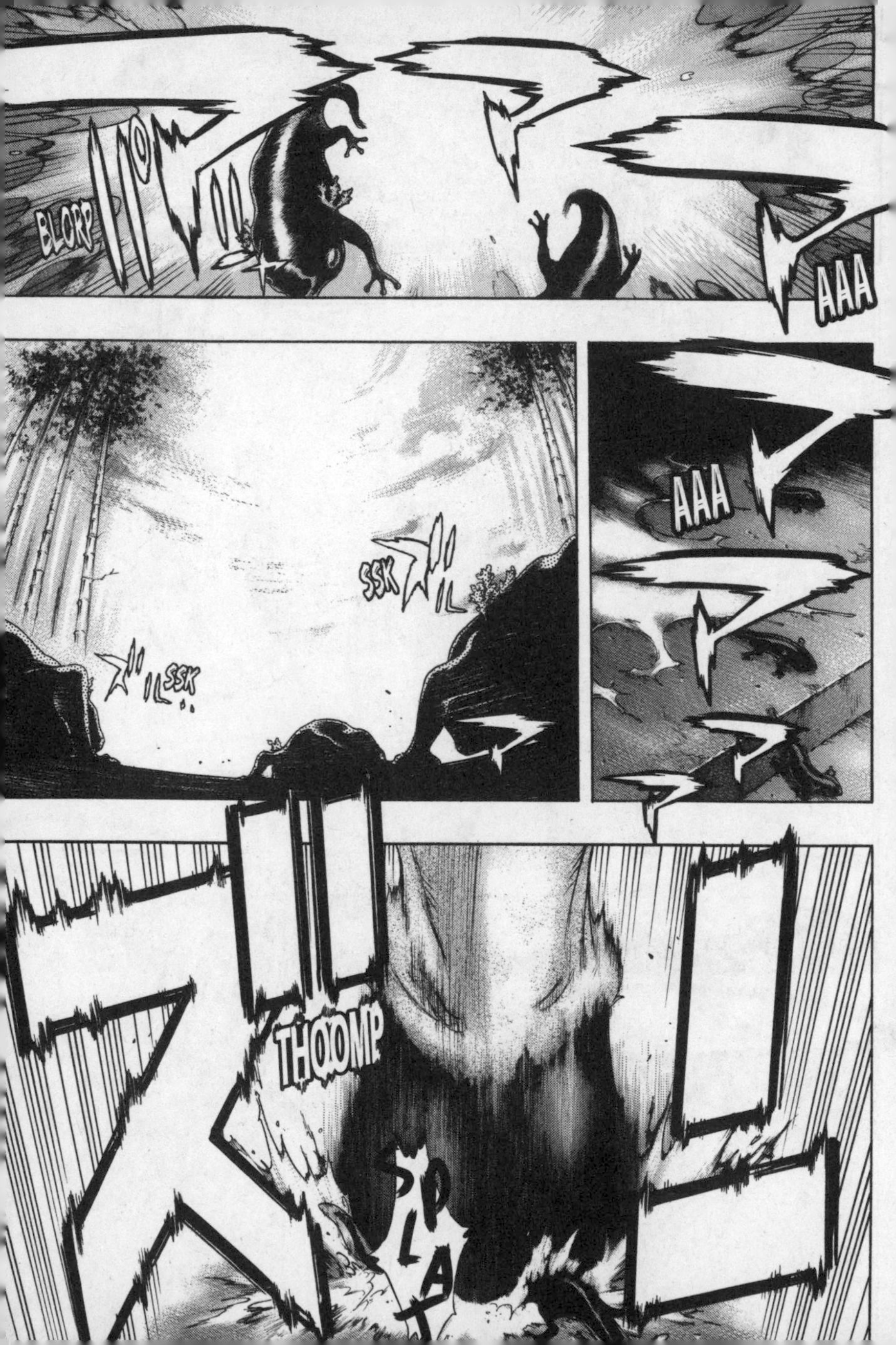
AAA
BLORP
AAA
SSK
SSK
THOOMP
SPLAT

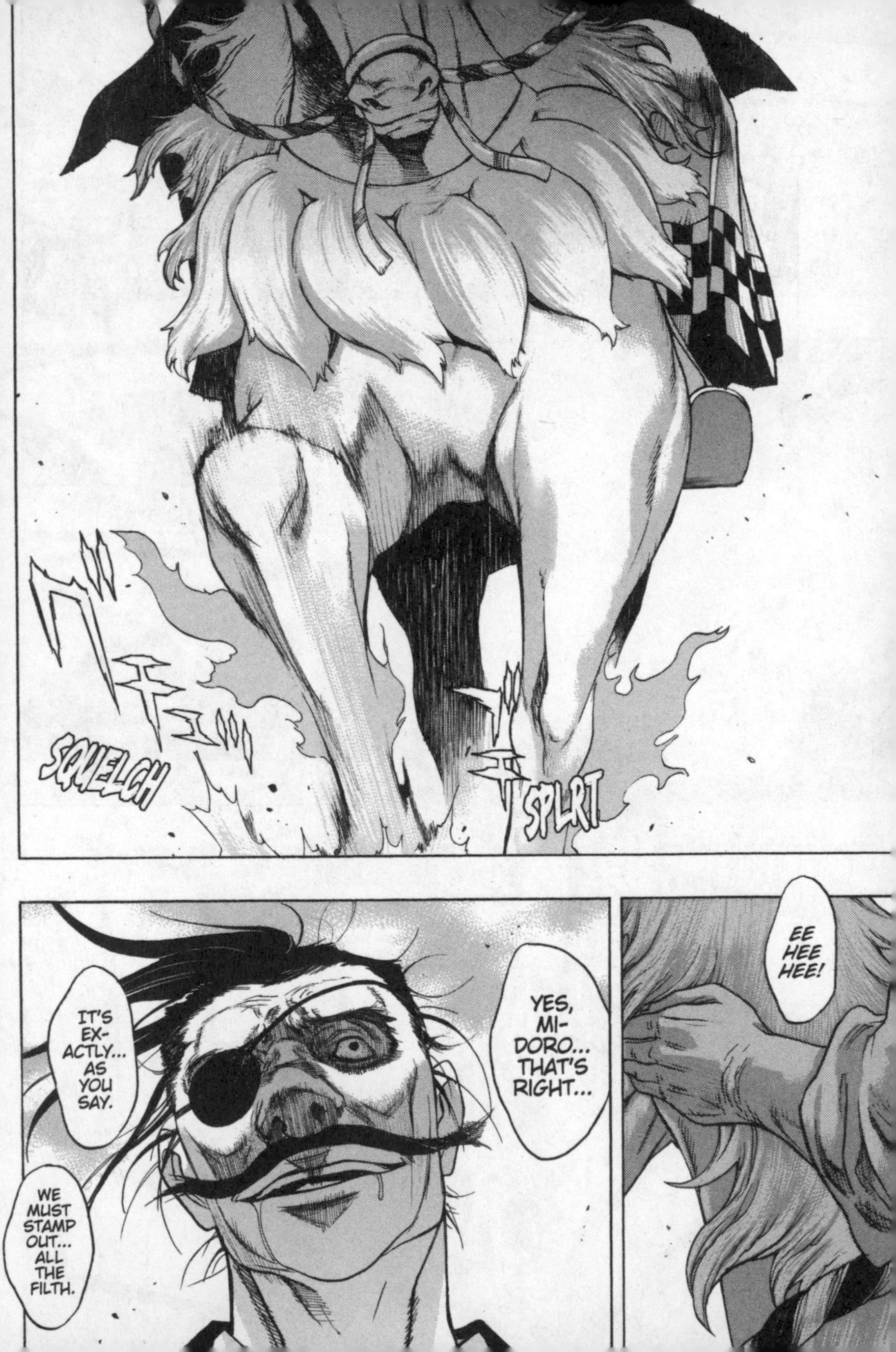
SQUELCH
SPLRT
EE HEE HEE!
YES, MI-DORO... THAT'S RIGHT...
IT'S EX-ACTLY... AS YOU SAY.
WE MUST STAMP OUT... ALL THE FILTH.

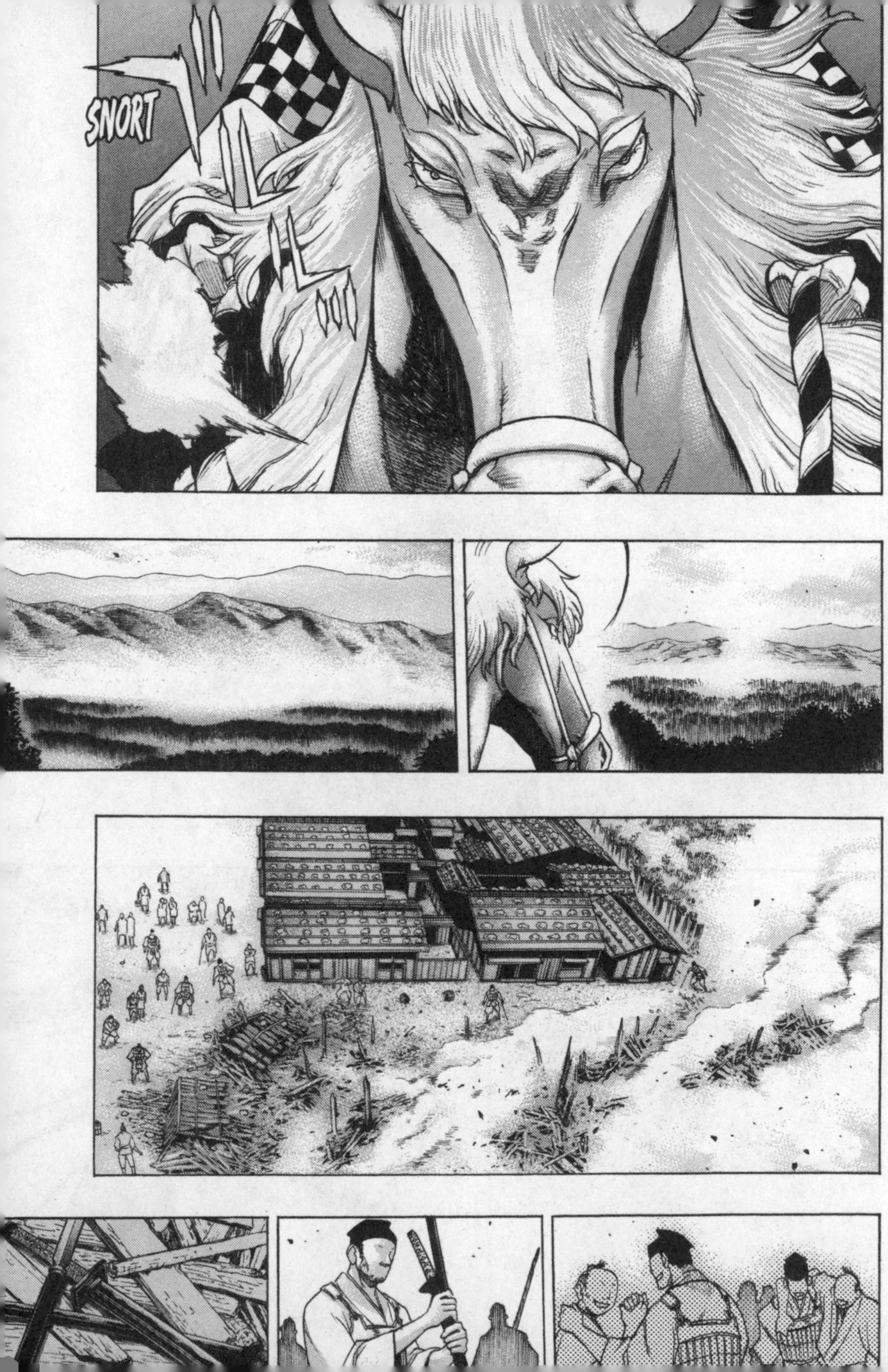
SNORT

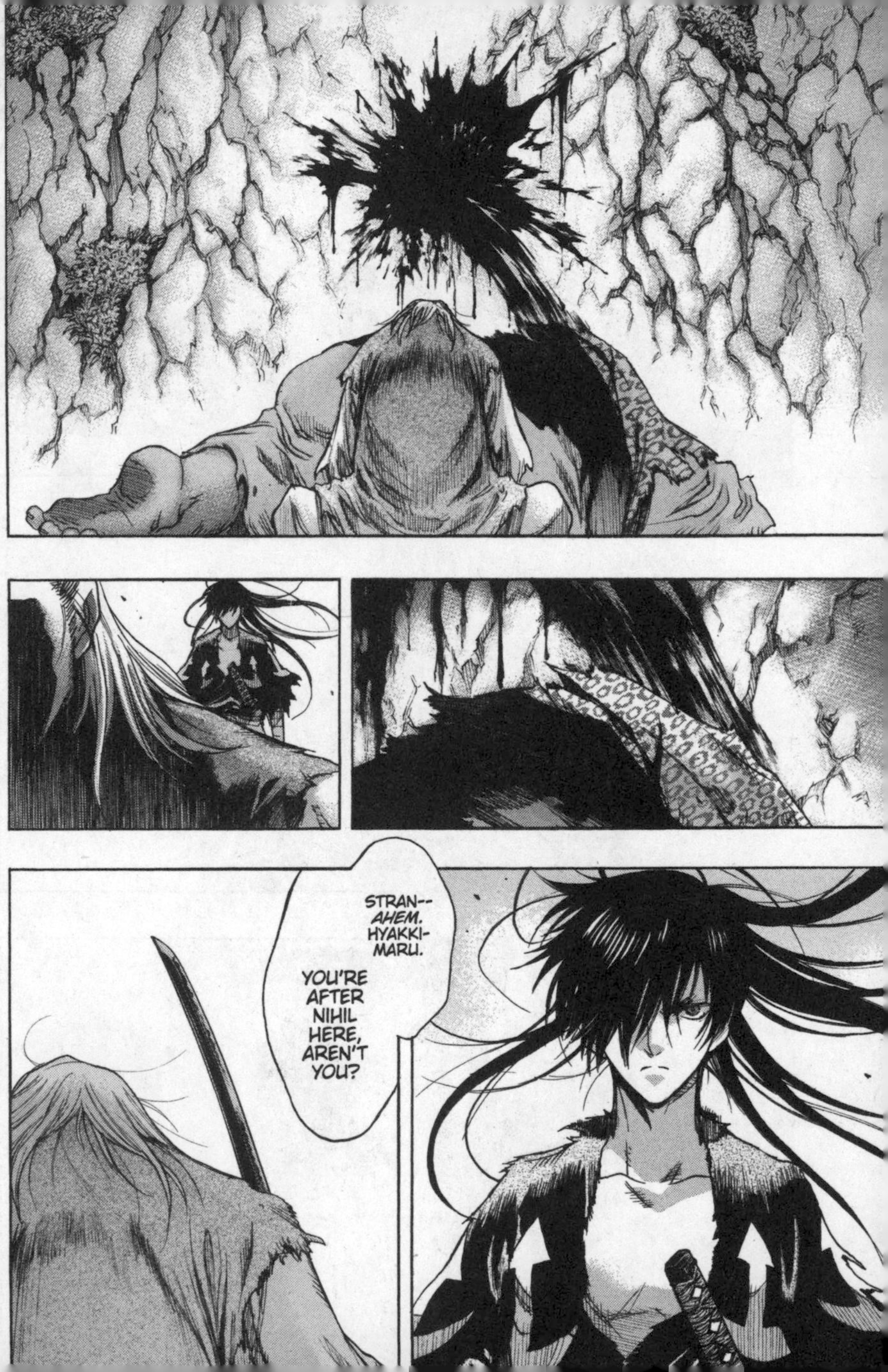
STRAN-- AHEM. HYAKKI-MARU.
YOU'RE AFTER NIHIL HERE, AREN'T YOU?

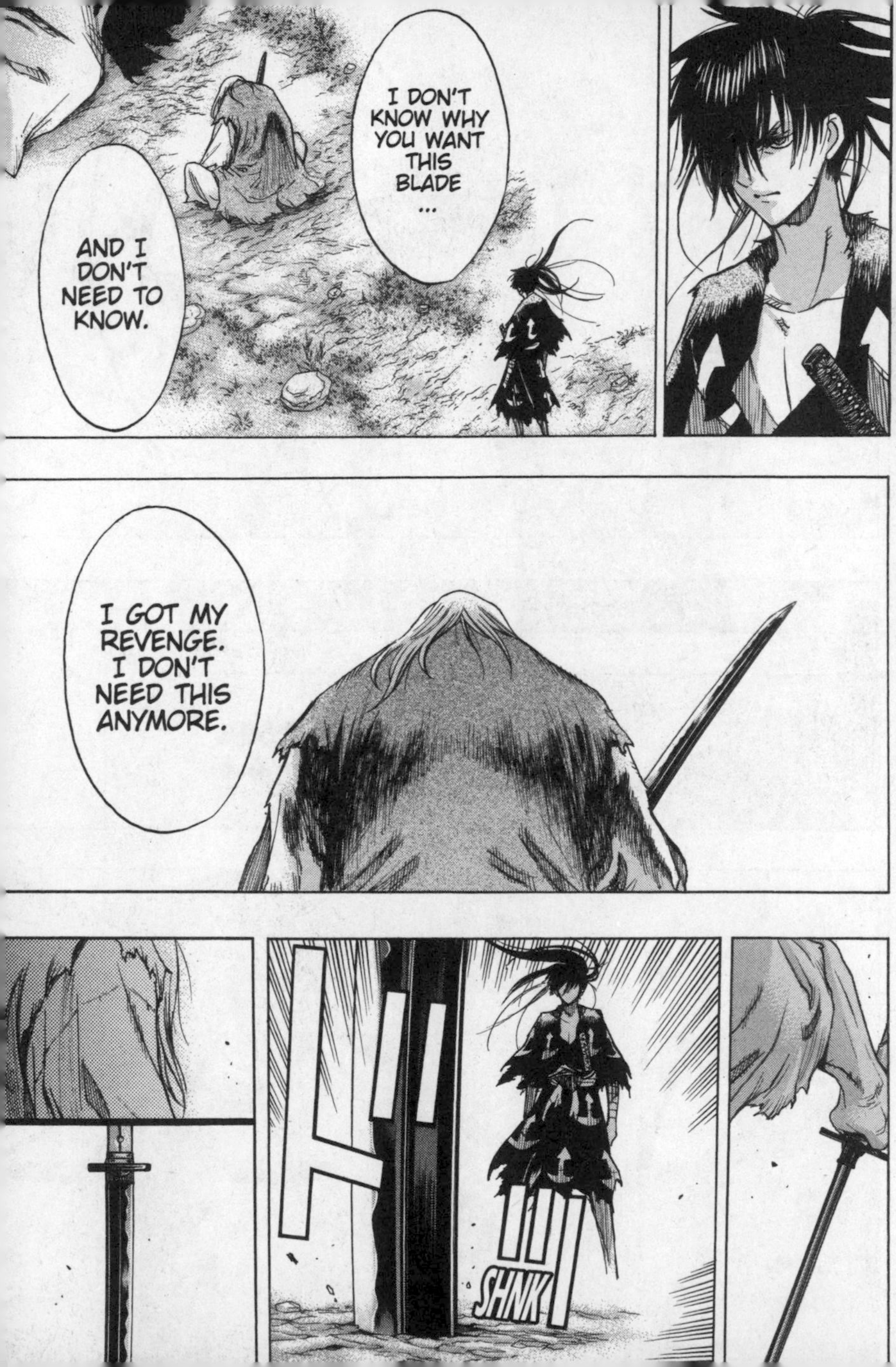
I DON'T KNOW WHY YOU WANT THIS BLADE ...
AND I DON'T NEED TO KNOW.
I GOT MY REVENGE. I DON'T NEED THIS ANYMORE.
SHNK

THANKS
FOR
LENDING ME
YOUR
STRENGTH
FOR SO
LONG.

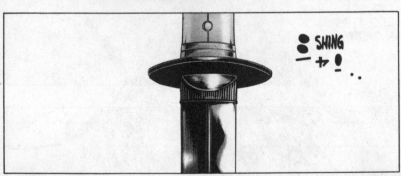

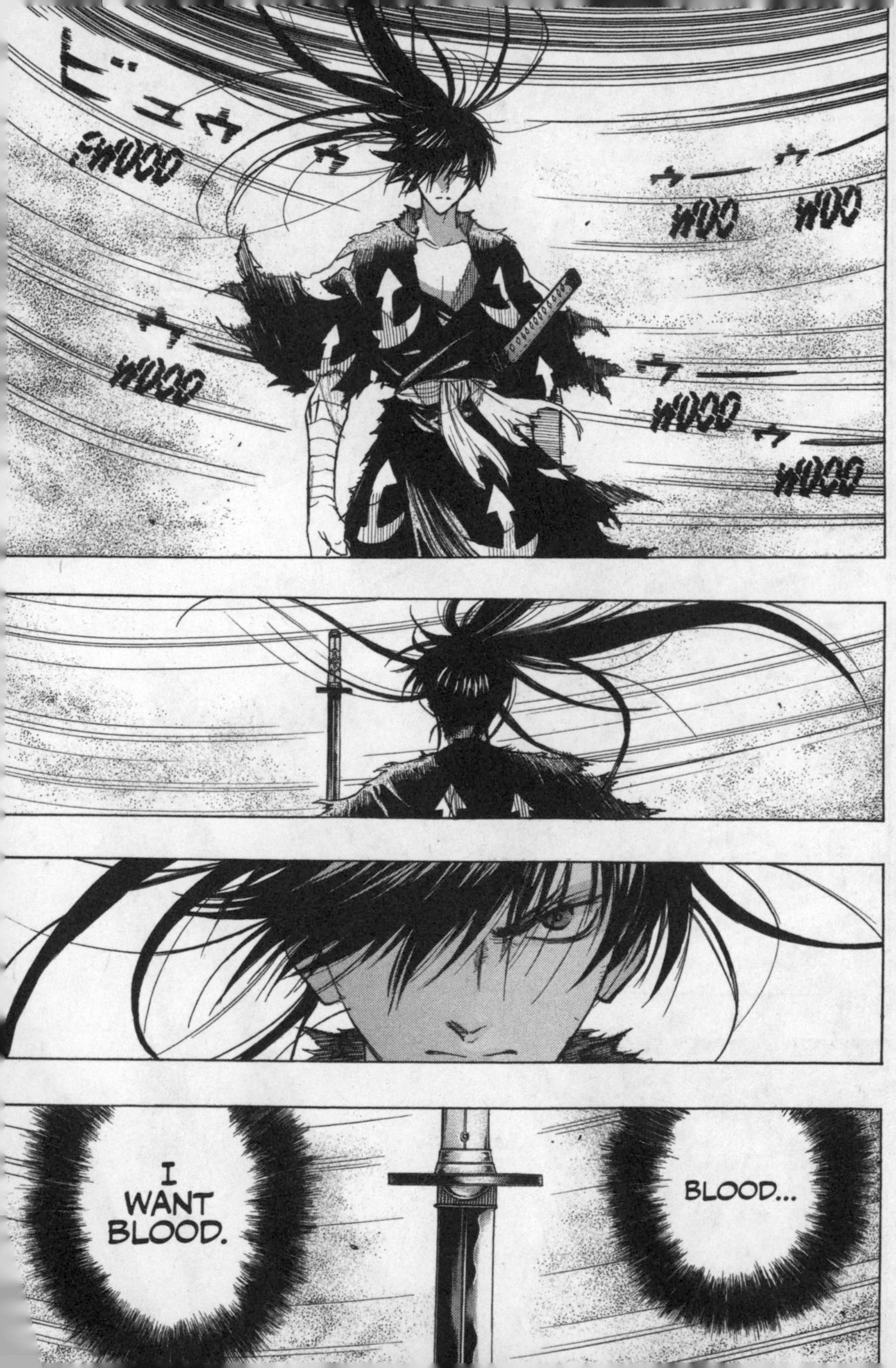
WOO WOO
WOOO
WOOO
FWOOO
WOOO
BLOOD...
I WANT BLOOD.

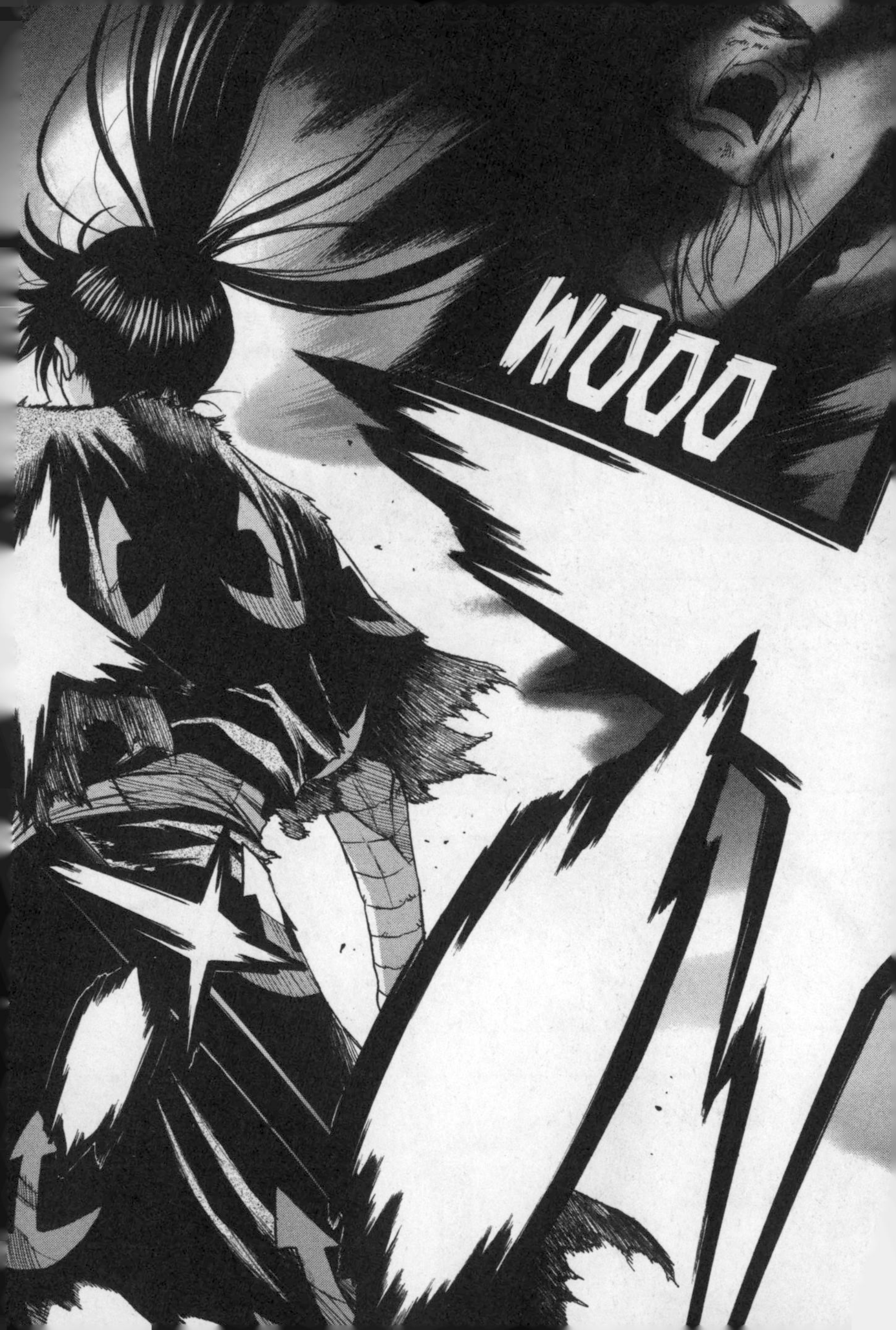
WOOO

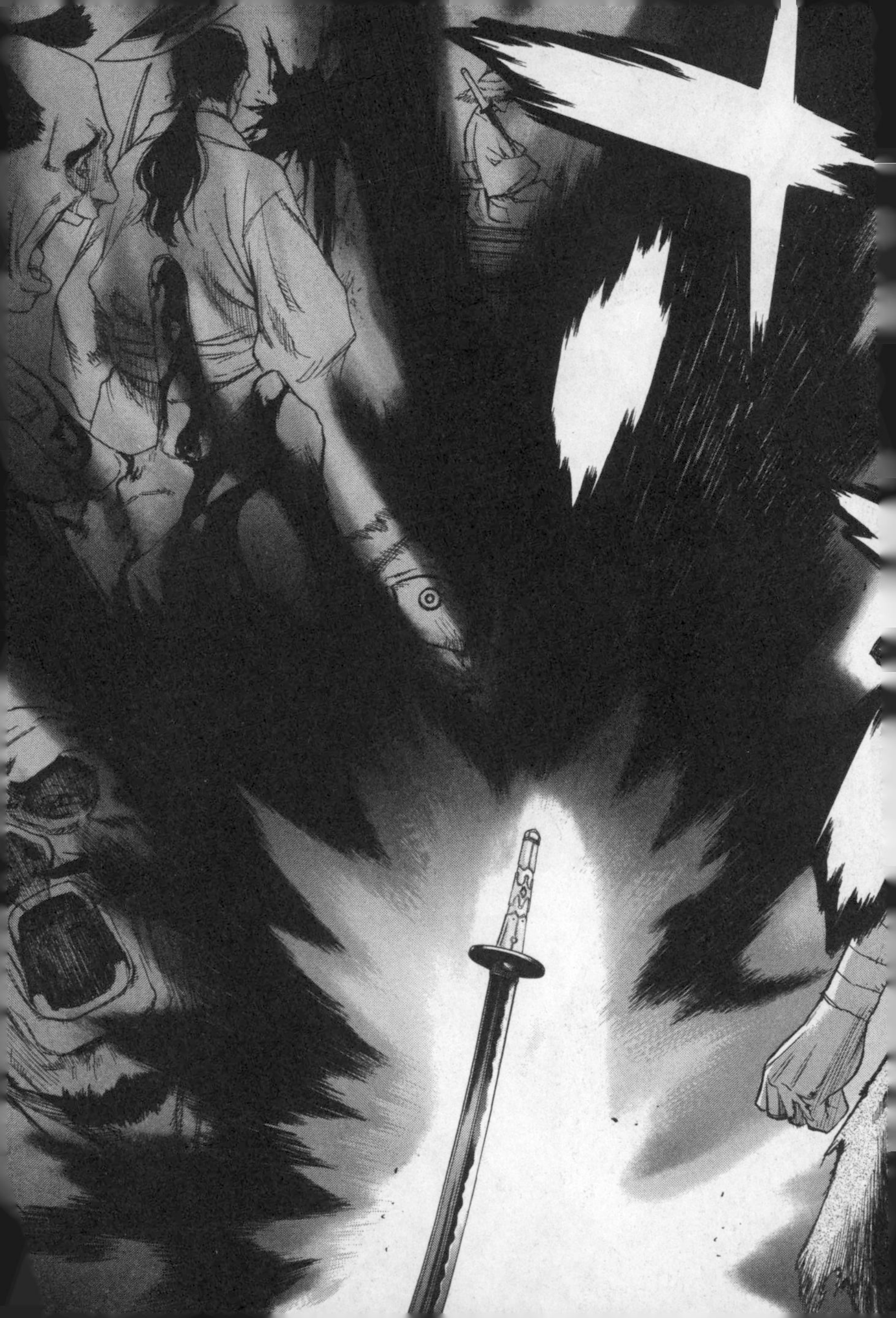

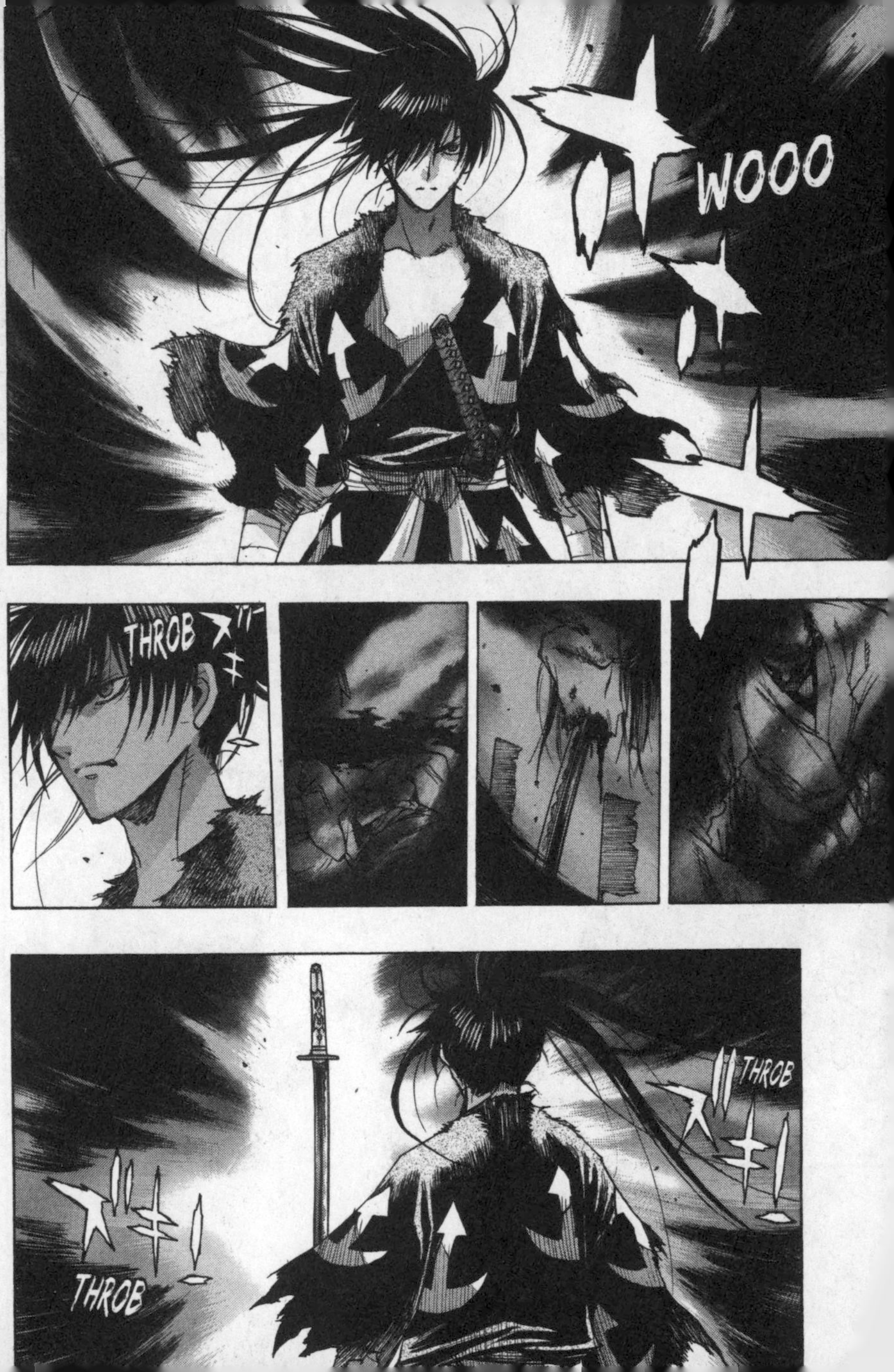
WOOO
THROB
THROB
THROB

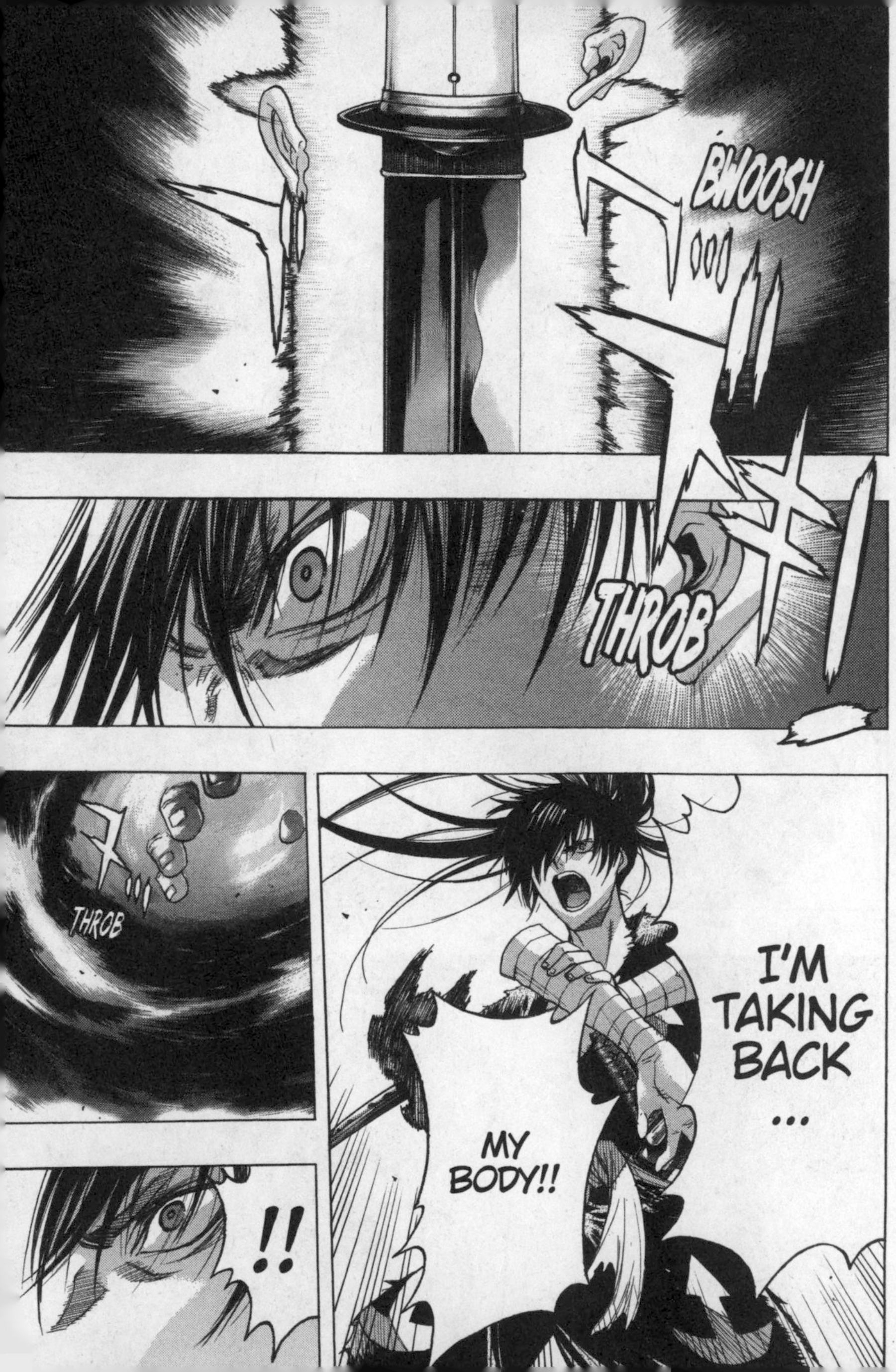
BWOOSH
THROB
I'M TAKING BACK ...
MY BODY!!
THROB
!!

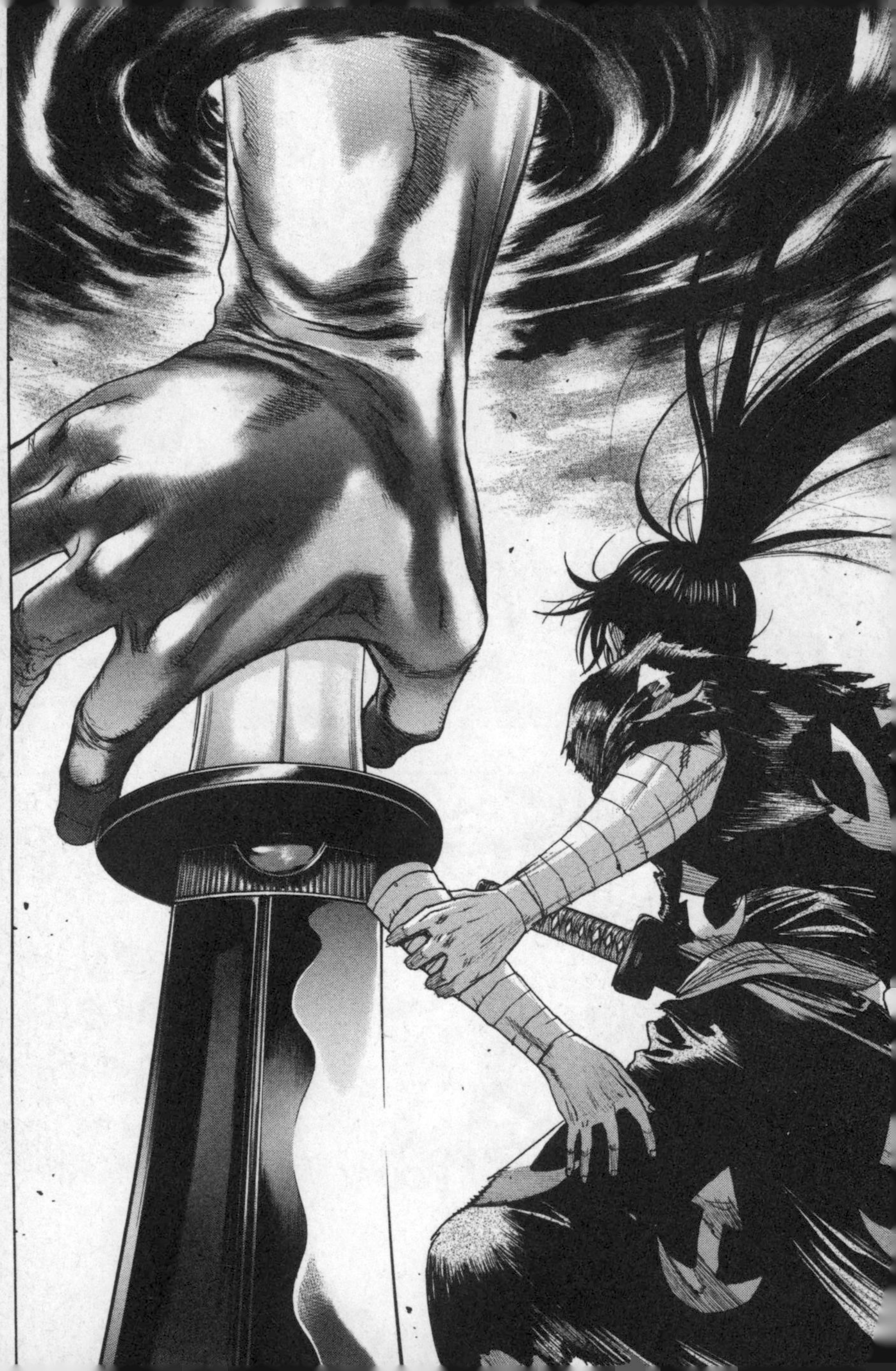

THE LEGEND OF
DORORO AND
HYAKKIMARU

どろろと
百鬼丸伝

THE LEGEND OF
DORORO AND **HYAKKIMARU**

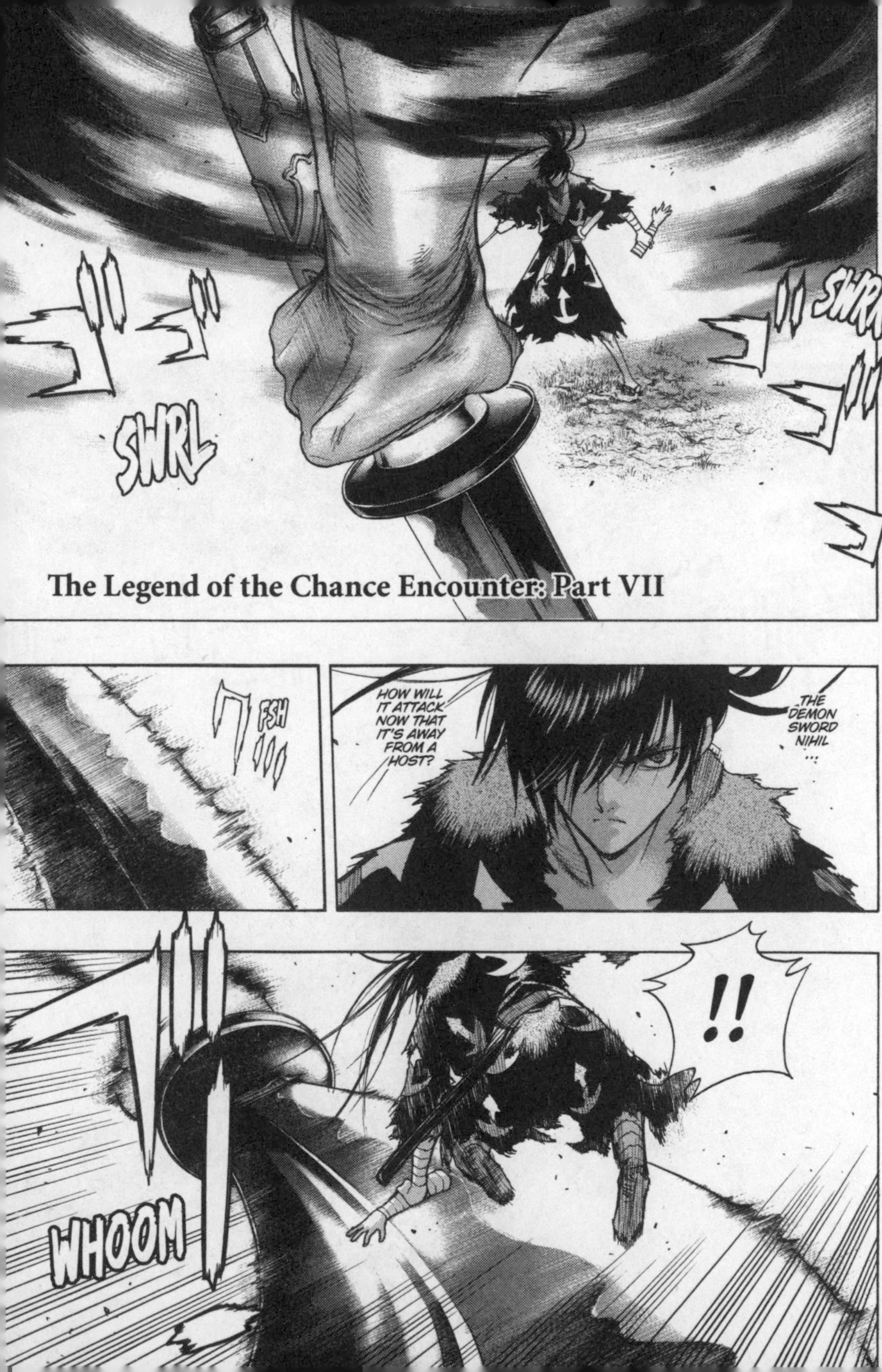
SWRRR
SWRL
The Legend of the Chance Encounter: Part VII
THE DEMON SWORD NIHIL ...
HOW WILL IT ATTACK NOW THAT IT'S AWAY FROM A HOST?
FSH
!!
WHOOM

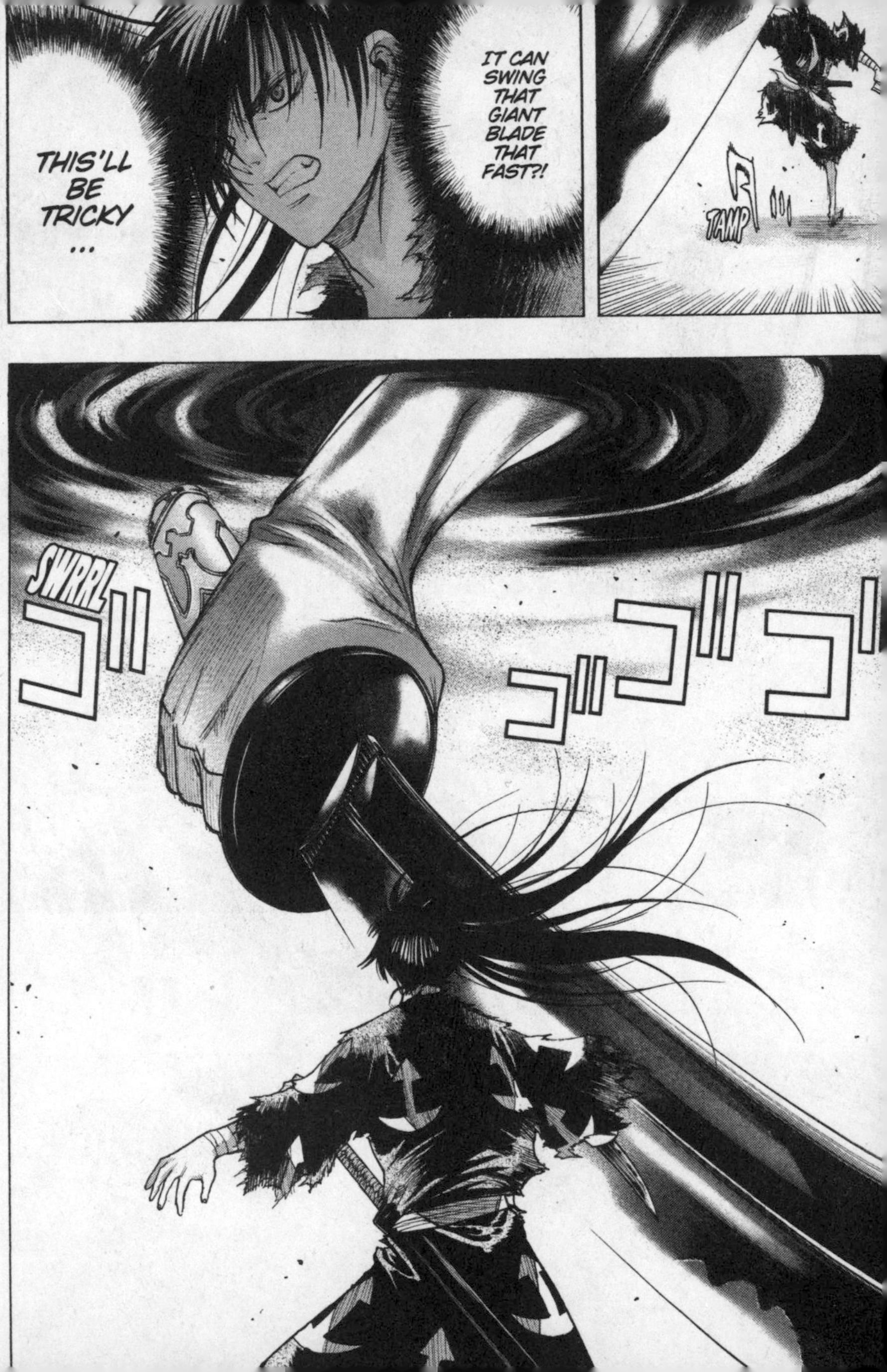
TAMP
IT CAN SWING THAT GIANT BLADE THAT FAST?!
THIS'LL BE TRICKY ...
SWRRL
ゴゴゴゴ

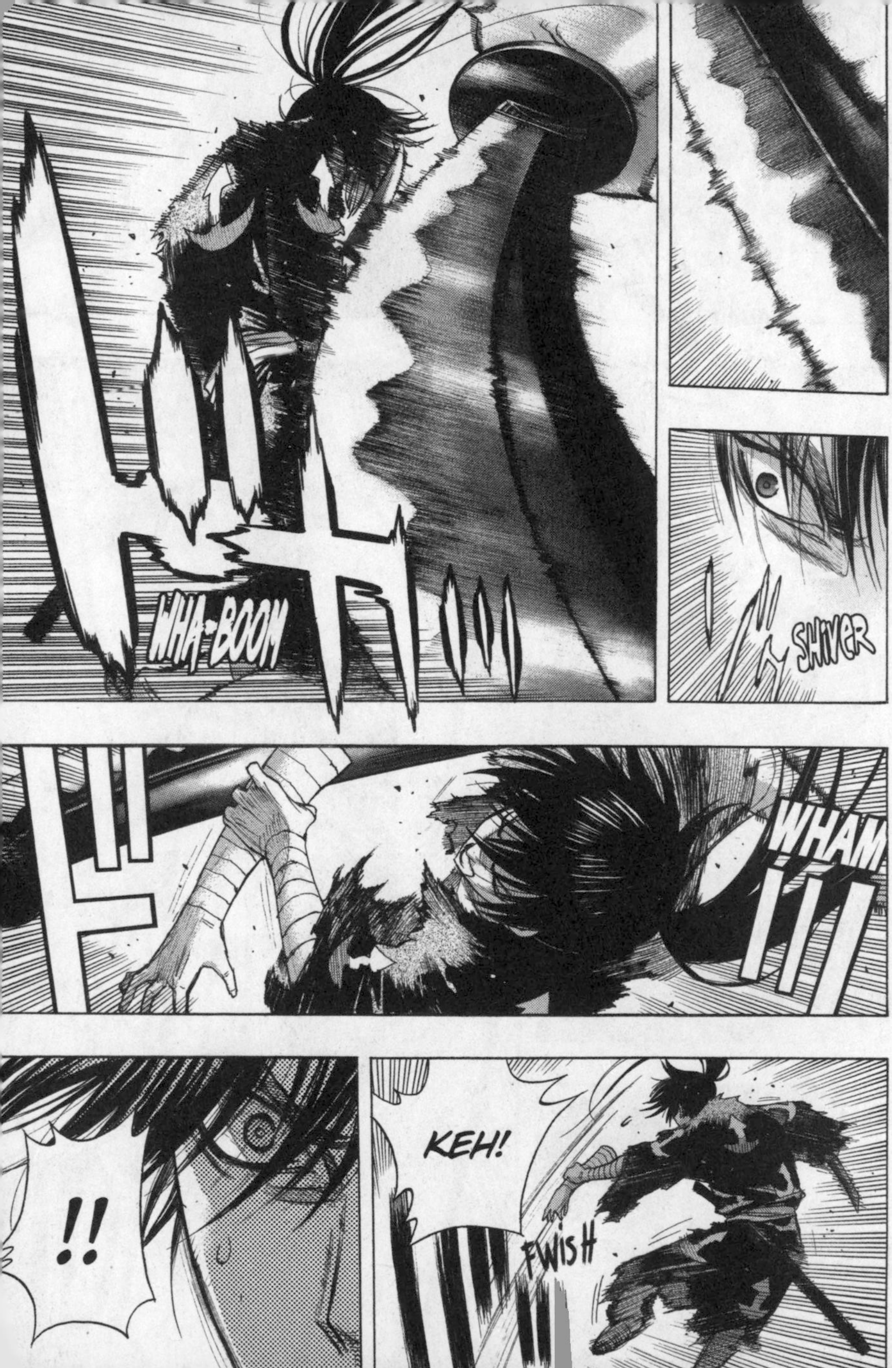
SHIVER
WHA-BOOM
WHAM
KEH!
FWISH
!!

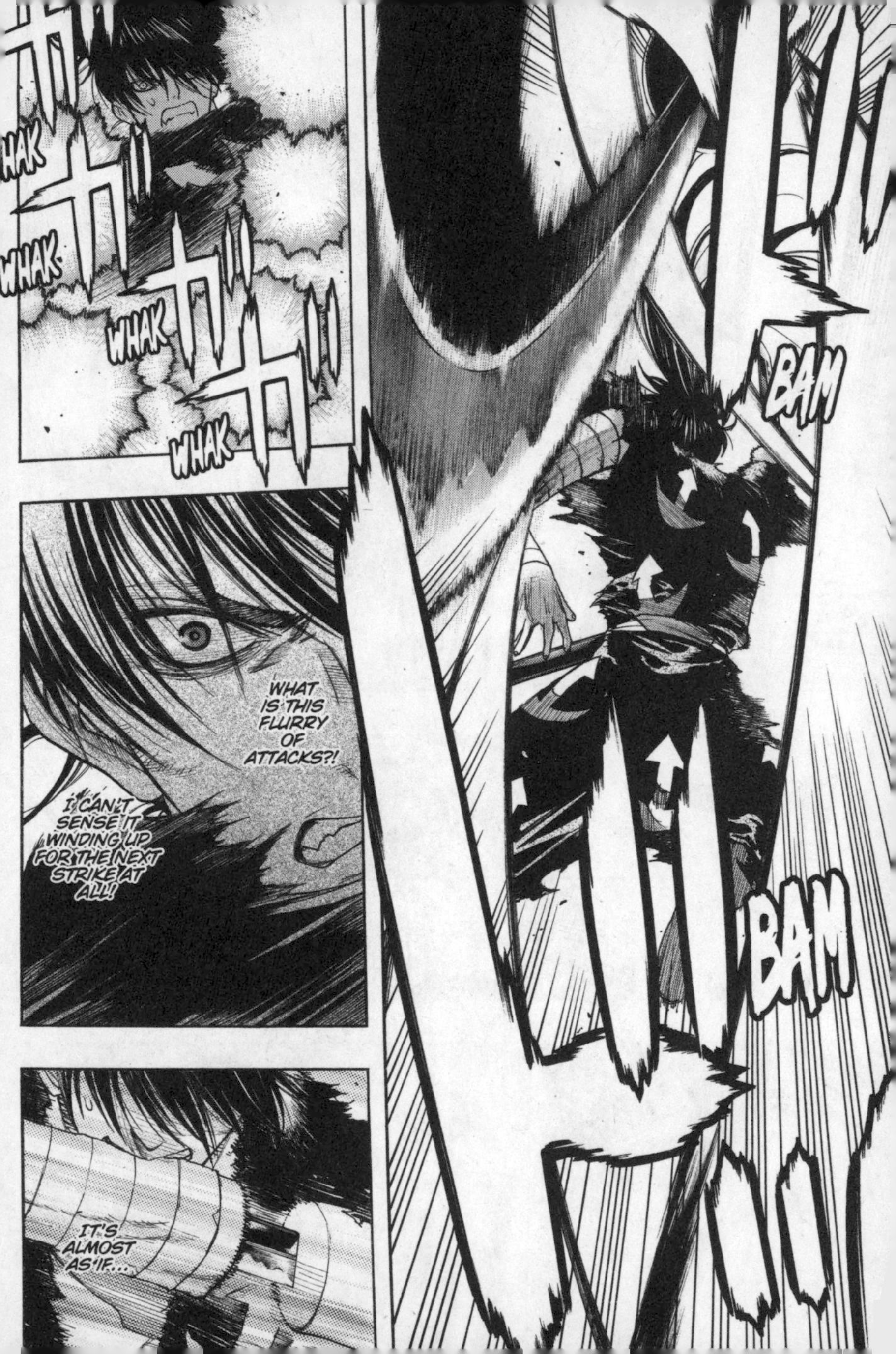
BAM
BAM
HAK
WHAK
WHAK
WHAK
WHAT IS THIS FLURRY OF ATTACKS?!
I CAN'T SENSE IT WINDING UP FOR THE NEXT STRIKE AT ALL!
IT'S ALMOST AS IF...

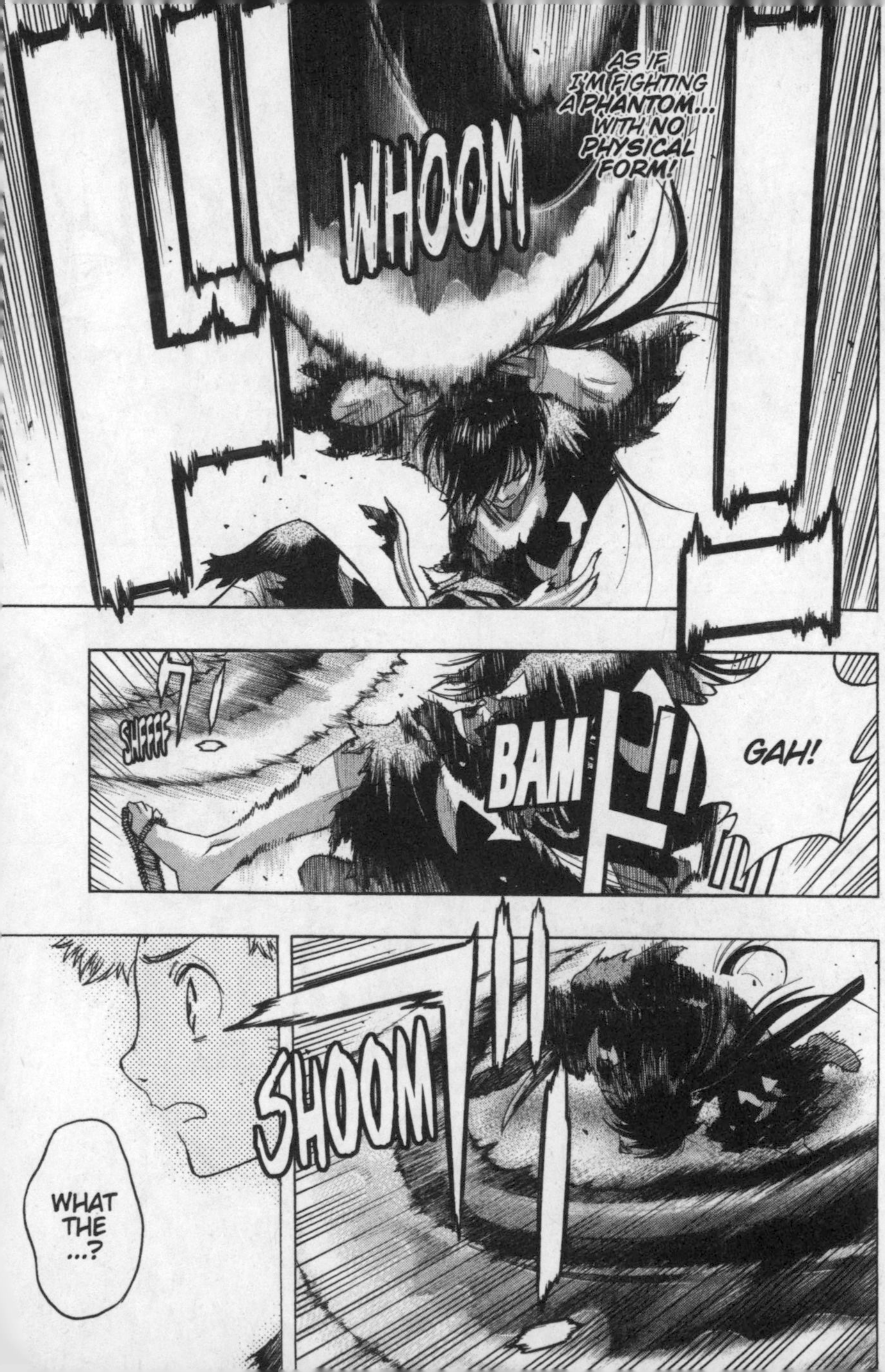
AS IF I'M FIGHTING A PHANTOM... WITH NO PHYSICAL FORM!
WHOOM
GAH!
BAM
SHFFFF
SHOOM
WHAT THE ...?

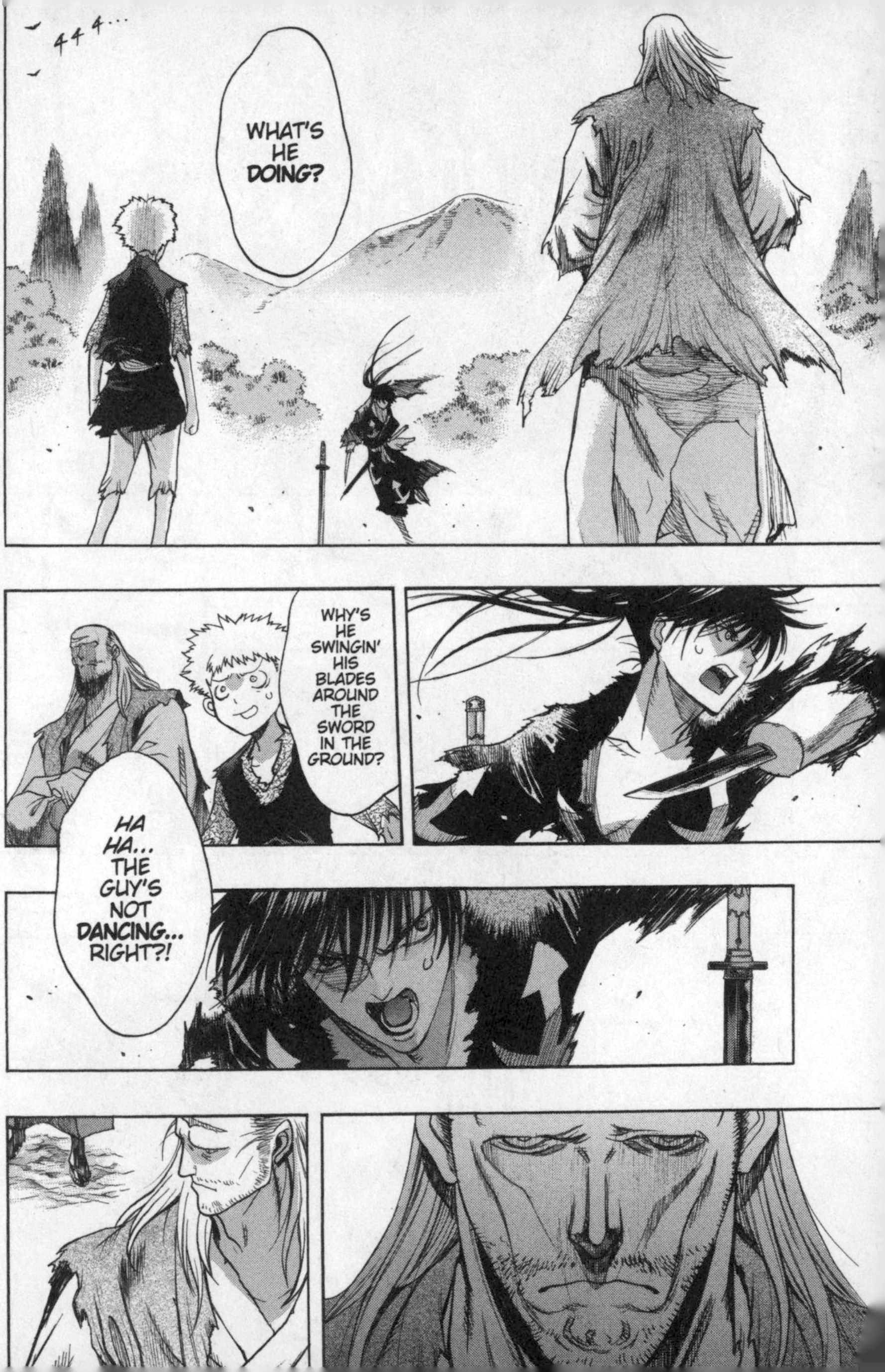

444...
WHAT'S HE DOING?
WHY'S HE SWINGIN' HIS BLADES AROUND THE SWORD IN THE GROUND?
HA HA... THE GUY'S NOT DANCING... RIGHT?!

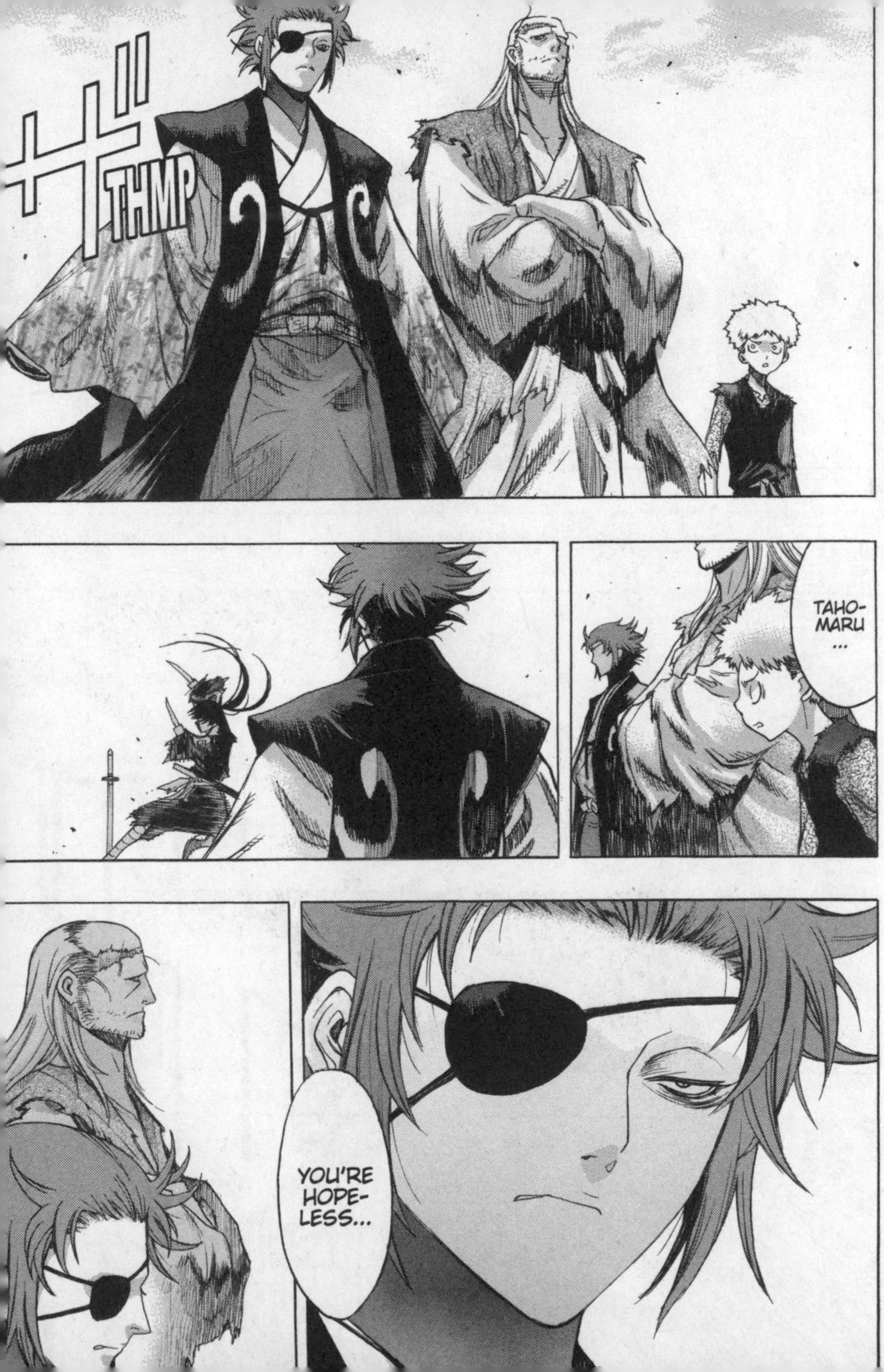
THMP
TAHO-MARU...
YOU'RE HOPE-LESS...

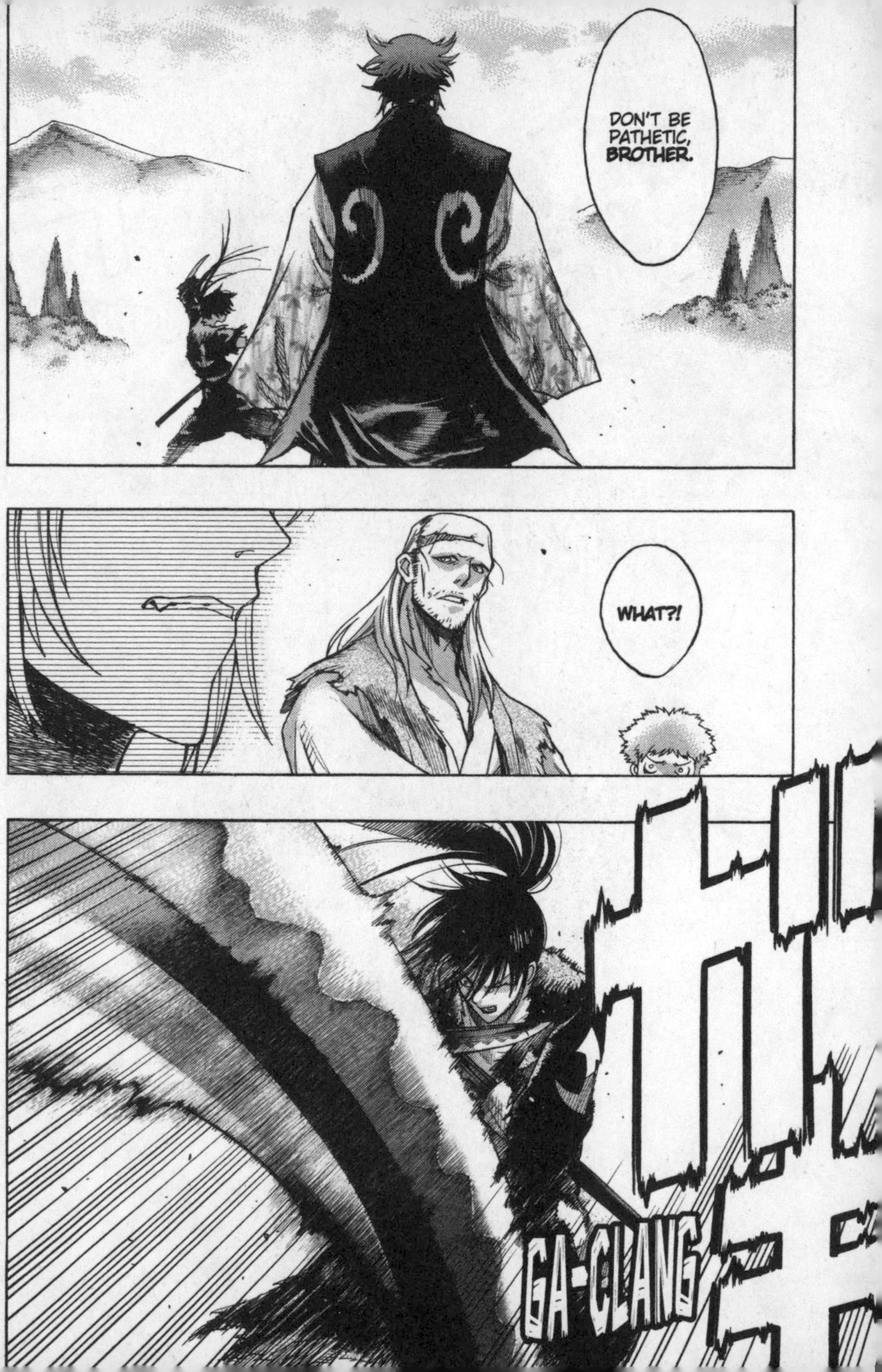
DON'T BE PATHETIC, BROTHER.
WHAT?!
GA-CLANG

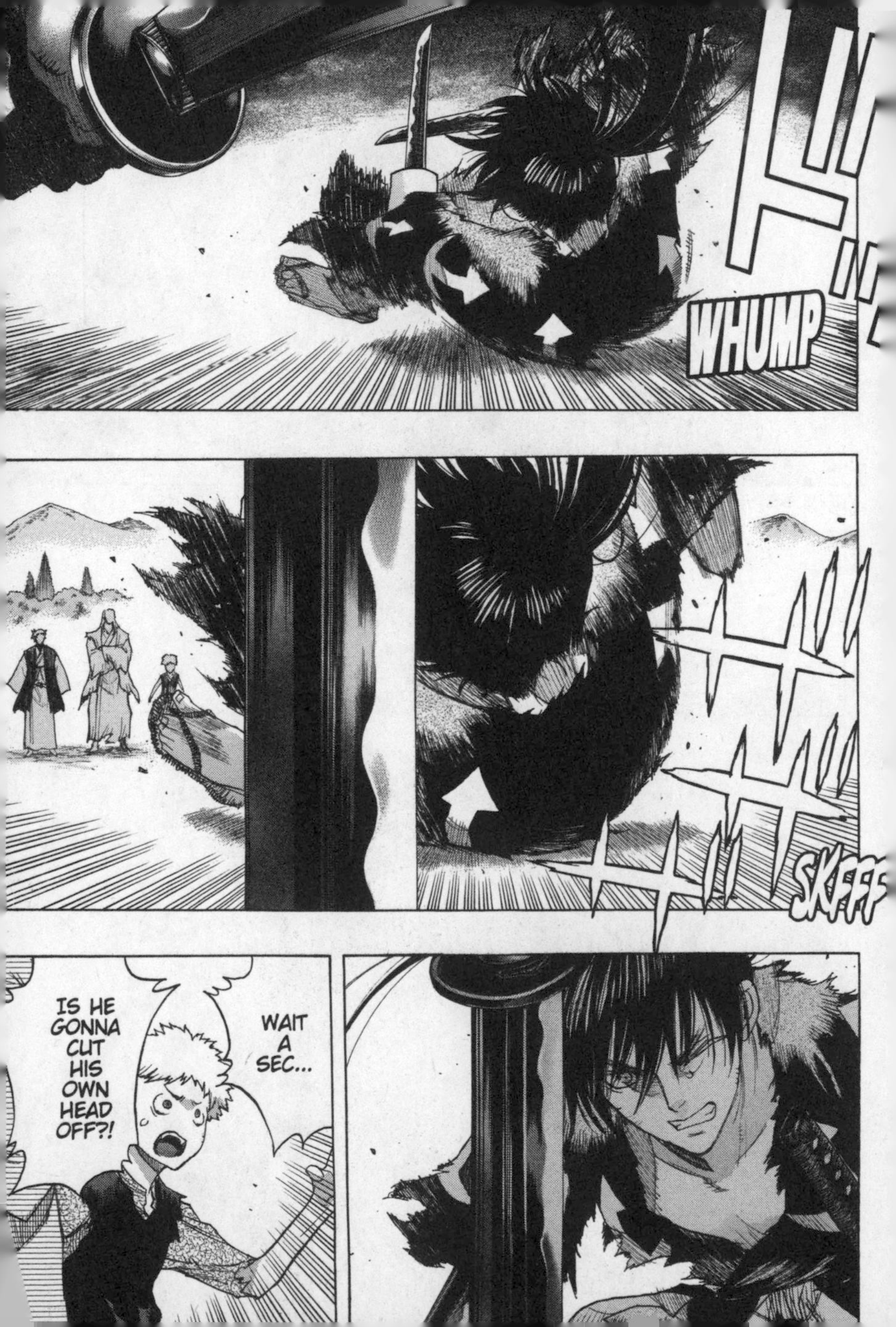
WHUMP
SKFFF
WAIT A SEC...
IS HE GONNA CUT HIS OWN HEAD OFF?!

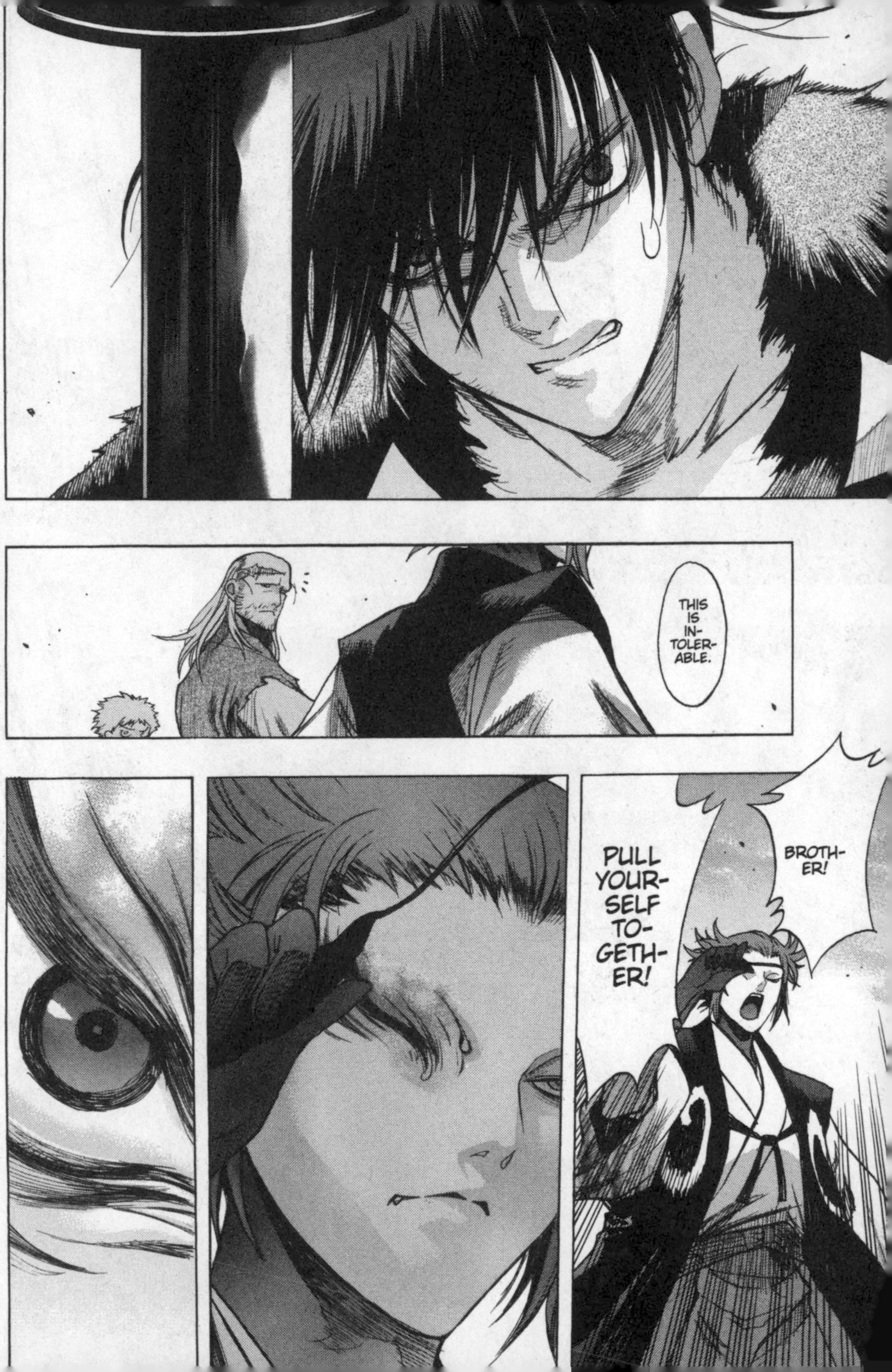
THIS IS IN-TOLERABLE.
BROTH-ER!
PULL YOUR-SELF TO-GETH-ER!

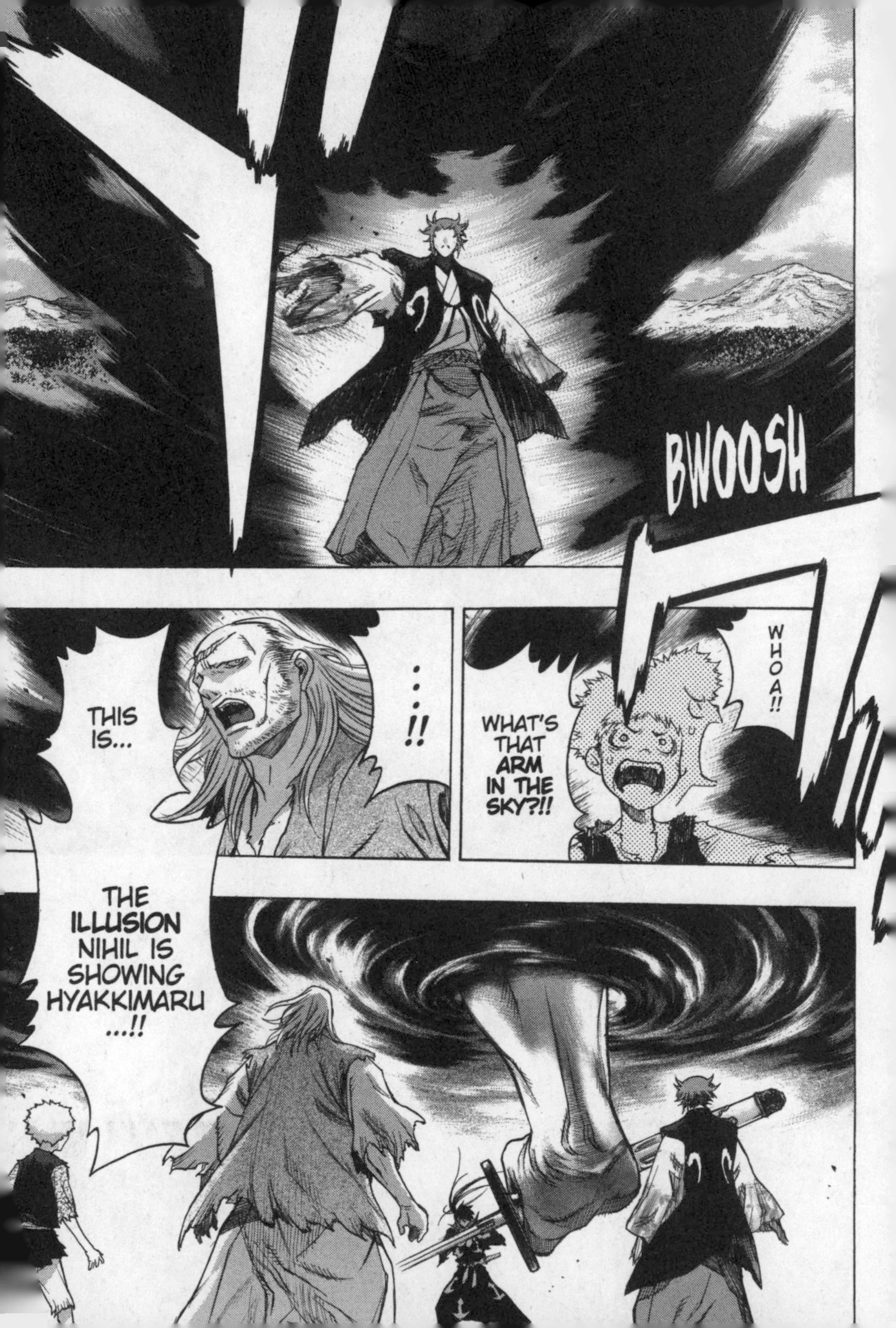
BWOOSH
WHOA!!
WHAT'S THAT ARM IN THE SKY?!!
...!!
THIS IS...
THE ILLUSION NIHIL IS SHOWING HYAKKIMARU ...!!

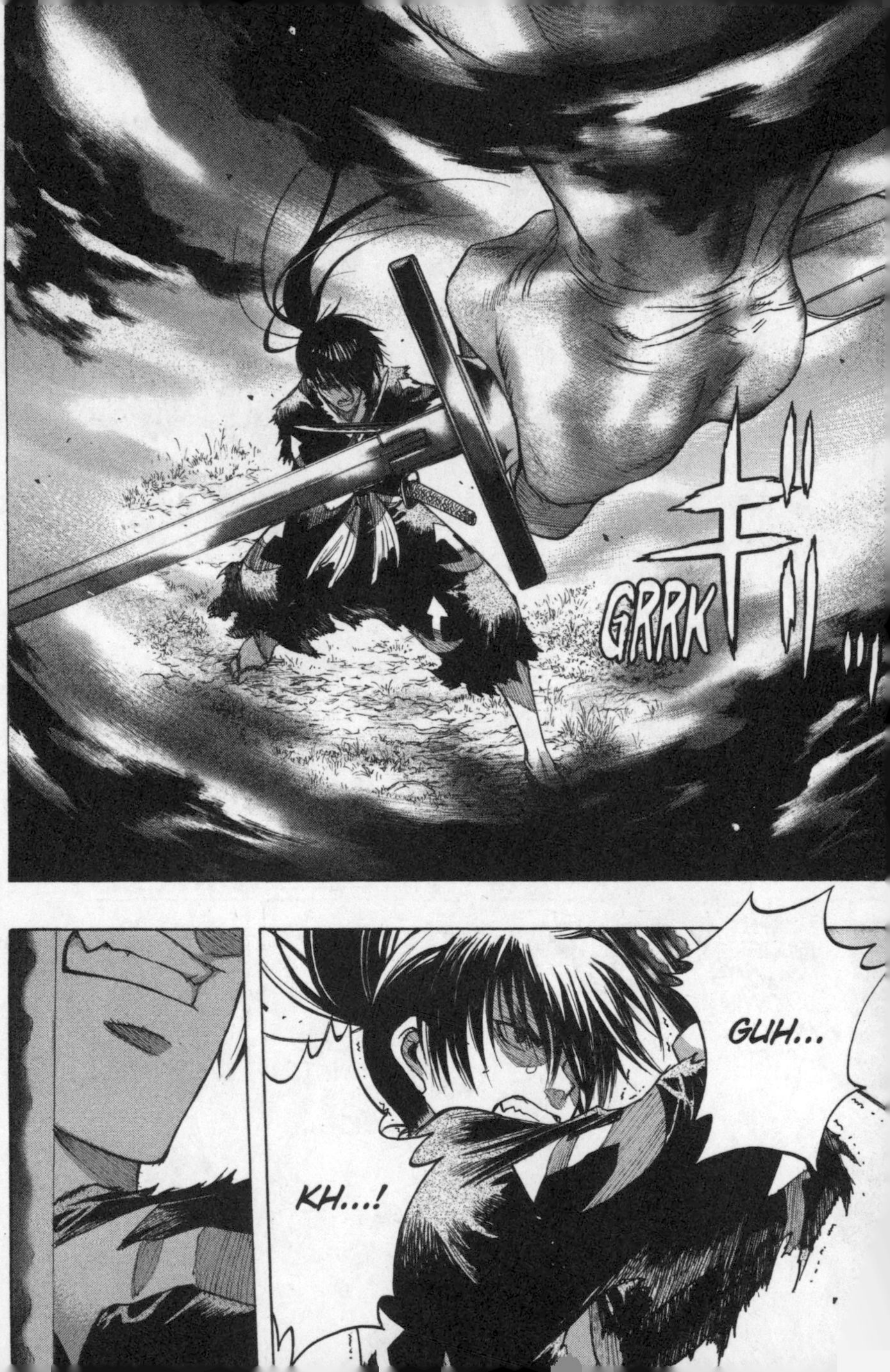
GRRK
GUH...
KH...!

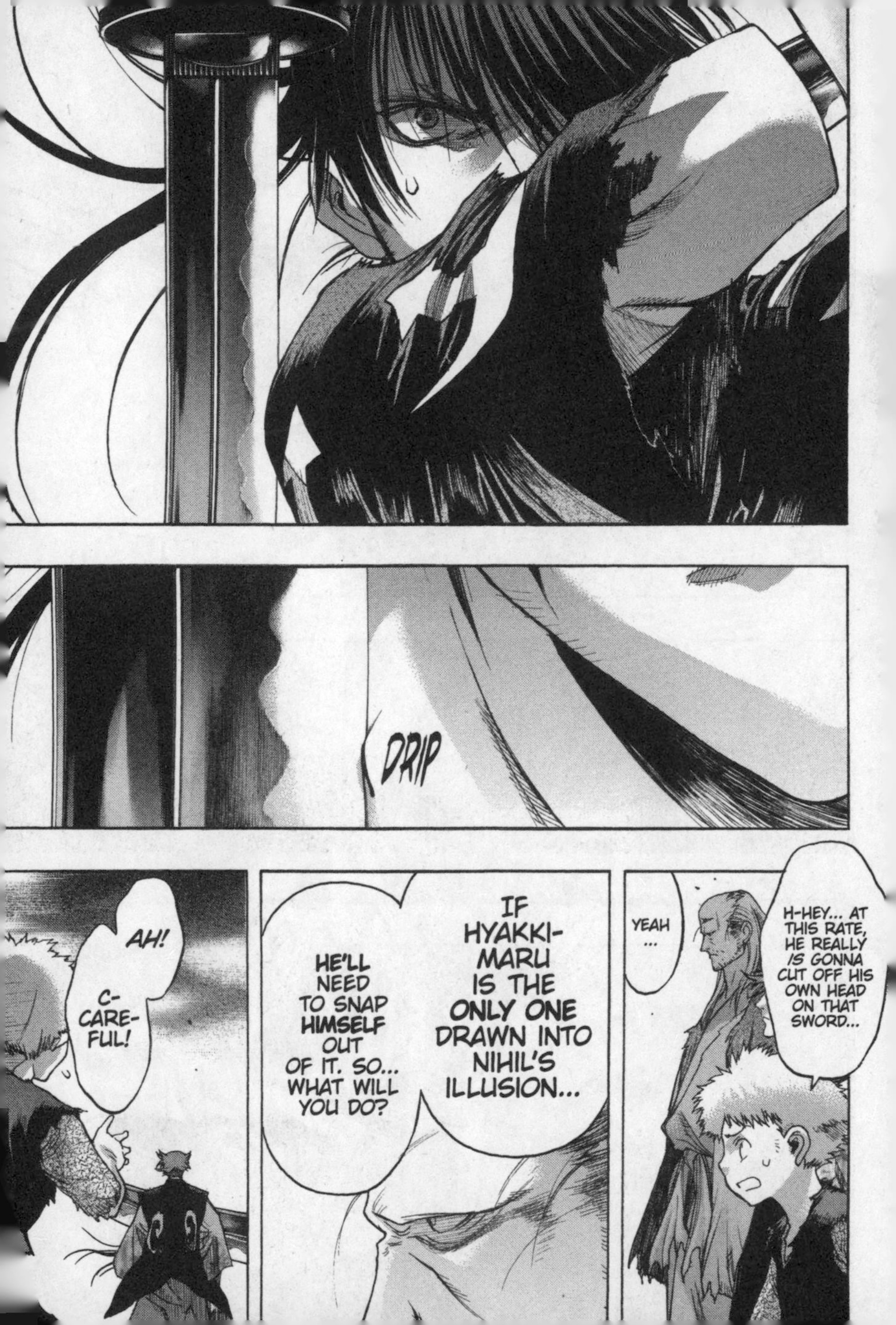
DRIP
H-HEY... AT THIS RATE, HE REALLY IS GONNA CUT OFF HIS OWN HEAD ON THAT SWORD...
YEAH ...
IF HYAKKI-MARU IS THE ONLY ONE DRAWN INTO NIHIL'S ILLUSION...
HE'LL NEED TO SNAP HIMSELF OUT OF IT. SO... WHAT WILL YOU DO?
AH!
C-CAREFUL!

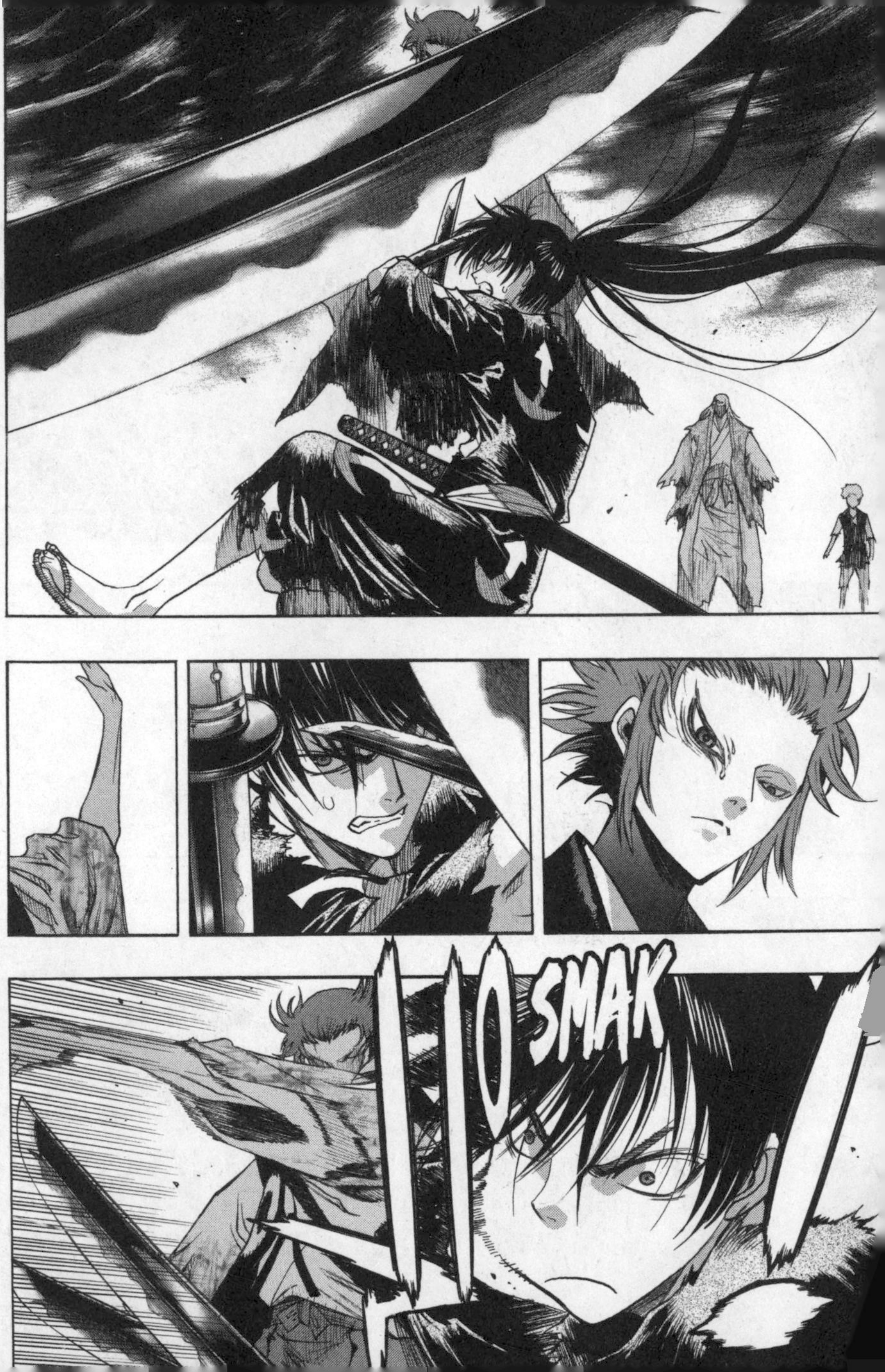
SMAK

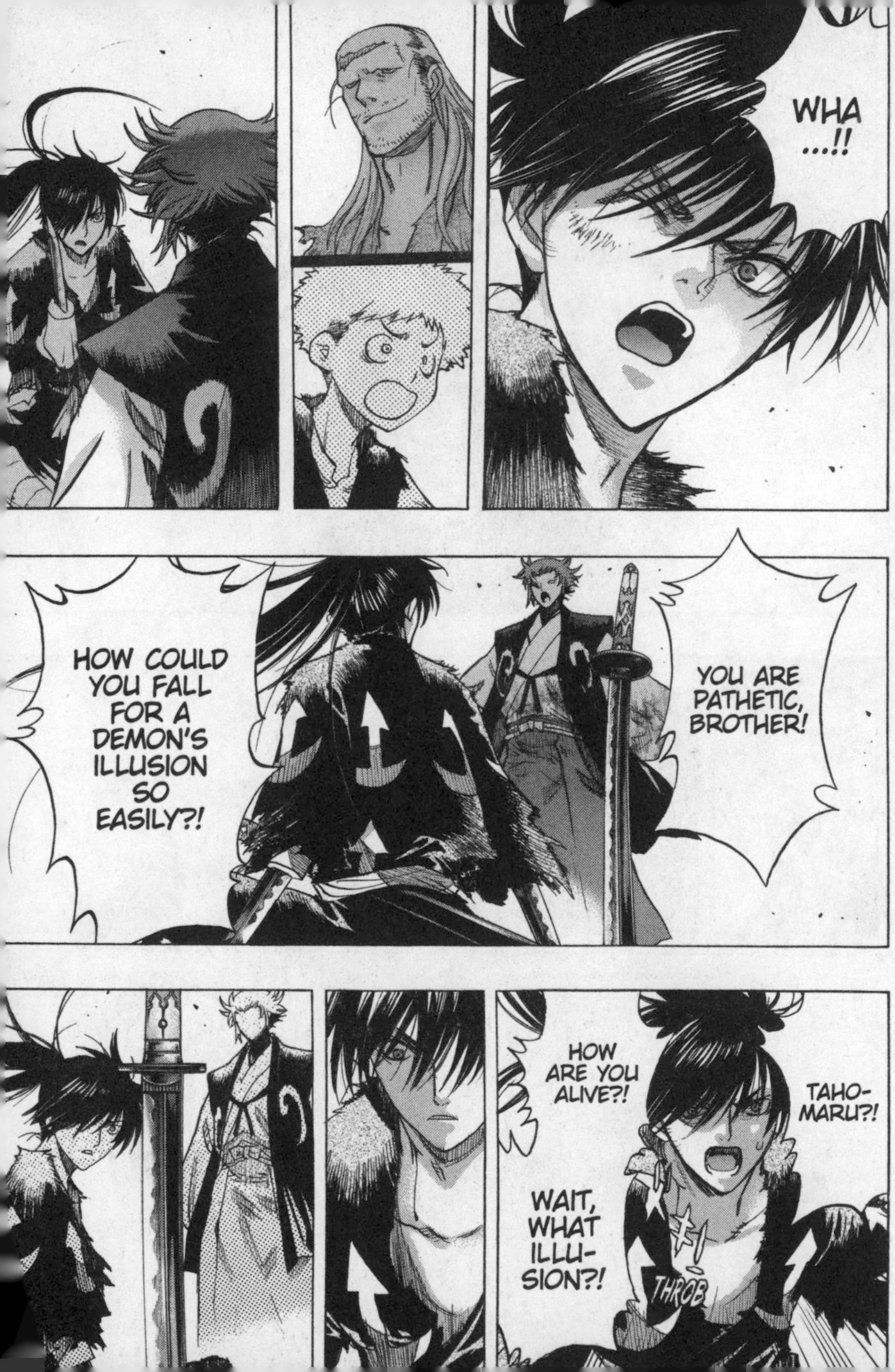
WHA ...!!
YOU ARE PATHETIC, BROTHER!
HOW COULD YOU FALL FOR A DEMON'S ILLUSION SO EASILY?!
TAHO-MARU?!
HOW ARE YOU ALIVE?!
WAIT, WHAT ILLU-SION?!
THROB

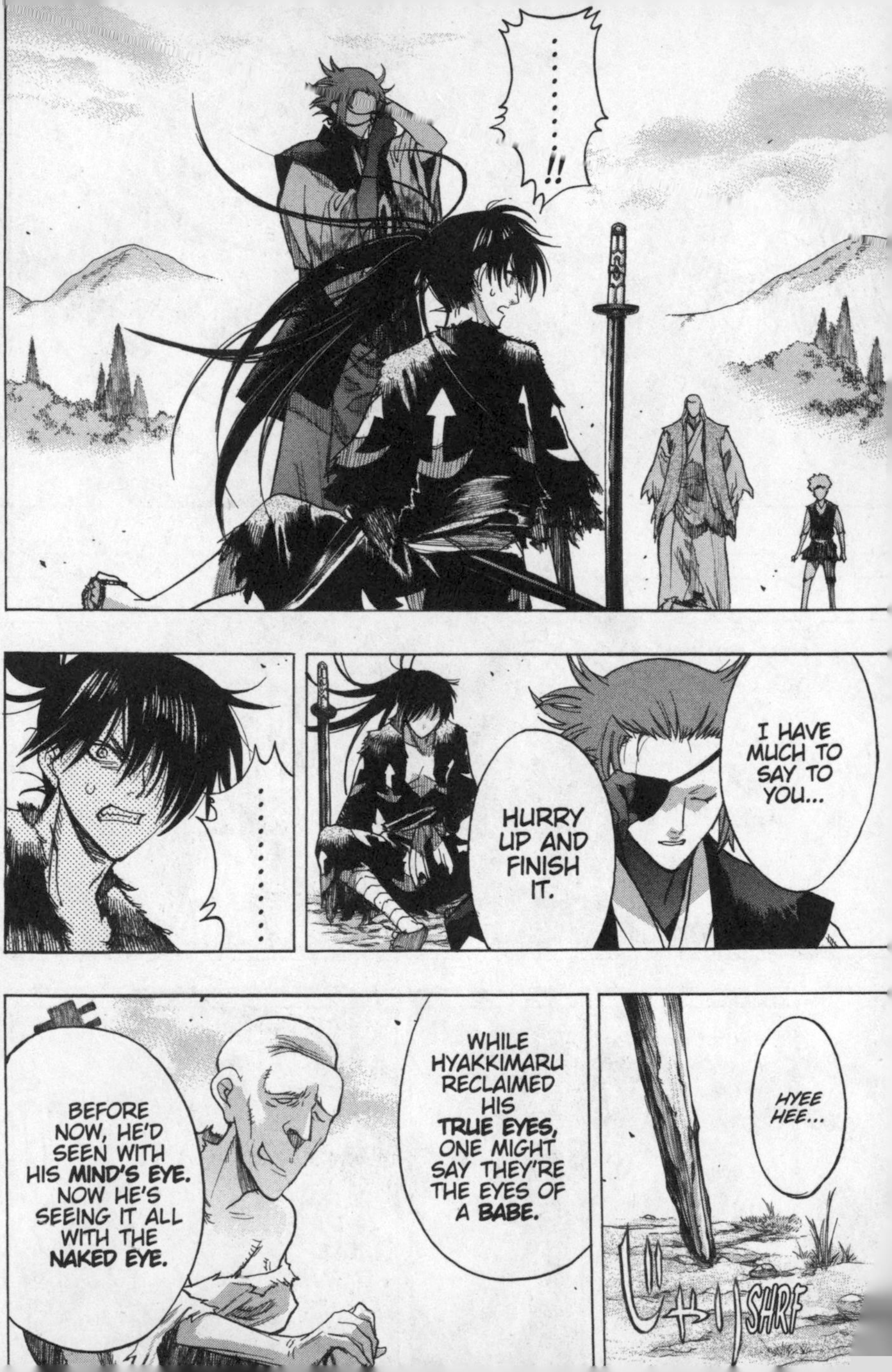
......!!
I HAVE MUCH TO SAY TO YOU...
HURRY UP AND FINISH IT.
......
HYEE HEE...
SHRF
WHILE HYAKKIMARU RECLAIMED HIS TRUE EYES, ONE MIGHT SAY THEY'RE THE EYES OF A BABE.
BEFORE NOW, HE'D SEEN WITH HIS MIND'S EYE. NOW HE'S SEEING IT ALL WITH THE NAKED EYE.

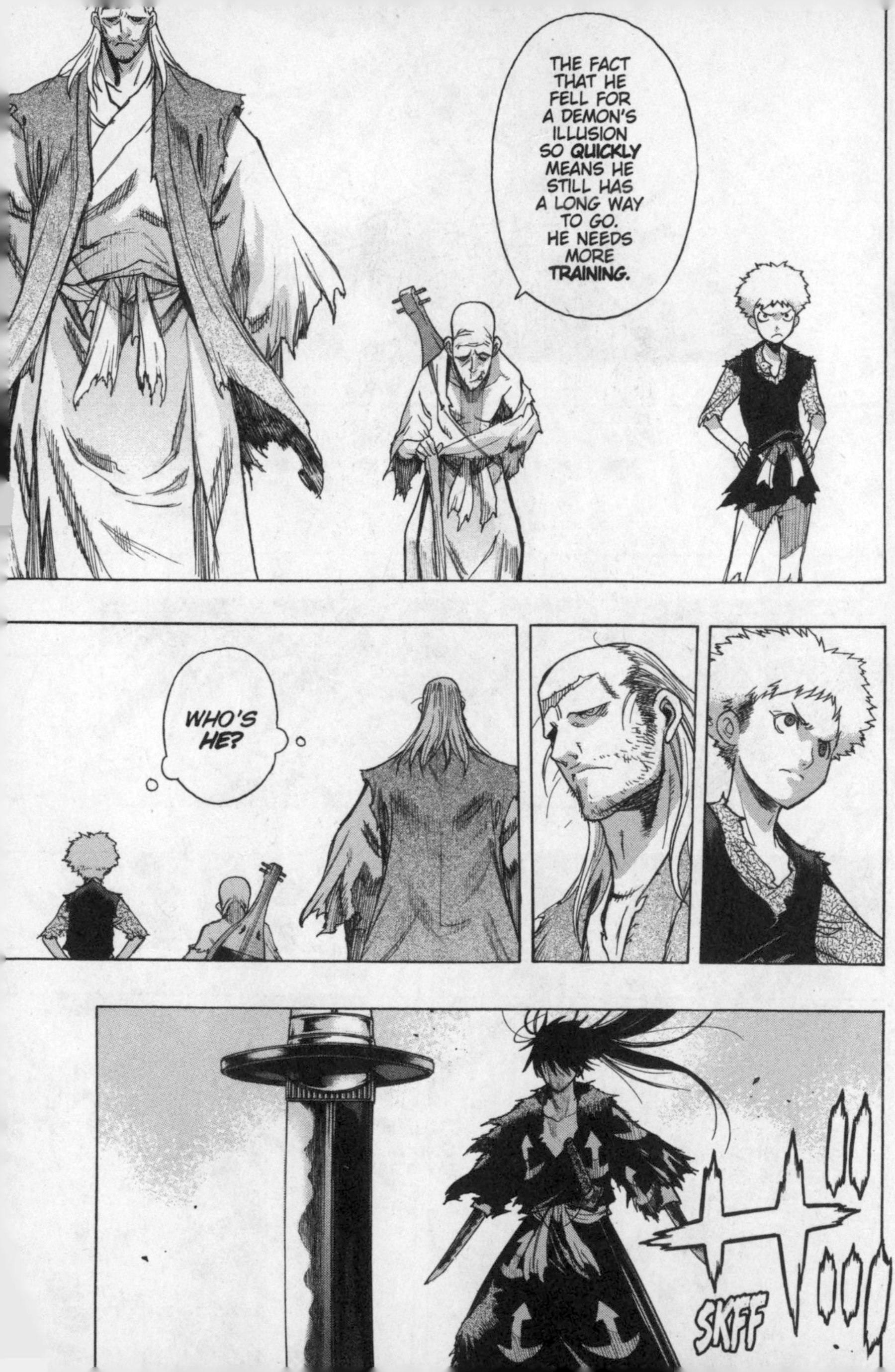
THE FACT THAT HE FELL FOR A DEMON'S ILLUSION SO QUICKLY MEANS HE STILL HAS A LONG WAY TO GO. HE NEEDS MORE TRAINING.
WHO'S HE?
SKFF

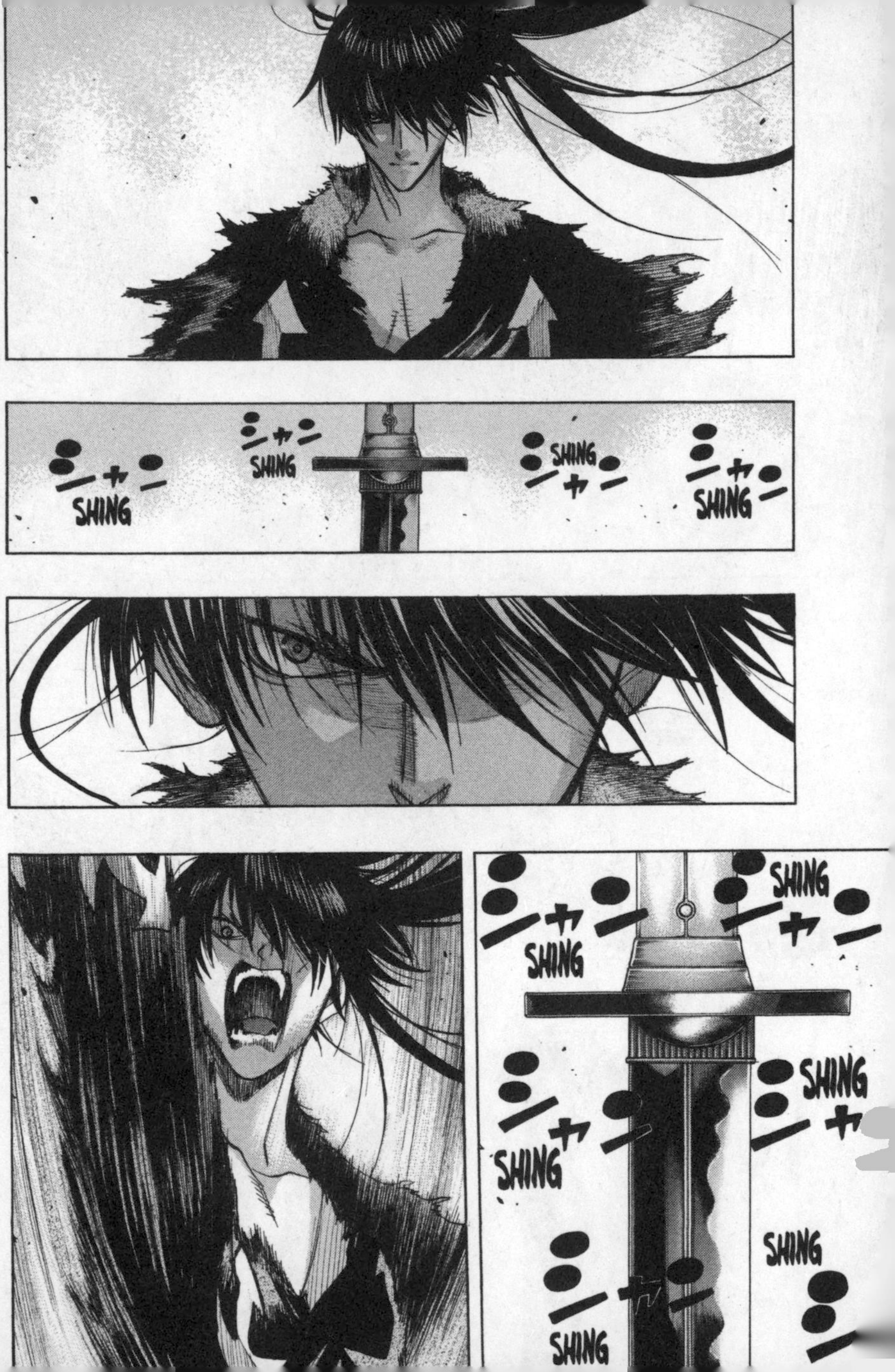
シャン
SHING
シャン
SHING
シャン
SHING
シャン
SHING
シャン
SHING
シャン
SHING
シャン
SHING
シャン
SHING
シャン
SHING
SHING
SHING

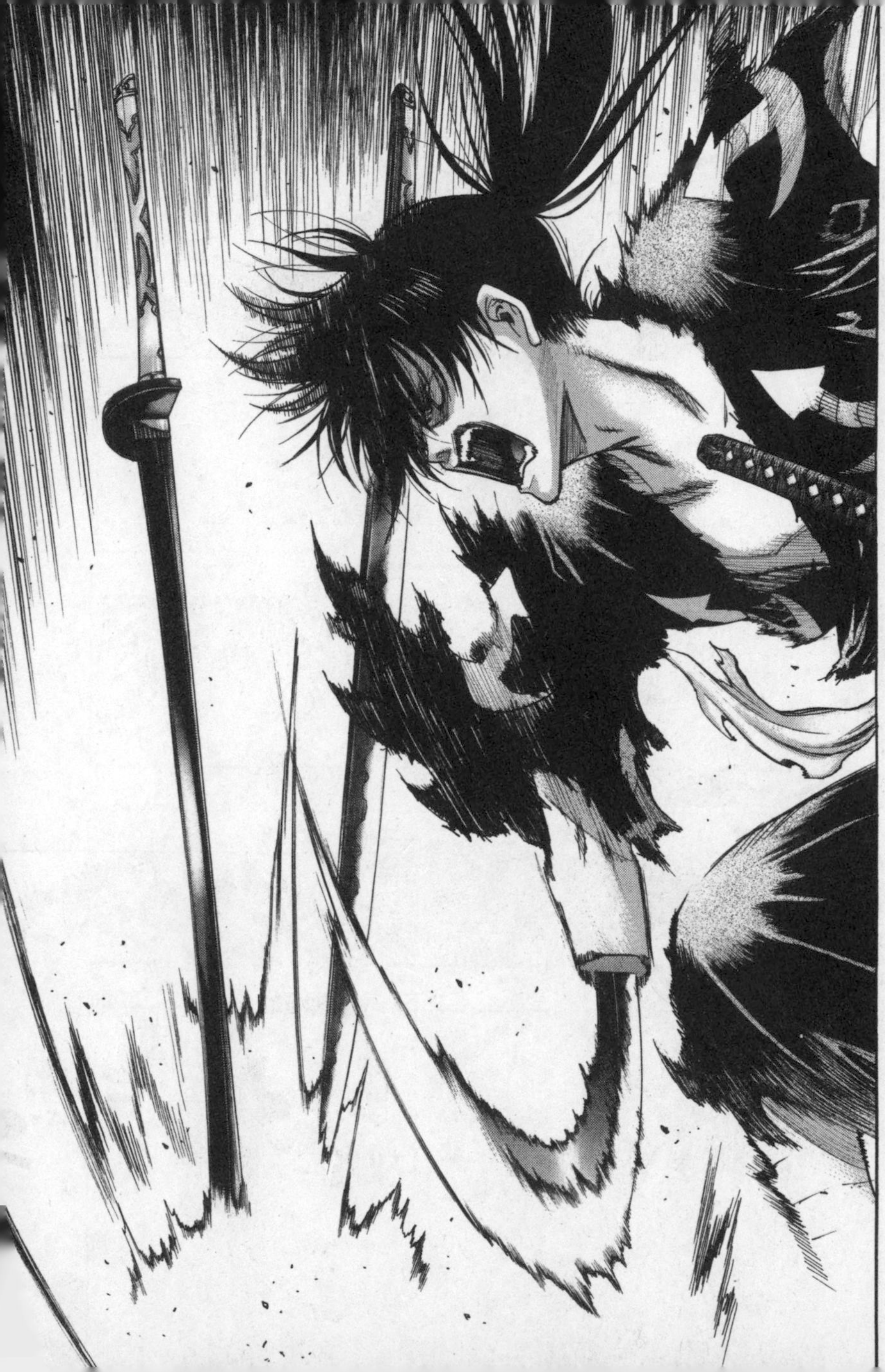

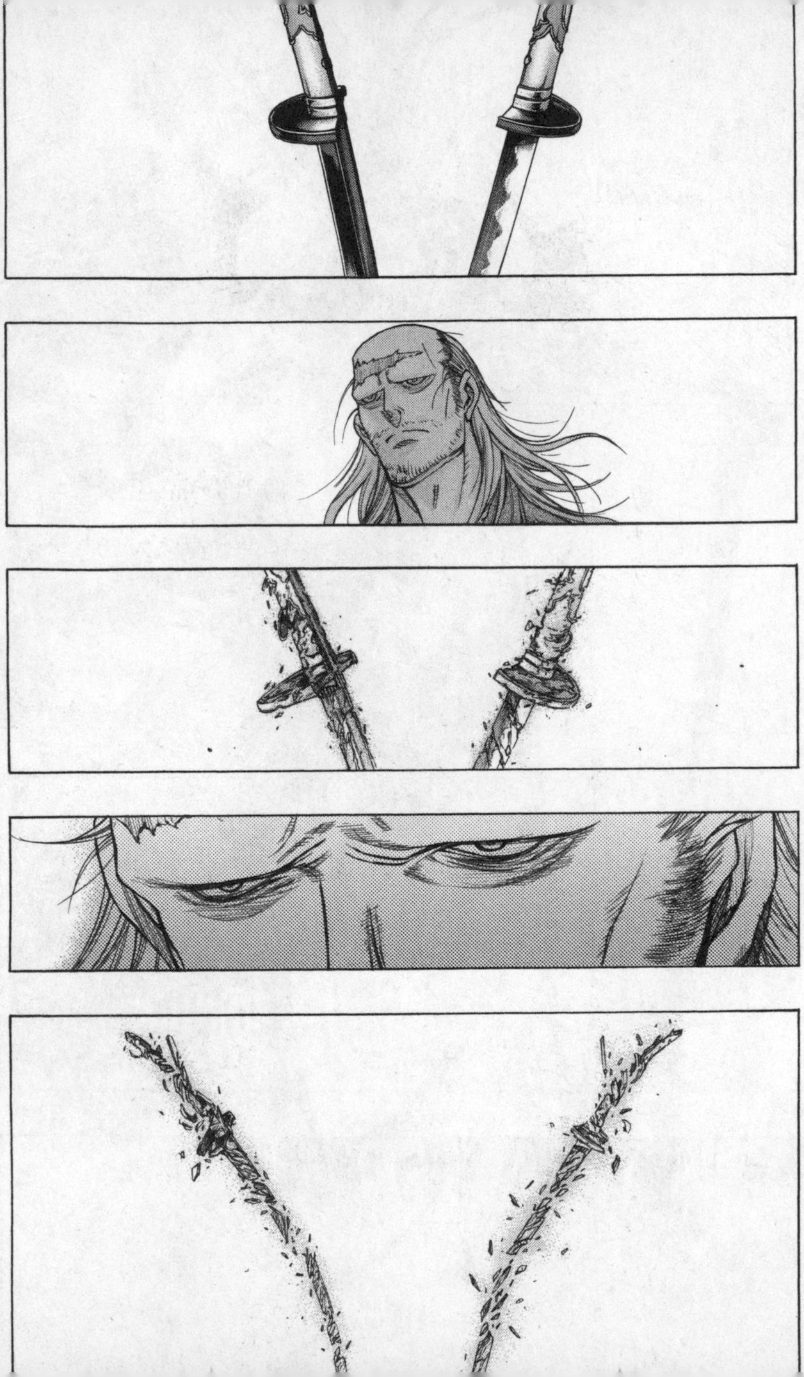

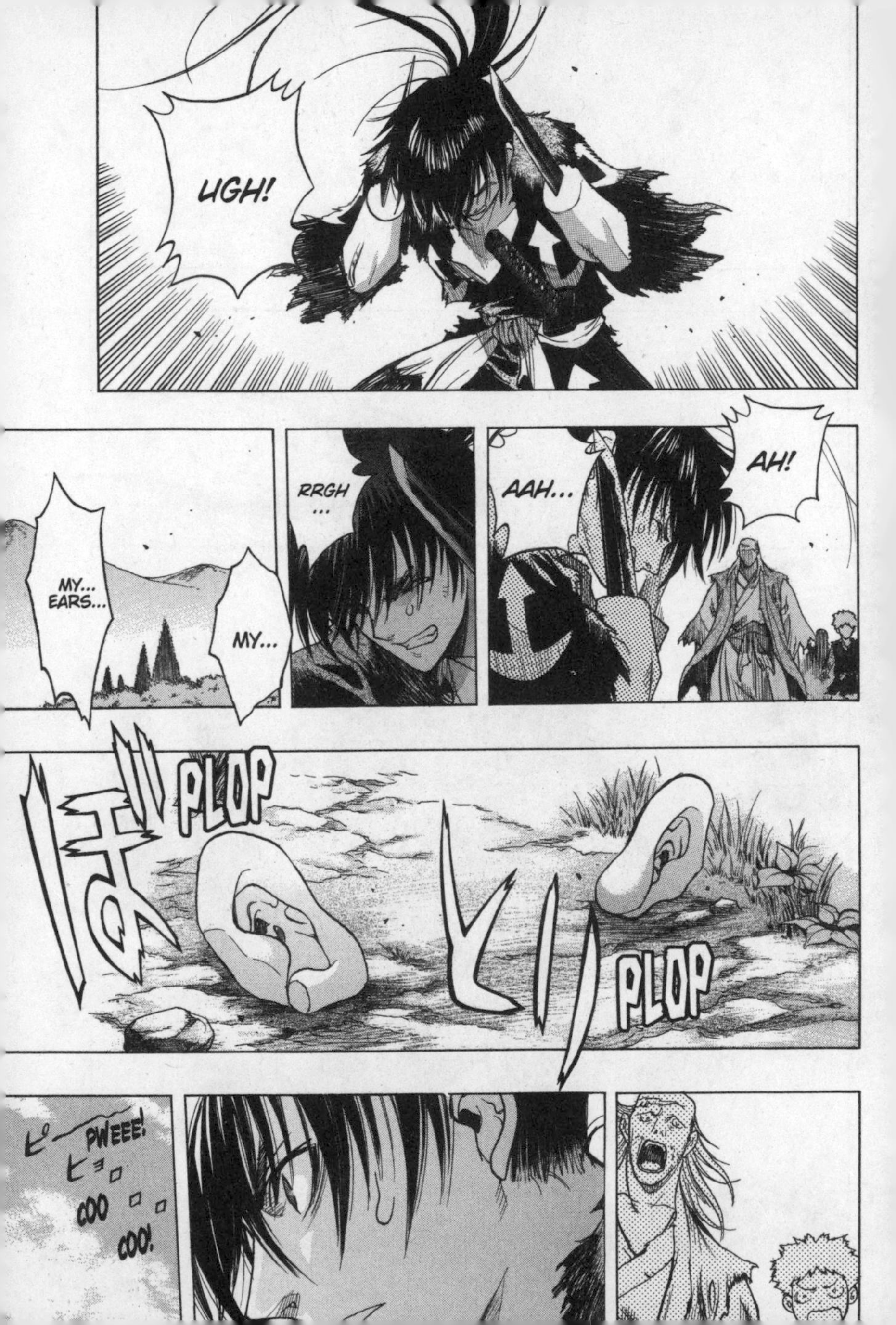
UGH!
AH!
AAH...
RRGH...
MY...
MY... EARS...
PLOP
PLOP
PWEEE!
COO
COO!

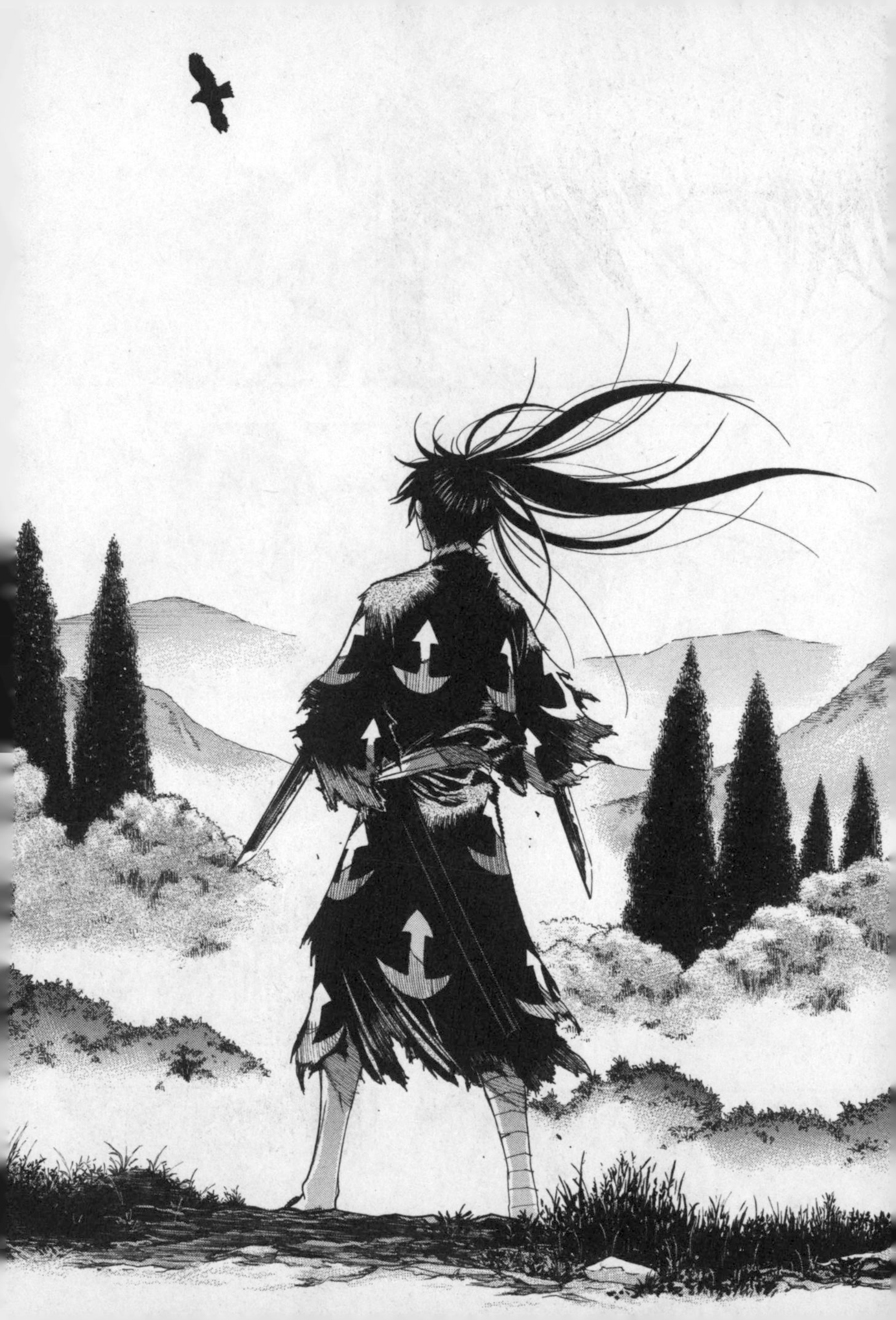

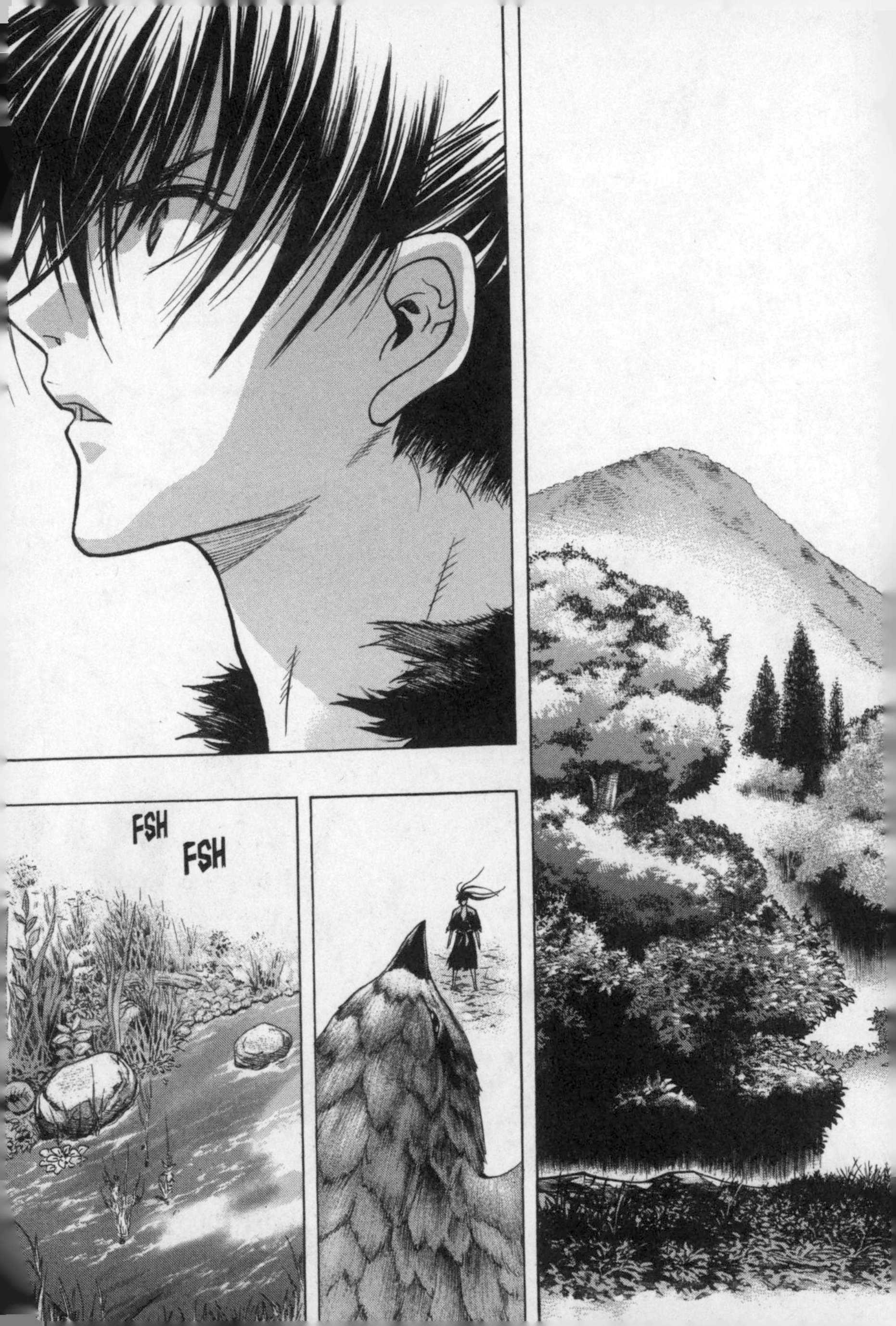
FSH
FSH

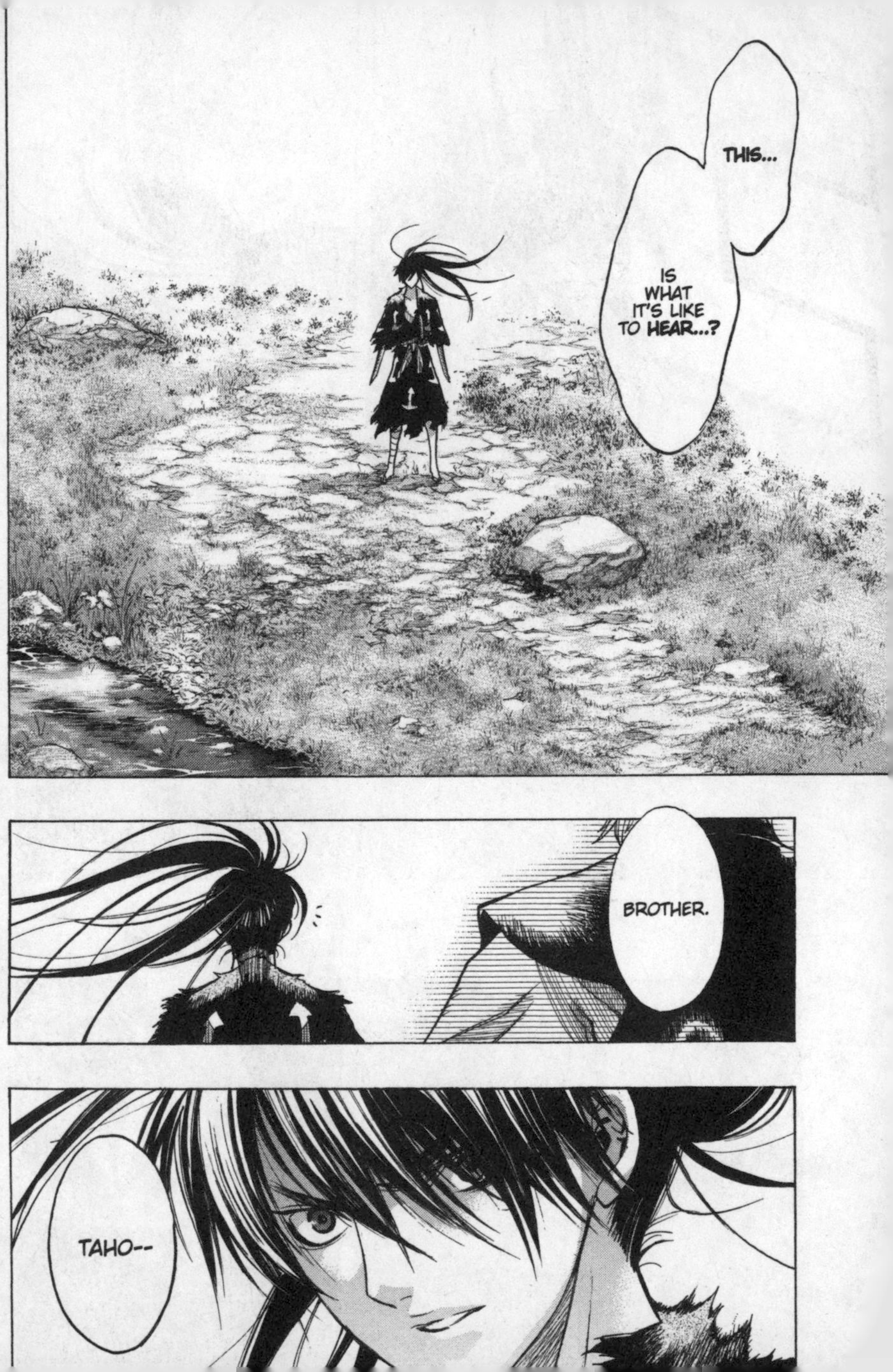
THIS...
IS WHAT IT'S LIKE TO HEAR...?
BROTHER.
TAHO--

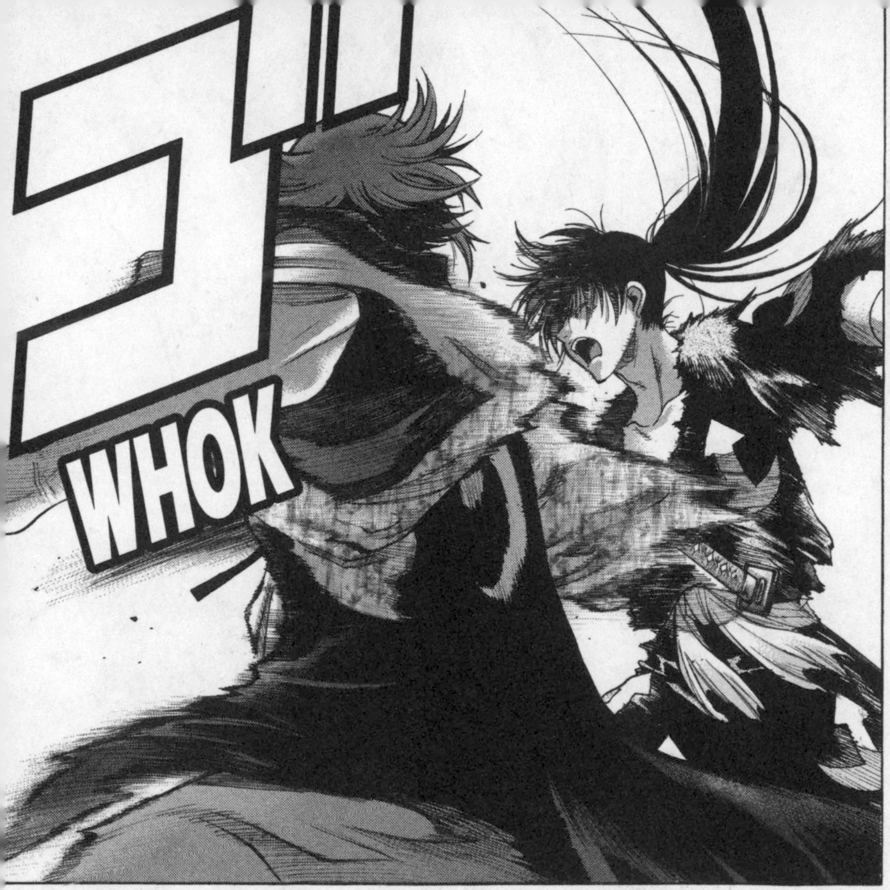
WHOK
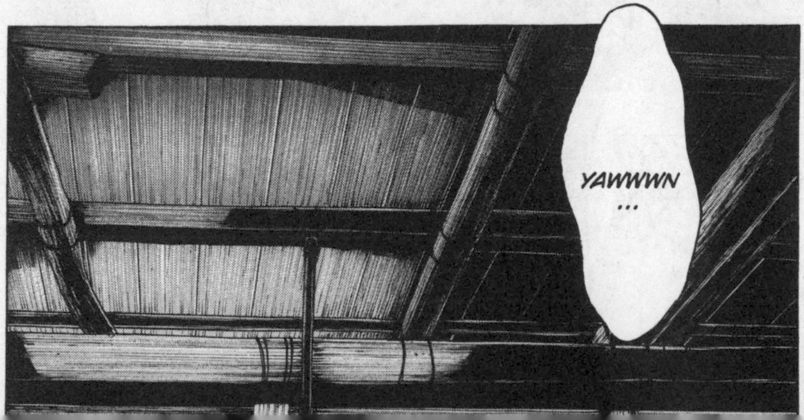
YAWWWN
...

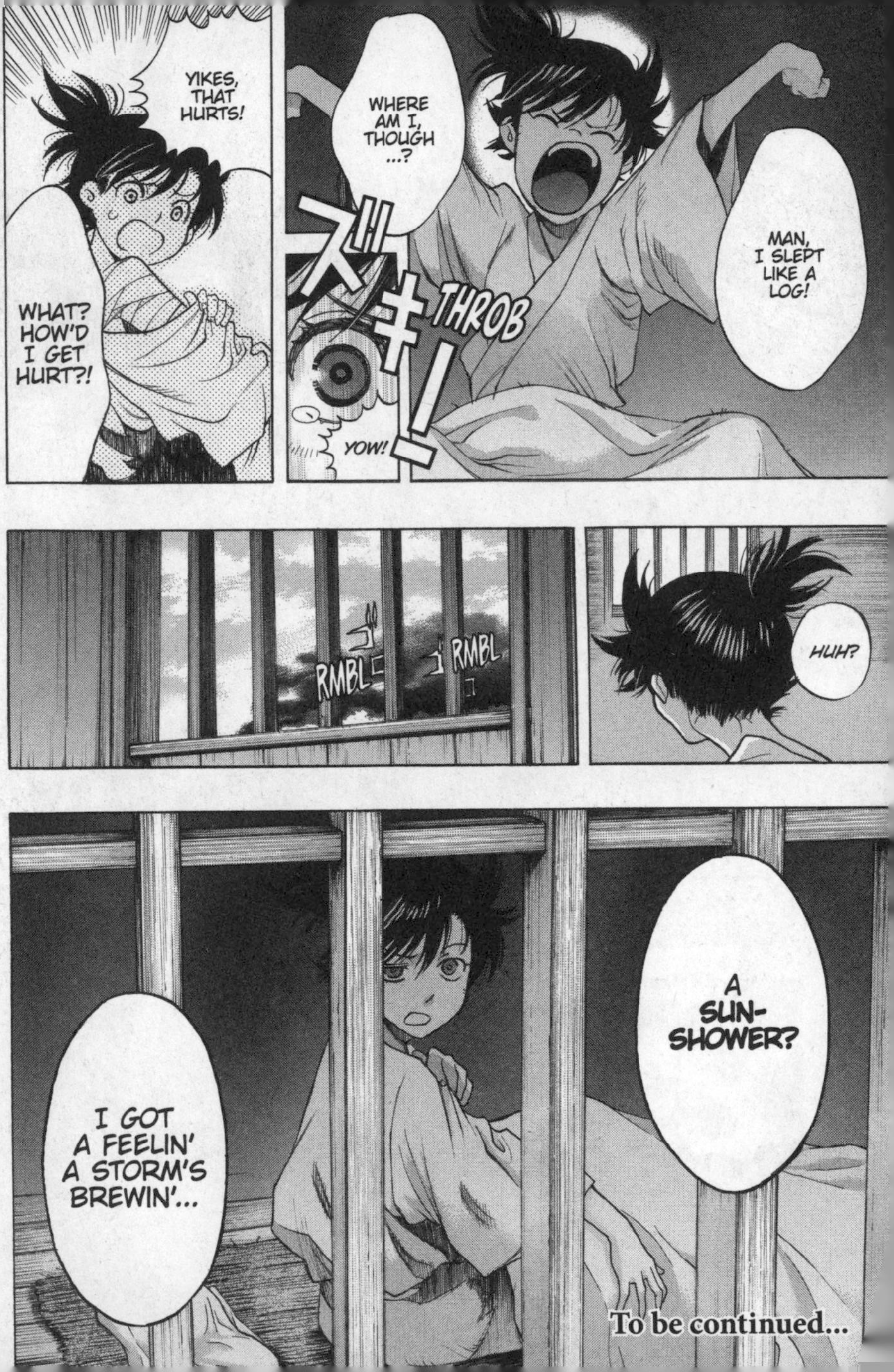
MAN, I SLEPT LIKE A LOG!
WHERE AM I, THOUGH ...?
THROB
YOW!
YIKES, THAT HURTS!
WHAT? HOW'D I GET HURT?!
HUH?
RMBL
RMBL
A SUN-SHOWER?
I GOT A FEELIN' A STORM'S BREWIN'...
To be continued...

THE LEGEND OF
DORORO AND
HYAKKIMARU

どろろと
百鬼丸伝

THE LEGEND OF
DORORO AND HYAKKIMARU

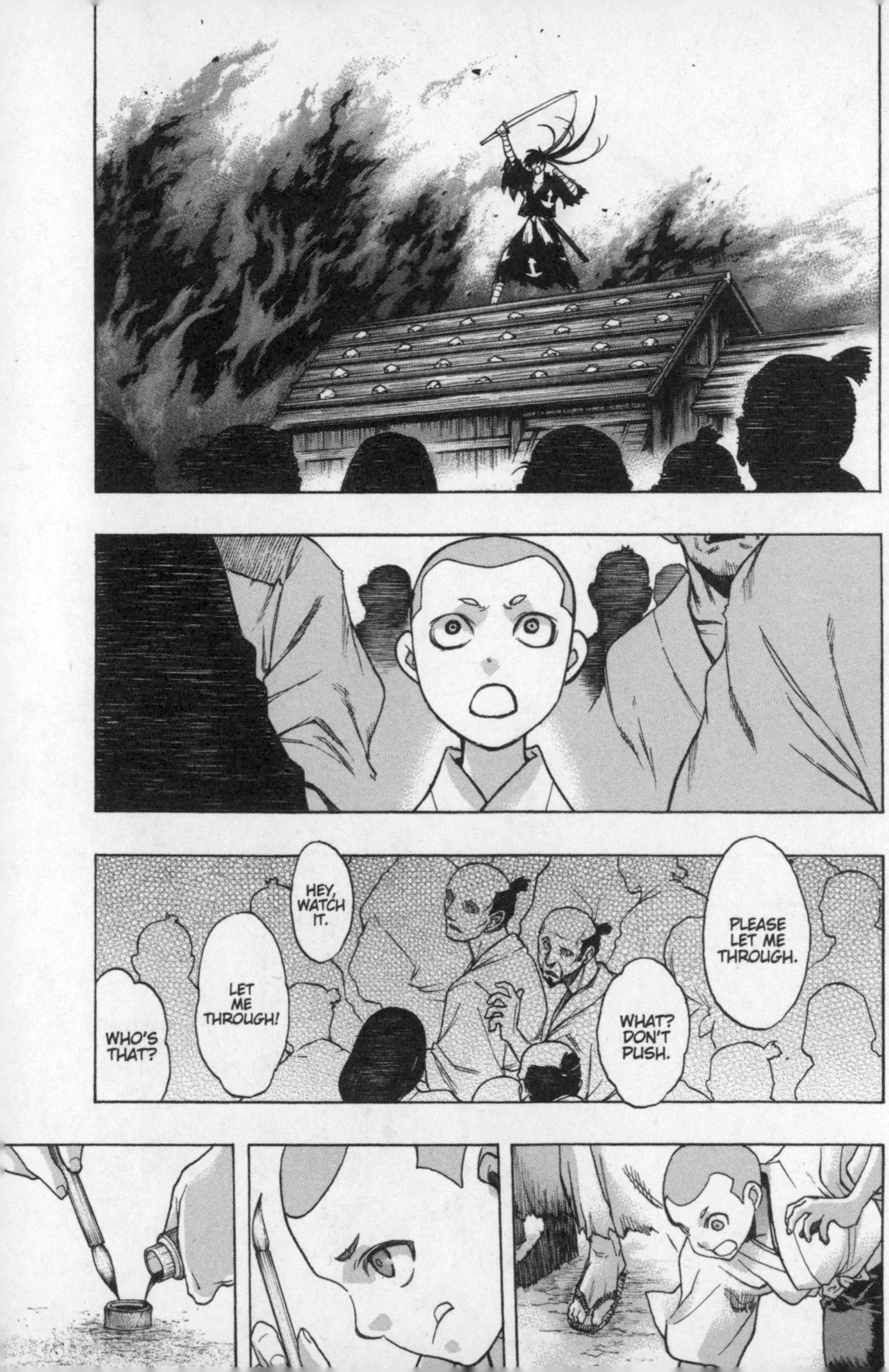
PLEASE LET ME THROUGH.
WHAT? DON'T PUSH.
HEY, WATCH IT.
LET ME THROUGH!
WHO'S THAT?

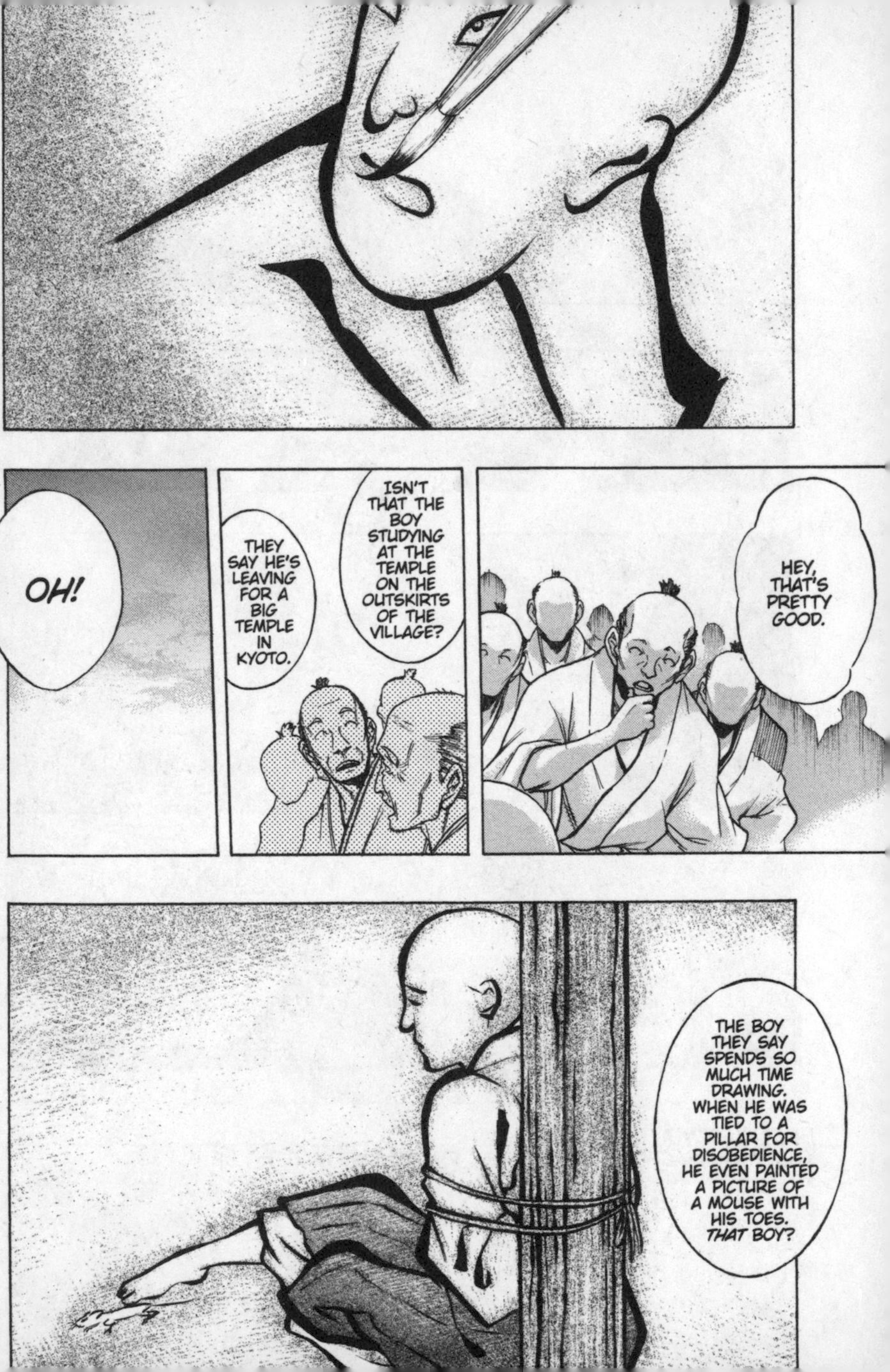
HEY, THAT'S PRETTY GOOD.
ISN'T THAT THE BOY STUDYING AT THE TEMPLE ON THE OUTSKIRTS OF THE VILLAGE?
THEY SAY HE'S LEAVING FOR A BIG TEMPLE IN KYOTO.
OH!
THE BOY THEY SAY SPENDS SO MUCH TIME DRAWING. WHEN HE WAS TIED TO A PILLAR FOR DISOBEDIENCE, HE EVEN PAINTED A PICTURE OF A MOUSE WITH HIS TOES. *THAT* BOY?

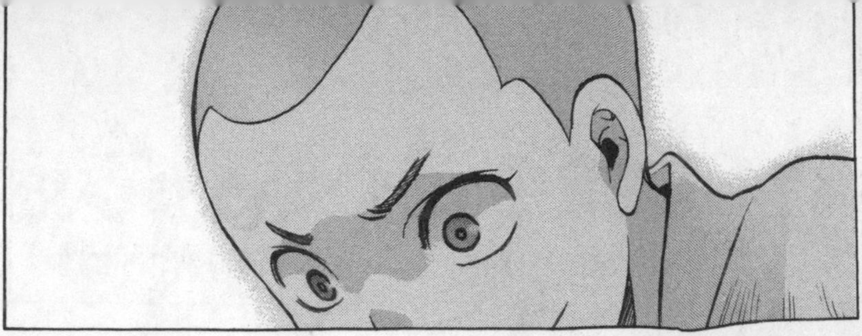

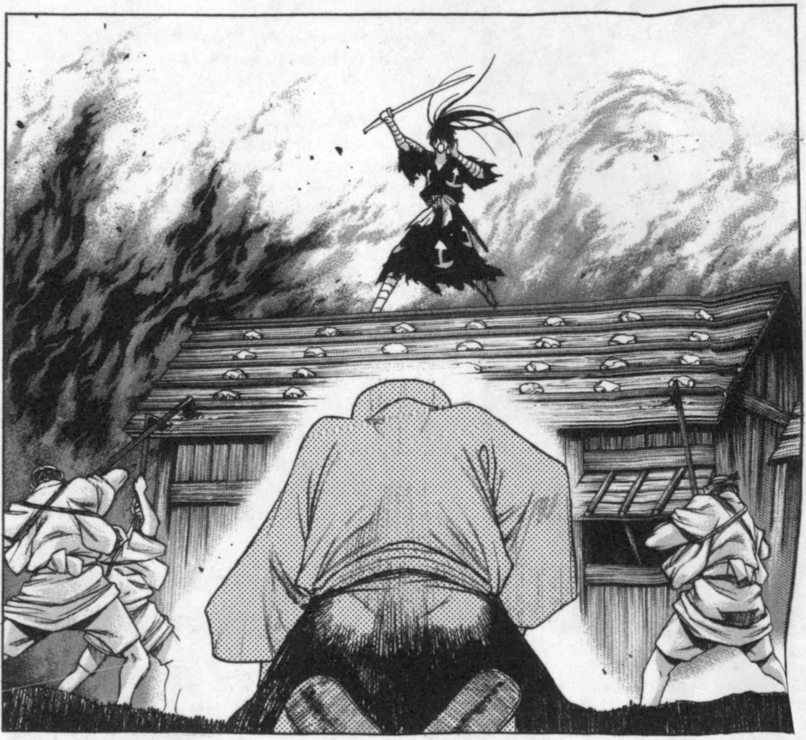

SESSHU TOYO (1420-1506)
THE MUROMACHI PERIOD'S MOST PROMINENT MASTER OF INK AND WASH PAINTINGS AND A ZEN BUDDHIST PRIEST. TO THIS DAY, SIX OF HIS PAINTINGS ARE DESIGNATED NATIONAL TREASURES OF JAPAN, AND HE REMAINS ONE OF THE MOST IMPORTANT FIGURES IN JAPANESE ART HISTORY.

SEVEN SEAS ENTERTAINMENT PRESENTS

THE LEGEND OF
DORORO AND HYAKKIMARU
VOLUME 5

story and art by **SATOSHI SHIKI**   original story by **OSAMU TEZUKA**

TRANSLATION
Amanda Haley

LETTERING AND RETOUCH
Sean Bishop

COVER DESIGN
Nicky Lim
(LOGO) **Kris Aubin**

PROOFREADER
Brett Hallahan

SENIOR EDITOR
J.P. Sullivan

EDITOR
Jay Edidin

PREPRESS TECHNICIAN
Melanie Ujimori

PRINT MANAGER
Rhiannon Rasmussen-Silverstein

PRODUCTION MANAGER
Lissa Pattillo

EDITOR-IN-CHIEF
Julie Davis

ASSOCIATE PUBLISHER
Adam Arnold

PUBLISHER
Jason DeAngelis

DORORO TO HYAKKIMARUDEN volume 5
©Tezuka Productions / Satoshi Shiki 2021
Originally published in Japan in 2021 by Akita Publishing Co.,Ltd.
English translation rights arranged with Akita Publishing Co.,Ltd.
through TOHAN CORPORATION, Tokyo.

Seven Seas press and purchase enquiries can be sent to Marketing Manager
Lianne Sentar at press@gomanga.com. Information regarding the distribution
and purchase of digital editions is available from Digital Manager CK Russell
at digital@gomanga.com.

Seven Seas and the Seven Seas logo are trademarks of
Seven Seas Entertainment. All rights reserved.

ISBN: 978-1-63858-238-0

Printed in Canada

First Printing: September 2022

10 9 8 7 6 5 4 3 2 1

FOLLOW US ONLINE: *www.sevenseasentertainment.com*

READING DIRECTIONS

This book reads from *right to left*, Japanese style.
If this is your first time reading manga, you start
reading from the top right panel on each page and
take it from there. If you get lost, just follow the
numbered diagram here. It may seem backwards at
first, but you'll get the hang of it! Have fun!!

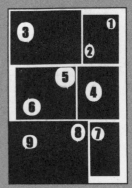